WENDOVER
WINDS *of* CHANGE

WENDOVER
WINDS *of* CHANGE

A History

by

RONALD R. BATEMAN

To Gert, Mark, and the long-time residents of
Wendover, this history is dedicated.

Mark and Gertrude Tripp

Mark Tripp, a native of neighboring community Callao, Utah, worked at the local potash plant during his career. He was tireless in developing a cemetery for Wendover. Mark and Gertrude raised their family of seven children and numerous grandchildren in Wendover.

Gertrude Tripp was instrumental in many church, civic, educational, and governmental affairs concerning Wendover. Gertrude assembled an extensive collection of Wendover photos, newspaper articles, and other local historical documents over the past half century. Her collection was the impetus for this history. Gertrude was named "Woman of the Year" in 1999 by the local newspaper, *High Desert Advocate*. She has been involved in education in Wendover for over forty years and is a Wendover City Councilwoman. She is also a cancer survivor.

On front cover:
– First train excursion on the salt beds, November 9,1908 *(Utah State Historical Society)*
– Western Pacific logo *(Union Pacific Railroad)*
– *Mormon Meteor (Utah Salt Flats Racing Association, Cris Shearer)*
– *Enola Gay* on Tinian Island *(childrenofthemanhattanproject, Joseph Papilia)*
– Wendover Will, 2002 *(Ronald R. Bateman)*

© 2004 Ronald R. Bateman
ISBN: 0-9745983-1-3 (hardback)
ISBN: 0-9745983-2-1 (softbound)
LCCN: 2004091984

CONTENTS

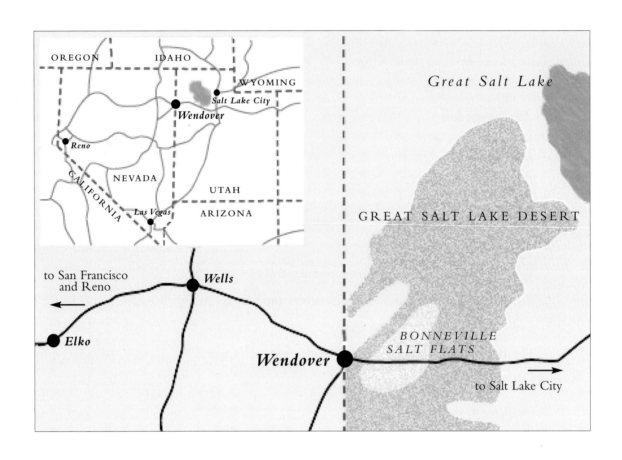

ACKNOWLEDGEMENTS

This undertaking could not have been possible without the assistance and cooperation of many individuals. In giving credit, the author assumes full reponsibility for the contents. Any omissions or errors are completely inadvertent. There is always a danger of leaving someone out in crediting people by name. Some who have helped include Gertrude Tripp who collected at least five scrapbooks filled with materials including writings, photos, and newspaper clippings over the past fifty years. She also compiled a history of the local Relief Society, a women's religious and service organization. Gertrude asked if I would undertake this history project. To her, major credit and thanks are given.

Jean Draper has the ability to put into words and to detail past events, some of which she was a part. She wrote several local historical articles for the *High Desert Advocate,* a Wendover newspaper.

Louise Ann Noeth's book, *Bonneville Salt Flats Land Speed,* and Ab Jenkins' book, *Salt of the Earth* were valuable resources for chapter six on the Bonneville Raceway. A cardboard box full of videos, photos, books, and articles was freely shared by Chris Shearer of the Utah Salt Flats Racing Association. Connie Disney masterfully designed the volume and Kirsty Evensen and Jani Fleet edited the pages. Record-setting racecar driver Marvin Jenkins and home-grown salt flats announcer Ron Christensen offered unconditionally their valuable salt flats knowledge and photo collection of Wendover. Most importantly, Phyllis Bateman provided the funding for publication of this volume. My beautiful wife, Beverly, gave immeasurable support and encouragement for which I am grateful.

Others who contributed are Kerrie Supanich, Linda Brown, Russ Draper, David Jennings, Jim Petersen, Loyd Hall, Don Hall, Mike Devine, Mark Tripp, University of Utah Special Collections, Bob Lee, Betty Lee, Kyle Bateman, Harold Bell, Chris Melville, Richard Dixon, LaMar Melville, Vaughn Tripp, Margaret Wheeler, Glenn Wadsworth, Loneta Wadsworth, Jay Hicks, Jeddy Cook, Pie Linares, Gene Jones, Dale Stewart, Sheila Stewart, Gordon Stewart, Bonnie Tilbury, Shirley Peterson, Dennis Weder, Utah State Historical Society, Nevada Historical Society, John Hernandez, J. Ronald Anderson, Wayne Shields, Terrance Holdeman, Brent Peterson, Barbara Cole, Janis Hutchinson, Marie Johnston, Dr. Bruce Lamus, Dr. Charles P. Bean, Norma Christiansen, Karen Christiansen, Mollie Hewitt Taylor, Dr. Duncan Metcalfe, Bernece Marquardt, Goldie, Glenda, Nancy, and Marie "Pokey" Green, Irene Peterson, Brock Treglown, Elaine Dahlstrom, Luanna Dean, Billie Ann Devine, John McKellar, Ouida Blanthorn, Charles Freudenthal, Wester Potter, Alison Moore of the California State Automobile Association, the West Wendover Branch Elko County Library, Norman Holmes of the Western Pacific Feather River Route Portola Museum, Roland Anderson, David R. Kendziora who is historian at Hill Air Force Base, Kirk Petersen, Su Richards, Auer Jensen, Dan and Pat Matthews, and William White. Also Dan Park, William B. West, Colonel Paul Tibbets, Richard Campbell, Joseph Papalia, Janell Tuttle, Doug Misner, Charles Hibbard, Donn Frisk, Gerry Newhouse, Armando Rodriquez, Dr. Verl Jensen, Randy Bateman, Jay Evensen, and Wallace Gwynn.

PREFACE

On the surface, all one sees are the lights of Wendover. But there is a rarely-known history of the little town that is fascinating and complex. The story of Wendover is a puzzle with many and varied pieces that do not always fit neatly together. The task has been to gather them into a readable and understandable manner. Does one begin with the geologic past, at the railroad's founding, the early explorations, or the boom of the 1940s? What made and sustained Wendover? Was it the railroad, the air base, gaming, the highway, the salt flats with its potash, salt production, and speedway? Or was it all of the above? As former resident Blair Lamas mused, Wendover is "a town without parallel." It is indeed unique.

INTRODUCTION

Wendover, USA

WENDOVER, UTAH
population: 2,842★
altitude: 4,230 ft.
time zone: Mountain

WEST WENDOVER, NEVADA
population: 6,500★
altitude: 4,230 ft.
time zone: Pacific

A shimmering, alkali plain gives way to barren, dirt-colored hills where the twin cities of Wendover, Utah, and West Wendover, Nevada, are located. The towns lie in a cove surrounded on three sides by the dead, brown mountains. They straddle two sides of the line on the Utah/Nevada border. They are politically two towns, but geographically one town in two states.

This seemingly unremarkable spot was not mentioned in the accounts of those who survived the desert crossings of 1846. Instead, these early strangers to the land trudged forward to the refreshing waters of Pilot Mountain twenty-five miles north and then on to California or on to tragedy, as in the case of the Donner party. Nearby, archeologically rich Danger Cave predates the birth of Christ by thousands of years. The 1860s Pony Express route, Overland Stage, and the Old Lincoln Highway traversed a common route sixty miles to the south at the Ibapah community, thus avoiding the white, salt plains.

The life-giving water of Pilot Mountain replenished the mighty steam locomotives of the Western Pacific starting in 1907. Wendover sprang into existence with the construction of a railroad roundhouse, water tank, and workshops. Sturdy gandydancers were needed to provide manpower at each railroad section. These railway workers haphazardly erected dirt and tent-roofed shacks with tar paper coverings. The tiny village of Wendover was connected to the rest of the

★ 2000 census

world by the tenuous tether of the railway and later by the ribbon of road paralleling the railroad tracks. A decade later came Prohibition, prostitution, and lawlessness associated with trafficking moonshine whiskey. Few people know that the first transcontinental telephone lines linking the east coast to the west coast were joined at Wendover in 1914. In 1917, a rail spur led southeast to the mineral rich mines of Gold Hill. By 1926 Wendover was connected to Salt Lake City by a highway remarkably engineered over the barren expanse of the Bonneville Salt Flats. The resulting Victory Highway opening celebration was well publicized by Ab Jenkins when he outraced a dignitary-filled passenger train to Wendover.

Modern motorists speed east and west across the broad, white expanse of the Great Salt Lake Desert, in a hurry to get somewhere, yet oblivious to the history in the area. How could there be a history of man in such a desolate, bleached scene? Yet there is much recorded information originating near the crusty-skinned salt where mirages appear and vanish over the roundness of the earth! Here pioneers barely succeeded in crossing the treacherous salt with muddy underlayment. Here Native Americans subsisted in the protected cave shelters of the adjacent northern hills. Here the railroad breeched salt, and superbly-built race cars found a friendly, cool, snow-like surface on which to perpetually set speed records. Less spectacular, but equally important to the existence of the populace is the history of man's laborious efforts starting in 1916 in designing the miles of crisscrossing canals, ponds, and mills of the long-running salt and potash harvesting operations. Since its inception, Wendover has also been a supply center for cattle ranchers and sheepmen.

An enterprising, young man, Bill Smith arrived in Wendover in 1924 and immediately saw the tourist potential along the highway. Two years later he established the Cobblestone service station with a perpetually glowing light bulb, welcoming weary travelers to town. Bill's business survived and soon he expanded. His State Line business included a café, hotel, and casino services. Bill and his wife Ann eventually added a neon cowboy, "Wendover Will," in 1952 which became a symbol of Wendover. Other businesses such as the A-1 and Western Service followed suit with motels, cafés, and gas stations. Thus the tourist trade, the lifeblood of Wendover, was firmly established.

Tiny, drowsy Wendover barely survived the Great Depression. Its survival was due in part to Salt Lake racer Ab Jenkins and his British counterparts who put the Bonneville Speedway permanently on the international map. The Bonneville Salt Flats where the land speed races are held is one of very few places on land where one can actually see the curvature of the earth.

Following the Great Depression, Wendover was shocked into wakefulness when a military city of 20,000 boomed overnight right across the street from the home folks. World War II had arrived in Wendover with the building of a gunnery range and an air base! The Army Air Corps established training of B-17, B-24, and B-29 heavy bomb groups at Wendover Field. The groups received superb training due to the moving target Tokyo Trolley, the dummy, tar-covered, salt battleships, and the mock enemy city built of salt. The various bomb groups later flew sorties in Nazi Germany, Japan and the South Pacific among others, and were cited for their bravery and heroism in the heat of battle. Several crewmen received Medals of Honor. Many were shot down and survivors suffered as prisoners of war. The self-contained 509th Composite Group, under a shroud of secrecy, trained at Wendover Field for their singular mission, to drop atomic bombs on Hiroshima and Nagasaki, Japan. Their mission, headed by Colonel Paul W. Tibbets, Jr., ultimately ended World War II and

was credited with saving a bloody invasion of a half million U.S. servicemen into Japan. The base saw limited use after the war and was dismantled and abandoned to decay until recent efforts to restore the remains as a unique World War II air field museum.

Wendover reverted back to a quiet, tourist town for the duration of the 1950s through the end of the century. Water is a key to Wendover's existence. The Western Pacific railroad sold its water rights and two sections of ground to Wendover City for $90,000 in 1960. Wendover Air Force Base transferred Johnson Springs water to Wendover on July 9, 1976. Wendover achieved status as an incorporated town in 1950 and as a third-class city in 1982. The desert on the Nevada side of Wendover began to blossom in the 1980s. The little gambling center made up of the A-1, the Hideaway steak house, Jim's Casino, and the State Line Hotel and Casino (now the State Line Nugget) was quickly joined by the Nevada Crossing, the Silver Smith (now Montego Bay Resort), the Peppermill, the Rainbow, and the Red Garter casinos. Such businesses created jobs and a resultant increase in population. A new city, West Wendover became official when it was incorporated in 1991. The two Wendovers grew remarkably fast, especially West Wendover. There were 2,500 residents in 1985 and 6,500 in 2000 with a promise of more growth to come. Shopping centers, more planned casinos, movie houses, a water park and a championship-caliber golf course were amazing proof of the unprecedented expansion. And just as astounding, there was enough water to support the ongoing expansion in the middle of the desert.

To top it all off, after congressional committee approval, the two towns voted in a non-binding referendum in 2002 to combine as one, with Wendover, Utah, seceding to Nevada. Such a move had not happened since the Civil War! But there were problems to overcome in the plan to change the state boundaries (see chapter seven). These difficulties may never be overcome. Only time will tell.

People who have lived a significant time in Wendover praise the community and consider it home. They have no desire to live anywhere else. That is the real story of Wendover—the people.

Wendover Timeline

PRE-HISTORY

Lake Bonneville covered western Utah. Later, Native Americans used springs and caves of Pilot Range for sustenance and shelter.

1827

"Trapper, trader, explorer, and frontiersman Jedediah Smith was perhaps the first white man to cross the salt flats while returning from his first expedition to California."

1832-36

Captain Benjamin L. F. Bonneville, French-born U.S. Army officer, explored the Rocky Mountain region. Bonneville Salt Flats, Bonneville Speedway, and Lake Bonneville were later named in his honor. He employed Joseph Reddeford Walker who crossed the northern perimeter of the salt flats.

1833

Fur trapper Zenas Leonard traveled through the area and wrote, "We came to the mountains described by the Indian as having its peak (Pilot Peak Mountains) covered with snow. It presents a most singular experience—being entirely unconnected with any other chain."

1834

Isaac P. Rose claimed to have crossed the salt desert.

1841

Bartleson-Bidwell wagon train was first to cross Utah, camping "at the east base of Pilot Peak, the first white persons known to have visited those springs."

1845

John C. Fremont, along with vanguard scouts Kit Carson and Joe Walker, crossed from Grantsville to the west boundary of Utah at Pilot Mountain (then well within the state of Deseret); it became known as "Hastings Cutoff." He was scouting a route to California from the Salt Lake Valley.

1846

Lansford W. Hastings promoted Fremont's shortcut, shortening the distance between Fort Bridger and the Humboldt River.

MAY 28. Hastings' party camped at the base of Pilot Peak.

JULY. Heinrich Lienhard kept a detailed journal of the salt desert crossing he made with four men. They camped at Pilot Springs on AUGUST 19 and remained in the vicinity until AUGUST 24.

JULY 20. Edwin Bryant in company with William Russell, described the salt desert in his writings as his group of nine men on horseback camped near Pilot Peak.

JULY 20. The "desert of mud" claimed wagons and live-stock of the George W. Harlan and Samuel C. Young group of forty wagons.

SEPTEMBER 8. The ill-fated Donner-Reed Party found water at the base of Pilot Mountain.

1847

Miles Goodyear led an expedition of horsemen from California to Salt Lake crossing the "salt plane" about JULY 3, traveling 22 hours constantly without finding water. Reported the trail as unfit for wagons.

Captain James Brown returned from California with pay for the Mormon Battalion Sick Detachment. It took his expedition three days to cross the salt desert without water. They burned portions of the Donner Party's abandoned wagons for warmth. Arrived in Salt Lake City DECEMBER 1.

1849

OCTOBER 29. Captain Howard Stansbury Expedition reached the base of the Pilot Range. Dr. John McNulty and the Colony Guards took the Hastings Cutoff and "suffered much" on their way west.

1850

JULY. John Wood with the Ogle-Robinson party kept a journal of his desert crossing, reaching Pilot Peak.

JULY 29. Jno. B. McGee reported in a letter from Pilot Creek the need for "2 gallons of water to each animal and one gallon for each person" and a supply of grass in order to successfully cross the 80-mile desert (salt flats). Gold seekers in the California Gold Rush crossed the salt flats in a constant stream of traffic that summer.

AUGUST 7. Other crossings are detailed by John Udell, William P. Bennett, Carlisle S. Abbott of his friends, and Madison Berryman Moorman with upwards of 500 to 600 immigrants using the Hastings Cutoff across the salt desert that summer.

1854

Lieutenant E. G. Beckwith made a survey for a transcontinental railroad following a route on the south edge of the salt desert near Granite Mountain, thus bypassing Hastings Cutoff.

1855

Captain J. H. Simpson surveyed a new wagon road west of Salt Lake, "crossing the extreme southern tip of the [salt] desert at Fish Springs."

1857

Newfoundland Mining District founded in the early 1870s.

1858

Silver Islet Mining District begun.

1869

Transcontinental railroad joined at Promontory, Utah on May 10, eliminating wagon travel from east to west.

1876

"Eugene Munsee homesteaded one of the springs at Pilot Peak thirty years after the emigrants stopped there."

1880s

The Federal government used Pilot Peak, Nevada, as a triangulation point while surveying the mountains of the area. Heliograph beams were flashed 130 miles from Observatory Peak (Mount Ogden) and other peaks in adjoining states to assist in mapping.

1884

Thomas Stevens pedaled across the desert of northwestern Utah skirting the salt flats around the northern end of the Great Salt Lake on a transcontinental ride.

1896

The salt flats' potential for racing was first recognized in 1896 by W. D. Rishel who was scouting a bicycle race course from New York to San Francisco. He crossed the flats in 22 hours, but discounted the desert as a suitable course for the race.

1900

Charles and Joseph McKellar built a log cabin and lean-to kitchen a few miles north of Donner Springs. During the first decade of the century, limited mining of lead, gold, silver, and copper was done in the northern portion of the Silver Island Mining District, producing about $90,000 in valuable ore.

1903

MARCH 6. Western Pacific Railroad incorporated in San Francisco, California. The Western Pacific Railway was organized to build the San Francisco to Salt Lake City route to compete with Southern Pacific. Western Pacific was part of George Gould's Rio Grande Missouri Pacific system.

1906

Construction of the Western Pacific Railroad begins at Oakland, California, and in Salt Lake City, Utah.

1907

MAY 14. Tracks of the Western Pacific reached the Utah-Nevada state line. Western Pacific Railroad built a water tower at Wendover. W. D. Rishel returned to the salt flats with a four-cylinder Pierce Arrow, but turned back after sighting a shimmering lake which he later found out to be a mirage.

1908

L. C. Thomas and Ferdinand Johnson opened the first store on William Morgan's mining claim in a large lumber-floored tent.

1909

William Lamb took the first bag of mail from Wendover to Gold Hill by stage. Wendover was laid out as a railroad town and established as a round house center. Western Pacific Railroad completed construction of tracks across the salt flats on the Salt Lake City to San Francisco route.

1910

JUNE 1. Robert Works appointed postmaster. Ab Jenkins traveled 60 mph on the salt on a Yale motorcycle.

1911

JANUARY. J. W. Johnson Jr. was justice of the peace at Wendover Precinct.

MAY. C. A. Jackson was the first weather observer at Wendover, Utah. The station was established and observations furnished in cooperation with Western Pacific Railroad.

William Rishel, famous bicycle racer, accompanied Ferg (Ferd) Johnson of Wendover in Johnson's Packard touring car on the salt flats as they roared to a speed of 50 mph.

AUGUST. Joseph Conley was justice of the peace at Wendover Precinct.

DECEMBER 8. Ferdinand M. Johnson was appointed postmaster; served until 1923

1913

J. A. Vinable, Justice of the Peace.

Conley's acre deeded by the railroad to Joe Conley to establish a business (ca. 1913).

Elsie Lord taught at Wendover Elementary School.

Actual construction began on the Wendover Cutoff or Northern route using meager Utah State Road Commission funding, circumventing the more southern Lincoln Highway route going through Ibapah, Utah.

FEBRUARY. Arsonist set fire to the livery stable, burning three horses tied in the barn. A duel was fought soon after with duelists facing each other on opposite sides of the Utah-Nevada line next to the saloon which was built on the line.

1914

Teddy Tezlaff, driving a Blitzen Benz started the beginning of a great tradition, the first unofficial speed record of 141.73 mph on the Salt Flats. Production of salt began at Salduro; dikes are constructed during World War I.

JUNE 17. Final splice in the coast-to-coast telephone line was made at Wendover.

JULY 29. Coast-to-coast telephone line declared operational.

1915

JANUARY 25. Coast-to-coast telephone line was formally opened with great celebration.

1917

First road across the "Great American Desert" completed between Knolls and Wendover.

Deep Creek Railroad completed to Gold Hill, Utah.

1918

The California Automobile Association commissioned a study to determine the best route across western Utah. The study recommended a route which went through Wendover. By 1924, they raised and donated $40,000 to the state of Utah for the Wendover section.

1919

William A. Lyman, justice of the peace at Wendover Precinct.

Victory Highway begun after World War I victory in Europe.

1920

Salduro had a population of 194 during potash production.

Nelson (Ed) Lamus and his wife Faye came to Wendover "in 1920 or there abouts."

MAY. Secretary of Agriculture Henry Wallace announced approval of federal aid for the Wendover Cutoff road across the Salt Flats.

DECEMBER. The Utah State Road Commission designated the Wendover road as eligible for federal funds under the Federal Highways Act of 1921.

1921

DECEMBER 3. Fire burned Ferd Johnson's Spencer Mercantile Co. and the Cooley hotel and store. New brick school built about this time.

1923

MARCH 5. James A. Lyman was acting postmaster and Nellie M. Trezona was appointed postmaster June 11.

1924

JUNE. Bill Smith decided to stay in Wendover when he was tossed off the train.

Ab Jenkins established a time record as he raced a train from Salt Lake to Wendover and won.

JUNE 23. A PW 8 military plane was able to complete the first successful dawn to dusk crossing of the USA, landing at Salduro, Utah, to refuel.

1925

JUNE 13. Wendover section of the national Victory Highway was completed as part of the first modern highway. Dedication ceremony took place at Salduro on the same date.

Western Pacific Hotel, Tri State Merc, and J. A. Leyman Jr.'s (J.A. Lyman) store first listed in the Polk Directory.

1926

Bill Smith and Herman Eckstein opened the Cobblestone Service Station with $500 savings and put a light bulb on a pole in front that was never turned off: "the light in the desert."

OCTOBER 18. James A. Lyman Jr. appointed postmaster of Wendover.

OCTOBER 20. The Lincoln Highway Association executive committee changed a portion of the Lincoln Highway running from the Goodyear Cutoff through Gold Hill and Ibapah to the Victory Highway route going from Grantsville directly west to Wendover. The change was finalized on December 2. The U.S. Bureau of Roads then assigned numbers to all interstate highways and the Wendover road became U. S. Highway 40.

1927

APRIL. Road between Wendover and Ely, Nevada, completed.

NOVEMBER 9. W. A. Lyman set apart as presiding elder of the Wendover branch of the Church of Jesus Christ of Latter-day Saints; he was later succeeded by President Peter McKellar.

1931

Gambling legalized in Nevada.

1932

Smith and Ekstein installed a roulette table in the Cobblestone, opening one of the first gambling establishments in Nevada.

White building built by the W.P.A. was used for LDS church services and for community activities such as dancing.

SEPTEMBER 18-19. Ab Jenkins averages 112.935 mph during a 24-hour period driving alone. Not recognized by the Automobile Association of America as they were not present. He stayed on a cot upstairs using his own bedding at the Western Pacific Railroad station as there were no other facilities in town.

1933

Ab Jenkins set first official 24-hour average for speed at 117.77 mph.

Bill Smith's Cobblestone Service added cabins for rent as did the Western Service station, unlike the previous year when Ab Jenkins came to town.

The Wendover Gliding Club was organized. Gliders were built and rebuilt and "numerous experimental flights" were flown over the salt flats.

OCTOBER 2. Mrs. Anna Clancy becomes acting postmaster.

NOVEMBER 22. Mrs. Millie M. Lyman becomes acting postmaster.

1934

AUGUST 7-8. Jenkins beats his 1933 24-hour record by racing an average of 127.229 mph in a twelve-cylinder Pierce Arrow.

1935

Western Pacific Railroad forced into bankruptcy, reemerged in 1944.

JULY. John Cobb sets 24-hour record of 134.85 mph average.

AUGUST. Jenkins regained the 24-hour record at 135.58 mph.

SEPTEMBER. Captain George Eyston improves the 24 hour record by racing at 140.52 mph average.

SEPTEMBER 3. Sir Malcolm Campbell set land speed record for one mile of 301.13 mph in his *Bluebird Special*.

1936

MARCH 3. Mrs. Erma G. Sullivan appointed postmaster.

APRIL. Briton Eyston set two records with a diesel-engined vehicle traveling 159 kph for one kilometer and 158.87 mph for a mile in his *Flying Spray*. Eyston set sixty records in July including 135.5 mph in 48-hour average in the *Speed of the Winds*.

AUGUST-SEPTEMBER. John Cobb breaks many of Eyston's records, raising the hours average to 150.16 mph.

    Ab Jenkins in "Mormon Meteor" sets 72 new world records on a circular track. He set the one-hour record at 170.99 mph, the 24-hour average at 153.823 mph, and the 48-hour average at 148.641 mph.

    Modern day Bonneville potash operation started by Bonneville, Ltd., a division of Kaiser Corp.

    C. E. McDonald, then J. J. Duggan, were trainmasters and G. W. Curtis was division superintendent on Western Pacific at Wendover.

NOVEMBER 20: Mrs. Millie M. Lyman appointed postmaster, office advanced to presidential with more status and pay in 1938.

1937

Robert F. Heizer of the University of Utah visited the Wendover area as part of a widespread survey of anthropological sites in the Great Basin.

NOVEMBER: Eyston jumps the measured mile speed record to 311.42 mph in the *Thunderbolt*.

1938

Pilot Mill potash plant constructed.

Will Smith previously won sole ownership of the State Line Casino business with the toss of a coin, Nevada-style. He subsequently built the State Line Hotel with restaurant, casino and air conditioned rooms.

SEPTEMBER 16. Capt. George E. T. Eyston in *Thunderbolt #1* set a one-mile land speed record of 357.5 with 5,000 horsepower.

1939

AUGUST 2. President Franklin D. Roosevelt received a letter from Albert Einstein telling him of nuclear research being done in Germany on "an extremely powerful bomb" being developed.

AUGUST 26: "John Cobb became the world's automobile speed king by driving his car 369.74 [367.910] mph."

    Elmer R. Smith began exploring the Wendover area for anthropological purposes and continued for three summers.

1940

Wendover Bombing and Gunnery range opened as a sub-post of Fort Douglas, Utah.

Mrs. Elizabeth C. Elliott was acting postmaster September 1 and postmaster February 20, 1941. She was later murdered in a jealous fit of rage by her husband "High-pockets" Elliott, the local sheriff.

1941

AUGUST 12. First contingent of ten men and two officers arrived at Wendover Field.

DECEMBER 6. Roosevelt authorized money to begin a highly secret nuclear research project called "The Manhattan Engineering Project." Pearl Harbor was bombed the next day.

1942

APRIL. 306th Bombardment Group was the first outfit assigned to Wendover, followed by the 302nd BG in July, the 100th BG in September, and the 308th BG in October.

    First transcontinental all-weather buried cable joined at Wendover. Wendover Field achieved official army air base status.

OCTOBER: Los Alamos, New Mexico, atomic bomb facility opened under J. Robert Oppenheimer.

1943

Federal government constructed a new six-room elementary building and turned it over to the Tooele County School Board for staffing and administration. Deeded to county in 1945.

Juke Box Cave floor leveled and a concrete dance floor was poured by World War II airmen with help from Spike Birdzell.

Byron R. Christiansen owned a riding stable across the road from the State Line Casino with his two teenaged sons, B. Ray and Max, operating it all summer.

A grocery store, a drug store, a beauty parlor, and a bakery are among the additions to Wendover's economy.

JANUARY 2. 384th Bombardment Group consisting of the 544th, 545th, 546th, and 547th Bombardment Squadrons assigned to Wendover Field to receive combat training in B-17 bombers. Began departing in April.

JANUARY 31. Wendover post office discontinued. Mail was thereafter sent to Wendover Field Branch of Salt Lake City post office during the course of the war.

OCTOBER 11. 489th Bomb Group assigned to Wendover, arrived in December

1944

JULY 19. Officers Club burned to the ground.

APRIL–SEPTEMBER: 180 fighter pilots successfully trained in P-47 aircraft. Training halted with pending arrival of 509th.

SEPTEMBER 1: Colonel Paul Tibbets Jr. given command of the 393rd Bombardment Squadron which became part of the completely self-sufficient 509th Composite Group assembled at Wendover in top-secret preparation for atomic bomb mission, activated in December. The hand-picked "GI's knew only what was necessary to do their own job. They named the unknown thing they were working on 'The gimmick.' The Wendover base itself was given the code name 'Kingman' and work in the ordnance area was termed 'Project W-47.'" The code name "Silverplate" instantly got them anything they wanted.

DECEMBER 9. Federal Recreational Building dedicated, operated originally by the USO Council; later referred to as the Wendover community building.

1945

AUGUST. $2 million fire caused by an explosion in #1 hanger, destroying the hangar, five warehouses, and an office building plus six airplanes at Wendover Field.

AUGUST 6. Colonel Paul Tibbets Jr. flying the *Enola Gay* dropped the atomic bomb on Hiroshima, Japan, bringing an end to World War II.

1947

The Church of Jesus Christ of Latter-day Saints purchased the red brick school for $1,350 for use as a chapel.

Electric power came to Wendover, not tied to federal operations.

SEPTEMBER 16. John Cobb set a land speed record of 394.2 mph in his *Railton Mobile Special*.

NOVEMBER 1. Wendover Post Office re-established. Mr. Lynn B. Smith appointed acting postmaster.

1948

Utah Salt Company founded with salts coming from the ponds of Bonneville, Ltd. near Wendover.

1949

Western Pacific-Denver and Rio Grande inaugurated the California Zephyr streamlined transcontinental train between Oakland, California, and Chicago, Illinois (passed through Wendover).

AUGUST: Bonneville National Speed Week sponsored by Southern California Timing Association was first held; becomes an annual event. Bonneville Speedway became official course for land speed records.

University of Utah survey party operating out of the base camp at Wendover, uncovered Raven Cave, excavated Juke Box Cave, and began excavation of Danger Cave.

1950

AUGUST 7. Wendover approved for incorporation as a town; population less than 500.

Roland E. Free set world's motorcycle record of 156.71 mph.

1951

MAY. 17-year-old male hanged himself in Wendover City jail.

1952

"'Wendover Will,' the world's tallest cowboy sign, made his appearance and was an instant hit with the public."

Colonel Goldie Gardner in MG Special set record 202.02 mph.

1954

JUNE 17. Telephone officials dedicated a concrete and bronze monument on the site of the "golden splice"—the point at which the transcontinental telephone line was completed in 1914 at Wendover.

Brick gymnasium built for the school.

1958

Bill Smith died. Ann Smith took over and Gene Jones was appointed general manager of the State Line.

1959

Clouds of radiation in deadly levels spread toward U.S. Route 40, Knolls, and Wendover, following 8 tests at nearby Dugway Proving grounds.

1960

The Western Pacific Railroad turned over the Pilot Mountain water system to Wendover City.

1961

MAY 28. "Two microwave repeater stations and an underground cable repeater station on the main transcontinental communications route were blown up" by saboteurs at Wendover Notch, Cedar Mountain, and Knolls.

1963

Craig Breedlove reached a speed exceeding 400 miles per hour on the Bonneville Salt Flats.

Boy scouts found ten live hand grenades from 9 Mile Ridge area. The clips were out and they were rusted. Hill Air Force Base sent a crew out to blow them up, circa 1963.

1964

Tom Green beat Don Campbell's Australian record of 403.135 mph with a land speed record of 413.20 in Walt Arfon's *Wingfoot Express*, a jet-powered vehicle at Bonneville Speedway. Art Artfons and Craig Breedlove took turns breaking the speed record four times during the year.

1965–66

High school students bussed to Wells, Nevada. The first high school building was constructed in Wendover.

Bob and Bill Summers used a four-engined, wheel-driven race car to set a land speed record for piston engines that would stand for 26 years. The run was 409.277 mph.

NOVEMBER 7. Art Arfons in the *Green Monster* set a record of 576.553 mph in the two-way run.

NOVEMBER 15. Craig Breedlove made two perfect runs of 600.601 mph in his jet-driven *Spirit of America Sonic I.*

1966–67

New highway, Interstate 80, begun across the salt flats; completed in 1972.

1967

MAY 26. Nine students were in the first graduating class of Wendover High School.

1968

First kindergarten class in Wendover.

1969

Four boxcars filled with unfused bombs disintegrated in an explosion between Wells, Nevada, and Wendover; cause unknown.

Church of Jesus Christ of Latter-day Saints chapel dedicated in Wendover.

1970

"On October 23, 1970, *The Blue Flame* set a world land speed record of 622.407 mph driven by Gary Gabelich."

Ab Jenkins of *Mormon Meteor* fame was inducted into the Utah Hall of Fame as a charter member. Named as #11 in list of Utah's "50 Greatest Athletes of the Twentieth Century" by the *Salt Lake Tribune*, December 26, 1999.

1971

The state of Utah tried unsuccessfully to promote the Great Salt Lake Desert as a future space port for the space shuttle.

Highway I-80 bypassed Wendover to the north.

AUGUST 18. Wendover volunteer fire department organized under Chief Lamar Melville.

1972

Jim's Casino took the place of the A-1 Casino.

Lynn Poulsen began 17-year tenure as Wendover justice of the peace.

1973

JANUARY. A 1966 Pontiac ambulance was purchased for $1,508 for Wendover City. Elko County donated $750 toward the purchase. By September the city was looking at purchasing a $4,800 Suburban to use as a second ambulance. Gillette ambulance service still operating across the salt flats. New State Line Casino was constructed.

1974

Sixty-sixth annual Utah State Firemens' Association convention was held in Wendover, Utah.

1976

Wendover air base water system sold to Wendover City including Johnson's Springs.

John Palmer was in charge of promoting a Wendover tourism complex which was unsuccessful after a several-year effort.

1977

Part of Wendover air base transferred to the city and placed on the National Register of Historic Places.

1979

A missile crashed and stuck in the ground at Blue Lake.

1980

Wendover had a population of 1,099 people.

GAPA launch site and blockhouse were added to the National Register of Historic Places.

1981

Fred D. and Elma Lynn West deeded a 40% share of their West Wendover property to the Wendover Land Company.

1982

Nevada Crossing opened as a casino in Wendover. It would join the State Line, Jim's Casino, the Hideaway, and the Gold Rush.

MARCH 25. Wendover became a third-class city with a population of 1,099.

1983

The Red Garter Casino began operation at Wendover.

Heavy precipitation creates a 20-inch deep "Lake Bonneville" causing cancellation of annual speed racing.

JANUARY 11. Western Pacific Railroad Company became a subsidiary of Union Pacific Railroad.

1984

Silversmith Casino began operation across from the State Line Casino.

Vitro mill site tailings were relocated from Salt Lake City to Clive, Utah (an old Western Pacific Railroad section), and placed in an above-grade disposal cell.

JULY 23. Jim's Casino closed.

1985

Peppermill Casino opened in West Wendover.

Lt. Governor Oveson suggested that Utah ask Congress to secede Wendover, Utah, to Nevada.

1986

Swedish artist Karl Momin created *Metaphore Tree of Utah* sculpture at a cost of $2 million on the salt flats.

West Wendover library built on 2.25 acres.

1987

SEPTEMBER 24. Bureau of Land Management sold 6.54-acre parcel of land in West Wendover north of old U.S. Highway 40 to the State Line Hotel and Casino for a record $610,000.

1988

Kaiser Aluminum and Chemical Corporation sold its potash plant to Reilly Wendover.

A radioactive materials license was approved for Envirocare of Utah, Inc. Contaminated soils were thereafter shipped from Denver, Colorado, to the west desert of Utah.

1990

Wendover population at 1,626 with an area of 8.5 acres.

Ten-acre parcel of land set aside as the Wendover cemetery.

Envirocare of Utah, Inc. received a permit from Utah to dispose of mixed radioactive and hazardous contaminants near Clive, Utah, in the desert fifty miles east of Wendover.

BLM began a three-year study to investigate salt deterioration on the salt flats.

FEBRUARY. Wendover, Utah, chief of police June (Junius) Carter was arrested along with his wife and was subsequently sentenced and served prison time on drug-related charges.

AUGUST 25. 509th Memorial Dedication, "A Celebration for World Peace," at the Wendover USA Visitors Center.

Hazel Sorensen recognized as "Woman of the Year" in Wendover for her four terms as president of the American Legion Auxiliary and her service to children at Christmas each year.

1991

The City of West Wendover, Nevada, incorporated, making it one of the newest cities in Nevada; articles of incorporation filed with state of Nevada on May 2.

Al Teague set world land speed record for a single-engine streamliner with a run of 409.986 mph.

1993

The Federal Nuclear Regulatory Commission licensed Envirocare of Utah, Inc. to dispose of uranium and thorium by product tailings at the company site near the Bonnevlle Salt Flats.

1996

West Wendover High School built.

1997

The State Line and Silver Smith Casino launched a $50 million expansion, doubling its size.

SEPTEMBER: First two stop signs installed on Wendover Boulevard where Alternate 93 intersects.

LaMar Melville's John Deere tractor was "borrowed" by makers of the movie *Con Air*. The producers ended up renting the tractor for several months for much more than it was worth.

1998

Utah Senate passed a resolution supporting return of *Enola Gay* bomber to Wendover for permanent display.

1999

Wendover received a loan for $3.4 million to upgrade the water line.

Gertrude Tripp was recognized as "Woman of the Year" for her many civic contributions to Wendover.

2000

U.S. Census showed Wendover, Utah, with a population of 1,537 and West Wendover, Nevada, with a population of 4,721.

2001

Congressmen from Nevada and Utah along with commissioners from Elko County, Nevada, and Tooele County, Utah, join Wendover and West Wendover officials in annexation bid for the two Wendovers to become one within the state of Nevada.

AUGUST 2-5. 56th and 509th Composite Group Reunion held in Salt Lake and Wendover.

At Speed Week, Don and Rick Vesco join the elite group of 400 mph racers in their jet-powered car with a run of 458.45 mph.

Rocketeer enthusiasts blast away their rockets on their annual weekend on the salt flats.

SEPTEMBER 13. Collision of a 250-passenger, 18-car Amtrak train and a Union Pacific freight train pulling seventy-five empty coal cars powered by three locomotives left an Amtrak engine and a sleeper car in flames and several derailed. There were only minor injuries at the sight about 12 miles east of Wendover. Several of the wrecked cars were subsequently buried in the salt near the crash site.

Air Force training exercises held on the million-acre Utah Test and Training Range with bombing missions targeting Afghanistan look-alike camps. The training was in preparation for attacking Al Qaeda and Taliban terrorist strongholds in response to the New York City and Washington, D.C., terrorist attacks of September 11, 2001.

2002

JANUARY. State Line-Silver Smith Resorts file for Chapter 11 bankruptcy protection allowing for a reorganization.

MARCH 7. The U.S. House Judiciary Subcommittee on Commercial and Administrative law pass a bill enabling the Utah-Nevada line and Wendover, Utah, to be moved into Nevada. It required the two communities to vote on it in a referendum within two years.

JUNE 11. U.S. House committee voted for succession of Wendover to Nevada.

AUGUST 12. Nolan White became the fastest driver in the world in a race piston-driven car with twin engines at 411.25 mph. He later died on October 20, three days after crashing at 422 mph on the first half of the required two-way run while trying to break his own record.

Tanis Hammond became the fastest woman in the world at the World of Speed when she made a world record run of 299.701 mph, going 305.994 on the first half of her two-way run.

OCTOBER. The State Line Hotel and Casino and the Silver Smith were purchased at auction.

Jeanne Pflum, M.D. set new women's land speed record at 302.179 mph.

OCTOBER 25. Two $19 million F-16s from the 388th Fighter Wing collided in midair and crashed twenty-five miles southeast of Wendover on the Utah Test and Training Range. One pilot ejected safely and the other one was missing and found dead the following day. Twenty-two planes had crashed on "the 11-million acre military range" over the previous twenty-year span. Two weeks later another F-16 crashed northeast of Wendover, killing the pilot.

NOVEMBER 6. Residents voted in a non-binding referendum to unite as one city. Wendover (110 for and 61 against) and West Wendover (248 for and 191 against).

2003

MARCH. Wendover's first traffic light installed in front of the Rainbow Casino.

MARCH 12. A recreated version of the Wright Brothers'

Flyer was successfully flown at Wendover Airport. The *Flyer* was built by Utah State University engineering students.

MAY. Juke Box cave was vandalized.

AUGUST. Syrian-born Father Fawaz Ayob arrived as the new Catholic priest in Wendover. He was fluent in French, English, Spanish, and Arabic.

SEPTEMBER: A 40-megawatt thermal oxidation power plant proposed for Wendover.

Marv Jenkins drove the *Mormon Meteor III* 60 mph on the salt flats and John Hollansworth raced his exact replica of Ab Jenkins' 1934 Pierce-Arrow during the World of Speed.

OCTOBER. The U.S. Army Corps of Engineers commenced conducting the first coordinated and comprehensive field work in the Wendover Air Force Auxiliary Field environmental restoration program by collecting and analyzing samples of soil and groundwater across the entire former facility in order to determine specific types of contamination that may exist.

NOVEMBER. Marine C-130 cargo and troop transport aircraft practiced landings in the dark over a three-day period at the Wendover Airport.

Montego Bay celebrated its three-day grand opening featuring Herman's Hermits with Peter Noone.

Tooele County School District announced plans for a new soccer/track stadium and baseball diamond at Wendover High School to be built immediately, west of the school.

The Rainbow Hotel Casino commenced remodeling 149 rooms in the Nevada Crossing Hotel purchased by the Rainbow in August 2003.

DECEMBER. The restored *Enola Gay* bomber was placed on permanent display at the Udvar-Hazy Center, Smithsonian Museum in Washington, D.C.

Sixteen years of local bus service ended in Wendover and West Wendover.

The Spanish Baptist Church hosted two different Christmas plays.

2004

JANUARY. New Wendover City Council members Steve Lawrence and Karl Jorgenson began new terms, replacing Brett Shelton and Shawn Wadsworth. Gertrude Tripp began a second term in office as a council member after winning November reelection. The mayor was Steve Perry.

West Wendover City Council members were Mike Miera, Jimmy Carter, Mike Gunter, Viola Troyan, and Jamey Reilly. The mayor was Josephine Thaut.

MARCH 31. Reilly Industries, Inc. sold its Wendover, Utah, potash business to Denver-based Intrepid Mining, LLC.

1.

Wendover's Beginnings
The Good, the Bad, and the Ordinary

"Yes the desert country of Utah and Nevada does have a unique quality—and little Wendover is set in the center of so much history making!"

—E. Wardell-Hall

Surveys were completed and construction of a new railroad, owned by the Western Pacific, progressed with new towns and terminals located along the route. Wendover, Utah was founded as one of those railroad towns. Starting in 1907, a roundhouse, depot, water tower, and other essential buildings were commenced and the first train officially arrived from Salt Lake City, Utah, in 1909.

Sixty-one years earlier in 1846, westbound covered wagons had used nearby Pilot Mountain as a scepter as they struggled across the Great Salt Lake Desert on their way to California. The remote, treeless cut-off was then abandoned for the next half century until the railroad came looking for a water source to quench the thirst of the giant *"Malley"* steam engines and the smaller *"Crocodile"* locomotives.

Railroad workers located a spring about twenty-six miles north of the proposed route on the side of Pilot Mountain and recognized the opportunity to pipe water from the spring to the railroad. The water and railroad junction point became the townsite of Wendover.

Salt mining would begin during World War I. It would sputter to a halt after the war and then be revived several times until it became a staple for the economy of the little village. Land speed racing on the salt flats appeared simultaneously and added further life and color to the area.

World War II brought a startling transforma-tion to Wendover as it was chosen as the sight for one of the most important phases of the war effort. Wendover Field was rapidly built and it played a pivotal role in winning World War II.

Twenty-one heavy bomb groups trained at Wendover Field with over 20,000 personnel stationed there. In addition the 509th Composite Group carried out secret preparations under the direction of Colonel Paul W. Tibbets Jr., contributing to the abrupt end of World War II with the atomic bomb drops on Hiroshima and Nagasaki, Japan in August 1945.

In the early days of the community, there was very little organization to the tiny town. People built shanties haphazardly over the landscape because the railroad owned all the land. Pete McKellar said when he first came to Wendover, it looked as though someone had dropped a handful of buildings and they landed helter-skelter along the countryside.

Early residents constructed simple frame houses with tent roofs, tarpaper covered shacks, or tie houses with dirt and canvas roofs. They used old railroad car decking which they found piled near the round house. They tacked cardboard to the walls for insulation and then painted or added tarpaper over the cardboard.

According to William G. "Rusty" Howell, Western Pacific Railroad, Superintendent Eastern Division, *"In those days Wendover consisted mostly of shacks built out of odds and ends—mostly refuse from freight cars which had been cleaned at Wendover or other salvage taken from the railroad.*

Most of the houses were built into a bank, with three dirt sides and the front patched up with tin, cardboard, and other material."

Historian Garn Anderson described what happened next. He said, *"As time went on, the town improved a great deal. Many of the tent houses were remodeled with board coverings. Soon after the end of World War I, six houses were brought in from Salduro to be used for homes. A few years later [1932] more frame homes were moved from Gold Hill, Utah[,] when the mine closed down.*

"There were no fences, flowers or lawns in the beginning. The first trees in town were brought in from McKellar's ranch and planted at Mr. Dempson's place in 1918. Soil was hauled in and this brought about flowers, grass and some gardens. There weren't many vegetables in town. Gran Lamus would raise them in her garden and sell them to a few people. Some peddlers would bring vegetables in on the railroad to sell to the townspeople." Mrs. Letty Hewitt had a cultivated, beautiful yard by the 1920s with rose vines, a lawn, a fence and grow boxes.

People heated their homes with pot-bellied stoves fueled by coal from the railroad. Kerosene lamps were used for lights and boxes were used for furniture. Outside toilets were built at the end of a path.

In 1908, L. C. Thomas, a young switchman on the Southern Pacific at Montello, Nevada, from Louisville, Kentucky, joined Ferdinand M. Johnson of Montello in establishing Wendover's first store which they called the Spencer Mercantile Company. They located the store on William Morgan's mining claim near the Utah-Nevada state line in a large tent which was floored and walled to a height of about six feet with lumber. Johnson and Thomas made concrete blocks during quiet periods for the purpose of constructing a more substantial building for their store.

In late 1909, the partners sold their property to Mr. Robert Works. Works immediately obtained a lease on a town site lot from the Western Pacific Railroad Company and constructed a building 40 by 80 feet in dimension with the concrete blocks.

After an unsuccessful try at the real estate business in Salt Lake City, Ferdinand Johnson returned to Wendover in 1910 and re-purchased the store from Mr. Works. Johnson immediately began construction of a warehouse and dwelling.

Mrs. Johnson arrived from Salt Lake City on the first train that carried a paying passenger. Ferdinand said it was a real replica of the *"slow train from Arkansas."* Mr. Johnson gave the date of his wife's arrival as New Year's Eve, December 31, 1910. There was no place in town for her to sleep and the Johnsons had to devise sleeping quarters within the store. Mr. Johnson stated that it was *"pretty rugged going for her, [how] well*

Faded photos of Wendover taken in 1926 after a snow storm. Note the haphazard layout of the houses. Top and middle photos are combined in the bottom photo. *(Leland Scott Tanner, Gertrude Tripp)*

Eugene Munsee, an early settler in the Wendover area, homesteaded at Pilot Springs, circa 1876. *(Utah State Historical Society)*

I remember the crying spell she had—caused, I suppose by the [dismal] *outlook for the future."*

At that time many herds of sheep were trailed from northern Utah and Idaho for winter grazing on the surrounding open range: Gold Hill, Callao, Ferber Flats, White Horse Pass, Ibapah, Dolly Varden Country, Steptoe, and Antelope Valley, and numerous other locations where winter grazing was abundant. Many of the outfits obtained part or all of their supplies from Wendover and helped considerably to make Wendover quite active during the fall, winter, and spring seasons.

The early years of Wendover were a seemingly lawless period in the town's history. It was the beginning of prohibition and *"due to Wendover's isolation, it became the center for much illicit traffic in moonshine whiskey."*

Prohibition in the United States lasted from 1920 to 1933 due to Amendment 18 of the U.S. Constitution. However, a wartime food-control act went into effect earlier which made alcohol illegal to manufacture or sell. After September 8, 1917, no

whiskey was legally manufactured and no more beer was made after May 1, 1919. By July 1 no intoxicants could be sold and saloons were illegal also.

Prohibition in the 1920s generated numerous tales nationwide. In nearby Ibapah all the ranchers annually gathered their cattle at the Wade Parrish Ranch in the center of the valley. After they were all together, they trailed the calves to Gold Hill where they loaded them aboard cattle cars on the Deep Creek Railroad for shipment through Wendover to market.

Their immediate reward was moonshine whiskey from the stills around Gold Hill. Some of the partying cowboys had more than a little difficulty staying atop their horses on the 15-mile ride back to Ibapah.

A humorous incident related to the illegal trafficking of liquor near Wendover was told by Jay Hicks. The comical experience happened to him and his grandfather, John A. Erickson. Erickson owned the Last Chance Ranch on the southern edge of the salt flats. He supplied beef for the railroad camp of Wendover twenty-five miles away.

At that time (probably about 1920) there were whiskey stills in the hills around Wendover. On certain weeks large sacks of corn were dumped from the train and other weeks, sugar was dumped into the sage brush. When John Erickson and his grandson Jay Hicks rode looking for cows, they would notice the sugar and corn sacks.

One day, while driving the cows out of the hills, Jay saw one cow do a flip flop with its tail in the air. He rode over to see what happened and discovered the cow had fallen into a hole with a moonshine still inside. Mr. Erickson came to look.

Sheepmen trailed through the middle of Wendover with their herds and bought supplies from Ferd Johnson's store. *(Molly Hewitt Taylor)*

Early A-1 cabins in West Wendover. They were formerly owned by Joe Conley and the Tri State Merc. *(Gertrude Tripp)*

John and Jay saw that the cow had fallen through the roof of a dugout built into a hillside with a log wall on one side. The dugout was camouflaged by trees. It was full of whiskey mash—eight barrels full. She had knocked over all eight and the stench was horrendous.

Another time, Mr. Erickson stopped at a working still with a fire going but no one was in sight. He found a jug and filled it, which took quite a while. He later met the moonshiner, Jimmy Holden of Wendover, and told him that he had taken a gallon. The man responded that it was all right because *"I eat your beef too."*

Joseph Conley and Thomas Conley appeared with the horde of new-comers following the building of the railroad and purchased a mining location on the Nevada side of the line in Wendover. They erected a building within which they allegedly carried on bootlegging, etc.

The Conleys made a homestead entry on the land Western Pacific had selected for a town site within Utah. The railroad was very anxious to locate the terminal within Utah to avoid the tax laws of Nev-

ada. The railroad began construction of several buildings including a hotel and round house when they found out that the Conleys had previously homesteaded the land.

The railroad worked a deal with the Conleys whereby the railroad obtained title to the town site for $10,000 and deeded one acre of land and water rights to the two homesteaders. It was not long until Joseph had Tom's interest in the property and had erected a building in which he conducted a hotel, store, pool hall, feed corral, and restaurant. The property became known as Conley's Acre.

Mr. Ferdinand Johnson operated an adjoining store and felt that *"as a natural consequence,"* he and Conley were unfriendly to one another. He found Mr. Conley *"a constantly active and uncompromising adversary"* and related several examples of his *"annoying acts."*

In 1920, Ferd Johnson added an extensive, supposedly fireproof addition to his store (the property was owned by Marie Johnston in 2004). Johnson carried mostly groceries and men's clothing in his store. He purchased a large amount of merchandise in the fall of 1922 amounting to $20,000 to augment the usual

First two homes built near the upper highway on Wendover's east end, circa 1920. The house with the trees still stood in 2004, immediately west of the Wendover City offices. The home belonged to Mr. & Mrs. Percy Hewitt. *(Molly Hewitt Taylor)*

Last Chance Ranch

Swedes John and Hilda Erickson were called on a mission to Ibapah, Utah, in 1882 by the Church of Jesus Christ of Latter-day Saints. Ibapah is located sixty miles south of Wendover by road. They moved to Ibapah before Wendover was in existence. They worked among the Goshute Indians at Ibapah. The Ericksons homesteaded the Last Chance Ranch half-way between Ibapah and Wendover on the edge of the salt flats in 1898. They raised alfalfa hay, livestock, fresh fruit, and had an excellent garden thanks to the fertile soil containing potash. John Erickson later operated a mail route three times per week after William "Wid" Lamb of Gold Hill and Wendover gave it up. The route included Wendover, Gold Hill, Callao, Trout Creek, Pleasant Valley, and Deep Creek. Mr. Erickson delivered mail by horseback and then with a Kiesel truck. His wife Hilda was a dentist, midwife, missionary, and merchant. She lived to age 108 and was the last living Mormon pioneer who had crossed the plains before the coming of the railroad.

In 1923 the Ericksons sold the Last Chance to a wealthy New York family named Dunlap. Mr. Dunlap, a stout, balding man of about forty ostensibly manufactured whiskey to be bootlegged during Prohibition. Fred Boyd of Ibapah worked there as a ranch hand for a time. He told of an incident in which Revenue agents came to investigate. The farm hands were ordered to hurriedly feed the unprocessed mash for the alcohol to the hogs. The animals consequently became intoxicated.

The bootlegging operation had potential because of being remotely located, yet near the Deep Creek Railway, and so the product could be shipped east to a ready market. Apparently, the whole thing became too risky because the impressive two-story mansion the Dunlaps had built abruptly burned to the ground. Mr. Dunlap caused the conflagration when he reportedly filled an open container with gasoline and floated a lighted candle on the surface of the flammable liquid, causing a delayed explosion as the fumes reached the candle when it burned lower. He was able to leave the vicinity of the ranch until after the house burned. Hired man Byron Christiansen and others tried in vain to save a beautiful player piano used in the parlor. "The Dunlaps left the area" and were not heard from again. They had attempted to collect an insurance claim, but to no avail.

stock of supplies. He did so to accommodate the numerous sheep outfits that came each winter on the vast grazing ranges adjacent to Wendover. Ferd wrote *"The post office was part of the same building."*

Mr. Johnson stated that on December 3, 1922, at 4:30 a.m. he was awakened *"by unusual sounds. I sprang to the window and could see a small blaze on the upper floor of the Conley Hotel building and I immediately thought there would be no trouble to extinguish it with the water usually available.*

"The Conley acre laid between our property and the railroad water tank from which the water was piped up town and several openings and water faucets had been installed there for different uses. When we undertook to draw water from the line for use in extinguishing the blaze, we found to our utter disappointment that no water could be had." Ferd discovered that every tap between his property and the water source was open.

Johnson continued "[On] *account of the extremely low pressure no water was passing through so there was nothing could be done except to stand and watch the fire progress to the complete destruction of the Conley hotel building, the small dwelling on the Conley ground, and finally catching our property [including] the original building we had constructed for occupancy when we first came in 1910.*

"The complete loss of the buildings and stocks amounted to not less than $50,000. I had been carrying sufficient insurance to cover but by this time the lucrative business we had enjoyed during the first World War had begun to decline quite seriously and on September 1, 1922, had asked the insurance agent to reduce our insurance one half. So we were not sufficiently covered when the fire occurred a few months later." A railroad employee was burned to death in the fire.

Johnson's store faced south. It also faced the railroad and the space between the front of the buildings and the railroad was known as *"Main Street."* Johnson opened another store he called the *"Lumberyard Building"* after the fire. He subsequently left Wendover and sold his holdings to J. A. Lyman. Lyman's building eventually burned also. Lyman had the misfortune of being robbed by a person with his face dyed red with

Dunlap mansion on the Last Chance Ranch. *(Molly Hewitt Taylor)*

and some common in modern day.

Charges recorded in the dockets included crimes of riot; indecent assault; burglary; many cases of drunkenness; vagrancy; removing horses and wagons from a lady who was the sole supporter of her family; indebtedness, usually to the A. J. Spencer Mercantile; having intoxicating liquors and 300 gallons of fermenting mash; and willfully, maliciously, and knowingly obtaining goods, food, and lodging under false pretense.

All the lawlessness created a need for a jail. One old-timer claimed to have been the first occupant. It happened this way. He was awarded the contract to build the jail. It took the balance of the summer to construct the edifice. When he and his partner were paid for the job, *"they staged a monumental celebration"* that was wild in nature. They wound up in the newly built jail as a consequence.

Allegedly, Jack Dempsey (the famous boxer), A. V. Smith, and Bert Christie were accused in October 1917 of putting one Earl Barnes in fear with a deadly weapon by force and without consent and did take,

mercurochrome and his belly stuffed with a pillow. Lyman was robbed twice, which put him out of business.

There were law enforcement officers and other rudimentary elements of government locally in Wendover to handle lawbreakers. At that time, D. M. Dave Adamson was sheriff of Tooele County and he kept Charles McKellar in Wendover as his deputy. William Mieklejohn had been a Wendover deputy prior to McKellar.

Early justices of the peace were J. W. Johnson, 1911; Joseph Conley, 1911 to 1913 (yes, the same Joe Conley previously mentioned); J. A. Vinable 1913 to 1918; William A. Lyman, 1919; J. F. Cameron, 1920; and O. W. Hargreaves, 1921. Wendover had postal services also. Ferdinand M. Johnson was postmaster from 1911 until he left Wendover in 1923. Johnson was followed as postmaster by James A. Lyman, Jr., Nellie M. Trezona, and Millie Lyman.

One old-timer claimed Wendover was as *"wild as all get out"* in the early days. That claim is backed up by local justice of the peace court dockets from 1911 to 1921. A perusal of crimes before the court shows some problems unique to that time period

The old swimming hole south of Wendover, November 1921. It had hot, tepid, and cool spring water coming from the bottom. It was won-derful. Eight or ten local girls would take off their dresses, leave on their underwear and petticoats, and jump in. Of course, they didn't know that boys were hiding in the rocks just above the swimming hole behind them. When the girls finished they would run across the salt flats to the bushes and the hot wind and sunshine would dry them off. *(Glenda Green)*

steal, and carry away the sum of $243 from Earl Barnes' possession. A change of venue was filed for showing bias and prejudice.

More than one defendant was accused of assault with intent to kill with a deadly weapon, one of whom *"did beat, strike, and bruise the body of the accuser."* Other crimes were of forgery; transporting liquor into Utah; interfering with an officer searching an automobile; and use of vile, vulgar, obscene language on the premises of the Western Pacific Hotel.

Other charges included refusing to go to work; stealing an ivory jewel case containing jewels worth $100 or more; carrying a concealed weapon; stealing and selling an auto tire and tube; willingly and feloniously taking from the freight depot of the Western Pacific Railroad three bundles of sheep hides or pelts valued at $100; arson; taking two yearling bulls and one yearling heifer from John Erickson; and swiping one

plate of meat from the ice box of the Wendover Mercantile and Hotel. One man was accused of stealing and riding away a horse belonging to William Lamb.

William M. Lamb operated a livery stable in the early days of Wendover. He also regularly drove the stage between Wendover and Gold Hill, Utah, and later ran a general store at Gold Hill for years. Still later, he and his wife moved back to Wendover where they operated a café and service station.

William Lamb's daughter was Edna "Ted" Pankratz who grew up in Wendover starting in 1908. She lived among the greed, arson, gunplay, prostitution, and tragedy, and lived to tell about it. She and her father calculated that the railroad men, bums, drifters, and teamsters needed food for their bellies so they opened up *"Ted's Boarding House"* inside a tent with a long wooden slab for a table.

Conley's Acre

In 1951, Mr. Blair Lamus wrote: *"I came to Salduro in early 1923. Although only 10 miles apart there was no amount of contact between the two communities and I did not get acquainted in Wendover for a considerable time afterwards. As a result what little I know about early day Wendover I acquired by hearsay and contact with some of the old timers such as Joe Conley and Jack Jensen who were partners in the Tri State Mercantile.*

At the time of my arrival the Conley Hotel, the Cooley Hotel, the Spencer Mercantile Company's store operated by Ferd Johnson had already been destroyed by fire."

Blair Lamus stated in a letter that allegedly *"Joe Conley was a great and controversial figure. He was a man of great generosity, strong convictions and violent temper. He had considerable foresight and business ability and was civic-minded to a greater extent than any of his contemporaries in Wendover. Conley was engaged throughout his time in Wendover in violent feuds with many different people, and he was accused directly or indirectly of arson, armed burglary and other crimes as well."* Auer Jensen who subsequently owned the Tri State Merc said Conley did more good than bad in the community. He said he had a heart of gold. School teacher Elsie Lord said Conley funded the local elementary school to get it started. Conley was a lawyer by training.

Conley's first controversy in Wendover was with the Western Pacific Railroad which wound up in litigation. He acquired the Wendover town site from the federal government ahead of the railroad company and they undertook to condemn it. It was finally settled by the Western Pacific paying Conley $10,000 for the town site and giving him the right to all the water he could use on the acre of ground which he retained as long as the Western Pacific Railroad Company pipe line to Pilot Mt. was in existence. Further they agreed to build the depot for the railroad immediately adjacent to the so-called "Conley's Acre," which they failed to do.

Joe Conley had the only tourist cabins in Wendover, to begin with. His cabins were the precursor to the A-1. Later on, Bill Smith built some cabins in conjunction with his Cobblestone Service (see chapter 2). Bill heard that Conley was going to burn him out because of the competition he was giving him. Consequently, Bill stood guard each night with a gun, even though he didn't like guns. Sure enough, Joe reportedly came along with a can of gas. Bill hesitated in shooting Joe. He didn't want to kill him or even shoot him in the leg, so he hit him over the head with the gun. It saved his cabins.

Later on, Fred West bought the A-1 from Joe Conley with Bill Smith as a silent partner. Fred didn't have the money to buy it alone. Obviously, Joe did not like Mr. Smith and was not aware that he was a partner in the deal.

A customer inside Lyman's store. James A Lyman built the Castle Service with his own hands. *(Glenda Green)*

She whipped up meals of mutton, beef, vegetables, soup, and dessert. It was not fancy and only cost thirty-five cents a plate. The word went out and the place became popular and profitable.

She told of a sheepherder finding an unidentified skeleton in the Nevada desert. Her dad decided the man should have a decent burial so he made a wooden coffin complete with a padded lining. They put the skeleton inside and nailed the lid shut.

They wanted to give the poor soul a funeral and the only place available was the local saloon. Her father preached a brief sermon and she sang "Rock of Ages." They carried the coffin into the desert and buried it in an unmarked grave.

William Morgan's mining locations in Nevada were about the only land that was available which was not owned by the railroad. Consequently, Morgan sold a parcel of the claim to a woman known as Mamie Morris who erected the New-house Hotel in partnership with Mrs. Chris Schrieber and another woman. According to Mr. Johnson, it was *"very well conducted and well-known for its hospitality, and was really a place of*

prostitution." It was located next to a deep gully or ravine.

Dr. Joseph H. Peck, a physician hired by the railroad during the construction of the Deep Creek Railroad, related stories of his acquaintance with a madam named Mamie whom he said operated the Blue Goose bordello in Wendover. Whether the Blue Goose and the New-house Hotel were owned by the same woman is unclear. The Blue Goose structure consisted of six or eight small 8´ x 8´ rooms lined in a row. The main entrance had a desk and chair inside and a curtain hanging in the back. It had a piano with grand sounding tones. A red lantern hung over the front door.

Glenda Lyman, as a little girl, delivered newspapers around town and to the Blue Goose, too. Her mother told her to never go inside. Glenda said the girls wore pretty dresses and nice smelling perfume, and they were nice to her. They would sit around and talk and give her sarsaparilla to drink.

Jay Hicks remembered his grandfather talking with Mamie outside the Blue Goose and said she had no nose, only two holes in her face for nostrils. Mary Kemp was the last to operate the sporting house and had a diseased face, according to another remembrance. They are probably one and the same person. Mary took care of the down-and-out winos and others who needed help after she went out of business. The Blue Goose was down on the flats where the army base was eventually built. The army closed it

Left: Lyman's Castle Service Station had peaked towers. *(Glenda Green)* Middle: postmasters Millie & James A. Lyman. *(Chloe Parrish collection)* Right: Millie Lyman was postmaster of Wendover with the post office in her home. *(Glenda Lyman Green)*

The building on the right was the Wendover Elementary School and the white building was used for all community activities. The smaller brick building was erected in the 1920s and the larger white one was built in 1932. Both were also used for church. Above the chimney in the photo is the peak called Needlepoint. The distant telephone pole between the buildings is near Highway 40. *(Brent Peterson)*

when they moved in about 1940. It was located where the Hideaway Club operated in 2003.

Young, single girls looking for work found it at the potash plant closing the sacks of potash by hand sewing. When the Depression hit and they lost their jobs, some of them resorted to working at the Blue Goose in Wendover. Several of them eventually married railroad men.

Schools

"There was no school in Wendover, Nevada, in the early years, only two saloons & brothels and two or three one-room shacks," wrote one author. An original school building was built on the Utah side sometime prior to 1915 and Elsie I. Lord (later Jensen) was teacher from 1915 to 1919.

Mrs. Lord said the building was somewhat of an old shack. The Munsee children who were nieces and nephews of Gene Munsee who homesteaded Pilot ranch were some of the first pupils as was Varian Anderson. There were fifteen to twenty students each year. In 1915 three students graduated from the 8th grade from three different families.

The school came under the supervision of the Tooele County School District in 1915. 1915 was the year schools in Utah were consolidated by law. District records in 1915 show Elsie I. Lord was paid a salary of $75 per month and the janitor, a Mrs. Clark, was paid $15 monthly.

All the teachers were required to hold a teaching certificate approved by the state board of education. One early school teacher was said to be allergic to men!

Mrs. Lord wrote that a new brick building was erected by Tooele School District while she was teaching there. The steam-heated school house was a one-room building which served for school, recreation, church, etc. A male teacher fired up the boiler early in the morning before school to warm it up. Bruce Lamus did so for church when he was in the upper elementary grades.

Community Center

The nation was in the deep throes of the Depression when a new white community building was built in 1932 in Wendover. Workers for the WPA (The Work Progress [later Work Project] Administration) complet-

Students swinging next to "Saltona," Wendover's first elementary school, circa 1920s. *(Molly Hewitt Taylor)*

There was a small movie projector window facing northward, where movies could be projected on a screen on the north end. There was also a small elevated stage at the north end where plays were put on.

A man from out of town came through every two weeks with a movie projector and would show a Hopalong Cassidy movie or *"The Hunchback of Notre Dame,"* etc. The building had hardwood floors which made it ideal for dancing, especially when corn meal was strewn across the dance hall. Folding chairs provided the seating. You might see three or four generations on the dance floor at once.

Downstairs was used for roller skating at recess and other times. There were also restrooms and kitchen facilities. The electricity was furnished by the Western Pacific boiler room and conducted at low voltage. Consequently, the lights would sometimes be dim due to line loss.

ed the building. The WPA was a program designed by the Franklin Roosevelt administration to put people to work who were out of work during the Depression. The WPA built highways, parks, buildings, swimming pools, sewers, and athletic fields throughout the nation.

This building stood for forty-six years until it was *"demolished to make way for a two-story duplex"* in 1978. The white building was used as a movie house and a place for dances. If you walked up the steps and entered through the double doors, one of the first things you would see was a small elevated booth on the south wall, accessed by a ladder with six or eight rungs.

To the south of the school and community building was an open dirt and gravel field where the children played football and baseball at recess. To the east were the main residential streets of old Wendover. The first house on the north of the street was Varian "Chunky" and Ada Anderson's. Chunky maintained the water line from Pilot Peak to Wendover and

Fifth-through eighth-graders in 1939 with teacher Ernie Barlow (back row) posed on steps of new school. First-through fourth-graders used another room of a two-room school with a second teacher. *(Bruce Lamus)*

Wendover, Nevada, elementary school in 1942. *(Gertrude Tripp)*

worked for the Western Pacific railroad. The telephone company owned a white house across the street from Chunky's. Next was Lind Hutchinson who traveled on his small railroad scooter between Wendover and Elko as a track inspector. Two houses further east was Melvin "Spike" and Mary Birdzell's home.

Food

Local historian Garn Anderson remarked that *"Where man lives man*

1947 Wendover Elementary class. *(Shirley Peterson)*

must eat." Obtaining, transporting, and storing *"food was somewhat of a problem during the early period from 1907 to the late 30s."* The railroad was about the only means of getting supplies to and from Wendover until the Victory Highway was built in 1924.

People from Wendover and *"isolated points along the way"* placed their orders to be delivered from Salt Lake City on the "Way Car." Cured meats came by the refrigerated way car. Fresh fruits, vegetables, and meats were delivered by a faster method, the passenger train engine.

Anderson reported that *"individual and family orders were placed with Tom Hannigan, round house foreman. These were sent to the Colorado Market in Salt Lake City. Each order was packed separately and the individual's name written on the outside. All were then placed together in a large box and delivered at the depot in Salt Lake just before the train pulled out. They were placed on top of the engine tender for a fast three[-]hour run to Wendover.*

"On arrival, everyone met the train. The boxes were dropped to the ground, opened up and each person issued his package of meat which he or she rushed home to the ice box. On days when the train was late there was some anxiety over the condition of the roast ordered ahead for Sunday."

The Spencer Mercantile and later the Tri State Merc furnished basic food needs for Wendover families. By the 1930s, peddlers from Grantsville made house-to-house deliveries of butter, fresh vegetables and fruits, and meats. Orders were taken for future delivery each time they dropped by.

Peter McKellar and Charlie Orme furnished local residents with

Mrs. Sigmon's fourth-grade class 1957-58. *(Ron Christensen)*

First grade, Wendover Elementary, 1955-56. *(Glenda Green)*

made for keeping food cold. Ice was kept in a storage compartment at the top of the unit. As the ice melted, the water drained into a pan under the ice box. The pan had to be regularly emptied or it overflowed onto the floor and had to be mopped up. The ice came from the railroad ice house.

An earlier method of refrigeration involved a hand-made wooden frame covered with fabric such as flannel or burlap or canvas. A typical size would be six feet high including the legs on which it stood and two to three feet square. Insects were kept out by a screen around the sides with a solid top and bottom.

A pan of water on top furnished moisture which was wicked out by the cloth draped over it. As the moisture in the fabric evaporated, it caused a cooling

fresh milk and sometimes fresh meat from their dairy. People would buy meat from local ranchers and hang a side of fresh pork or mutton or a quarter of a beef in a shed during the colder months of the year and cut from them as needed. Mr. Orgill sold t-bone steaks for forty cents a piece in the early 30s.

Families stored their perishable items in ice boxes

Tri-State Merc and Victory Garage in 1926. *(Gertrude Tripp)*

Setting telephone poles in the mud. *(Utah State Historical Society)*

Distributing telephone poles near Wendover. *(Utah State Historical Society)*

effect inside. A breeze added further cooling. The home-built cooler worked similarly to modern swamp coolers except they were used to keep food cool.

Transcontinental Telephone was Joined at Wendover

President Theodore Vail of American Telephone and Telegraph began planning the final link of telephone service across the U.S. in 1910. Telephone service was in operation from New York to Salt Lake City by 1911. Bell Telephone Company of Nevada was incorporated on January 13, 1913, to provide construction of the last link in the transcontinental telephone line.

Workers surveyed a line between Wadsworth, Nevada, and Wendover, Utah, within five months after crews were sent into the field in November 1913. Property lines had been determined and easements had been purchased. The company had worked out the problem of *"an adequate repeating device that could amplify voice communications at a constant level over great distances."*

By 1914, the final 400 miles of transcontinental telephone service were completed across the deserts of Nevada and Utah. Telephone construction crews faced the same perils of sand, floods, snakes, desert heat, lack of water, hard ground, and blizzards as the

wagon trains and railroad builders had experienced previously. The section across the salt flats was a tremendous problem because of glaring heat reaching 130 degrees at times. Crews strung open copper wire on green glass insulators on 130,000 poles.

Phillip Earl of the Nevada Historical Society described the process. *"An army of 100 men, 34 wagons, 116 horses, four trucks, three automobiles and a crawler tractor had meanwhile descended upon Nevada, but a worse time could not have been picked.*

"The spring of 1914 was one of the wettest in 30 years and crews often found the stakes underwater when they

Drilling holes to set telephone poles during the wet spring of 1914. *(Utah State Historical Society)*

Telephone crews lived in mobile horse-drawn trailer wagons. *(Utah State Historical Society)*

newsmen. For three days they feasted on roast duck and other catered gourmet delicacies in a dining tent. In addition, champagne was flowing on the Nevada side of the line, served in glass insulators.

Two flags were nailed to the cross arm atop the final pole by a lineman. The flags included an American flag and another which proclaimed "S.F.-N.Y.

arrived. *Roads had to be built the whole way to haul in poles and wire as well as every crumb of food, piece of bedding and drop of water. In some areas, the vehicles bogged down in the sand; in others, they mired in the mud. Mosquitoes swarmed out of the sagebrush in such numbers that the men had to make blankets out of barley sacks to keep the horses from being eaten alive and they had to be constantly on guard against rattlesnakes.*

"There also were personal hardships aplenty, but the men persisted since each and every one of them felt a sense of mission and history as they went about their daily tasks. A total of 13,900 poles were erected; each man had perhaps taken a million steps in the cause of the four-month project and the line-men had climbed another half-million steps up and down the poles." The disabling sands necessitated American Telephone and Telegraph Company sending an extra fleet of Model-T Fords to help out.

The final splice was made on the Utah-Nevada state line at Wendover on June 17, 1914, by crews of Bell Telephone of Nevada from the west and Mountain States Telephone and Telegraph which built from the east. Local festivities were attended by telephone executives in dark, heavy business suits, as well as locals and

Completion of the first transcontinental telephone line in Wendover, June 17, 1914. *(Utah State Historical Society)*

Toll Line Completed June 17, 1914."
At a signal, two teams and wagons with
their crews crossed under the last pole
while a cameraman recorded the event
on motion picture film.

The Panama-Pacific Exposition of
1915 was chosen as the time for the
first official message to be sent from
New York City to San Francisco. On
January 25, 1915, Alexander Graham
Bell in New York sent a message to his
former assistant Thomas Watson in San
Francisco with perfect reception. They
were joined by AT&T president
Theodore Vail in Florida and U.S. pres-
ident Woodrow Wilson in Washington,
D.C.

Utah Salduro Company trenchers were used to build the Wendover Cutoff
highway across the salt flats. *(Gertrude Tripp)*

AT&T had placed 32 repairmen and repair equipment on horseback along the desert route to make sure
there would be no interruption in the communication. AT&T initially set the cost of a three-minute call
at $20.70 and each additional minute would be $6.75.

The Wendover Cutoff of the Victory/Lincoln Highway

Since there was no highway going west across the
desert, the people initially depended on the railroad for
transportation. However, traffic could come to
Wendover indirectly by road from the south via Callao
and Gold Hill. This road may have been the so-called
"commissary road." By 1917, the Deep Creek Railroad
was completed, making the stage and freight line road
less of a necessity.

In 1917 also, the first auto road was completed
between Wendover and Knolls. Prior to that time,
some of the early travelers drove directly on the salt
from Knolls to Wendover. Later when the road was
built, it was only wide enough for one car with
turnouts every so often for passing. If two cars met, one
would have to back to a turnout. They weren't good at
backing and would often end up stuck in the muddy
salt. One old-timer made a good amount of money
with his team of horses pulling the hapless travelers
out. He charged $10 per vehicle to pull them out.

The route leading from Gold Hill to Wendover
was an offshoot of the Lincoln Highway which was
created as a result of a desperate need to improve roads

all across the nation. Mass production of automobiles
made owning them more affordable to increasing
numbers of Americans. Roads used by wagons and the
like were not suitable for use by cars. Furthermore
these roads were not connected and only useful in
leading to a market or railroad center in a local area.

At first, government did not provide for highways
either monetarily or in any oversight manner. Consequently, business stepped in, including the Lincoln
Highway Association. This association was organized in
July 1913 with the goal to develop a highway leading
across the continent from New York to California. The
founders of the Lincoln Highway intended on using
*"already-existing roads that went in the general direction for
their desired route and then incorporate these roads into their
highway."*

The route through western Utah went west to
Grantsville, south through Skull Valley, and then south-
ward to Fish Springs where it joined and followed the
Pony Express trail to Callao and Ibapah. From 1919 to
1927, the highway went directly west across the mud
flats (salt flats) past Granite Mountain to Gold Hill.
This was named the Goodyear Cutoff, Sieberling
Section.

On the state level, officials were initially promoting a southern route (Lincoln Highway) to California
leading to Los Angeles rather than the destination of
San Francisco. One official of the Utah State
Automobile Association apparently reflected the atti-
tude of many Utah officials. He said: *"Any road across
the western section of our state is valueless to Utah. . ."*

Wagon hauling gravel in Wendover for the Victory Highway. *(Molly Hewitt Taylor)*

location north of the same hill. The gravel used in paving it came from a gravel pit located near what was later the Western Motel north of the modern U.S. 40. It was named the Victory Highway or Wendover Cutoff.

There is little written information concerning the Victory Highway. A brochure published by George L. Clark in 2002 gave some details. He wrote that the Victory Highway Association was incorporated in 1921 at Topeka, Kansas. It was organized to remember the Americans who served in *"the World War"* meaning World War I. It went from New York City to San Francisco along a 3,271-mile automobile route which passed through Wendover when it was completed.

Conversely, Northern California civic groups felt that a cutoff across the salt flats would greatly enhance travel to their part of the state.

At the same time, Governor Spry told a Lincoln Highway official that his intentions were to build a new road leading directly west across the salt desert, including forty miles of mud flats and salt beds. One author explained it this way: *"Spry encouraged the improvement of the miserable path that went west of Salt Lake City across the salt flats to Wendover."*

In September 1914, the Salt Lake, Tooele, and Grantsville business communities met along with the governor, the state road engineer, and the Utah Automobile Club and passed a resolution *"that supported a road to Wendover."* The resolution also stated that the Lincoln Highway would be changed to follow the same route, contrary to the intentions of the Lincoln Highway Association. Such lobbying efforts were further strengthened by support of the Salt Lake Commercial Club and the Salt Lake Rotary Club, according to Lincoln Highway historian Jesse G. Petersen.

In January 1915, the Utah Legislature appropriated $30,000 and the Salt Lake City Council contributed another $10,000 to the building of the Wendover highway. The road, when built, was gravel and was originally parallel to the railroad as it went through the hamlet of Wendover.

Consequently at Wendover, the road passed along the south side of the hill which juts out into the desert on the west side of Wendover. Later, where the Utah-Nevada state line exists the route was changed to a

Clark quotes *The Bulletin of San Francisco* in September 1922 which triumphantly proclaimed on its editorial page, in part: *"When the Victory Highway is completed, it will constitute the greatest monument in all history. From the pyramids to the peace palace at The Hague there is nothing that compares with the gigantic enterprise of proclaiming our part in the World War by means of a paved roadway crossing the continent and linking the two oceans with a concrete chain 3,300 miles long. The most colossal of the triumphal arches, ancient or modern, becomes a minor circumstance when contrasted with the Victory Highway. And like the roads of ancient Rome, it will be an enduring monument preserved as long as the Untied State remains the great republic of the West."*

The plans were to have statues of soldiers and bronze eagle monuments erected along the highway at the borders of each state. These were to be funded by the efforts of political and community leaders. Few were actually placed. However, in the end, the highway was marked with orange, diamond-shaped Victory Highway road signs along the way.

In 1920, construction began on the section of the Victory Highway east of Wendover. By 1923, the Secretary of Agriculture decided at the federal level to fund the Victory Highway west of Salt Lake City. It was known as federal aid project number 51-A. The road paralleled the Western Pacific Railroad located immediately to the south in a 41-mile straight line from Knolls to Wendover going west. *"Because of the construc-*

tion difficulties involved, the road 'furnished the most novel example of road building methods of any highway constructed in 1924.'"

Ben Blow, president of the Victory Highway Association wrote an article in *Good Roads: The Journal of Highway Engineering and Transportation* about the Victory Highway in June of 1924. He said that conditions across the Great American Desert (Bonneville Salt Flats) were so unusual *"as to be unmatched in the history of highway building."*

Mr. Blow referred to the salt flats as *"the stumbling block which confronted all highway organizations in their plans for road development. . ."* He was one who, early on, recognized that the salt was *"as hard as rock, as smooth as a billiard table, and as non-skid as un-surfaced concrete . . . forming a great national speedway for automobiles upon which no matter how high the automobile tires keep cool due to the refrigerating properties of the salt."*

Many of the same problems were encountered as in building the railroad bed. Three basic problems arose in construction. The first problem involved how to build a solid base, the second was how to provide for and protect from the back-and-forth flow of water, and the third involved the logistics of building across the salt flats.

The salt beds were a combination of salt particles and clay silt, a remnant of the bottom of Lake Bonneville, an ancient inland sea. Much of the time, the soil deposit is damp a few inches underneath and becomes *"a quagmire many feet in depth."* At other times there is a foot or so of water which shifts from one end of the flats to the other by wind action, making one end dry and the other covered with two feet of water.

Louise Ann Noeth informatively wrote in her book entitled *Bonneville Salt Flats: "The Wendover cutoff section, just like the railway line, was built directly upon the heavy rock salt bed, using the notorious slimy clay mud excavated immediately next to the roadway. Blair and Ed Lamus, Wendover construction men who won the contract to build the salt section, knew that the gooey mud would produce a thoroughly satisfactory sub grade for the road when dried.*

"Lamus shared the knowledge with highway engineer Lee Wendelboe, and the discovery helped reduce the cost to a mere $9,000 per mile, far below the average of the day. The construction method was unique. . ." The costs along the *"Great White Way"* were less than other sections of the

Wooden culverts lasted much longer than metal ones for the highway across the salt beds. Wooden pins held the culverts together. *(California State Automobile Association/ Louise Ann Noeth)*

highway, due in part to the ease of digging in the salt and clay.

As was mentioned, the newly-formed construction company of Lamus, Zimmer, and Lamus received the contract to build the grade across the salt portion of the highway. Ed Lamus was general foreman, Blair Lamus was his son, and R. C. Zimmer was the superintendent. They all worked for the Solvay Process Company, harvesting potash from the salt plain and were granted a leave of absence to work on the highway. They lacked experience in building roads but had extensive experience in dealing with the salt beds.

Jesse Peterson quoted R. E. Dillree who worked as an engineer on the Lincoln Highway Seiberling Section across eighteen miles of the salt beds. Dillree stated: *"In one place . . . it was necessary to use four tons of hay before work could proceed in order to secure traction which would allow for the movement of the grader, and even the three caterpillars with a combined horsepower of 230, were required to pull one elevating grader.*

"Breakdowns were frequent, and it was only by the exercise of ingenuity and all available resources that many places were completed. Underground flows in many places caused saturation of desert material, and often sunk [sic] the vast caterpillar tractors half way underground as if in quicksand." Similar conditions existed in building the Victory Highway further north.

Charles Kelly described in detail how they built the highway. He said: *"Profiting by previous attempts, and conducting numerous experiments, the engineers in charge evolved a unique method which had never been employed* elsewhere. They found that if the roadbed was built directly on the salt, it would sink, due to the percolation of water through the salt bed underneath, which is porous.

"The road embankment, being absolutely level for forty miles, constitutes a dam across the salt flats. If water collected during the winter on the surface to a greater depth on one side than on the other, the pressure on the higher side would force the water through the porous bed of salt beneath, dissolving it away and allowing the roadbed to sink.

"To overcome this, a novel method was adopted. A trench three feet wide was dug down through the salt to the mud beneath. Other trenches were dug at some distance from the first to a depth of fifteen feet."

Highway engineer Lee Wendleboe added that a key trench next to the roadbed was necessary to act as a seal between the clay under the salt and the clay used in the road bed. As many as six trenches were dug outward from the road bed at regular intervals. An excavation machine with a twelve-foot diameter digging wheel did the digging. It was leased from the Solvay Process Company. A conveyor moved the clay to the proper position on the roadbed.

Wendleboe later wrote: "The salt from these trenches, which in some places was four feet deep, was discarded but the mud from below the salt was used to build the grade, directly on top of the first trench. Thus the mud in the first trench, connecting with the embankment above and the mud beneath, formed a dike which was impervious to percolating waters and prevented the salt from being dissolved away. The grade was then topped with eight inches of gravel, and the road was complete."

All-wood culverts were a unique feature of the Victory Highway. The heavy timber box drains were suited better than metal culverts which were quickly eaten away by the salt. The wood for the culverts was pickled in the salt brine of the salt desert and lasted almost indefinitely. They were pinned together with round wooden pegs. The engineers designed eighty-one wooden culverts and six wood-pile bridges.

Wendleboe described the all-wood culverts as "heavy timbers 6" x 18" formed into box culverts and secured together with hard maple wooden pins. . . The ends of the culverts were trimmed to the slope of the embankment."

On December 24, 1923, a second contract was signed which involved the grading and graveling process over the forty miles of salt. Croft and Bundy of Ogden and Lamus, Zimmer, and Lamus were the contractors. Pratt Matthews and Paul Wrathall of Grantsville were subcontractors during the graveling phase of construction.

Using scrapers to level the highway at the east end of Wendover. (Molly Hewitt Taylor)

Utah Governor Dern on the left, along with U.S. Secretary of Agriculture William Jardine and Nevada Governor J. Schrugham, participated in the opening of the Victory Highway by shoveling away a salt barrier. The official ceremony took place just east of Wendover on June 13, 1925. *(California State Automobile Association/Louise Ann Noeth)*

The Western Pacific Railroad agreed to load gravel with steam shovels and haul the gravel on flatcars from their pit fifty miles west to the site of construction. The railroad used a large blade, powered by the train engine to push the gravel off the cars on the north side of the track in windrow stockpiles. A horse team was used to pull a wooden slip scraper filled with gravel up and over an A-frame to load the wagons. Incidently, a slight scratch to a horse's leg when coming in contact with the salt would render a horse useless.

The gravel was then hauled by a team of horses to the roadbed. The wagons were 4´ x 6´ x 10´ in dimension with 4´ x 4´ boards on the bottom held together with a twisted chain. The side boards were about one foot in height. The bottom boards were pulled from the bed to let the gravel fall to the ground. It was a slow and tedious process.

Many different types of machinery were used in construction. One kind of machine would work in one situation while another type was required for another section of the road. Tractors were used for hauling and leveling. Plows, scrapers, draglines, clamshells, and trenching machines were rented from the Utah-Salduro Company. The ditching machines cut a three-foot wide trench using buckets on an endless chain, turning on nine-and twelve-foot wheels.

During the winter, the No. 10 Buckeye trencher worked day and night in fourteen inches of water. The trencher was used to throw up windrows of mud after which gravel was filled in for the road base. The temperature dipped to zero with continuous cold winds blowing. The men were chilled to the bone as they had to work in the ice-cold salt water. The contractors floated barrels of gas and fresh water in the brine-filled trenches to supply the trencher.

On one particular, cold, windy November day, two inspectors came to visit the project. The chief of the San Francisco office of the bureau of roads accidentally stepped off a plank walkway and fell into a water-filled trench. The *"colder-than-ice brine"* quickly

Race car driver Ab Jenkins in a black Studebaker roadster, racing a trainful of dignitaries to Wendover on June 13, 1925, the day the Victory Highway was opened to transcontinental traffic. Ab beat the train by five minutes, but the car had to have major repairs due to damage from the rough road. *(Marvin Jenkins)*

and the governors of Utah and Nevada, aided by the U.S. secretary of agriculture officially opened the road to traffic.

Previous to the official highway opening, Bill Rishel challenged Utah race car driver Ab Jenkins to race the celebration train to Wendover. A $250 bet ensued between Jenkins and the Salt Lake City Rotary Club.

The morning of the train's departure on June 13, 1925, Jenkins was ready in his black, Studebaker roadster complete with new-fangled, air-filled, balloon tires. He carried two passengers, Miss McCafferty, who was the secretary to the local Studebaker dealer T. W. Naylor, and a Salt Lake City policeman, Englishman Tommy Dee. The train was carrying dignitaries which

chilled him to the point of turning blue before he could be rescued. Dry clothes, the warm bunkhouse, and a warm drink revived him. His clothes were filled with brine salt which took several days to get it all out.

Wendleboe felt that the construction went smoothly overall due to the contractor's familiarity with the salt beds and the cooperation of the salt company in allowing the use of their equipment. The salt company's machine shop also proved invaluable in repairing machine breakdowns.

The Wendover portion of the Victory Highway was completed in June of 1925 after five years of labor across the salt flats. The total cost of the new road from Mills Junction, 29 miles west of Salt Lake City to Wendover, was estimated at $1,092,000. It cost $390,000 or $9,500 a mile to complete the salt bed section.

The section from Knolls to Tempie going east took longer than the projected completion date of October 28, 1926, due to the inexperience of the contractor, the *"failure of their gravel plants to work advantageously, and the sandy conditions of the area."* This section cost another $249,598 or $7,077 a mile.

Wendover was connected to Salt Lake City and traffic was passing through the little community daily. A victory arch (a barrier made of salt) was erected near Salduro to celebrate this "path across a mud puddle"

The Lincoln Highway Association eventually changed their main route which was south of the salt flats through Ibapah. The association added their name to the Victory Highway, Wendover Cutoff, by the late 1920s. The photo above shows the flooded Victory/Lincoln Highway across the salt flats. The new highway initially had two sharp turns (without cautionary signs) located near Salduro, Utah. *(Lincoln Highway Collection, Transportation History Collection, University of Michigan)*

included Nevada governor J. Schrugham, Utah governor George Dern, and U.S. secretary of agriculture William Jardine. Several hundred others were also in attendance.

The race start was signaled by the Salt Lake City mayor using a whistle and a flag. Jenkins lurched away as the train steadily began to gain momentum from the dead stop. Jenkins's passenger Tommy Dee was to throw a small bag of flour onto the railroad tracks each time they made a crossing. This patch of splattered flour signaled to the

U.S. Highway 40 going west from Wendover. *(Gertrude Tripp)*

train's passengers that Jenkins was in the lead. Dee was bounced and jostled along on the bumpy ride and was thrown into the front seat several times.

Jenkins beat the train by five minutes with a time of 2 hours and 40 minutes. It normally took five and a half hours to travel from Salt Lake to Wendover. It was a time of celebration. A brass band was on hand to greet the arriving racers, both train and car. Other cars met the train out on the salt beds a few miles east of Wendover and honked and waved as they overtook the train, fell back, *"and then overtook it again and again."* At the same time, the passengers on the train *"cheered from the windows and from in between the cars"* as the locomotive's bell rang.

Officials from the states of Utah, Nevada, and California rode the special train to Salduro. They were guests at a luncheon *"at the famous revolving tables at the Salduro clubhouse."* After lunch they proceeded to a speaker's stand improvised on truck beds nearby.

At the official ceremonies, the dignitaries were dressed in white as they shoveled away the salt barrier to officially open the Victory Highway. Jenkins held an unplanned race on the salt flats with ten cars racing each other. The governor was the winner. Residents from Wendover watched the whole spectacle from atop the Wendover hills as the cars bedecked with flags arrived for the ceremony.

"The completed highway,. . . was a remarkable piece of construction and a fine example of early highway engineer-

ing" proclaimed the narrative on a historic American engineering record map.

According to *Motor Travel* magazine of that year, the Wendover improvement was a *"Big California Aid."* An anticipated 90% of motor travel west of Salt Lake City would use the Victory Highway and it would become the principal connection by motor vehicle between northern California and the east.

At the same time, roads were being built all across the nation at a rapid pace. It became necessary to have a national standard for developing a system including designating and connecting each region. For example in 1925, *"there were over 250 named highways, each with their own colored signs often placed haphazardly, a fact which created great confusion,"* according to one author on the Lincoln Highway.

Consequently, the highways across America were given a standard numerical designation. The highway through Wendover was known at various times as the Wendover Cutoff, the Victory Highway, Lincoln Highway, or the Main Line (the *"Shortest, Safest, Fastest"*). In tribute to the armed forces that have defended the USA, it was called the Blue Star Memorial Highway or Eisenhower Memorial Highway. Finally, it became U.S. 40 and still later Interstate 80.

It is of interest to note that the old U.S. 40 two-lane highway hosted Burma Shave signs past Grantsville at the edge of the salt desert. They were small red signs with white letters. Five signs were placed 100 feet apart. Each sign contained one line of a four-line couplet and the fifth sign identified Burma Shave. For example:

DROVE TOO LONG

DRIVER SNOOZING

WHAT HAPPENED NEXT

IS NOT AMUSING

★★★ BURMA-SHAVE ★★★

or

PASSING CARS

WHEN YOU CAN'T SEE

MAY GET YOU A GLIMPSE

OF ETERNITY

★★★ BURMA SHAVE ★★★

Another note of interest: the Pacific Greyhound Line began operating over U.S. Highway 40 in 1932. Fares from Salt Lake City to Wendover in 1951 were $2.98 for a one-way and $5.29 for a round-trip including federal tax. The depot was located in the State Line Hotel and Restaurant on the Nevada side. The schedules allowed for a ten-minute rest stop at Wendover.

A last item of interest: sometime after Highway 40 was built, a set of petition fences was erected alongside the highway at different locations by contractor Pratt Matthews of Grantsville. The slatted fences were strategically placed to prevent drifting salt and sand from blowing across and covering the highway. Another modern convenience of the time was barrels of water strategically placed along steep grades for use in cooling overheated engines.

As time went on, with more and more travelers crossing the desert, the need was apparent for a new, divided highway. In fact there was a need nationwide during the 1960s for faster, wider superhighways. Consequently, highway planners and federal funding engineered and produced a system of interstate highways linking main U.S. cities across the nation.

The new interstate highway system had a marking system of red, white, and blue route markers. East-to-west highways were given even numbers and north-south highways were odd numbers. Lower numbers for routes were in the south and west. Interstate 80 was planned and built with a section of it crossing the salt flats and skirting Wendover.

Construction was begun across the salt in 1966-67. Parsons Construction Co., Healy and Hess, and Industrial Construction Company completed sections of the highway across the flats. Tons of fill dirt were hauled from gravel pits northeast of Wendover. *"In fact, part of the once-famed gunnery range"* was removed. A port of entry was built three miles east of Wendover. A pass was blasted through the mountain near Danger Cave to the east of Wendover. In the process, a large water-filled cavern was uncovered. The water was several hundred feet in depth. The cavern opening was subsequently and purposely filled with rock from the blasting to seal it.

Two interchanges were built. One entered from the east end of town just before the pass, connecting to the old Highway 40 as it entered the city limits. The second exit was located at the west end of town near the junction of Highway 40 and Highway 93 going south to Ely, Nevada.

Interstate 80 through Wendover was finally completed in 1972. The new interstate has significantly increased the safety, speed, and ease of travel across the salt desert.

2.

A Community Without Parallel

Wendover developed as an outpost of civilization
in the midst of isolation.

Wendover owes much of its prosperity to *"a visionary man by the name of Smith."* It was the year 1924 when unemployed mechanic William F. Smith decided to travel east to Salt Lake City on a Western Pacific boxcar after searching unsuccessfully for work in San Francisco. He was discovered on board three miles east of Wendover and tossed off the train.

He had no money as he stood forlornly watching the train disappear over the horizon of the shimmering salt flats. Bill noticed a cluster of buildings nearby. He learned that it was a potash plant in the small settlement of Salduro. He was an ambitious fellow and immediately went looking for a job at the plant.

Bill located the plant manager, Ed Lamus, and told him that he needed a job. Ed informed him that the plant had been productive earlier during the war, but that Germany was shipping in potash cheaper than the local plant could produce and ship it. Prospects for work at the plant were dismal at best.

Even though the hiring for the plant was done in Salt Lake, Bill convinced Ed that he would be a first-rate mechanic if he would give him an opportunity. Bill implored *"Give me a chance. If I can't do the job I'll walk away and you don't owe me anything."* Ed Lamus later said it was the best decision he ever made.

Bill worked at the potash plant for two years until he had saved $500. He then opened a gas station in Wendover in partnership with Herman Eckstein. They called it the Cobblestone because it was a small building made of cobblestone. Their living quarters were in the rear. One old-timer remembered that Mr. Smith first sold liquor under a bowery on the north side of a log cabin covered with a gabled roof. The liquor had to be brought inside at night.

Bill hung a light bulb atop a pole in front of the service station and kept it burning twenty-four hours a day. The light signified a friendly oasis in the desert.

> Bill Smith hung a light bulb atop a pole in front of the service station and kept it burning twenty-four hours a day. The light signified a friendly oasis in the desert. It was the beginnings of the State Line Hotel and Casino.

The following anecdote illustrates the importance of Bill's service station. *"One night, two Utah ranchers were traveling this road headed for Salt Lake City. It was the custom in those days of infrequent service stations to carry extra gasoline on the long and lonely Nevada roads. When the man who was driving stopped at the light in the desert for gas, his partner asked, 'Why stop here? We have enough gas in the back of the truck to make Salt Lake City easily.' 'Yes,' said the driver, 'but I want to buy gas from Bill Smith anyway. I don't want that light ever to go out!'"*

Gene Jones came to Wendover in 1931 with his mother. He spent most of the next fifty years working for Bill Smith and later his wife Anna. He gives interesting insights into the beginnings of the State Line Casino. At first, Gene worked at the Cobblestone Service. He earned fifty cents a day, seven days a week, for

eight-hour shifts, and he was furnished a lunch. Bill required him to wear a white shirt and white trousers with a bow tie, and Gene had to furnish his own outfit.

When Gene went to high school in Tooele and later Grantsville, Bill required him to start the day after school ended, and kept him sometimes two weeks into the school year in the fall until the tourist season dropped off.

Bill treated Gene very well but taught him some lessons at the same time. Gene said, *"One day I gave a fella $5 too much. Sure enough at the end of the day I was five dollars short. Mr. Smith said, 'Gene, I'm going to make you pay for that. If you pay for it you'll remember.' (That was ten days of work) 'The next time you won't give wrong change out.' He made Gene pay for it. Gene never forgot it. "He taught me to really be careful. If he'd a paid for it I'd've forgotten it.*

"He'd say 'Tell your boyfriends, don't come around. There is always something to do. There will be no chairs, no books, no radios. Put a rag in your pocket and if nothing else there is always something to wipe down.' Those were his rules. We never sat down. I'd work 12 hours as I got older. I'd go to work at five in the evening and work 'til five in the morn-

Cobblestone Cafe, service station and cabins, December 29, 1933. Above, William Smith, owner and operator of the Cobblestone. Later, the business became the State Line Hotel and Casino. *(State Line Casino/William and Anna Smith family)*

Building the State Line Hotel, circa 1938. *(State Line Casino/William and Anna Smith family)*

ing. I'd do that all summer. I worked 'til I was making three dollars a day and thought I was doing great. People now would think you're out of your mind.

"Times were tough and you needed a job and there weren't many jobs in Wendover. Mr. Smith fired me once. He had me on a shift and I was supposed to be back at one o'clock in the afternoon. It was hot and we lived downtown then. I came ambling in five minutes late. He happened to be standing there. He looked at his watch and said 'What time are you supposed to be here, Gene?' I said, 'One o'clock.' He said, 'You're five minutes late. I don't need you anymore.' He taught me another lesson.

"What could I do? I went down and saw Mrs. Moore. She and Mace ran the Western Café. I washed dishes. In those days, when you washed dishes, you scrubbed the floor, took out the garbage, fixed sandwiches, you did everything. I was just a kid. I swore if I got through that summer, I'd never work in a kitchen again in my life. I never did. No air conditioning. Hot! Mr. Smith taught me a good lesson about being on time.

"California tourists traveling through after school was out were good for business. School was the factor. When school would start then trade would slow down. . . We would send

[customers to] businesses on U.S. 40 further west because Mr. Smith had business ties to Elko, Winnemucca, and Lovelock.

"He told us to discourage people from going on the Ely route. We had little cards that showed stops along the way of Highway 40. We still used gas pumps that you pumped up. They had the glass. Mr. Smith would always say don't over-fill it. We'd wash all the windows. Check the oil. Get under the hood. You might sell a quart of oil. Look at the fan belt.

"Mr. Smith would tell us to check the car over and see if there was anything we could sell the customer. We'd look at the tires and see if we could sell them a new tire. We were really salesmen rather than pumping gas. He gave us a commission if we got a fella to grease his car or change the oil. We had a book you'd write your name in and what you did. It was 10 cents on an oil change for example. It gave us extra money."

Behind the Cobblestone Service Station was the fifteen-room Newhouse Hotel that had reportedly been a house of ill repute previously. Smith and Eckstein purchased the wooden building with the idea of making it into a *"first class hotel."* The hotel was renovated and renamed the State Line Hotel. Gambling was legalized in Nevada in 1931 and so the new own-

Car on hoist at the State Line Garage. *(State Line Casino/William and Anna Smith family)*

He insisted on first-class quality service to his customers and borrowed $40,000 in the spring of 1937 or '38 in order to build a new hotel complete with air conditioning and steam heating as well as space for a bar, slot machines, and a blackjack table. For those days, the hotel was a major achievement and a huge step forward for Wendover. Mr. Smith had been denied a loan in Salt Lake, Elko, and Reno, but received a loan from a bank in San Francisco after they visited Wendover and saw the need. They gave him a loan on the spot!

ers installed a roulette table. No slot machines were included at first because there was no room for them. It is claimed to be the first gaming establishment in Nevada.

Smith and Eckstein built cabins about 1933 for travelers to stay in. Tourists brought their own bedding and food in those days. The State Line trucked in water and stored it in a huge tank on the hill nearby. They did that for 35 years.

Mr. Eckstein died and his son became Mr. Smith's partner. Eventually, it became apparent that the two new partners could not agree on policy and they each wanted to buy out the other. They decided to settle the question of who would buy the business by flipping a silver dollar in the presence of witnesses and a justice of the peace in Elko. Bill Smith won the coin toss when it came up heads and took over complete ownership of the business.

The Depression of the 1930s took a toll on local businesses and many of them closed down. Bill Smith stuck it out knowing that Wendover was the main stopping off point between Elko, Nevada, and Salt Lake City, Utah, where travelers would look for cold refreshments and a cool spot in the desert heat.

In the meantime, a girl named Anna Sorensen from Mt. Pleasant, Utah, came to work at the State Line coffee shop in 1933. She was introduced to Wendover by relatives Spike and Mary Birdzell who later owned a coffee shop and service station at the east end of Wendover. Anna made her first hot, dusty, 7-hour trip to Wendover in the rumble seat of a car.

The Cobblestone added a roulette wheel in 1932, making it one of the first and longest continuously operating gambling establishments in Nevada. The Smith family operated it from 1932 until 2002. *(State Line Casino/Smith family & Hill Air Force Base);* Byron Dussler said the man's name was Eldor Bernine, a soldier in civilian clothes when photo was taken in 1941.

Upon arrival, she was invited to a dance in nearby Ibapah. She traveled another hour and a half, danced all night and returned to her first day of work which started at 6:30 a.m.

She worked hard and sent every penny she made home to her family. She waitressed in the coffee shop and then cleaned the travelers' rooms. She had to spray under the mattress buttons for bed bugs and she carried water to the hotel to use for bathing, cleaning, cooking, and drinking. It was depression times and money was hard to come by.

Bill Smith courted Anna

State Line slot machines in operation. *(State Line Casino/William and Anna Smith family)*

and in 1935 they were married. She joined him in building their business as an able, hard-working and willing partner. She *"did a lot for others."* She would give money to strangers if she felt they needed it. She contributed to the local schools with books, playground equipment, copy machines, scholarhips, etc., and was largely responsible for funding the constuction of the local LDS chapel. She helped whomever asked her and contributed much to the community of Wendover.

Mrs. Anna Smith on her 80th birthday.
(Gertrude Tripp)

The events of World War II abruptly changed Wendover from a small stopping off point for travelers to *"one of the busiest places on earth."* The people of Wendover all of a sudden had a huge city appear almost overnight two blocks from their doorsteps.

As described elsewhere in this volume, Wendover Field by 1942 became a vital center for training bombardment groups of the Army Air Corps including the pilot, crew, and support personnel which dropped the atomic bombs on Japan, ending the war.

The officers and enlisted men frequented the State Line Hotel and Casino as a place of relaxation and recreation, a place to spend their money. There were 20,000 men stationed in Wendover and they, when off duty, could be seen forming a single file line from the railroad tracks to the State Line, waiting their turn for a table to dine. They remembered in their memoirs going to the State Line with high hopes of *"breaking the bank."*

Garn Anderson listed the menu selection and prices in 1940 at the State Line Hotel as furnished by Gene L. Jones, manager. Coffee was ten cents or just five cents with a meal. Sandwiches included hot pork or beef with potatoes for forty cents, hot fried ham plain was twenty cents, a Club House sandwich was fifty cents, and lettuce and tomato salad was thirty-five cents.

Top: The State Line Cafe on the Utah side with no slots. Bottom: The State Line bar on the Nevada side with gaming tables in the rear. William Smith is at the far end of the bar. The back room later became the Red Garter dining room. *(State Line Casino/William and Anna Smith family)*

East half of panorama showing the State Line Hotel and Casino complex. *(Courtesy of the State Line Casino and Smith Family)*

West end of the State Line complex showing the garage, State Line residences, and motel accommodations. *(State Line Casino, Bill and Anna Smith family)*

Breakfast choices were stewed prunes or applesauce with choice of cereals, toast, and coffee for thirty-five cents. Tomato juice served with ham or bacon, one egg and toast and coffee was fifty cents. A breakfast steak with cereal, sautéed potatoes, toast, and coffee was the most expensive at sixty-five cents a plate.

For dinner at the State Line, you could have chicken fried steak for sixty-five cents, Salisbury steak for fifty cents, T-bone steak for $1.15, or New York cut steak for $1.10. Later on, rationing of food items during the war made choices more limited.

After the war Gene Jones came home from serving in the military and became assistant manager. The Smiths built a new motel. They added a 60-foot electric sign in 1952 which became known as *"Wendover Will,"* after Bill Smith.

Mrs. Smith initially was concerned that the cost of the sign was an unneeded extravagance to the young and growing family of three daughters, Marian, Billie Ann, and Carol, and a son, Jim. In the end, *"Wendover Will"* proved to be a success. The smiling cowboy, bedecked in blue jeans and hat with his arm beckoning to the casino, has become an icon of the State Line and of Wendover.

On Christmas Eve 1958, Bill called Gene Jones from Salt Lake and said he thought he would stay in town for the night and return to Wendover the next day. He never returned. He died in his sleep.

Anna Smith was left in charge of the State Line. She felt she had to sell the casino, but Gene Jones offered to help her operate it. She knew Gene was a good and competent individual so she named him as general manager. They decided to enlarge the casino restaurant and lounge area. In 1973, the old building was torn down and a new facility was built with an expanded parking lot. (See chapter seven for the conclusion to the story of the State Line and other gambling establishments in Wendover.)

Recreation

Neta Wadsworth stated that the only real recreation people of Wendover had was to get out and wander around in the hills. The cool, wet spring-time was especially beautiful. The desert came alive with color.

There were the short purple flowers and little white flowers carpeting the hillsides and flats. Cacti came out in bloom in every color.

There were other activities the community participated in. Neta Wadsworth mentioned progressive suppers where the participants dressed up like hobos or teenagers. There were clubs with card games using eight decks. They gambled using chips and pocket change. During the war, liquor was rationed and Bill

State Line Hotel lobby. *(State Line Casino, Smith family)*

Smith sold *"Southern Comfort"* which was a rotten homemade recipe. Many men went to Wells to buy a better grade of liquor.

After Christmas, locals gathered all the Christmas trees and piled them in a vacant lot. They then started a huge bonfire and baked potatoes in the hot ashes. The girls wore dresses *"no matter what"* the activity was.

When the base was in operation, the service club held dances. The club had a balcony where people could sit and watch the dancers below. Busloads of girls came from Salt Lake on Saturday night to dance with the soldiers. The local girls were also invited, sometimes with parents accompanying them.

Movies were shown, both on and off base at different times. Leo Waters and his wife ran the movie projector for the Lion's Club and later bought the equipment and showed movies regularly in the early 1950s. *"There was a show house at Salduro. Before the coming of the highway, many people put their cars on the tracks and rode over the ties to Salduro to see a show."*

A local drama group provided winter entertainment for the *"entire population"* of Wendover. They rehearsed, and subsequently performed both in the red school house and in the Western Pacific Beanery. Once in a while, locals would board the train to Salt Lake City and attend Handel's *Messiah* at the old Salt Lake Theater. *"Many people from Wendover also helped with its production."*

The base had big name talent come in. Bing Crosby and Bob Hope performed several times. The local kids were allowed in free of charge. They would sneak through the fence and watch. Bob Hope called Wendover *"Leftover"* and Bing Crosby named it *"Tobacco Road with Slot Machines."* Apparently, Bing liked the area as he bought and operated several ranches in the Elko, Nevada area in the late 40s and the 50s.

Bonnie Brown Tilbury came from a family of nine brothers and sisters. She recalled their family activities in Wendover. Her mother owned a beautiful player piano. Both she and her grandmother were wonderful singers. Her mom would prepare a large pan of popcorn and the family would sit on the floor, eat popcorn, and everyone would sing.

The Brown family played ball in their back yard. Mr. Brown also set up a boxing ring where the kids boxed. When any of them insisted on arguing, they ended up putting on boxing gloves and duking it out in the ring. The family rode into the surrounding hills in a 1930s pickup truck, modified with a flatbed and attached car seats on the back. It even had homemade seat belts. Bonnie said *"We had ice chests before anyone heard of ice chests."*

Garn Anderson reported that *"William Lamb had the first car in Wendover. Many times he would load up and take many people for rides on the salt flats. Out on the flats they would have bonfires with big dinners. Then they would dance around the fires on the flats."*

The townspeople formed a softball team during the Depression years. The government provided funding. The team competed against other teams from Tooele, Salt Lake, Elko, Ely, and Ruth, Nevada. It was *"rated among the best."* The women also had a softball team which regularly played on the edge of the salt flats east of town. There was even a golf course south of the tracks before the air base was built.

A professional wrestling/boxing event was spon-

"Wendover Will" sign sometime after it was built in 1952. The sign became a symbol of Wendover and of the State Line Casino. *(State Line Casino/William and Anna Smith family)*

sored on one occasion by the local Boy Scout troop. Bill Smith furnished his garage for an arena. The boxing ring was constructed of ties and car decking furnished by the Western Pacific Railroad. There was enough comfortable seating with an unobstructed view for between two and three hundred spectators, and it had excellent overhead lighting.

The 24th of July is Mormon Pioneer Day in Utah.

Downtown Wendover about 1960 looking eastward with the State Line Casino in the foreground. *(Gertrude Tripp & Ron Christensen)*

The Hewitts and Combs visit the "exotic" Salt Springs (now known as Blue Lake) south of Wendover on a recreational jaunt. *(Molly Hewitt Taylor)*

Gordon Stewart collected pop bottles around town and turned them in for a huge bag of candy. He deliciously devoured all he wanted on those days. Some of the local boys collected aluminum cigarette pack liners for recycling during World War II and turned them in for money to buy candy and pop. Others earned spending money by manually setting the pins at the base bowling alley.

The boys would sneak onto the air base when the buildings were vacant in the 1950s. They knew all the ins and outs of the hallways and could outfox the MPs for hours.

During the 1960s there were several swimming pools in Wendover where the young people and their families could gather. The base pool was still available. Other pools were at the Lewis Brothers' Motel, the Western Motel, Poulson's Best Western, and the Patio Motel.

It is a state holiday and celebrations are held throughout all communities of Utah. In Wendover it typically went like this: *"A miniature parade at 10 a.m.; races contests, ball games, and refreshments from 2 to 5 p.m. The day before[,] a truck would go to Elko to pick up watermelons. It came back to store the melons in the Western Pacific Railroad ice house. At about 5 p.m. on the 24th, these would be taken out on the salt flats south of the tracks for a melon bust."*

After dark a fireworks display was set off. It was separated into three timed sections to be set off in a beautiful array. Much preparation went into this extravaganza. $5,000 to $6,000 were donated by townspeople to spend. A committee ordered the explosives through Jack Jensen's Tri-State Merc. They then traveled to Salt Lake and Murray to choose the array of fireworks, and then they bought them wholesale. The Wendover Branch of The Church of Jesus Christ of Latter-day Saints sponsored the all-day event. The same kind of preparation went into *"the Christmas program, scouts, Red Cross, and other civic needs."*

One summer in the 1950s, the neighborhood boys hatched a plan to have some fun. They surreptitiously borrowed their mothers' brooms each afternoon and headed for a large cement pad where apartments had been torn down. They then proceeded to have hockey competition. The fun lasted for about six weeks until their mothers found out why their brooms were disappearing.

In the early days (probably 1930s), there was a community bathhouse located adjacent to the west side of the railroad roundhouse. People could shower in the 10′ by 20′ board building using steam channeled from the boiler to heat the water as it came through the pipes. It was really a luxury, but it had one draw-back! The wall boards were not fit tightly together and "peeping toms" could get an eyeful. Husbands,

Shirley & Ray Peterson and Glenda Green were honored in the local parade.

Wendover parade scenes in front of the Victory Garage, circa 1938. *(Glenda Green)*

A group of local Wendover kids who marched in the July 4th parade in 1938. *(Bruce Lamus)*

of necessity, had to stand guard outside so their wives could enjoy the shower.

Speed Week was and is a time to head by car or motorcycle to the salt flats to watch the races and time trials. STP t-shirts were given out freely in the 1960s. The youth would steal STP magnets and trade them back to the racers in exchange for packages of stick-on STP stickers. Teenagers talked and ate with the crews. They were allowed to move freely among the pit crews and be a part of the action.

What a breath-taking experience it was to watch the powerful cars lunge forward on the salt with the salt forming a plume high into the air behind! The faster the run, the higher the fan-tail sprays of salt.

Everybody knew everybody in those days and the

kids could feel at home. Anywhere in the town, a young person could knock on a door to use the phone or get a glass of water. *"It was a good place to live."*

Religion

Wendover is not a usual "cookie-cutter" Utah town, according to Jean Draper, a local resident. In other words, Wendover is not a typical Mormon community. Most Utah towns were started with an agricultural base and were planned, even mapped out, beforehand. Mormons were called by Brigham Young to settle each one. Not so with Wendover. Even though one writer claimed salt made Wendover, it was in reality a railroad town, and later a gambling town, with salt providing a stable side industry. There was no effort to colonize the area by the Mormons.

Wendover may not have been founded by members of The Church of Jesus Christ of Latter-day Saints as a Mormon settlement, but Mormons came to Wendover early in its history and established permanent roots there. Part of the history of Wendover is in the Mormon activities in the community. They kept a record of their doings. Many community activities were organized and conducted under the auspices of the local ward.

Minutes of the first Wendover LDS Sunday School and Relief Society indicate that they were organized on November 9, 1930. President Alfred L. Hanks of the Tooele LDS Stake was present and in charge of organizing the Wendover Branch. He appointed W. A. Lyman

Wendover chapel of The Church of Jesus Christ of Latter-day Saints.

as the presiding elder. A. B. Callister was assigned as superintendent of the Sunday School with N. F. Jensen and L. Sorensen as first and second assistants.

The officers for the local Relief Society women's organization were chosen by balloting. Sister E. Olson was president with Cleora Brockbank as first counselor and B. Anderson as second. The branch was discontinued the following spring with no explanation as to the reason.

Mission San Felipe Catholic Church.

The branch began functioning again in October 1937 with Peter McKellar as branch president, Chas. Orme, Jr., and Alfred M. Nelson as counselors. Myrtis A. Hutchinson was Relief Society president with Mary M. Birdzell and Nell Marie Palmer Lamus as counselors.

The branch was involved in providing activities for all ages. Much of the work was done by the Relief Society. Christmas pageants included nativity scenes, community singing, musical choruses complete with piano accompaniment, scenery, and lighting. Games, singing, and refreshments on the salt flats, quilting and sewing of dresses, pajamas, and quilts for welfare purposes, pot-luck luncheons, and health talks in Sacrament Meeting, with a health parade at school the next day were some of the activities.

In 1940 the LDS branch put on two one-act plays, "A Paternity Case" and "Mushrooms Coming Up." On October 31st, a program entitled "Hall of Horrors" was given along with an apron sale, fish pond, candy and popcorn, cider and donuts, and fortune telling, followed by a dance. Prizes were awarded throughout the evening for different costumes.

Wendover became increasingly involved in the war effort as Wendover Field mushroomed. The branch Relief Society made two quilts and eight blankets for the *"emergency campaign."* The branch held a community dance and music was furnished by the Wendover Post orchestra. At a branch conference in 1942, Tooele Stake President Alex Dunn gave instructions concerning entertainment with the branch for soldiers and defense workers.

Spike and Mary Birdzell ran a café and Spike turned the café over to the branch ladies. They served Spike's fried chicken special to a Lion's Club group. The branch singing mothers went to Salt Lake and sang with the Mormon Tabernacle Choir.

Hildred McKellar and Ruth Steele made dozens of meat pies to serve to guests visiting from the Tooele Stake. On November 6, 1941, 178 hours of labor were donated in making draperies for the local PTA. A paper and magazine drive was held earlier in September to raise money for welfare needs of the poor.

Ruth J. Steele was Relief Society president in 1943, and she was also chief clerk of the ration board of which L. B. Smith, Pete McKellar, and Blair Lamus were board members. She remembered Mr. L. B. Smith who was not a member of the LDS faith asking, *"Ruth, when are we going to have another Relief Society party?"*

Ruth stated *"Being with the ration board, we issued rations to the people on the air base so I knew a lot of people on the air base. I contacted the lady in charge of the USO as I heard they were going to discard some old pianos. We needed one badly at our church house. I went to the base and got the piano. I signed a paper that stated we could use it until they might need it again—for some reason they couldn't just give it to us. We enjoyed it. It was painted white.*

We had several plays and a fashion show. We had a big 4th of July parade, children participating and Easter egg hunts out on the flats where the air base is now. We helped a needy

Wendover Field Chapel. *(509th Pictorial Album)*

family move from Wendover. The husband was in the Air Force and was shipped out. They had several small children. We got clothes and food and helped the lady pack. When the commander of the base heard what we had done he said, 'I have never heard of any church doing so much good to strangers and non-members of their church.'

J. Ronald Anderson, as bishop of the Wendover Ward, had ample opportunity to serve. He held the hands of the young people when they were sick. He often traveled to Ibapah where he sometimes helped with funerals. He would speak and then help fill in the grave. He baptized dozens of children at nearby Salt Springs also known as Blue Lake.

When Ed Lamus died, the potash plant, where he had been foreman, closed for his funeral. At the funeral in Tooele, J. Ronald Anderson attended as a friend and when he walked in, Mr. Lamus's family asked him to organize and conduct the funeral on the spot. He quickly selected the music, called on J. U. Hicks as the first speaker and Pete McKellar as a friend who knew Ed Lamus as a pioneer of Wendover. Pete said Ed brought in tourists and could show them the Donner

party tracks, etc. Bishop Anderson then concluded the service and closed the meeting with prayer. He always had to be prepared.

He worked with the Boy Scouts. He took them camping, sometimes to Tracy Wigwam in Millcreek Canyon east of Salt Lake. He remembered one time when he and his scouts slept over a nest of polecats. He told the boys not to throw out their cans of beans or none of them would be able to go home. He figured they would be sprayed by the skunks.

He and the ward members hosted the state American Legion banquet for 500 people. They fried chicken at home and kept it warm in electric roaster ovens. They used a blow torch to warm water for coffee and tea. The chicken was served hot and tender, not burned. Every woman in Wendover cooked pies. They washed the dishes in large tin wash tubs. The meal was served quickly and efficiently and the Legion members were impressed enough that they came back the next year for their annual banquet.

Most local laborers slept on the Nevada side of Wendover where there were no state taxes and worked in Utah. Therefore, they were entitled to refunds from Utah. Anderson helped people get state refunds on their taxes and became a very popular individual among the workers. One man *"chewed up his legs"* in a power saw accident and Bishop Anderson helped him get medical claims.

Many of the workers donated some of their money back to the church because of his help. This in turn helped the ward with their welfare assessment as there was no tillable ground in Wendover to raise crops of any kind. It was common for other wards to raise grains or vegetables to sell to pay for church welfare needs.

The Relief Society also helped raise money for the welfare needs. As an example, minutes of the ward Relief Society noted *"throughout the year of 1947, a united effort was put forth to aid in meeting the ward cash welfare assignment. A Valentine party was enjoyed by (Relief Society) members and partners. Also an excellent amateur hour program was held, featuring 35 children and young folks. In March a very outstanding musical centennial pageant 'A Story of Granite and Bronze' was presented, with all special music rendered by singing mothers chorus."*

Relief Society minutes recorded: *"Three successful free health conferences were sponsored by the Relief Society. 192 children were inoculated for typhoid and tick fever. Later* *inoculations and vaccinations were given for small pox, diphtheria and whooping cough. May 5th, the annual bazaar was held displaying 185 beautiful articles, also a food table yielded cash receipts of $235.39. 383 donated articles of clothing which were and boxed for shipment to European Saints.*

"For the first time summer Relief Society was held. Opening social was held with a delicious hot dinner for all the members and their husbands. Fifty attended. On November 2nd, a very inspirational ward Relief Society conference was held with special music, readings and talks. On November 18th a special demonstration of Christmas gifts was given. In December, several boxes of clothing and shoes were prepared and sent to Indians in Arizona and New Mexico.

"A splendid Christmas party was held December 16th in connection with the literature lesson. The hall was exquisitely decorated, delicious refreshments were served and an exchange of gifts followed. An apron bazaar was held. The amount of $328.67 was raised and presented to the Bishop to help meet the ward welfare assignment."

Some of the young men stationed in Wendover in the military came to church. They were homesick and needed support and counsel. Bishop Anderson was able to advise and console them.

The ward members began raising money for a chapel as early as 1957. The ground-breaking ceremonies were held October 30, 1968, at 6 p.m. The Wendover District was created on January 4, 1998, with James Conrad as president, Dale Stewart and Michael Miera as counselors. Wendover had in the past been part of Grantsville and Grantsville West stakes. Pilot Mountain, a Spanish branch, and Ibapah were also part of the new Wendover District.

Past church leaders have been President Peter McKellar, J. Ronald Anderson, Alfred B. Callister, Phillip Garrett, Leonard F. Mauer, Monte G. Hammond, Dale E. Skinner, Robert L. Arthur, David M. Baker, Lynn Poulsen, Preston Nuffer, Wayne Shields, Dale T. Stewart, Kent Peterson, Brett Shelton, Matt Ekker, and Cathem Beers.

Other churches have functioned in the town since World War II. The Wendover Air Base Chapel held non-denominational services during the war. Mission San Felipe Catholic Church held services at 604 Aria Blvd. Khosrow Semnani donated land north of I-80 where the Catholic Church was built.

Earlier, a small Catholic chapel served patrons northeast of the A-1 Casino for many years. Father Vanski and many others at various times traveled once a week from Wells, Nevada, to hold services. The local diocese helped finance the local church and they had a 99-year lease from Twain West. Mr. West fired up the furnace at the church on cold mornings. It was torn down in 1972. There were also the Christian Fellowship located at 530 E. Airport Way, the Spanish Baptist Mission, 810 E. Pilot, and the West Wendover Baptist Church on Alpine Street in 2003.

McKellar Ranch

The first McKellars to settle near Wendover were Charles and Joseph McKellar, the sons of John McKellar and Margaret McIntyre who were from Scotland. The McKellar brothers built a log cabin and lean-to kitchen north of Donner Springs near the turn of the century.

They made a living selling horses at Lucin and the railroad. They also mined at Silver Island and nearby locations. They were life-long bachelors. Charles was a tough cowboy. He got in an argument over water rights or cattle with a man name McCustion on one occasion. McCustion reached for something under his buckboard tarp. Charley drew his pistol and shot McCustion dead, thinking that he was reaching for a pistol. McCustion turned out to be unarmed. Charles went to prison for the shooting and never got over it. He returned to the Wendover ranch and could often be seen brooding over the incident.

Hildred and Peter McKellar. *(John McKellar)*

McKellar's Pilot Mountain ranch. *(John McKellar)*

John M. McKellar was a brother to Charlie and Joe. He left Tooele in 1908 with thirty head of horses and a wagon and journeyed seven days to the McKellar ranch. He took his son Peter with him. Peter kept a detailed diary of the trip.

Peter McKellar and Charlie Orme left Tooele for Wendover during the Depression. Peter began ranching on the McKellar ranch, raising grain, corn, alfalfa, and cattle. They also raised fruits and melons. They purchased a house in Wendover and opened a dairy north of town where Interstate 80 was later cut through the mountain.

Peter and Hildred, his wife, became leaders in Wendover. Peter was an early church leader of the LDS branch in Wendover and he and his wife served two missions to nearby Ibapah. Pete was an original trustee on the Wendover town board. Hildred served in the local PTA.

Life on the ranch was interesting. Over the years, individuals stopped at the ranch on their quests looking for Donner Party buried treasure (read of the Donner Reed tragedy in chapter five). No one has been able to locate the elusive treasure. Peter did find some Donner artifacts while digging a potato cellar.

The McKellars worked hard from early morning 'til late evening but took time to picnic on the salt flats on occasion. The family amused themselves by throwing fire cinders into the wind, creating a fireworks display of sorts. They used paper plates as Frisbees, seeing how far the wind would blow them.

At the ranch in the evenings, they listened on the battery-operated radio to church conference, Joe Louis prize fights, or farm news. They sang to the tunes played on Hildred's piano or listened to stories while sitting on a screened-in porch.

Peter sometimes rescued tourists who ventured onto the salt flats, not knowing that they would sink. He made several rescue trips over a period of years often with a team of horses, plus water and food to help stranded tourists when their car axles sank deep in the sand and salt. These tourists were much luckier than were the desert crossing emigrants eighty years or so earlier.

Peter's nephew George recalled that *"Life on the ranch could be dangerous. . . Peter was cutting hay near the ranch house with his young son, John on his lap. Something spooked the horses and they ran away. Peter threw John clear of the mower and then jumped off. The horses ran and ran around the field like in a chariot race, until they got caught in a fence, destroying the mower.*

"Another time Peter's nephew, Eldon McKellar, came out of the ranch house after lunch and heard a hiss. The truck was parked by the bunkhouse and Eldon thought the truck tire was going flat. When he looked near the truck a rattlesnake was coiled ready to strike a rabbit. Eldon went to the ranch house and told Pete. Pete got his rifle and shot the snake."

Another nephew, Glen, wrote of a visit to the McKellar ranch. He said, *"After a hard day's work, Uncle Pete, Aunt Hildred, and I were sitting on the front porch when a badger ran up through the field. Since badgers eat chickens and eggs, Uncle Pete and I grabbed the guns and took off after him. He ran way up to the top of the field. Uncle Peter finally turned back because it was getting dark, but I continued on.*

"The badger ran under the fence and into a culvert that was under the old road. However, the other end of the culvert was buried, and by the time he saw his mistake, I had him trapped.

"I ran up and fired two or three rounds into the culvert.

Then I set my rifle down and kneeled down to look in and see if I got him. As I started to set my hand in the pipe, I saw a slight movement. There, no more than six inches from my hand, was a huge rattler, coiled and weaving back and forth. He was shedding his skin and he couldn't see me so he didn't rattle, but he sensed something was near. I certainly knew he was there.

"I jumped back and grabbed the gun. It was a twenty-one shot repeater, and I emptied the magazine into the creature before I even took a breath. When I was finished with him, you would not have been able to tell it had been a snake.

"I looked into the culvert to be sure I had gotten the badger and then I staggered back to the house, trembling and [as] pale as the moon-drenched clouds above me. Ever since then, I have felt a special loathing for those slithering symbols of Satan."

The ranch also turned out to be a romantic location for Glen. *"At night, the moon would reflect off the Salt Flats like a body of water."* Glen took his girlfriend to a spring on the edge of the salt flats and asked her to marry him as they gazed across the flats by the light of the moon. She accepted, by the way.

Early Potash Production

Author Garn Anderson documented the history of the salt business near Wendover. He reported that *"in about 1914 or 1915, Capell and O'Neal came into the Salduro area and started a salt business. This was followed with the development of potash and the construction of the potash plant at Salduro from 1917 to 1920."*

The name of the parent company was the Solvay Process Company and its subsidiary was the Utah Salduro Company. It was located seven miles to the east of Wendover. The Utah Salduro Company ceased operation forever after World War I for economic reasons. However, salt production at the Salduro plant continued until about 1926, apparently under new ownership.

Garn Anderson recorded: *"The Morse Brothers Equipment Company of Denver, Colorado, took over the plant and dismantled it in 1929. Buildings from Salduro were moved to Wendover starting in 1927 with the last buildings and cabins moved to the A-1 Casino by 1932."*

Potash production revived in the middle of the 30s with the development of the Kaiser properties, Bonneville Ltd. Division located four miles east of Wendover.

Aerial view of the new potash plant after being moved from Salduro prior to World War II. Highway 40 and railroad tracks on the right. *(Gertrude Tripp)*

Joseph L. Silsbee of Salt Lake City founded Bonneville Corporation about 1920 according to authors Lallman and Wadsworth. They stated that the title to forty square miles of land was given to the company through a "Special Act of Congress." This was in addition to the forty-nine square miles they acquired of the old Utah-Salduro Company property. This made a total of 57,500 acres.

For sixteen years the Bonneville Corporation tried unsuccessfully to extract potash from the salt flats. *"In 1936 a new operating company known as Bonneville Ltd. was formed."* It took three years before it became a viable, recognized operation.

Anderson further explained: *"Nelson E. Lamus (Ed) and his two sons Blair and Nelson had stayed in the area from the Salduro days and brought their past experience and knowledge of the flat into the new operation.*

"Ponding began about 1936. The Pilot Mill construction began in February of 1938. The first two cars of potash were shipped out in 1939."

Salduro trencher.

Early view of potash plant.

Salt wagons circa 1918. *(All potash photos courtesy of Gertrude Tripp)*

Shoveling potash, circa 1917 at Salduro. *(Gertrude Tripp)*

taxes, freight, and purchases.

Later, Standard Magnesium Corporation purchased the plant for one year, from February 1963 to March 1964. Kaiser Aluminum & Chemical Corporation then purchased the operation and operated it until Reilly Industries took over in 1988 (see chapter seven for more on modern potash production in Wendover).

Prior to World War II, Wendover remained a quiet, sleepy, little village remotely removed from civilization. Oh, there was the matter of the speed racers who brought waves of followers into Wendover for short periods of time in the later 1930s. Wendover became the temporary headquarters of the British racers and Utah racer Ab Jenkins.

Years later, potash employees J. L. Ritchie and Bird Draper were using draglines to clean out several old Bonneville canals. They dug up two perfectly preserved horses, perhaps ones used in building the canals in the first place. The salt had pickled them.

Blair Lamus followed his father Ed Lamus as the superintendent of the Bonneville Limited chemical potash plant. Blair was civic-minded as shown by his record of service. He served as the first president of the Wendover Town Board. He was a member of Lamus-Zimmer-Lamus, a construction company that designed and constructed the highway across the salt beds. Blair was employed by the state of Utah in maintaining the highway after its completion.

He was president of the Wendover Lion's Club and vice president of the Tooele County Chamber of Commerce. He was a director of the Tooele County polio campaign, a member of the Bonneville Speedway Association, and he designed, built, and maintained the Bonneville Speedway in co-operation with famed Utah auto racer Ab Jenkins.

Bonneville, Ltd. produced more than 70,000 tons of potash annually in the 1960s. The company employed more than sixty persons and paid millions in payroll,

Potash plant superintendent Blair Lamus on left with his father Ed Lamus. *(Bruce Lamus)*

Dryer at Salduro. It was still standing in 2003. *(Gertrude Tripp)*

Salduro salt wagons and steam engine powered conveyor. *(Gertrude Tripp)*

Salduro potash plant just after it was built. *(Gertrude Tripp)*

The Utah Solvay potash plant was fully operational with a community of homes surrounding it when this photo was taken November 26, 1917. *(Gertrude Tripp)*

A-1 Cafe in 1939. The original buildings were located on the south side of the Lincoln Highway. When US 40 was completed, the A-1 Club was turned around and relocated along the north side of the new highway. *(Gertrude Tripp)*

by gasoline distributorship which he later expanded into a café, service station, and motel. There had been three stores, but only one remained because the other two burned down prior to 1935. The Tri-State Mercantile was the sole remaining store and movies were held there on Saturday night sporadically.

The buildings were all made of wood in 1935 except one. The post office and half of the other building were constructed of *"railway sleepers"* which Englishman George Eyston described as *"thick, heavy timbers which kept out the heat and the cold and, when lined inside, provide excellent shelter."*

At that juncture in Wendover's early history, there were thirty-five families living there in one-story homes mostly moved in from Salduro. Most had verandas. The Cobblestone by that time had cabins for tourists as did Bill Moore's Western and the A-1. All three businesses had service stations, cafés, and $1 per night cabins. The Cobblestone and Western also had garages. The Cobblestone had an inn, a dozen small tourist cabins, and a *"wood and corrugated iron garage."* Sir Malcolm Campbell sheltered his Bluebird racer in the garage. The A-1 or its predecessor consisted of a bar, a recreation hall, a gas station, six wooden cabins, and a bar with a bartender from Northumberland County, England.

The Western Service on the east end of town had electric lighting, compressed air, and water from an elevated tank. Bill Moore's garage was used as a corn granary by sheepmen in the winter. Spike Birdzell had a near-

The railway roundhouse was the center of Wendover's economy. There were dahlias growing outside the roundhouse, thanks to the foreman. The chief engineer at the time was Irishman Tom Hennigan. The sheriff was "High" Elliott. High and his deputy had green lawns gracing their properties. They enforced the 50 mph speed limit through town, at least until

A-1 Hotel. *(Gertrude Tripp)*

Panorama of the A-1 Cafe, Hotel, and Casino in West Wendover. *(Gertrude Tripp)*

A-1 Shell service station. *(Gertrude Tripp)*

Open 24 Hours
Air Conditioned
Authentic Highway Information

Breakfasts
Lunches
Dinners
Fountain
Service
and Beer

WESTERN SERVICE, INC.

Service Station -:- Garage -:- Cafe -:- Modern Cabins
WENDOVER, UTAH

Just Opposite the Great Wendover U. S. Bombing Range
5½ Miles to Bonneville Salt Flats — World's Famous Speedway

127 Miles to Salt Lake City, Utah   120 Miles to Ely, Nevada

Faded business card from the Western Cafe and Service.
(Bruce Lamus)

who camped out on the ground. The travelers took advantage of Wendover's gas supplies and refreshments because they knew it would be awhile before they found such supplies in either direction.

Then things changed dramatically for Wendover from being a sleepy village to a city of over 20,000 almost overnight as World War II thrust Wendover into the world-wide conflict. But first, a history of the Western Pacific Railroad follows in the next chapter because the railroad is what started it all in the first place!

they were severely criticized in a Salt Lake City newspaper letter to the editor by an irate motorist. High murdered his wife in the Wendover Post Office during a marital dispute, and then turned himself in to Pete McKellar, the local clergyman. The murder caused quite a stir in the small community.

Tourists who came through varied from New England society ladies to rough miners, a truck full of Goshute Indians from Ibapah, to families with mattresses tied to their car roofs

The Western Cafe *(Crystal yearbook, 1967).*

Wendover, Utah, c. 1930s. *(Mary Tripp Peterson)*

3.

Western Pacific
The Second Transcontinental Railroad

*The Western Pacific "led its iron stallions down
to drink" in the waters of the west!*

—The San Francisco Call

For nearly fifty years the Southern Pacific had no competition in its overland trade activities. Due to the mountainous terrain and related costs of operating in rugged country plus the fact that the Southern Pacific was a monopoly, high rates were charged on freight and passenger service.

In 1905 in New York City, fifty million dollars worth of mortgage bonds were sold to finance the construction of *"a second transcontinental railroad."* It was called the Western Pacific Railway on its westernmost leg. It had earlier been organized on March 3, 1903, in California.

The Western Pacific, when completed, extended 924 miles from Oakland, California, to Salt Lake City, Utah. Passengers and freight cars rode a ferry between Oakland and San Francisco. The existence of numerous smaller railroad lines along the way made it possible to deliver supplies easily, thus speeding up construction and allowing simultaneous work on different sections. The Western Pacific was planned with maximum grades of 1% *"in spite of its several mountainous crossings."*

Western Pacific logo. The Feather River runs through Northern California. *(Courtesy Union Pacific Railroad)*

The Wendover site was at the juncture of 100 miles of flat grade to the east and thirty-three miles of one percent grade for tracks west to Shafter. Western Pacific engineers calculated that the company would save $100,000 in operating costs yearly by building the subdivision in Wendover.

The savings included access to fresh water by installing a pipe-line to supply the steam locomotives. Wendover had access to better water than the high mineral content water at Shafter. Such minerals in the water caused problems for the engine boilers.

Wendover was also a natural place where helper engines could be added to get over the mountains to the west. Also, the location on the Utah side of the state line was chosen to avoid Nevada tax laws.

Locating and constructing the Western Pacific Railroad across the *"Great American Desert,"* as the salt flats was then known, was a tremendous feat. The vast desert was foreboding and desolate. An eyewitness reported *"considerable apprehension"* as the first group of surveyors penetrated the area. The

New Wendover roundhouse in 1909 with a turntable in front for turning around locomotives. *(Utah State Historical Society, Shipler collection)*

and gravel for a more permanent road bed.

The labor was long and slow and difficult. The railroad bed was constructed mostly by manual labor and horse teams. A few steam shovels were used *"on the big fills and cuts."* On December 13, 1906, tragedy struck. A high wind blew the night before and caused waves to undermine the sands of the road bed. Engine No. 1 tipped over into the lake, killing the conductor and injuring several other crew members.

As work progressed to the edge of the salt flats and beyond, soft, deep mud was encountered, especially at what became Arinosa and Barro sidings. Temperature extremes and *"the killing glare which often blinded men after a few hours[']* *work"* took their toll on the workmen. At some points, the workers had to lay twenty miles of plank before they could place the ties and rails. On other areas of the salt beds, progress was rapid. A record ten miles of track was set on a good day.

Turnover of workers was a major difficulty, especially when more pleasant work was available. Such

doomed remains of an early emigrant train headed for the gold fields of California were still in evidence along a desolate stretch between Low Pass and Pilot Mountain.

The Utah Construction Company was under contract to build the rail line west from Salt Lake City. The first rails for the Western Pacific were spiked in Salt Lake City on May 24, 1906. The crews initially laid tracks to Buena Vista which was three miles west of Salt Lake City.

Large amounts of materials were arriving daily, so a supply yard was built to accommodate the supplies. Rails, spikes, ties, etc., were unloaded and sorted until needed by the track laying gangs. The *"one engines"* came in December 1906. These engines were used to haul supplies and to spread gravel.

The crews ran into obstacles almost immediately. Near the edge of the Great Salt Lake were huge mud holes. The track layers dumped several carloads of hay into the holes so they could cross with ties and rails. They later filled the mud holes with rock

Governor Spry and other dignitaries preparing to travel to Wendover on March 3, 1909. *(Utah State Historical Society)*

large numbers of men quit at times that the railroad engineer in charge sent detectives among the track gangs to see what was stirring up trouble. No specific cause was ever found. Drunkenness was an evident problem. The Western Pacific bought up all saloon licenses adjacent to work sites to lessen the opportunity to obtain alcohol.

The depression of 1907 helped with the supply of manpower. *"There were plenty of men available—and at lower wages. Had it not been for this unexpected break all of the contractors would probably have gone bankrupt since the work proved considerably more costly than they had figured,"* wrote Gil Kneiss in the *Headlight* magazine of 1983.

The *Headlight* magazine reported an interesting find. *"Location parties (for laying the railroad bed), on their first trip across the desert in the vicinity of Arinosa found an old wagon and the skeleton of a man lying in it, as well as the skeleton of a horse with harness still on, hitched to a wagon.*

"Two miles further west, they found a skeleton of another man and a horse. Apparently the man in the wagon was

Mayor Bransford of Salt Lake addressing dignitaries in Wendover on October 22, 1909. *(Utah State Historical Society)*

seriously ill. When one of the horses died, the second man unhitched the other horse and started for help, but made only a couple of miles where he too collapsed."

No further details are known of the construction across the salt flats. It was *"tedious going"* beyond Wendover as they built rails across the Toano Range of mountains and dropped into Steptoe Valley, then going westward to Flower Pass Tunnel.

The financial panic of 1907 slowed the building of the Western Pacific for a year or so, while at the same time it accommodated the railroad's need for crewmen by drawing from the ranks of the unemployed. The 1906 San Francisco earthquake, the California floods of March 1907, crew turnover and drunkenness, the salt flats, and the rugged Feather River Canyon had all delayed the building of the Western Pacific, but did not stop it from coming to fruition.

Furthermore, there had earlier been complications with regard to the building of the Western Pacific Railroad caused by lack of cooperation by the Southern Pacific Railroad. The Southern Pacific Railroad held title to the waterfront and

Coal hoist and water tower in Wendover 1909. *(Utah State Historical Society)*

Big Malley coal burner; one of seven fast freight locomotives which ran between Elko and Salt Lake City. *(Western Pacific Mileposts, Summer-Fall 1975)*

would not allow Western Pacific access to an outlet on the eastern side of San Francisco Bay. The WP needed a waterfront site in order to ferry passengers to and from San Francisco.

Consequently, on the night of January 5, 1906, there was a war of sorts on the waterfront in Oakland, California. *"Two hundred workmen from Western Pacific and 30 guards armed with carbines and sawed-off shotguns"* seized the north wall of the waterfront and began laying tracks. Over the next few days they laid a rail line connecting the WP with the shoreline.

The land on which the track was laid was not within the title of the Southern Pacific as the *"shoreline had progressed westward as tidelands and marshlands had been filled in."* Southern Pacific objected but could do nothing about it. With the previously mentioned bold move, the Western Pacific gained access to ferry service across the Bay to San Francisco.

The crews finally pushed west-bound to Wells, Nevada. Elko, Nevada, was reached on December 23, 1908.

Mileposts magazine reported *"trouble, mud, sand and high winds persisted, but grim perseverance brought together the track gangs from east and west near Sand Pass about October 1909."* On October 22, 1909, just a few days before the driving of the last spike in California, President E. T. Jeffery ran a complimentary excursion out of Salt Lake City for legislative and other Utah bigwigs. Salt Lake City Mayor Bransford congratulated the Western Pacific on *"a fine new railroad, a fine train, and a fine lunch in the diner. . . ,"* according to *Mileposts*.

Arthur W. Keddie sent a telegraph dated November 1, 1909, to the vice president and chief engineer of the Western Pacific Railroad, congratulating him and the company on the *"completion of the bond of steel by which the Western Pacific this afternoon gave to California a great transcontinental railroad."*

Earlier, a special train traveled to Wendover carrying railroad and government officials on March 3, 1909. Utah Governor Spry was among the dignitaries. The *Salt Lake Tribune's* Harold Shipler took valuable photos in reporting the occasion.

The *Milepost's* Western Pacific railroad history continued: *"On November 1, 1909, the track gangs from east and west met on the steel bridge across Spanish Creek near Keddie and foreman Leonardo di Tomasso drove the final spike. In contrast to the gold spike ceremonies on the first overland railway just forty years before, no decorated engines met head to head before a cheering crowd; no magnums of champagne were broached. The only spectators were a pair of local women and their little girls."*

Meanwhile, the Western Pacific company needed powerful steam locomotives to pull the long lines of heavily-laden freight cars. They ordered twenty freight engines from Baldwin and forty-five engines from the American Locomotive Company. The freight engines had a tractive [pulling] effort of 43,300 pounds. Thirty-five ten-wheel, passenger locomotives were ordered with a tractive effort of 29,100 pounds. The passenger engines had higher wheels so they were capable of traveling at faster speeds. The 100 new, coal burning

Malley oil-burning locomotive type which ran between Wendover and California on the Western Pacific. A total of ten operated between 1931 and 1952. *(Western Pacific* Mileposts, *Summer-Fall 1975)*

locomotives became the excellent workhorses for several decades for the WP.

Later, in 1938, at the high point in the company's history, the Western Pacific ordered eleven brand new Malleys. Four were oil burners and seven were coal burners. The Western Pacific then owned twenty-seven huge Malleys. The Malleys were some of the *"most powerful"* steam locomotives ever built anywhere in the world. They were two-pistoned with twelve drive wheels. They were *"designed to handle heavy fast freight trains both in the mountains of California and the open plains of Nevada."* The WP utilized them from Wendover west to California. The Malleys remained in operation until the more powerful diesels began replacing them in 1949.

Through-freight service began on December 1, 1909. Local freight service began earlier, primarily between Salt Lake City and Shafter where the Nevada Northern made the connection between Shafter and the *"flourishing mines in Ely."* Freight traffic to begin with was *"disappointingly slim"* until a fifty-car trainload of nails and wire was shipped from Illinois to Salt Lake City on December 25, 1909.

Winter hit hard in California and landslides, snow banks, and floods caused havoc for the railroad. There were washouts in the Nevada desert and the waters of the Great Salt Lake ate away the earth fill of the track. Even so, passenger service was inaugurated on August 22, 1910.

The railroad's financier, George Gould, son of wealthy Jay Gould, came through Wendover soon thereafter, riding in his cushy business car named *"Atlanta"* where white tie and tails was the norm at dinner. He was on an inspection tour with his pretty ex-actress wife and children in the rear of the Overland Express. It is interesting to note that air conditioning in those days was achieved by opening the

Salduro building on the salt beds. Probably the boarding house. *(Gertrude Tripp)*

Western Pacific maintenance buildings in Wendover 1909. *(Utah State Historical Society, Shipler collection)*

window, probably with the aid of the conductor, the porter, and two or three husky male passengers.

G. H. Kneiss recorded: *"Rates of pay at the opening, shed light on the passage of time. Locomotive engineers drew $4.25 per ten-hour day; firemen, $2.75. Conductors were paid by the month, $125 and no overtime. Brakemen got $86.25. In the office, a chief clerk found eleven twenty-dollar gold pieces and a five in his pay envelope; the stenographers $60 or even $75 if they were extra competent."*

A roundhouse, coal hoist, workshops, and other facilities plus a water tower were in place in Wendover by October of 1909. *"Three garden tracks were added in 1911."*

The Beanery restaurant provided food for travelers and crewmen. It was originally out-of-doors and was made of a half circle of wooden boxes for a bar to eat on. Later, a two-story depot was built which housed the Beanery with second floor sleeping accommodations for railroad crew members. The new Beanery featured a half circle counter with no tables.

By 1923 *"Wendover Yard consisted of three yard tracks in addition to the main line; and the Deep Creek Railroad had*

its terminal in Wendover," wrote Wendover yardmaster Scott Howell. During the Second World War, several more tracks were laid *"at Wendover to accommodate the base."* It became one of the larger train yards of the Western Pacific by the early fifties, but by then it was not needed.

Sections

The Western Pacific Railroad had stations or sections across the desert every ten miles where repair crews were located. Many sections had sidings. The sidings were a side set of tracks where extra train cars or cars used for the crew's housing could be sidelined. In cold weather, the switches used to turn a train onto the sidings were heated with propane heaters during the later years.

Some sections had sidings and some did not. Knolls, Salduro, Arinosa, and Wendover were some with sidings.

Salduro was established on the railroad as a section eight miles east of Wendover. It is sometimes referred to as Saldura. The name Salduro is a combination of Spanish and Latin and means rock or hard salt. It was most prominent during the 1930s and 1940s when salt and potash were mined in the area. The settlement which at one time had 200 inhabitants was

Bird's-eye view of Wendover rail yard in 1909. *(Utah State Historical Society, Shipler collection)*

finally abandoned in 1944 when the potash plant closed and, shortly afterwards, a fire swept through the small community.

Mary Millward was a school teacher in Salduro. The Ed Lamus family were long-time residents of Salduro.

Lee Wendelboe moved with his wife and son to Salduro in 1923 to oversee construction of the Victory Highway as the engineer for the project. He described living there. He said *"life at Salduro was more interesting than any place where we had previously lived. There was a picture show once a week, and several trains came every day. We had our groceries shipped by express from the United Grocery Co. of Salt Lake. There was generally something more or less exciting going on among the Solvay Company employees, which amounted to nearly a hundred.*

". . . we enjoyed the association of our neighbors and the people of Salduro, as we took part in the daily routine of living in the camp. In the evening we could see the headlights of the trains as they rounded the curve at Knolls, and we would estimate the time it would take for them to come the thirty-five miles to Salduro.

"Then there was the company boarding house, where, in the dining room, there was a large, circular table twelve feet in diameter, with a revolving top. A diner had to be quick to grab what he wanted as the food passed around in front of him. And then there was Andy the cook, whose pies were most

Early Western Pacific Railroad Depot at Wendover with Letty, Fred, Molly, and Hilda Hewitt in foreground. *(Molly Hewitt Taylor)*

delicious, really 'out of this world,' and one could keep eating as long as the table kept revolving. . . And then there was the 'honey wagon': that took care of the sanitary problems of the company houses, as there were no water or sewer lines in the salt beds. . .

The Solvay Company, during the First World War, had established this little town of Salduro, where they were experimenting with different processes of producing potash. About the time the company's experiments became fruitful, the war ended, and the company turned their plant into a salt producing business. With an outmoded plant, they could not compete with the salt manufacturing plants already in this business; so in a few years the Solvay people withdrew their support from future work at Salduro. About this time a new company was formed called The Bonneville Ltd. . . . ."

A Curtiss Hawk military plane used Salduro as a refueling stop on the first dawn to dusk cross country trip in 1924. A Curtiss Hawk aircraft, piloted by Lt. Russell Maughan of Logan, Utah, took off from Mitchell Field on Long Island, with refueling stops at Dayton, Ohio, St. Joseph, Missouri, Cheyenne, Wyoming, and **Salduro,** Utah.

Western Union sent a telegraph notifying the people

Looking westward at the Wendover rail yard as snow flurries begin to fall. *(Louis L. Stein in "Railroads of Nevada and Eastern California" by David F. Myrick)*

Overland Lumber Company at Salduro. *(Gertrude Tripp)*

of Salduro that Lieutenant Maughan of the U.S. Army was flying the historic flight from New York to San Francisco. He was to stop at Salduro to refuel. There were about 200 people assembled to meet him upon his arrival which took place in the early evening. He followed the railroad line, flying low, and landed on the salt bed. After refueling he took off and finished his flight to San Francisco.

One source claimed that Salduro was abandoned after 1921-23, leaving only the station and old machinery. Nelson E. Lamus and son, Nelson, obtained the contract to wreck the machinery and sell it for scrap. By 1932-1935 nothing was left at Salduro but a station house. This account contradicts the notion that Salduro was in use until 1944, as earlier mentioned.

Arinosa was nineteen miles east of Wendover in the heart of the salt flats. Today it is a seldom used siding with no permanent residents on the Western Pacific Railroad near I-80. It was a railroad maintenance camp, but it was abandoned in 1955 because it lacked culinary water and also because of improved transportation. The exact source of the name is unknown but it

is probably a corruption of the Spanish "arido" meaning "dry" or "arid."

Barro was 10.4 miles east from Arinosa. Barro as well as Arinosa at one time had corrals for horses used in the building of the first road across the salt flats. Feed and water had to be shipped in by rail for the livestock's needs.

Knolls was a siding on the Western Pacific Railroad on the eastern edge of the Great Salt Lake Desert forty-one miles from Wendover. It was a camp for railroad construction and maintenance men and later for I-80 highway construction personnel. The name refers to the numerous knolls in the area.

Ouida Blanthorn informatively reported: *"The station at Knolls was described as 'primarily a train order depot used to facilitate the movement of trains.' A large wooden water tank was installed at Knolls on a nearby hill and track was laid to haul water up to this elevated point. Water was shipped in by rail twice weekly from Wendover.*

"Sometimes the train crews would leave a tank car con-

Wendover Railroad Depot in winter. *(Glenda Green)*

taining a few feet of water on the hill. As one man wrote, 'this soon warmed and sure did make a good place to take a bath.'"

A small roundhouse was built at Knolls in 1909 but the ground was too soft. The first engine that was rolled into a stall sank and had to be raised to be recovered. The roundhouse was consequently torn down without being used. Both the railroad and the highway department had maintennce crews stationed at

Train derailment near Wendover. *(Glenda Green)*

Knolls. Later, a gas station, an outdoor restroom, cabins, and a café were built along Highway 40 at Knolls. A sign painted on each outhouse door read: *"If you are going to complain about the outhouses, DON'T USE THEM!"* Modern restrooms were out of the question as they hauled their water fifty-seven miles. Electric power lines were installed in 1960. Todd and Kenyon Riddle ran the station for over thirty years (1951 to 1984) after they purchased it from Harvey Naylor.

Clive Siding was ten miles east of Knolls on the Western Pacific Railroad where I-80 and the railroad pass over the Cedar Mountains. This temporary maintenance camp and siding was abandoned in 1955. It is the present site of Envirocare, a low-level radioactive waste storage facility.

Low was a Western Pacific Railroad siding at the northern tip of the Cedar Mountains on the eastern edge of the Great Salt Lake Desert. The settlement was established as a construction and maintenance camp. Local water was unavailable and the camp was abandoned by 1955. Dr. Joseph H. Peck visited there in 1917 and said: *"It consisted of a depot and two saddle horse[s] tied to the stockyard fence. The telegraph operators slept in the freight room and cooked their own meals on the office stove."*

Railroad worker Harvey Naylor worked at Low and talked about a rattlesnake problem as quoted by Ouida Blanthorn. He said: *"In the mornings the pesky creatures liked to snuggle up along side the rails to absorb a little of the heat held over from the day before and later in the*

day they took shelter under an old tie or rock or anything to get out of the sun. . . Some of us would ride to and from the work site on the push car or flat topped trailer attached to the motorcar, but we were careful not to dangle our legs over the side."

Delle was ten miles east of Low and seventy miles east of Wendover on I-80. It was a maintenance camp and dispatch center for the Western Pacific Railroad where it crossed the Great Salt Lake Desert. Today there are only a gas station, café, and siding. An early name was Dalles Spring but this was shortened to Delle by railroad personnel for telegraphic efficiency. "Dalles" is French and refers to paving stone.

Lee Wendleboe described living in a tent house at Delle under a large willow tree behind the railroad depot. He bought two tents, and connected them end to end. He connected a water line to the railroad water supply so they had running water in their kitchen.

In cold weather they heated their home with the kitchen stove. One morning after Mr. Wendelboe had started the fire, he went back to bed to get warm. Suddenly there was a loud knocking on their door and they could hear someone yelling that the tent was afire. Lee quickly doused the fire with water. A transient had spotted the fire and alerted the family. He refused to stay for breakfast as he was anxious to catch the next freight train.

The Wendleboes refrigerated their food in a large ice box which they supplied with ice from the *"reefer"*

First official train excursion on the salt beds Nov. 9, 1908. *(Utah State Historical Society)*

train when it came through. They threw large chunks of ice off the train onto the ground and climbed down to retrieve them. They wrapped the ice in burlap to make it last longer. The ice was an "absolute necessity" at Delle.

Mr. Wendleboe claimed that *"life at Delle for Pearl* [his wife] *was rather monotonous, but some times in the evening we would stroll to the contractor's camp, where there were women cooks, and Pearl would enjoy her conversations with them. Sometimes we would walk along the railroad tracks to the different mile posts, and the evening air and sunsets were the best that the world had to offer."* He said his wife made a fine, neat home in the desert.

Modern Delle has a gas station with a selection of fast foods and notions. Towing services have been available intermittently as well as motel rooms. The cafe burned to the ground in the 1970s and was rebuilt. There is an exit off Interstate 80 at Delle.

Going immediately west from Wendover the railroad sections were as follows.

Ola was a section eight miles from Wendover. It consisted of a house for the foreman and his family,

and a boarding house for the three or four gandy dancers (workers in a railroad section gang). There was a shed behind the main house where the foreman's wife washed clothes. It had a water barrel on the roof which was heated by the sun and used to wash clothes and as shower water for the workers.

Water was hauled in on the railroad and deposited into two large underground barrels for use by the workers. Rattlesnakes congregated near the cool barrels in the hot summer. One week the Richins family, who lived there in 1939-41, killed eighteen rattlesnakes in the vicinity. The three daughters stayed close to the house because of the prevalence of rattlesnakes.

One of the daughters, during an illness, slept in a cellar under the house where it was cooler. She noticed empty fruit bottles moving slightly on a shelf and then one fell off. She called her mother who investigated and found a huge rattlesnake moving among the bottles apparently enjoying the cool basement.

The Richins children attended school in Wendover one year. The other year their mother schooled them at home. They posted their mail in Wendover but

Western Pacific locomotive. *(Utah State Historical Society)*

ordered their food and other supplies by catalogue from Salt Lake. The train delivered them periodically. On delivery days, it was like Christmas unwrapping the newly arrived packages.

There were no trees in Ola but the Richins family planted a tamarisk bush. The bush is the only sign of civilization left at Ola in 2003.

Pilot was located 10.4 miles northwest of Wendover. The Pilot Peak Mining District was organized in the late 1870s but little ore was produced. In 1908 two saloon owners from Cobre worked some claims but produced very little.

In his book, *Old Heart of Nevada: Ghost Towns and Mining Camps of Elko County*, Shawn Hall wrote: "*With the completion of the Western Pacific Railroad, a stop and signal station named Pilot came into being. The railroad constructed some buildings to house the section crew and their families. A school opened in 1910, and Edna Ross was the first teacher. The railroad phased out the Pilot station in the 1920s. It moved the section crew elsewhere and dismantled the buildings for use at other stations.*"

More recently a section station was listed at Pilot during the 1930s and 1940s. A passenger train turned over as it derailed and fell on the section houses at Pilot. No one was killed in the accident, but a body was found that had flipped out of a coffin that was

being shipped in one of the freight cars.

For four years starting in 1934, there were several silver mines which produced small amounts of silver and copper, contributing to the local population and economy. Most recently in the 1980s, a lime plant has produced quick lime. The California Trail passed through the area and has been duly marked.

Clifside and **Proctor** were stations with telegraph offices located between Pilot and Silver Zone.

Silver Zone was located 6 1/2 miles northeast of Shafter. Researcher Hall states: "*The pass at Silver Zone was part of the Hastings Cutoff of the California Trail. The Donner Party navigated the pass before they met their fate in the Sierras, and signs of the trail are still visible in the area. The name Silver Zone came about after Major Robert Goldman discovered silver in the area in May 1872. . . .*

"*It was not until 1907 that Silver Zone revived when construction of the Western Pacific Railroad led to the organization of a work camp. T. J. Connelly built a saloon a short distance away from the camp. But it violated the Western Pacific's three-mile limit for alcohol consumption. Officials arrested many workers and had Connelly's license revoked. When the railroad completed construction in the area, the camp disbanded, and Silver Zone became a siding and housed a section crew.*

"*At 5,875 feet, Silver Zone pass is the highest point on*

Wendover Western Pacific railway depot. *(Brent Peterson)*

Shafter, who was a commander in the U. S. Army in Cuba during the Spanish-American War.

"As the Western Pacific neared Shafter, numerous lots were sold in the town. The first store, the Morgan-Spencer Mercantile Company, opened in early 1908. Orsen Spencer [see story of Ferd Johnson's Spencer Mercantile in Wendover in chapter one. Ferd was Orsen Spencer's son-in-law.] became the first postmaster when the office opened in his store on August 28, 1908. The Western Pacific began regular operations on November 9, 1908.

"A community of about forty lived in Shafter for years, and both railroads maintained section crews and small depots there. A school opened at Shafter in 1909 and did not close until 1933, when the county ran out of money. Schoolteacher M. J. Williams formed the Shafter Literary Society in October 1932 and

the Western Pacific between San Francisco and Salt Lake City, and it has had its share of railroad accidents. The most serious of these took place in March 1936 when Engine No. 9's boiler suddenly exploded, killing [two] brakemen. The two were in a caboose that the engine was pushing, and the explosion threw them through the roof. The conductor. . . was severely scalded and died five days later. Three men in the nearby section house were also badly scalded, but they survived."

The boiler blew up due to hard chemicals in the water which caused the boiler water to foam. Foam prevents steam from forming, causing locomotive boilers to malfunction. This problem was thereafter prevented by putting chemical cakes in the water tanks of the tenders.

". . . While trains still rumble through Silver Zone pass, there is little left there except for the concrete ruins at the railroad siding. At the old mines, a few signs of the short-lived boom camp remain."

Shafter (Bews) was located twenty-two miles west of Wendover and seven miles southwest of I-80. Author Shawn Hall reported: *"Bews was established as a siding for the Nevada Northern Railway in 1906. It was named for Richard Bews of England who established a ranch there in 1897 and ran a stage and freight station.*

"In April 1906 the railroad organized a construction camp that contained 150 Greeks and Italians. Bews was renamed Shafter when the Western Pacific Railroad reached there in September 1907. It was named after General W. R.

Clam shell shovel on coal hoist in Wendover. *(Molly Taylor)*

the Nevada State Herald *reported on society happenings. The society folded when Williams left after the school closed. In the early 1930s Clarence Neashum opened a general store. . . [Bob Scobie operated the coal chute at Shafter until he moved to Wendover].*

"In the 1950s Shafter's importance greatly diminished, and in September 1953 Joe LaFrance was named postmaster, mostly because he was the only eligible resident. The office closed on April 19, 1957. All businesses closed in 1957, and Shafter was basically abandoned after that. The Railway Express Agency officially discontinued its Shafter office in March 1959. Until a few years ago, a couple of buildings still stood at Shafter, but they have since been dismantled. Numerous concrete foundations are now all that make the site, and a small cemetery is located nearby."

Sonar, Jaspar, and Luke were stations with telegraph offices between Shafter and Ventosa as listed in the subdivision timetables of 1934 and 1945.

Ventosa was located five miles east of Tobar. Shawn Hall wrote: "*Ventosa was a stop on the Western Pacific Railroad and the next depot east of Tobar. The depot and stop were used primarily as a shipping point for Spruce Mountain ore, and a special siding was built to load the ore. A school was opened at Ventosa in 1912, with G. E. Brown as teacher, and it remained open until the 1920s. From the*

Local Wendover Western Pacific employees standing on the clam shell shovel. *(Molly Hewitt Taylor)*

teens through the 1940s about ten people, most of whom worked for the railroad, lived at Ventosa.

"In 1929 a plan to build a railroad spur to Spruce Mountain with Ventosa as the terminus attracted a considerable amount of interest, but trucks came into vogue before the line could be built, and the railroad never materialized. In the early 1950s the depot and section buildings were abandoned, sold, and removed.

"Ventosa made the news one more time in August 1950 when a broken draw bar derailed thirty-two cars there. A fire broke out, and all the cars were destroyed at a loss of $250,000. Only concrete foundations are left at Ventosa today."

Tobar was originally a construction camp for the Western Pacific Railroad in 1908. The name of the town which grew up around the railroad depot stemmed from the tented Rag Saloon. The saloon's owner hung a sign which read "To Bar," meaning go this way to get to the bar or saloon. The message was shortened to one word and hence the name of the town. Marbled posts lined the well-laid streets at one time in Tobar's history.

Dry farms supplemented the railroad town by 1910 and the next year

Wendover roadhouse and water tanks. *(Molly Hewitt Taylor)*

Smoke coming from the Wendover roundhouse. *(Molly Hewitt Taylor)*

Ruby and **Wells**, Nevada, were the next two stations or sections spaced at ten miles apart along the line west of Wendover. And so on.

Living Along the Railroad Sections

Bonnie Tilbury talked of life along the railroad sections. She said Ray Peterson from Wendover drove an ice truck. The ice was brought in on the ice train to Wendover and to the sections along the way. The people had water boxes which they would fill and then throw a block of ice in to keep it cold. If a family needed ice water, they would take a bucket with a rope on it and dip into the water box similar to getting water from a well. The water was brought in on railroad tankers, except at Delle where water was available.

Tilbury's grandfather took mail and water to Knolls and dropped off and picked up mail in boxes along the highway sections. The sections were ten miles apart *"so you always had neighbors if you needed anything."* The sections organized baseball teams and even played in the state tournament. They would play where the old Knolls airport was at one time about half way between Knolls and Clive. They would have a picnic with everybody bringing potluck. This was before World War II.

The need for section crews to replace rotted ties and warped rails eventually became obsolete. With the introduction of creosoted ties and heavier rails, the closely spaced railroad sections were no longer necessary and were closed.

During the second World War, Wendover was booming and a large contingent of workers manned the railroad in Wendover twenty-four hours a day. They operated the roundhouse, the freight yard and depot, the ticket office and the rip-track crews, all under the direction of section foreman Brent Peterson.

A trainmaster was in charge of operations at each railroad terminal. C. E. McDonald was trainmaster at Wendover followed by J. J. Duggan and J. F. Lynch. Leo Waters was the station and freight agent. He brought

there were seventy-five residents in twenty homes at Tobar and a post office. In 1913 a school was opened and the two-story White Elephant Hotel was built in conjunction with a promotional campaign which included brochures dubbing Tobar as the *"home of the big red apple"* to lure new residents to the town. Tobar was then the hub of shipping for ore hauled in from surrounding mining districts.

Tobar went through a series of booms and busts, and even a temporary name change to Clover City, all caused by droughts, jackrabbit invasions, and metal price fluctuations. The 1920s saw the last of Tobar as a viable town and during the 1930s all that remained was the railroad section crew and their families.

"On June 29, 1969 there occurred an event in the Nevada desert that could not have happened in a better place if it had to happen at all." One mile west of Tobar, a train carrying carloads of bombs destined for Vietnam exploded at 4:00 p.m. in the afternoon and left a huge crater. The explosion injured two railroad crewmen and slightly burned two transients.

There were seventy train cars pulled by four diesel locomotives, including twenty-two boxcars loaded full of 750 pound bombs. Each forty-foot boxcar held one hundred and twelve un-fused bombs. The first detonation occurred in the 61st car, which set off a chain reaction of explosions, completely disintegrating four boxcars behind it plus a gondola. *"Except for the door of the 61st car, no identifiable piece of the four boxcars was ever found."* No definable cause for the explosion was determined.

his family to Wendover in 1938 and they lived at the depot as they couldn't find suitable housing in town. Edith Peterson, the wife of yard foreman Brent Peterson, held several jobs with the railroad, including one titled simply a "call girl," but of a different type than the usual. She was responsible for going to the various crew members' homes and calling them out to work.

The huge locomotives were refueled with coal stored in a wooden building referred to as a coal bunker. A clam shell crane was used to unload gondolas (a railroad freight car

Wendover railroad stockyards. *(Molly Hewitt Taylor)*

with no top) loaded with coal and dump the coal into the coal bunker. The same self-propelled steam clamshell also went up an elevated track and loaded the coal onto the tenders.

The local people bought coal from the Western Pacific which freighted it in for them. The local store also carried coal to sell. Residents used the coal to heat their homes. Some of it was in large lumps. Bruce Lamus remembered the chore as a kid of breaking the lumps into small pieces and putting them into a coal scuttle for use by his mother in their cooking stove.

The yard crews switched cars in and out of trains and changed the cabooses. Each conductor was assigned his own caboose. Engines were also changed from the small crocodiles to the giant, noisy Malleys going west out of Wendover and vice-versa going east.

The yard crew was made up of permanent employees. They operated switch engines to move cars and engines from train to train, etc. The hostlers built fires in the engines and moved the engines around in the roundhouse. Jobs did not overlap. Maintenance personnel did not run the engines and hostlers did not do maintenance.

Brent Peterson had a yard crew which, besides their regular duties, also *"took care of the town."* Mr. Peterson and his workers maintained the roads. When

they needed patching with oil or gravel to fill mud holes, the yard crew did it. When large pools of rainwater or runoff were present, the yard crew sprayed them with oil to keep the mosquito population under control. They performed the same function when cesspools frequently bubbled to the surface, providing breeding grounds for insects.

When squatters and prostitutes, who would come in from Wells and Ely, Nevada, on pay-day, started setting up structures on the hillsides, Brent Peterson and his yard crew took care of the problem by tearing them down.

The yard crew unloaded livestock, corralled them, and fed and watered them overnight. There were no long haul trucks, and livestock would have to be taken off the trains periodically on their way to market. Wendover was one of those livestock stops. The rail yard crewmen also took care of the town water system. Sometimes in the winter the wooden pipe would freeze and Peterson and his crew would cut into the line and by-pass the frozen section.

Thom Anderson of the Western Pacific Railroad Historical Society wrote: *"Wendover was manned 24 hours a day and was the away from home terminal for crews from Elko and Salt Lake City. The crews would report to the station office upon arriving to turn in their paperwork and go off duty.*

"Other functions included calling crews to man the trains and issuing them the paperwork for the train, sell tickets for passenger trains and handle paperwork for freight being shipped, as well as providing office space for the trainmaster and road foreman of engines. The station had a hotel on the second floor that served as a dormitory for train crews and other employees."

Freight train crews went off-duty and fresh crews replaced them in Wendover, but not passenger train crews. The passenger trains traveled faster at fifty miles per hour than freight trains and could cover a longer route from Salt Lake City to Elko, Nevada, which were two subdivision locations.

Freight trains traveled between 100 and 120 miles in sixteen hours. They averaged twenty-five miles an hour due to time waiting at siding while other trains passed by, as well as time taking on water, etc. Engine crews could work no more than sixteen hours per day by law. Wendover was a place to stay for off-duty trainmen.

Freight trains came through Wendover daily in the 1930s. Trains going west had uneven numbers and trains going east had even numbers. The first west bound train, #61, arrived in the middle of the night at 2:15 a.m. and left at 3:00 a.m. The second westbound train, #77, came in at 4:00 p.m. and left at 5:00 p.m. At 3:50 a.m. #62 arrived heading east and departed to the east at 4:40 a.m. In the afternoon #82 stopped at 6:00 p.m. and departed at 7:00 p.m.

During the 1930s, the *"Scenic Limited"* provided daily passenger train service, going west as train #1 arrived in Wendover at 9:25 a.m. and left at 9:35 a.m. Train #2 of the *"Scenic Limited"* going east came in at 6:40 p.m. and departed five minutes later. This passenger train was discontinued in 1939 on June 11.

A new passenger train in 1939 was called the *"Exposition Flyer."* It was inaugurated to take passengers to the San Francisco Golden Gate Exhibition 1939-40 World's Fair. The lavish event, complete with the large man-made Treasure Island, celebrated the

> Toward the end of World War II, several trains pulling eight or nine cars filled with coffins of soldiers, killed in the war stopped periodically in Wendover to take on coal and water. Each time the engines were shut down, complete silence followed. All the passenger seats had been removed to make room for the caskets, and the doors and windows were sealed with bolted steel covers. It was a solemn sight which brought the town of Wendover to a standstill. A feeling of reverence and a quiet hush came over the town when the trains stopped.
> *(Related by Wendover Western Pacific yard foreman Brent Peterson and his daughter Barbara Cole)*

construction of the world's largest suspension bridges, the Golden Gate and San Francisco-Oakland. The Western Pacific's *"Exposition Flyer"* carried many passengers to and from the exhibition. Westbound #39 arrived in Wendover after midnight and eastbound #40 went through Wendover in the late afternoon.

Changes were made periodically to the timetable over the years and a third pair of scheduled freight trains was added for a time. Sometimes a train was *"annulled"* on a given day and did not run at all. At busy times, an extra train was added. It was train Extra #765 carrying bombs which exploded at Tobar in June of 1969. The trains used paired tracks west of Wells to just east of Winnemucca, Nevada. Eastbound trains used the Western Pacific and westbound trains used the Southern Pacific tracks.

Signals and Communication

All communication along the Western Pacific was initially done by telegraph. From 1948 to 1952, the Western Pacific constructed a pole line between San Francisco and Salt Lake City and installed a signal and communication line.

The code line consisted of two wires. The wires were sometimes damaged due to poor weather conditions such as wind or freezing temperatures. Signal crews were stationed along the rail line to make repairs. Night or day they were on call. They climbed the poles and made temporary splices using a twisted pair of lines if the distance was short, maybe between four or five poles. If they needed to communicate with controllers in Elko, Nevada, or Portola, California, they could climb the pole and tap into the code line.

The signal crews installed and repaired a variety of useful signals. There were fire detectors, high and wide detectors, mud detectors, snow detectors, high water detectors, and hot box detectors. The journals on train wheels were filled with oil and occasionally would get hot and catch on fire. Sealed ball bearings were used later on.

Later model Western Pacific diesel locomotive. *(Utah State Historical Society, Shipler collection)*

Before hot box detectors were installed, track walkers watched for the hot journals and would signal the hand-under *"Wash Out"* sign to stop the train. A hand-over *"High Ball"* signal meant everything was O.K. Important telegraphed orders were relayed to engineers as they slowed down at sections by means of a note attached to a hook atop a bamboo pole held up near the passing engine. The engineer grabbed the telegram with his hand.

With the advent of automatic hot box detectors, the hot journals were identified electronically. The high and wide signals indicated sections of broken track or separated spans which could potentially de-rail a train. Incidentally, there were five major de-railments on the Western Pacific line between 1967 and 1970 for various reasons.

The crews either walked or used small motor cars to travel along the track. The motor cars could travel up to fifty miles per hour. The men had a schedule of trains and the times they came through so they knew when they could be traveling on the track. They repaired signals or exchanged fresh batteries in signal houses along the track.

The Western Pacific ran on a strict time schedule. In fact, according to Wendover section foreman Brent Peterson, *"The railroad was run by time."* All workers were required to have a 21-jewel, five-position railroad watch. A railroad watch inspector came by periodically to check each watch to make sure it was operating at peak efficiency. Such exact time schedules by railroads led to the formation of times zones across the country.

Sometimes there were mistakes made and close calls. One signal foreman who worked out of Wendover said he could quickly and instinctively lift his 500-pound car and flip it off the track in a hurry. He had the misfortune of miscalculating a schedule one day east of Beowawe, Nevada, and peered out from a signal house where he was checking batteries in time to see a locomotive plow into his motor car, eventually bringing the entire train to a complete halt.

The "California Zephyr" went through Wendover on its way between California and Salt Lake (*www.calzephyr.railfan.net*).

The "California Zephyr"

Until about 1952, Western Pacific trains were powered by steam. Three years earlier in 1949, the WP began converting to diesel. The *"California Zephyr"* was the first diesel-powered train. The *"California Zephyr"* was a streamlined, passenger train with five dome cars. The Vista-Dome cars were an instant success. Burlington's *"Pioneer Zephyr"* was the first and was a *"hallmark of the Burlington fleet."* There were two California Zephyrs: one went west daily and one went east.

The Budd Manufacturing Company produced them initially. Each stainless steel car was named with the beginning title *"Silver."* Eventually seventy-seven cars would be named with the prefix *"Silver,"* such as *"Silver Palace"* and *"Silver Schooner."* There were in the beginning six ten-car trains. The number was increased to eleven and then to thirteen cars per train later on.

The foreman was so upset that he couldn't remember his name for a few minutes after being asked by the conductor. The railroad gave him seventy-four demerits—seventy-five demerits meant immediate dismissal. He had just received the bid to work in the area, moved his family there, and purchased a new car. It was a close call in more ways than one!

In the late 1960s the motor cars were replaced by high roller pickup trucks elevated on railroad wheels. These high rollers were allowed to travel as a rule up to forty-five miles per hour but could go much faster if needed.

Railroad life was not easy, to say the least. Besides the dangers involved, there were the hot and cold extremes, the dust and long hours, rattlesnakes, and separation from family. Water, food, mail, and other supplies had to be brought in on the railroad.

March 19, 1949, was the official inauguration of the Zephyr which took place in San Francisco at the Pier 3 ferry building on the Embarcadero. After formal ceremonies were held, the first eastbound train left at 9:30 a.m. PST on March 20, 1949. *"Every female passenger onboard was presented a lavish corsage, of 'silver' and orange orchids flown in from Hilo, Hawaii for the occasion. To add to the festive atmosphere, the Western Pacific Employee Band was present to supply music for the departure. Thus a legend in passenger train history was born,"* according to Wilson and Radecki.

The route took 2½ days to complete, covering 2,525 miles. The Chicago Burlington & Quincy went from Chicago to Denver. The Denver and Rio Grande went from Denver to Salt Lake City and the Western Pacific took the Zephyr on to California.

At one time, a blood bank car traveled as part of

the Western Pacific. This military blood procurement car was called the *"Charles O. Sweetwood."* The car had four bedrooms which were used for giving blood. A fifth bedroom was used as an office and testing laboratory. It also had a lounge used as a waiting room and a dining room where refreshments were served to donors.

The car contained large refrigerators where blood could be temporarily stored until picked up by the California Zephyr daily for shipment to Berkeley, California. It was operated by four Red Cross nurses. It stopped in Wendover on one particular day and received forty-six donations of blood.

The California Zephyr maintained regular, daily services for passengers between Salt Lake and Wendover. It left Salt Lake at 10:25 p.m., arriving in Wendover at 12:25 a.m. Mountain Standard Time.

There was also a Zephyrette which was a streamlined passenger car powered by a diesel locomotive. The Zephyrette operated on Sunday, Wednesday, and Friday, leaving Salt Lake City at 8:30 a.m. arriving in Wendover two hours later. The single fare from Salt Lake to Wendover was $3.51 including tax with a round- trip fare being $6.33. Westbound trains were numbered 17 and eastbound trains were numbered 18.

The California Zephyr ran until March 22, 1970, having operated for twenty years and two days. It was discontinued because of financial problems. Travel by rail was being replaced by airlines and bus routes, *"though neither offered the opulence or service afforded to the rail passenger."*

Amtrak took over a modified service under the name of California Zephyr. Today most of the Zephyr's seventy-seven cars are owned by other railroads and have been modified.

The demise of the Western Pacific was gradual. Railroad historian R. W. "Dick" Bridges summarized the end. He said that in the year 1960, two events happened which por-

tended *"significant changes ahead for"* the Western Pacific.

The first change was the discontinuation of two passenger trains which provided service three times a week between Salt Lake City and San Francisco, California. Bridges stated that *"patronage on these two trains had decreased to the extent that employees being deadheaded by the Company from one work point to another often out-numbered revenue passengers. Operating losses too large to bear with no prospect of revenues increasing at a greater rate than expenses dictated the discontinuance of Trains 1 and 2."*

The second change that happened was on October 12, 1960. On that date, the Southern Pacific Railroad successfully applied for control of Western Pacific.

During the '70s, modernization of the Western Pacific Railroad was emphasized. Modernization included *"equipment, roadbed, operating procedures and administrative techniques."* Mr. Bridges wrote: *"One of the most significant of those modernization projects was the 'computerization' of the railroad. By the end of the decade train consists [manifests] were being produced and transmitted by computer with pertinent waybill data included, car inventories and switching movements at the several yards were computerized, as were payrolls, accounts payable, freight claims,*

Children of railroad engineer Percy Hewitt, Hilda & Fred, with their pet geese. The geese were kept to chase away begging vagrants. They did a good job until a rattlesnake killed one of the geese. The other goose pined and had to be returned to the Last Chance Ranch. *(Molly Hewitt Taylor)*

First train to Gold Hill, Utah, in January 1917, moving forward while laying tracks. *(Mervelle Lord Probert collection)*

demurrage, car accounting and locomotive maintenance functions.

"The railroad again operated in the black even in the face of huge cost increases and stiff competition during the decade of the 1970's. . ."

Even so, stiff competition made it difficult to maintain profitability of a small railroad like Western Pacific. Single-line carriers had the advantage of charging lower rates than carriers such as Western Pacific which was required to *"participate with other roads in joint rates to the same points served by the single-line carrier."*

The control of Western Pacific by Union Pacific was approved on January 23, 1980. Two years later, the Interstate Commerce Commission approved the merger which had been previously agreed upon by the board of directors of both companies. By approval, the Union Pacific also merged with Missouri Pacific at the same time.

Bridge's concluded: *"Western Pacific's independent corporate existence. . .may be* said to have terminated on January 11, 1983, when at a meeting of the Company's Board of Directors action was taken to confirm the Company's status as a subsidiary of the Union Pacific Railroad Company. . . The eightieth anniversary of the incorporation of The Western Pacific Railway Company would have occurred March 6, 1983."

Bridges further summarized by saying, *"One thing is clear— that corporation was merely an intangible legal entity; its spirit or soul or being, if you will, were people: people who planned its creation and constructed its facilities, people who operated its trains, maintained its tracks, bridges and assorted other structures, people who kept its records, sold its services, maintained its signal and communication facilities, kept its equipment in repair, in short all those people who, as Western Pacific employees, did the necessary jobs to keep the Company operating. It is to those people that this final salute goes."*

The Union Pacific continued to operate through Wendover as a new millennium dawned. Freight cars were parked on sidings, a small station house stood near the edge of the tracks, but few, if any, crewmen resided in Wendover.

Percy Hewitt in the middle was the engineer on the Deep Creek Railroad, his son Fred is on the right. *(Molly Hewitt Taylor)*

The Deep Creek Railroad

Talk of a railway going through Deep Creek or Ibapah, Utah, dates back as far as 1881. Deep Creek was then on the major Overland Stage route going west. Mining activity in nearby Gold Hill and Clifton, Utah also made the railway attractive to some. Even so, little came of the idea until after the Western Pacific was built across the salt desert.

The Utah Construction Company began building the bed for the Deep Creek tracks in November 1916. The route originated in Wendover and went south along the edge of the salt flats staying just inside the Utah state line for about sixteen miles and then went southeast alongside the Last Chance Ranch and Dutch Mountain to Gold Hill.

The Deep Creek Railroad Company began operations in 1917 as a spur of the Western Pacific leading to and from Gold Hill, Utah, southeast of Wendover. The Wendover depot was housed in a small building east of the Western Pacific depot. It had a small, shingle-sign which read DEEP CREEK R.R.CO./ OFFICE hanging above the door.

Dr. Joseph H. Peck humorously described the building of the Deep Creek Railroad spur in his book *What Next Doctor Peck*. The description was undoubtedly similar to the building of the rail line from Salt Lake to Wendover, at least while building across the edge of the salt beds.

He reported: *"The situation in the railroad camp was, as they say in the Navy, 'normal, all fouled up.'"* First came the survey crew. Their business was to find the easiest grade on which to build the railroad bed. Every hundred feet or so, the surveyors would drive small pine stakes into the ground with weird figures on them. The pine stakes pinpointed the center of the track to be built and they designated the height of the fill needed to lay the ties.

The level salt flats appeared well suited for laying the track until storms soaked them with moisture. The soil that was used to build the rail bed consisted partly of salt. Salt, soil, and water combine to form sticky mud. Dr. Peck recorded: *"There is no more distressing sight than watching a locomotive settle down into mud, especially salt mud, like an old hen on a setting of eggs."* The unsteady roadbed was like riding in a small boat on a stormy sea.

The crewmen would quickly become covered with *"the foul-smelling salt mud."* The clothes dried stiff complete with wrinkles due to the salt. The skin on

Two views of the Deep Creek Railway at the Garrison water tank near the Last Chance ranch. Note the 1890s passenger coach in top photo. *(Molly Hewitt Taylor)*

This 1920 oasis in the desert was created by the Englishwoman Lotty Hewitt, complete with lawn, trees, roses, and grow boxes. This was the Wendover home of the engineer of the Deep Creek Railroad and his family. *(Molly Hewitt Taylor)*

rails using huge ice tongs with long handles and laid the rails along the ties. For safety purposes, a man gripped one handle of the tongs on each side of the rail being carried. The tong point was interlocked over the groove of the rail. If a man tripped or lost his grip on the tongs, the rail would drop harmlessly between him and his partner. The rails were heavy. It took ten pair of tongs and ten men on each side of a rail to safely carry it to its position.

The spikers followed the carriers. They used spikes and angle irons to secure the rails to the ties and to other adjoining rails. A boss of the crew used a track gauge to ensure proper distances between parallel rails. While the spikers were fastening and the boss was gauging, other men held the rails steady with bars.

the workers' legs would become skinned and chaffed. The only way to put on the pants again the next day was to hang up their pants at night. They could then step into the pant legs as if they were a pair of stove pipes.

Following the survey crews came the men and mules with plows. They dug a barrow pit on each side of the surveyed roadbed. A second crew used mule-drawn scrapers to pile the dirt into the rough shape of a roadbed.

Muckers smoothed the piles into the finished roadbed using shovels. A small engine followed which pushed three flatcars. One flatcar was loaded with rails and two were filled with railroad ties. Teams of men carried the ties and laid them a designated distance apart for fifty feet ahead of the end of the laid track.

Other teams carried the

The crews left expansion joints between the rails to allow for the heating of the sun. The joints caused the clickety-clack sound made as the train wheels passed over the joints. The rails were thirty feet in length and the joints were staggered every fifteen feet.

For every twenty feet of new track laid, the work

Gold Hill, Utah, in the winter of 1924. *(Deep Creek Reflections, Thelda Boyd Swain collection)*

engine moved ahead the same distance. Laying a mile a day was a good day. The work day went from eight to five and the workers were paid two dollars per day. The ballasting crew came last. Their task was to pound rocks and cinders between and under the ties until everything was tightly pressed together.

Deep Creek train arriving in Gold Hill. *(Melba Nicholes)*

The train crews lived in a work train camp. The camp consisted partly of converted box cars used as sleeping cars or tents with straw tick bunks stacked three high, a dining car, and a kitchen. Each of the sleeping quarters accommodated fifteen to twenty men. The cars had a large stove in the middle surrounded by five or so stools or nail kegs. A *"smoky old lantern,"* hung from the ceiling, *"shed a light as soft as that seen through a thin fog."* The work mules were tied to a picket line not far from camp.

The superintendent had a solitary, eight-by-ten-foot, tarpaper shack in Wendover with an iron cot with springs. His desk was made of an old packing crate and he owned an armchair. Dr. Peck described him as efficient and a nice guy. The doctor was assigned living quarters in the chief engineer's tar paper shack. His office was five feet square in the headquarters building, which was twenty feet wide and forty long. His desk and stool were made of scrap lumber and discarded boxes, as were his shelves.

The camp cook stayed in a tent close to his kitchen. He kept a rolled canvas under his bed containing a jug of whisky and an assortment of razor-sharp butcher knives of differing sizes and lengths. He had helpers called *"swampers."* They slept in the dining tent and were the dishwashers and floor scrubbers.

The tables for most of the workers were made of rough lumber and had sawhorse supports. The table top was turned over when it became too greasy. Ten-man wooden benches surrounded the tables. The dinnerware consisted of enamel cups, saucers, bowls, and plates. Water was served in tin cups and they used tin silverware.

Arbuckle's packaged coffee was the usual drink. Dr. Peck said, *"It was rumored that it was made of navy beans soaked in carbolic acid with chewing tobacco added for coloring."* He jokingly added, *"I have heard it said that just after one of Brigham Young's wives had served him a cup of this potent brew he had his vision in which the Lord told him to class coffee along with tobacco and whisky as a sin."*

Abandoned Gold Hill freight office of the Western Pacific railroad spur. *(Molly Hewitt Taylor)*

Gold Hill, Utah, on the cover of the *Headlight* magazine, October 1944. *(Deep Creek Reflections)*

Scrambled eggs, beef stew, canned peas, and an orange or banana for a treat on Sunday were the usual fare. Dessert was generally dried fruit pie with a crust made of flour *"diluted with cement."*

There was a pecking order in the camps. The *"hog heads"* or locomotive engineers were the real aristocrats. The foremen were close behind followed by the doctor. They sat at a table with an oil cloth cover.

The youngest had to sleep highest and furthest from the stove. Rock workers and blasting powder technicians were above the common workers. Next came the teamsters above the scrapers; the spikers looked down on the rail placers who spurned the muckers. The lowest on the totem pole were the kitchen swampers.

The construction workers were experienced and some were well-educated, but most were *"castoffs of society."* Their morals were completely lacking and the majority were drunks. They came to Wendover as loads

"of human bodies soaked in alcohol." Apparently, the railroad company had an arrangement with police and hiring halls in California and Salt Lake City to take skid row bums and put them to work on the railroad. They were fed for one day and then given their choice of continuing working or leaving on the next freight train out.

When a shipment of prospective laborers arrived in Wendover, Dr. Peck checked them over. He eliminated those with chronic or infectious diseases. They were given a ticket back to where they came from. For those that passed, they were marched to nearby warm springs and told to bathe. They were then given hot coffee in mush bowls from which they could lap the drink as most were shaking too badly to pick up the bowls. They were fed a pint of canned tomatoes and later a substantial breakfast of ham, eggs, oatmeal, and creamed coffee.

The roadbed across the flat salt proceeded quickly

except for thirty-five wash-outs caused by a flash flood along a fifteen-mile section. Dr. Peck said there was salty water everywhere.

Next came the section by Dutch Mountain along its base. They had to begin elevating the roadbed because it had to climb nearly a thousand feet to reach Gold Hill. There were many fills and cuts along the way due to washes created by the mountain runoff. Culverts were boxes made of *"heavy timber twenty feet long and about three feet wide"* to fill the cuts.

The work near the mountain consisted of swinging double jack hammers, hitting the drills while another worker held the drills. The drills were used to make holes in the rock for purposes of dynamite blasting. Dr. Peck had to treat several different types of injuries including those caused by flying rocks from blasting, eyes filled with rock dust, and injured wrists from drilling.

After the dynamite blasting occurred, the workers shoveled away the broken rocks and dirt into dump cars. Mules were trained to pull the dump cars to a dumping site and then the mules dragged the cars back to be filled again. All this work was done automatically without the need of a mule skinner.

After laying the track around the northern and eastern bases of Dutch Mountain, Gold Hill was in sight. The final few miles of bed were graded and the tracks laid and the job was done.

The line was built quickly and freight service began in March 1917. Passenger service started in April. The cost to build the railway was $450,000. The expectation was that large amounts of high-grade copper and tungsten ore would be extracted from the area's mines and shipped away to have valuable minerals smelted out.

For about three years the copper deposits held out and then *"turned into arsenic ore."* A cotton boll weevil infestation starting in 1923 created a need for the arsenic ore to be mined and shipped for use as

an insecticide. The arsenic boom lasted for about two years. Overseas suppliers, cut off earlier during war time, began shipping again to the southern states.

"After this train service was reduced to daily, then twice-a-week, then for the next ten years once-a-week runs hauling copper, gold ore, tungsten and whatever else the miners could come up with," according to authors Stephen L. Carr and Robert W. Edwards.

A 1944 *Headlight* magazine article stated: *"The Deep Creek Railroad consisted of 46 miles of single tracks, two locomotives, one combination passenger coach, one freight car, and one water car."* There were a depot and a warehouse in Gold Hill.

The 1895 vintage passenger car was made of wood with an old-time coal stove bolted inside for warmth in winter. The car swayed from side to side while its windows rattled. It was illuminated by a faintly glowing gas lantern hanging from the ceiling. Worn-out linoleum covered the floor and formerly plush, red velvet seats faced the stove with fancy brass trimmings adorning the interior. The car's exterior was painted Pullman green and the interior was mahogany wood. It was a sixty-foot, combination passenger and baggage car.

The train traveled no faster than ten to fifteen miles per hour. It could only pull three cars at a time because of a poor road bed. Sometimes it stopped along the way for passengers to hunt rabbits or coyotes. Passengers could board or leave the train at any con-

Deep Creek Railroad at Garrison Monster water tower. Twospot was the name engineer Percy Hewitt used for the Deep Creek Locomotive. *(Molly Hewitt Taylor)*

venient point. In October 1917, the Deep Creek Railroad was held up by bandits who came away with a diamond pin, $243 in cash, and a box of .22 shells. One of the bandits was Jack Dempsey who later became famous as a world champion boxer.

Percy T. Hewitt was the engineer for the Deep Creek Railroad. Mason Moore was the superintendent, clerk, conductor, track repairman, stenographer, and road master. Cigar-puffing Walter Lord was the railroad agent in charge at the Gold Hill Depot from 1919 until his death in 1937. A railroad company phone line ran to Gold Hill on which Mr. Lord received and sent messages in the form of telegrams via the telephone.

The Western Pacific was insolvent by 1939 and the Deep Creek Railroad was running a deficit, so *"the Interstate Commerce Commission authorized immediate abandonment. The last train ran on July 31, and by October the rails had been pulled up, and one of Utah's most remote railways became a ghost,"* according to Carr.

4.

Wendover Field

Training Base for Bombers and a Secret Atomic Mission

*"Those who have long enjoyed such privileges
as we enjoy forget in time that men have died to win them."*

—Franklin Delano Roosevelt

At the end of the twentieth century, the use of atomic bombs on two Japanese cities ranked as the most significant happening of the century, according to a year-long survey conducted in 1999. The American public placed the bombing ahead of Neil Armstrong walking on the moon, the Soviet Union's collapse, penicillin's discovery, the invention of the Internet, and the war in Vietnam.

In 1941 when the atomic bomb was in the beginning stages of development, the United States economy was coming out of the depths of the Great Depression. Consumer prices were rising with a new car costing about $1,000, a steak sold for 23 cents, and the median income was $2,000. There were still five million persons unemployed, but things were looking up.

All the same, war clouds were on the horizon. Armed U.S. merchant ships were shipping supplies of food, medicine, and war materiel to Great Britain in protective convoys. The U.S. in 1940 had enacted a selective service act requiring military registration of sixteen million men between twenty-one and thirty-six. Germany was advancing throughout Europe. Signs of war were all around.

Even so, it was still a shock when Japan ferociously bombed Pearl Harbor at the beginning of December 1941. World War II came forcefully to America. The stunned, sleeping giant of a nation had been awakened. By nightfall on December 7, hundreds

walked to the White House and began to sing *God Bless America* as well as other patriotic hymns.

Elsewhere in the U.S., military vehicles blocked streets. Coils of barbed wire barriers were thrown up along the beaches and soldiers could be seen everywhere. Signs promoting civil defense, the military, and freedom were soon displayed throughout the land. Songs were sung which underscored loneliness and melancholy songs like *Don't Get Around Much Anymore, White Christmas,* and *You'd be So Nice to Come Home To.* Anything Japanese or German was a target of anger.

America was under attack. German submarine wolf packs patrolled offshore. Merchant ships were torpedoed, with bodies and debris floating ashore. Oil slicks formed from the sunken and damaged boats. Later on, Japan actually bombed American civilians in Oregon using giant, long distance air balloons.

Communities installed air raid sirens, and mock catsup-stained casualties were treated by civil defense trainees. The government issued dog tags for children to identify them in case of injury. Blackout curtains were draped over windows and air raid wardens checked for unconcealed lights peaking through. People kept their ears glued to the radio. Some people were fearful, others excited to get going.

One Alabama mayor galloped through town on horseback calling for volunteers. Eighty percent of the

First barracks at Wendover Field looking southward, 1941. *(Donn Frisk)*

fourteen days by using prefabricated parts. Henry Ford manufactured B-24 Liberators in the Willow Run defense plant outside of Detroit. The plant produced 8,685 planes by the end of the war. At first it produced one bomber a day, but by 1944 one bomber was produced every 63 minutes. Wendover, Utah played a significant role in this tremendous war effort.

During the middle 1930s, the axis powers of Germany, Japan, and Italy began their aggressions against foreign soil. The United States was fully cognizant of the ominous signs of war.

town came forward. Plane spotters were organized in 24-hour surveillance shifts. One hundred thousand private pilots flew their own aircraft on submarine patrols. Savings stamp programs, victory gardens, and salvage campaigns were supported by many loyal citizens.

In June 1942, four English-speaking German saboteurs landed near Long Island, New York, and later four more in Florida. They carried with them bombs, timers, flares, money, and incendiary pistols and were planning to hit dams, bridges, factories, terminals, and the like in planned attacks. They were caught and four were executed for espionage. It was a time of danger and what the future held in store was unknown.

American industry swiftly geared up for war production. Thirteen million workers and volunteers operated 185,999 factories all over the nation. Women stepped forward to fill acute labor shortages. According to James W. "Skip" Wensyel in an *American History* magazine article of June 1995, *"Former canneries now made parts for merchant ships; cotton-processing plants produced guns; bedspread manufacturers turned out mosquito netting; a soft drink company loaded shells with explosives; a shoe manufacturer forged cannon; and a former burial-vault builder now specialized in one-hundred-pound bombs."* There were 16,000 factories working 'round the clock by May 1942. Henry J. Kaiser, Henry Ford, and Donald M. Nelson, a former Sears and Roebuck executive, headed massive production efforts.

Kaiser led the building of Liberty ships and reduced the production time from eight months to

Prior to World War II the army paid scant attention to its air force division. The air corps was secondary to all other arms of the military. That would change in a hurry!

The U.S. Army Air Corps began building depots and stations with Congressional appropriations money in 1935. An air field at Wendover, Utah, was part of the Congressional funding. In September 1940, construction of runways and buildings was begun at Wendover. Wendover was designated as a bombing and gunnery range and was administered as a sub-depot of Fort Douglas in Salt Lake City. In turn, Fort Douglas was part of General Headquarters Air Force as of September 1940.

The United States War Department identified the Great Salt Lake Desert as an ideal location for a training range, defensively located inland. Colonel Thomas E. Gwyn, U.S. District Engineer, Salt Lake City District, later recalled: *"I was directed to build an air base at Wendover, Utah, but was given no instructions as to its location. After talking to Mr. Lamus, a desert rat who had lived in the area for years and who was interested in the potash plant located there—it was decided to build the base near the Nevada border.*

"The ground water level was only about a foot from the surface. Also, we were told by Mr. Lamus that when the wind was blowing to the north the salt flats would be covered with about 18 inches of water and when blowing to the south the flats would be dry. For this reason, it was necessary to fill in for the runways to bring them 18" above ground level. We were able to secure good fill material near

the site. Vic Newman was the hauling contractor and did a good job.

"The runways were about 10,000 feet in length. We also constructed barracks, officer quarters, shops, mess hall, hospital, etc.

"My directive for this base was to provide for a garrison of 350 men and for about 2500 men for summer training. This was forgotten, the camp and Wendover had about 7500 [closer to 20,000 population] at its peak on an area of 265,000 acres [1,822,000 acres].

"I made an agreement with the Western Pacific Railroad to purchase 1500 gallons of water per day at 50 cents per 1000 gallons, but we soon saw we were in trouble over water. I went over the waterline to Pilot Mountain, which supplied water to the camp. This line was about 25 miles long and made up of all kinds of pipe that was leaking at every joint.

"We built another reservoir to catch any surplus water when it rained and also ran another pipe line into camp. Major Dippey, the commanding officer put a guard on the railroad water tank and refused to let the railroad take water. He also placed very stringent regulations in effect for the use of water such as flushing toilets and bathing. The situation was very serious.

"We brought out our geophysicist who had found water for us at Tooele, to find water in Wendover. He found water but it contained 20,000 grains of salt. The most fresh water he could find was about 100 gallons per minute which was not enough.

"The State Line Hotel, the center of activity [for the air field], was situated right on the line. As the name suggests, one could dine in the restaurant on the Utah side, then go through a wall opening into Nevada and the gaming room." James Les Rowe *(State Line Casino/William & Anna Smith Family)*

"About 32 miles from Wendover was a beautiful spring of fresh water flowing about 4000 gallons per minute. This spring [at Johnson Springs Ranch], *which came out of the mountain at 70 degrees belonged to the Utah Construction Company who owned a cattle ranch in this area. We rented this spring for $12,000 per year. Within a short distance of its source it disappeared in pot holes.*

"About this time, Major Bowen, a geologist and water expert was sent to me to go over our water situation. After spending some time studying the situation he came into my office and said he recommended that the water be secured from the spring owned by the Utah Construction Company. While he was sitting there in my office, I phoned Washington and asked for $1 million dollars to bring this spring water into Wendover and if they did not want to appropriate this sum

Wendover was "a 2nd Army staging base for units preparing to move overseas."

—James Les Rowe

then I recommended that Wendover be abandoned. Washington's reply was to take the matter up with the Army Air Corps and let me know.

"Major Bowen's eyes about popped out. He said 'You mean to tell me you asked for a million dollars on just what I told you?' My reply was 'You heard what I said over the phone.'

"The next day Washington called and said 'Thomas, you can have the million dollars.' We then placed an order for 32 miles of pipe which, on account of priorities had to be placed the next day or so with the military. Our investigations had shown that the spring was the only available water." Thus, the Wendover Field construction was authorized on the basis of availability of a spring of water, much the same as the railroad earlier in the century. Local author Garn Anderson said, *"Wendover was originally intended as a temporary base and was built with only temporary materials."* Wendover soon became the largest bombing and gunnery range in the world. It encompassed 1,882,200 acres.

There were initially *"ten B-18 medium bombers, eleven B-17 heavy bombers, and six A-17A attack aircraft"* assigned to Fort Douglas and based at Salt Lake Airport with Wendover as a subdepot. The aircraft were part of the 7th Bombardment Group which flew into Salt Lake in August 1940. There were three bombardment squadrons and a reconnaissance squadron.

The 7th Bomb Group performed live night bombing at Wendover in November 1940. They were returning from a flying training mission to March Field, California. Eventually, in November 1941, the 7th Bomb Group was ordered to fly to the Philippine Islands to provide reinforcements for General Douglas MacArthur's air force. They left Salt Lake City in mid-November for California, and departed Hamilton Field, California, on December 6, 1941. As they approached Oahu, Hawaii, the next morning at 0800 hours, December 7th, they encountered the Japanese sneak attack. They were able to safely land eleven of their twelve B-17s. One landed on a golf course. One of their men was killed and one B-17 destroyed.

Wendover Field was in continuous use after that to

Engine maintenance of B-18 bomber at Wendover Field. *(Donn Frisk)*

> "During World War II there was no U.S. Air Force, it was the Army Air Corps. There were no air bases, they were air fields."
> —Jim Hubbard

train bomb groups prior to going overseas. Later in the war, the 509th Composite Bomb Group was especially outfitted and secretly trained at Wendover in the use of atomic weapons with the goal to end World War II.

One young soldier, James Les Rowe, and his wife described arriving in Wendover during World War II. He noted: *"When we arrived at our destination it was immediately apparent that the community of Wendover was even smaller than I had anticipated.*

"We found the entrance road to the base at the west end of the field. Turning left onto this road we shortly crossed railroad tracks. Just beyond was the base fence line, and we parked near the entrance gate. Leaving my wife in the car, I checked into the Base Headquarters. There, a lieutenant told me I was to report back the next morning for an interview.

"With this done my wife and I now had to find a place to stay. We tried the hotel, but the answer was still 'no.' We inquired at a number of other places but still with no success. Finally it was at the A-1 Café that we heard about a vacant room in the house across the road. We located the owner and rented the room so our immediate problem was taken care of—at least temporarily, since we could only rent the room for one week.

"Once we were settled, we decided to take another look at the town. It didn't take long—Wendover was tiny. There was only one paved road, the main highway (US 40). Geographically, as I knew it in 1945 there was only Wendover, Utah, but it spilled over into Nevada with two or three houses and the A-1 Café on that side of the state line. ...

"The State Line Hotel, the center of activity, was situated right on the line. As the name suggests, one could dine in the restaurant on the Utah side, then go through a wall opening into Nevada and the gaming room.

"The base was located on the Utah side, and its nearest fence line (east to west) was roughly parallel to the highway but a short distance to the south. In between the highway and the fence line of the Base there were four or five houses, one of which had a small post office in the front.

"Across the highway, opposite the base (to the north) was a gas station, a small store and a few more homes. About a block north of the highway were three trailers parked alongside a small building which housed the rest rooms, shower and clothes washing facility to accommodate those people living in the trailers.

"A dirt road ran by the trailer parking spot in the direction of Nevada and dead-ended or just petered out near the state line. Back of these houses and trailers was a range of hills running parallel to the highway.

"This was all there was to Wendover, and on this particular evening I expected to stay here just a few days like so many other military personnel who had temporarily stayed here and moved on to overseas destinations. Some of them had left their squadron numbers painted on the rock faces of the hills. . . .

"As it happened, the only places to which my wife and I went during this waiting period were to the café across the street for our meals and to the store on the Utah side of the state line.

"The terrain sloped upward to some extent from the nearest Base fence line to the highway and beyond. From out-

Johnson Springs Ranch from which Wendover gets much of its water. The small spots in the foreground are cattle. *(Hill Air Force Base)*

The first dispensary at left. State Line Hotel in the center distance, 1941. *(Utah State Historical Society, Byron "Casey" Dussler)*

side the store a person could get a fairly good view of the base so on each trip to the store I couldn't help but note the lack of activity. . . ." Thus we have one serviceman's description as he and his wife experienced their first day in the hamlet of Wendover.

The Utah Test and Bombing Range was developed on the territory once covered by the prehistoric Lake Bonneville. The land was federally owned, making it easily obtainable. The open expanse of the landscape and the relative closeness to *"major western air force bases"* led to the facility's development and sustained its usefulness in ensuing years.

The base site was equally distant from military bases in Los Angeles, San Francisco, and Seattle and was on a railroad line running to the west coast. There was a supply depot nearby at Ogden and training could be virtually year-round due to *"very little rain or snow"* in the area.

The infantry post of Fort Douglas in nearby Salt Lake City was re-designated an Army Air Base by the secretary of war August 4, 1940, with the Salt Lake City municipal airport as its airfield. The flat, smooth surface of the salt plain made it ideal for landing the huge B-17 Flying Fortress bombers and Douglas B-18 Bolos.

About the time construction

began, the local Wendover telephone operator knew something big was happening when the switchboard came to life. Phone calls began pouring in by the hundreds when, only days before, the phone line into Wendover was seldom used.

In October 1940 Utah governor Henry H. Blood heard from a group of cattle ranchers who protested the loss of the large area of government grazing land. They felt that it would *"wipe out 100 outfits"* of stockmen and cost the state economically. A war looming on the horizon took precedence over their concerns and the War Department assumed jurisdiction over the newly designated air base.

In the spring of 1941, *"the War Department allotted $1 million for grading, drainage, paving, and night lighting projects at Wendover and in the summer a bombing and gunnery range detachment was activated as a sub-post of Fort Douglas.*

"By this time the field sported four 63-man barracks, a 250-man mess hall, officers' quarters, an administration building, a telephone exchange, two ordnance warehouses, a bomb-

One of the first buildings at Wendover Field. *(Utah State Historical Society, Byron Dussler)*

78

Shown are several of the early crew of thirty-seven who arrived to begin work on Wendover Field, August 1941. They ate meals at the railroad "Beanery" when they first arrived because there were no mess facilities on base. The first ten men and two officers were Captain Darold Smith, Lt. Horace L. Woodard and enlisted men Staff Sergeant W. A. Roach, Sgt. Fred Rau, Sgt. Otis C. Wynn, Cpl. Howard P. Eidson, Pvt. Donn Frisk, Pfc. William L. Lingaman, Pfc. Gerald G. Booth, Pvt. Milton C. Bratley, Pvt. Joseph V. Weinberger, and Pvt. William F. Humes. *(Hill Air Force Base)*

site storage building, and dispensary. There were also three ammunition igloos and four powder magazines. A power system with its own generating plant was also under construction, as was a railroad spur and water and sewer systems," as stated on the Hill Aerospace Museum website.

By the summer of 1941, the Wendover bombing and gunnery range was the largest military reserve in the world. The complex extended into three counties of Utah including Box Elder, Juab, and Tooele. The approximately 1,822,000-acre site was 86 miles long and was from 18 to 36 miles wide. It was expanded in February 1941 from the original 1,560,000-acre site by authorization of President Franklin D. Roosevelt.

The air corp initially sent ten men and two officers to *"set up operations at Wendover."* The men were activated on July 29, 1941, as a bombing and gunnery subpost of Fort Douglas, Salt Lake City. They actually arrived in Wendover on August 12, 1941. Other men followed soon after. The original commander was reserve officer Captain Darold G. Smith. Col. Robert N. Dippey, Col. Curtis LeMay, and Col. Harris McCauley were other commanders during World War II.

One of the original thirty-seven soldiers who arrived in the fall of 1941 was 33-year-old, Private Byron Dussler who had been drafted in June. His military experience was unique because all his service was at Wendover. He was discharged because of his age on November 29, 1941, only to be recalled to Wendover the day after the attack on Pearl Harbor.

Upon returning to Wendover, Dussler was put to work filling flares with kerosene to use for night bombing target practice, and pouring crank case oil in huge circles for daylight target practice. After this assignment he tended coal furnaces. Finally he served as clerk in the 315th Army Air Force head-

Wendover Field tower construction. *(Richard Campbell)*

WWII postcard featuring Wendover Field. *(Ron Christensen)*

quarters, working on payroll and later with the flying training program. He was stationed in Wendover for the duration of World War II and eventually served as the base's highest ranking enlisted man, a sergeant major. The twenty-one bomb groups that trained at Wendover came and went, but he stayed.

He had a feeling of being in charge, and with good reason. He sometimes trained the officers supervising him because he had the experience! Things happened because he knew who to talk to. He controlled all the appointments for all officers at headquarters. He felt that things needed to be done promptly in war-time and was "exceptionally capable" at doing it.

Author Roger D. Launius surmised that *"No doubt, Dussler"s ability to circumvent the bureaucratic labyrinth to get work done quickly placed him in good graces with both his superiors and his fellow draftees."* He could

procure a truck for an officer or create an emergency furlough in a matter of minutes. In doing so, he was allowed to circumvent normal protocol and official directives and he *"made generous use of forged signatures."* He had little use for *"foolish or nonproductive"* regulations. There were times during his five years at Wendover when he had to send his laundry to California because of regulations. Paperwork caused one man to be sent to Wendover three times, only to be immediately shipped out again. Other men were transferred on suspicion of spying.

Dussler felt that the war was far removed and remote from Wendover. The war was scarcely discussed by him and his colleagues. He mused that maybe someone would let them know when the war was over. He both hated and enjoyed Wendover. He liked the weather, the beer, and sleeping, but he disliked hav-

"I couldn't help but think this evening when I relaxed a bit after chow that in spite of Wendover being a trying place, I've never had so many friends in my life. It sort of brings us all down to a common level. Personalities who didn't mix in civilian life go through the mill and come out a pretty homogeneous group. Wall Streeter and fruit peddler dress alike, do the same chores, and find they have something in common after all."

—Byron Dussler

Weapons class on Wendover Field firing range. Eyewitness Donn Frisk said one of the trainees laid his weapon down on the table after target practice and walked away. The high caliber firearm discharged hitting him in the back of the skull and passed out the top of his head. The man survived. *(Utah State Historical Society)*

Bomber machine gun turret training in 1943 at Wendover Field. *(Utah State Historical Society)*

B-17 in flight with no tail markings to indicate unit. *(Maxwell Air Force Base)*

dispensary, signal office, warehouse, powerhouse and part of the administrative headquarters in place.

For the first few months they had only three vehicles for the growing population of personnel. They had a theater which showed only silent movies. They reported that their morale was high, the food was good, and *"the men went to work with a will."*

Crews hauled in many tons of gravel to fill in the mud flats. The men made improvements to the facility at a steady but slow pace until Pearl Harbor was attacked on December 7, 1941. After the attack, rapid mobilization of troops began almost immediately and thousands of gunners and bombardiers were among those needing training.

The first phase of training took place on bases in Arizona, Idaho, Oregon, and Washington states where rudimentary bombardment drills were executed. Wendover Field was designated for the second phase

ing no sheets, the chow, arising at 6:15 a.m., bed checks at 10 p.m., double bunks, and everything else. He and his cronies drank a lot of beer at the State Line Hotel and Casino. He remarked that the State Line had a *"spirit and color that makes one feel the pep and tang of mischief."*

Dussler was discharged on October 14, 1945, at Boise, Idaho, after having been in Wendover for four years and immediately returned to Wendover as a civilian where he worked for another six months in processing soldiers' discharge papers. He was finally able to leave what he called a *"vast wasteland,"* an *"eternal changeless domain of some uninhabited planet."*

During the hot August days of 1941, the primary duty of the men was to maintain the targets. They also laid cement sidewalks and performed other construction tasks. It was a long process. Gerald Cook of neighboring Ibapah worked on the survey crew for 3 years, starting in 1940 laying out the barracks floors. When the intial crew arrived in August of 41 there were barracks, a mess hall, a

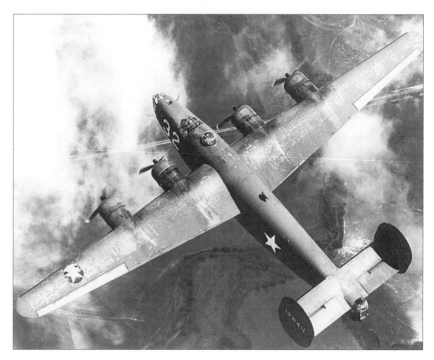

B-24 Consolidated Liberator. *(Maxwell Air Force Base)*

Needle Point

Bear Claw

Giant Rock

Grocery store, laundry, cafe, barber shop, drug store

Wendover Field housing project. *(509th Pictorial Album)*

"Wendover at night is a strange and eerie place. There are no street lights, only two giant search lights at each end of the field sending their beacons across the sky and there are a thousand red transformer lights on power poles. We hear the coming and going of army trucks, the roar of planes; there must be a war going on some place."

—*Byron Dussler, Jan. 12, 1943*

Above: B-17 vapor trails filled the sky, sometimes stretching for ninety miles on bombing runs over Europe. The 100th, 306th, 379th, 384th, 388th, 393rd, and 457th were among the B-17 Bomb Groups trained at Wendover Field. *(Maxwell Airforce Base)*

Left: Headquarters, Wendover Field. *(509th Pictorial Album)*

Inside the cockpit of a B-18 bomber. *(Donn Frisk)*

that developed marksmanship and accuracy of bombardment of the teams. Each bomb group followed a procedural checklist with individual commanders responsible for training their own crews. A third phase involved training for long range navigation and large formations. This phase took place near Sioux City, Iowa.

Wendover Field was officially activated March 1, 1942, by the Army Air Force as a training base for B-17 and B-24 heavy bombardment groups. Until then it had been a sub-post of Fort Douglas in Salt Lake City. The Wendover sub-depot was opened in April under command of the Ogden Air Depot in order to give local technical and administrative control for requisitioning, storing and issuing Army Air Force property needed by organizations while stationed at Wendover Field.

The 306th Bombardment Group consisting of 72 aircraft and 2,261 people arrived in April 1942 for training. The B-17s of the pioneering 306th would later serve in the European theater of the war, *"striking targets deep in the heart of the Third Reich."*

Twelve temporary buildings were available for living space. The headquarters was no more than a 50 x 20 foot room. Furnishings were sparse. Military clerks used boards laid across sawhorses in a U shape around the perimeter of the room as desks and cardboard boxes were used as cabinets. The 306th's training should have been completed in six weeks, but it took double the time. The men walked a mile or more

Aerial gunnery range at Wendover Field, located northeast of base. *(Donn Frisk)*

84

Unmanned Jeep moving target on firing range located northeast of Wendover. *(Utah State Historical Society)*

going to and from work and training except when the base provided a "trolley" of sorts consisting of a flatbed trailer pulled by a tractor.

The 306th built a machine gun range to the north of Wendover. They also constructed a city made of salt for target practice and installed electrical illumination for night training. They shipped out to England in August 1942 where they led the first bomber attacks inside Germany. One of their number, Staff Sergeant Maynard "Snuffy" Smith, was awarded the first Medal of Honor in Europe. He was a gunner on a B-17 and performed several acts of heroism during a fighter attack while on a bombing run.

The 308th Bombardment Group was assigned to Wendover Field on September 29, 1942. It was fully manned by November. Flight crews received training with the B-24 bombers while combat crews and ground echelons were processed and organized as well. Practice in combat missions, identifying targets, long range navigation, and flying in high altitude formations was done. The goal was to establish effective units as opposed to individual air crews.

Of necessity, training had to be done speedily. The 308th was transferred to China in early 1943 where *"they took the heaviest combat losses of any group in China."* The 308th led all other combat bomb groups in bombing accuracy throughout the world on final tally.

The 100th Bomb Group, consisting of thirty-six combat crews, arrived in Wendover in late November 1942 and brought their own desks, typewriters, and other equipment. They were assigned a one-story, tar-paper barracks building for use as their headquarters. It contained an office in the middle and a ground school

Air defense classes at Wendover. Models of aircraft were hung from fishing poles where firing angles, offensive and defensive positions, and different flying formations could be studied and adjusted. Note the pot-bellied stove at the far right. *(Utah State Historical Society)*

both morning and afternoons with different squadrons attending each. The coal heating stoves often exploded, blowing soot over everything in the room. The stoves would get too warm or not burn *"worth a damn."* Percy Hewitt, former engineer on the Deep Creek Railroad, was one of the firemen who faithfully tended the heaters. Up to ten tons of coal were used per week when the base was first operating in 1941. When any of the firemen got drunk, there might be too much heat. Steam sometimes came out of the toilets when that happened. More than likely, there would be no heat, especially if a firemen left his post to go dancing at the State Line. One night, the base commander sat in his car all night with the

lecture room *"devoted chiefly for identification instruction"* as well as map reading and combat intelligence. Classroom instruction required innovations. The lecture area was complete with aircraft and ship models. Models of aircraft were hung from fishing poles where firing angles, offensive and defensive positions, and different flying formations could be studied and adjusted. Huge maps on sliding boards were also employed in the training process. The 100th BG added a situation map of the world, covered with Plexiglas.

Classes were two hours in length and were held

motor running and the heater on. The same night, the fire truck pumps froze.

At the commencement of training, the commanding officer of the 100th called the combat crews together and reminded them they would soon be part of the reality of the war. He *"told them that some of them would be killed—that was part of the show—but that they were going to be part of a fighting outfit that was going to see plenty of action and do plenty of damage."*

The 100th and the other bomb groups abruptly came face to face with the real war as soon as they

---

Description of Arrival of 494th Bombardment Group in Wendover, 17 December 1943

"From all quarters of the compass, by train and bus, airplane and automobile, an apparently casual collection of individuals began to assemble in that Garden Spot of the Old West, Wendover, Utah. They debarked usually in flurries of snow, or a steady drizzle of rain, jostled each other in the muddy and salt-encrusted streets of the area, lost and found their personal gear in the growing mounds of baggage, and lined up for everything from going to a latrine to delivering 'name, rank & serial number' to anyone who required this information.

"Lives there a man with soul so dead who can forget the first impressions of Wendover! The chill bleakness of the hills North and West of us that was only equaled by the salt flats extending to the horizon to the South and East, with a haze of soft coal smoke hanging over the small ... town, the airfield and cantonment area day and night. It has been wisely observed that no better area could have been selected by anyone for the training of a combat outfit in combat scenery; Sherman on his march to the sea left more behind him to look at than our new home provided. In brief, it was a masterpiece of desolation." Source: http://home.att.net/kelleys_kobras/494history/written.htm

The "Tokyo Trolley" was known as the best in the United States for training realism. It was a railroad flatcar with three machine guns attached to it. The flatcar moved at forty miles per hour down a railroad track built for its use. The gunners practiced hitting moving targets along the route, developing *"excellent marksmanship skills."* An interphone system of throat microphones allowed the gunners to communicate with their instructors and each other. *(Utah State Historical Society)*

reached the front, far from the white salt plain they had left behind. It was common to be housed with "veteran" airmen, most of whom were also barely twenty years of age like themselves. Some of the flyers from Wendover noticed that there was little effort to make friends with the new squadrons arriving from the U.S. This social phenomenon occurred because many crews did not return from bombing runs. It didn't pay to make friends!

The freshly trained bomb groups were promptly pressed into action upon arrival, and joined bombing sorties which sometimes stretched ninety miles from beginning to end. There was helpless terror in the hearts of these young men (who were "not cowards") as they flew their bombing runs, not knowing if they would survive for even another instant. More than once, an armed 500-pound bomb stuck in the bomb bay and someone had to scramble onto an 8-inch wide catwalk and pry it loose. This was accomplished without the aid of oxygen at more than two miles of altitude while battling the gale force slipstream.

Flak blew holes in the metal skin of their aircraft. Flak exploded through engines and penetrated bodies. *"The sickening rattle of machine-gun bullets and cannon fire"* hit the airships. Enemy German or Japanese fighter planes attacked, coming out of nowhere. Bombers all around were sent limping home minus one or more engines or they fell hurtling from the sky with engines aflame. Some airmen were able to escape from the wounded planes and parachute into cold rough seas or into enemy territory. One man without a parachute grabbed his buddy as they jumped. He held on until the chute released, which abruptly halted the free fall and sent him plunging to his death.

Being rescued was the exception. If they survived the fall or endless hours in the icy sea water, capture

Donn Frisk in airmen's gunnery outfit holding a .50 caliber machine gun at Wendover. *(Donn Frisk)*

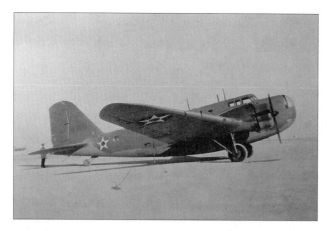

B-18 bomber at Wendover Field, 1942. There were 134 built or converted in the 1930s, based on the Douglas DC-2. The wingspan was 89 ft. 6 in. and the length was 56 ft. 8 in. Maximum speed was 217 mph at 10,000 ft. with a range of 1,200 miles. The crew of six had three .30 cal. machine guns and 4,400 lbs. of bombs. Capt. Smith kept one in the sole hangar available when the first group came to Wendover.

B-17D in 1941 at Wendover Field. The bombers dropped sacks of flour for practice. After the attack on Pearl Harbor, sandbag barricades were built around three sides of each parked bomber at Wendover.

Military truck stuck in the muck as usual somewhere near Wendover. (All photos this page courtesy of Donn Frisk)

Tracked military vehicle at the motor pool, Wendover Field 1941.

B-17D with Leppy Hills behind it.

Wendover fire engine, 1941.

The east end of Wendover Field is shown in this 1940s photo. Note the rail yard in the center. U.S. Highway 40 divides the town in the foreground. *(Molly Hewitt Taylor)*

A view of Wendover and Wendover Field in the late 1940's, as seen from the mountains north of town. *(Ron Christensen)*

845th Squadron party. Songs of the day included "Beer Barrel Polka," "Rose of Old San Antone," and "Pistol Packin' Mama." *(Charles Freudenthal)*

Massive military city was built almost overnight in Wendover. *(Richard Campbell)*

1944 winter scene at Wendover Field. *(Charles Freudenthal)*

usually followed, and then humiliation or torture, long, forced marches, and miserable internment in concentration camps. It can be safely stated that training at Wendover was a breeze compared with what came after that!

The weather in Wendover was unusually mild the winter of 1942-43. It rained occasionally and temperatures were above freezing every day. The midwest was experiencing below freezing weather at the same time it was mild in Wendover. The flying was *"interrupted only one day when a low overcast caused operations to be suspended."*

The 100th Bombardment Group left for Sioux City, Iowa, aboard a troop train on January 1, 1943. The conditions on the trains were dirty and cramped. Most were without ventilation and very little heat was available. Two men slept in a lower bunk and one in the upper bunk in order to accommodate everyone. Nobody got *"too much sleep."*

From there, the 100th was stationed in Thorpe Abbotts, England, where it flew 306 missions between June 25, 1943, and April 29, 1945.

As was mentioned, the army air force built a mock enemy city from salt near the Wendover mountains for bombing target practice. Enemy battleship targets on the salt gunnery range were built of tar, *"adding dimension and realism."* Lighting was installed which enabled bombing practice at night.

The bombers' only defense against enemy fighter planes was their own gunners. They needed to be proficient. The army installed skeet and rifle ranges and a stationary machine gun range with moveable targets. In addition, a circular pit was built in which an unmanned jeep guided by a wooden rail traveled in circles with a target mounted on it. The jeep traveled at speeds ranging from five to thirty miles an hour and was located at a distance of 170 to

Units Trained at Wendover Field During World War II*

100th Bomb Group (Heavy)	B-17s for European Theatre	November 1942–January 1943
302nd Bomb Group (Heavy)	B-24 replacement unit for U.S. duty	July–September 1942
306th Bomb Group (Heavy)	B-17s for European Theatre	April–August 1942
308th Bomb Group (Heavy)	B-24s for Pacific Theatre	October–November 1942
379th Bomb Group (Heavy)	B-17s for European Theatre	December 1942–February 1943
384th Bomb Group (Heavy)	B-17s for European Theatre	January–April 1943
388th Bomb Group (Heavy)	B-17s for European Theatre	February–May 1943
393rd Bomb Group (Heavy)	B-17 operational training unit in U.S.	April–June 1943
399th Bomb Group (Heavy)	B-24s for U.S. duty assignments	April–December 1943
445th Bomb Group (Heavy)	B-24s for European Theatre	June–July 1943
448th Bomb Group (Heavy)	B-24s for European Theatre	July–September 1943
451st Bomb Group (Heavy)	B-24s for European Theatre	July–September 1943
456th Bomb Group (Heavy)	B-24s for Mediterranean/European Theatres	June–July 1943
457th Bomb Group (Heavy)	B-17s for European Theatre	December 1943–January 1944
458th Bomb Group (Heavy)	B-24s for European Theatre	July–September 1943
461st Bomb Group (Heavy)	B-24s for European Theatre	July 1943
464th Bomb Group (Heavy)	B-24s for European Theatre and U.S. duty	August 1943
467th Bomb Group (Heavy)	B-24s for European Theatre	August–September 1943
489th Bomb Group (Heavy)	B-24s for European Theatre	October 1943–April 1944
490th Bomb Group (Heavy)	B-24s for European Theatre	October 1943
494th Bomb Group (Heavy)	B-24s for the Far East	December 1943–April 1944
509th Composite Group	B-29s for atomic warfare	December 1944–April 1945

*http://www.hill.af.mil/museum/

240 yards away from the gunners.

Gunnery crews built the Tokyo Trolley and it was known as the best in the United States for training realism. It was a railroad flatcar with three machine guns attached to it. The flatcar moved at forty miles per hour down a railroad track built for its use. The gunners practiced hitting moving targets along the route. This *"required excellent marksmanship skills."* An interphone system of throat microphones allowed the gunners to communicate with their instructors and each other. *"This training method simulated to the greatest extent possible the condi-*

Wendover Field airmen. *(Charles Freudenthal)*

Wendover 847th Squadron Operations. *(Charles Freudenthal)*

the tribunal received a "telegram from General Douglas McArthur praising Wendover's gunners as the best trained in the Army."

Crews installed an aircraft beacon atop the mountain immediately north of Wendover. It was powered by a gas generator. Herman Zahn, airplane commander, mentioned driving a jeep *"to the eye of the needle"* with a tank of gas for the beacon. A little to the east on the side of the mountain was a gigantic sign which read *"This is War. Kill or be Killed."* The vivid reminder of the war could be seen as far away as Salduro, eight miles away.

tions of aerial warfare . . . These training devices for the gunners were put into use by November 1942," according to author Roger D. Launius.

The machine gun range was located east of Wendover on the north side of Highway 40. The smell of the machine gun fire was strong enough at times in nearby Wendover to make residents sick to their stomachs, and the racket from the range was exceptionally loud also.

The officers in charge of constructing the machine gun range ordered midnight requisitioning of the lumber and building supplies from the government and government contractors without authorization in order to get the range built in a time of shortage. The men were known as *"Captain Keyes and his 1,000 thieves,"* according to Donn Frisk. Captain Keyes was to be court-martialed for the deed but was exonerated after

Four bombardment groups consisting of B-17s and B-24s had begun or completed training at Wendover by the end of 1942. At the end of another year, about 2,000 civilian employees and 17,500 military personnel were housed in Wendover. By late 1943 all phases of training were assigned and

489th Formation, winter 1944, Commanding officer Lt. Col. Chester Morneau, Group Operations Officer (in front). *(Charles Freudenthal)*

carried out at the Wendover Field. Fifteen groups completed training in 1943 and three groups were still undergoing training.

In December 1943, four bomb groups at Wendover included the newly arrived 489th Bomb Group. The 399th, 489th and the 494th were B-24 units in training and the 457th was a B-17 bomb unit. They lived in pyramidal tents until shortly after Christmas when they were able to move into tarpaper-covered, wooden barracks.

B-24s on the runway at Wendover Field, Utah. *(Charles Freudenthal)*

The base was definitely overcrowded at times. Lt. Col. Charles Freudenthal wrote a history entitled *"A History of the 489th Bomb Group"* in which he said, *"There were chow lines, movie lines, PX lines, lines at the mess halls and the clubs, and lines waiting for a sink to wash in, or to use other sanitary facilities. 'You have to get in line to get in line,' groaned a disgusted GI."* The State Line Casino was a popular attraction for the GIs. Officers were assigned to frequent there one night and enlisted men the next *"as the base authorities tried to avoid drowning the community in a sea of khaki."*

Once in a while, a pass to Salt Lake City was handed out which gave a break from the drudgery of work on the base. Lt. navigator Bill Wilkinson told of piling six or eight people into an old Cadillac and speeding to Salt Lake *"only to find it almost impossible to even get a drink in that strict Mormon town."*

Chuck Harkins of the 844th portrayed married life on Wendover's base as quoted in Freudenthal's history. He penned the following: *"Flo, my bride of a few weeks, arrived in Salt Lake City in January [1944]. I checked her into a motel and returned to Wendover to see what our chances were of getting quarters. You might remember that a wife had to work on base for a couple to be eligible for trailer quarters, so when the Officers Club hired her as a hat check girl we were assigned half a trailer. We moved in, feeling lucky to have anything. Our half of the trailer had the door; the other half had the kitchen and was occupied by a master sergeant and his wife. There wasn't much privacy in either half, but the sergeant's wife managed to get pregnant while we were there.*

USO sign reads "The Recreational Oasis of the Great Salt Desert Built in One Day." *(Utah State Historical Society)*

"The showers and latrines were about 30 or 40 yards away from our trailer, and it took two trips to get everything set up for a shower. There wasn't any heat in the building, so the first trip was to turn on the hot water, so the steam would warm the place up. The second trip, of course, was to take the shower. Usually we had to go fully dressed, because of the snow and often freezing temperatures. When you had to answer a call of nature at night, it was rough!

"Flo and I owned just one set of sheets, and slept on them much longer than we should have before

Wendover Field's "temporary" tarpaper-covered barracks. Byron Dussler lamented on the drafts of air coming through the barracks walls which chilled the men to the bones. The wind howled fiercely, picked up gravel, and hurled it against the side of the buildings like hail. The desert staged a *"dance of the winds,"* according to Dussler. *(Charles Freudenthal, L. Mitchell)*

laundering them. The first time she washed them, Flo took them to the clothes line and threw them over the wire. As soon as the two halves came together they froze—tightly. Solid. We slept without sheets that night.

"A couple of times a week we took a five gallon can and a broomstick and walked to a service station on the nearby

Byron Dussler wrote home and said, "While eating supper at the cafeteria tonight I noticed the motley crowd of soldiers, civilians, wives, girlfriends, all stranded at Wendover. I looked at them and thought of how many lives are turned topsy-turvy by the war. Will this last for endless time?

"School attendance charts at the office are a hodge-podge mess. Students don't show up for classes, or else the students show up and the instructor doesn't. Some work their heads off while others fritter away their time."

highway to buy kerosene for the heater in our half of the trailer. On the way back, we each took one end of the broomstick and hung the full can in the middle. It was a long trip with that 30 pound load!

"Flo was soon exposed to Air Corps humor. In her first week on the job, some practical joker asked her to page an officer who had a call on one of the public phones. She spent several minutes on the paging system trying to get Lieutenant Roger Wilco to come to the phone."

Training for the 489th got underway in January but not without *"an assortment of difficulties."* The group had to train using only eleven aircraft available to them and often only 40% of them were operational.

Training was carried out day and night. Weather conditions were marginal and required instrument practice in low visibility situations as a result. One condition was unique to the salt flats. *"Heavy rains would accumulate on the impervious surface, creating a mirror-like*

94

effect. On a clear night, the stars above were reflected in the water below, and without flight instruments, disorientation could easily result."

Ground training classes were too long and cut into the flying hours. Supplies and equipment were *"in short supply."* Qualified instructors were also not always available and crews had to train themselves.

On one occasion, Walter Wallace of the 846th remembered training at the gunnery range. The trainees began *"playing around"* with a Gibson Girl, a portable radio set used to send distress signals. They thought it was a dummy and turned it on, sending out a distress signal.

Wendover Field 1944. (*Charles Freudenthal*)

The crash crew responded by climbing the mountain. On the way up a real plane crash occurred and the crash crew was already half way to the scene thanks to the trainees goofing off with the radio set.

Walter Wallace continued: *"Another time up there we had a day off and went mountain climbing. We didn't know there was firing going on on the other side of the mountain. There were a lot of spent 50 caliber rounds laying around, but an old know-it-all said that was from air-to-ground firing. Well, it wasn't from air-to-ground firing. It seems like there was a little canyon up there and these 50 caliber slugs were ricocheting off the mountain side, up that canyon, back and forth off the walls, and out across our heads. Of course, we heard the things going 'Whirr, real close by, so we hit the dirt, and then got out of there real quick."*

Wallace recalled the time in Wendover when he refused to climb in and ride in the ball turret of his aircraft. The pilot threatened to court martial Walter until he saw that the turret wasn't properly bolted down and might fall off the airplane. On another occasion, Wallace passed out, standing up when the guns jammed in the top turret. Wallace was attempting to clear the jam caused by spent rounds when his oxygen bottle ran out.

Fruedenthal said that *"lack of experience was a prob-*

lem in nearly all the skilled positions." He gave the example of ground radio man J. D. Jordan working with a new, untrained man on a B-24. Jordan went to clear snow off a long-range transmitter which was on. He told the new man not to press the antenna key. He pressed the key anyway while Jordan was grasping the antenna. Jordan ended up with only the minor injury of a sore hand after falling off the wing from the jolt; but it could have been much worse.

One flight crew played a joke on one of their mechanics who didn't like flying. They took off with

847th operations offered training on recognizing various types of anti-aircraft flak. (*Charles Freudenthal*)

Wendover 1942 in the mess hall. *(Donn Frisk)*

him in the tail of the plane on a practice flight without a parachute for him. The plane unexpectedly went into a tail spin and could have crashed. It was missing three-fourths of the rudder and had a twisted fuselage. No more pranks were played by anyone after that.

There were times when two and three engines went out while on a training flight. During one crash landing the flight engineer was thrown through the center of the windshield and the co-pilot was killed when he went through the right side of the windshield and was pinned to the ground by the wing.

On a practice bombing mission, another crew was startled by a loud noise and found *"one bomb bay door flapping in the slipstream and two bombs were lying on the other unopened door. The third bomb had ripped the flapping door off its track and was somewhere below us, heading for an area on the range that was far, far from the target."*

The loose bombs were partially armed but the bombardier Chuck Harkins was able to pry them out over the open desert. They did not detonate as far as the crew could tell, because they heard no explosions.

At the conclusion of training at Wendover, the 489th flew a 36-plane simulated combat mission to Boise, Idaho. The following day, March 29, 1944, sixteen crews flew to Dugway Proving Ground near Tooele and participated in the largest chemical warfare field test ever conducted up to that time.

The lethal strength of phosgene gas was being determined *"at various distances from point zero"* and they were investigating how lethal the gas was against different protective devices and materials. The crews were required at the outset to enter a gas chamber in order to get a *"very short whiff of phosgene gas"* after which the tests were conducted at high altitudes. Both missions were highly successful according to Freudenthal's 489th history.

The 489th quickly headed overseas to England, the first of them arriving on April 7, 1944. *"They were assigned to heavy bombardment duty with the 2nd Division of Lt. Gen. Jimmy Doolittle's 8th Air Force."* They were some of the most successful in using radar for accurate navigation and as a jamming device. Years later, several of those who survived attributed their being alive to the training they received from instructors and drill sergeants in that far away time and place in Wendover, Utah.

Wendover was a very important part of the war effort. Over 1,000 aircrews were trained and incorporated into twenty-one groups from 1942 to 1944 at Wendover Field under the charge of the Second Air Force. They saw combat in support of D-Day, in bombing Germany and in other parts of the world. Several individuals were awarded the Medal of Honor.

On April 18, 1944, the 72nd Fighter Wing was given charge of Wendover Field. This was done to change the base's role to one of training fighter pilots. The first sixty trainees arrived at Wendover on May 31, 1944. The training involved ground and air instruction. *"Ground training consisted of photography, combat intelligence, chemical warfare, and a range orientation"* plus flight simulation.

"Air training consisted of air-to-ground and air-to-air gunnery, communications, and flight instruction." A mini-

Chemical warfare training at Wendover with gas masks. *(Donn Frisk)*

mum of eighty hours of flying was required to complete the training in a P-47 aircraft. The P-47 training was hurriedly discontinued in August at Wendover with 149 pilots trained. Incidentally, the P preceding

Wendover Field looking towards the east. The Federal Housing Administration Project built the Nev-Tah Apartments in 1942-43, alleviating some of the base overcrowding. The above picture includes the Nev-Tah apartments which later became the Patio Motel. It is of interest to note that John Huston, the famous motion picture director in the 1940s through 60s purchased the Patio Motel as part of 200 former Federal Housing Administration development units in Wendover. In 1959 Huston made an unsuccessful attempt to buy Western Pacific Railroad's water rights which Wendover City had agreed to purchase the year before. Huston was famous for directing several classics including *The Maltese Falcon* (1941), *Key Largo* (1948), *The African Queen* (1951), *Moby Dick* (1956), and *The Bible* (1965). Huston made several trips to Wendover incognito. He would fly to Salt Lake City, don an old trench coat and hat and hitch hike to Wendover. Upon completion of his business there, he would again dress in the overcoat and hitch a ride back to Salt Lake City. He was very conservative with his millions. He wouldn't buy a file cabinet to store motel records in. He kept the records in cardboard boxes strung around the office. After Huston, Russ Lewis owned the Patio Motel. *(509th Pictorial Album)*

B-17E or F side view on Wendover Field runway. *(Donn Frisk)*

B-24 L experimental ship. Left to right: Fred Sherrer, W. A. Borgne, A. E. Inselsberger, T. Dollard. *(Gwen Inselsberger)*

The B-17E had a redesigned vertical tail and the armor was substantially increased. Also, the turrets were remote-controlled. *(Donn Frisk)*

the number signified a pursuit aircraft.

There were numerous crashes while training pilots to maneuver planes in conducting bombing runs. Details of men were assigned to clean up the wreckage and to retrieve the bodies. It was sometimes gory. One time, spots of blood scattered across the salt left a trail 200 or 300 yards long. The trail led to a severed head.

Ralph D. Fry, instructor-mechanic, 603rd Air Engineering Squadron, spent two years in Wendover and remembered cleaning the wreckage from a B-29 plane crash off the highway east of Wendover in August 1943. The plane also hit a freight train, causing it to crash. Local resident Neta Wadsworth said the wreckage was *"piled all the way from the potash plant to Wendover."*

Western Pacific section foreman Brent Peterson helped with the cleanup. He said the B-29 touched the highway as it crashed and then hit the train. The train was loaded with supplies being sent to distant battle fronts. Forty-seven cars were piled up like an accordion. The cars contained such varied items as clothing, pillow cases, tractors, and one was filled with *"Red, White and Blue Beer."*

Plane crashes averaged one per day. The pilots didn't know how to fly, yet they were sent up before they were ready. Some were intoxicated, causing them to become disoriented.

At some times of the year, the salt flats were covered with water, hampering the clean-up efforts. Local rancher Pete McKellar, on more than one occasion, was requested to go with air force offi-

B-24 bomber on Wendover Field tarmac. B-24 bomb groups trained at Wendover included the 302nd, 308th, 399th, 445th, 448th, 451st, 456th, 458th, 461st, 467th, 489th, 490th, & 494th. *(Hill Air Force Base)*

Crewmen working on the Superfortress B-17D at Wendover, circa 1941-42. The B-17D & E had four Wright R-1820-65 Cyclone engines. The B-17D had a 67 ft. 11 in. wing span; the B-17E had a span of 73 ft. 10 in. There were 12, 731 built of all models. The maximum speed of the D was 323 mph and the E was 317 mph. 6,000 lbs of bombs was the typical load. The B-17 had a reputation for surviving even when damaged. *(Donn Frisk)*

"One B-24 caught on fire as it sat on the Wendover Field apron and was destroyed. A bombardier who had remained inside doing paperwork after it landed was burned to death."
—*Donn Frisk*

Special weapons test unit at Wendover Field, Utah 1944. B-17F #42-30514. *(Gwen Inselsberger)*

cials to rescue men, or recover bodies when planes crashed on Silver Island. Donn Frisk volunteered to help with a commercial airliner crash in the mountains north of Wendover. He said the only survivor was an infant whose mother had protected it during the crash.

Lynn Kenley, whose father was Wendover Field fire chief Fred Kenley, commented that some of the crashes were really successful emergency landings. When the

Wendover Field fire chief Fred Kenley and his wife Annie. *(Gertrude Tripp)*

planes over-ran the runways, they stopped in a hurry due to the muddy flats beyond. The flight crews considered any landing successful if you could walk away from it. The problem came in trying to explain goofs to commanding officers or to pass the buck to mechanical failure.

Researcher Scott C. Frischknecht reported that *"the reduced maneuverability of bombers in comparison to fighters, and the lack of requisite experience in team flying, caused an abnormally high number of crashes (157) and fatalities (121) among these 'transition' pilots. Approximately 93 percent of the accidents proved to be caused by pilot error. The Army therefore canceled the plan to send thousands of fighter pilots to Wendover to teach them to fly heavy bombers."*

Another problem was sabotage. Even though security was tight on Wendover Field, Fire Chief Fred Kenley claimed that there were instances of sabotage. Kenley possessed at least one photograph of an airplane in flames caused by vandals. He said saboteurs would leave an inconspicuous fire stick or pencil which ignited hours later and could destroy an aircraft. Base telephone operator Jeanne

Kenley reportedly thwarted two different cases of sabotage by her alert intervention. The saboteurs were captured in both instances.

Eventually, the Second Air Force took control again of Wendover Field and soon the 393rd Bombardment Squadron of B-29s was relocated to Utah from Fairmont Army Air Field, Nebraska. It took only four days from September 10, 1944, when the 393rd was given orders until the unit arrived on September 14.

"Without question this was a very special squadron, for the 393rd became the nucleus of the 509th Composite Group, the only unit ever to drop an atomic bomb in combat," stated historian Roger Launius. On December 14, 1944, the 509th Composite Group was activated with 1,767 officers and men, which included a team of civilian and military scientists making up the First Technical Detachment.

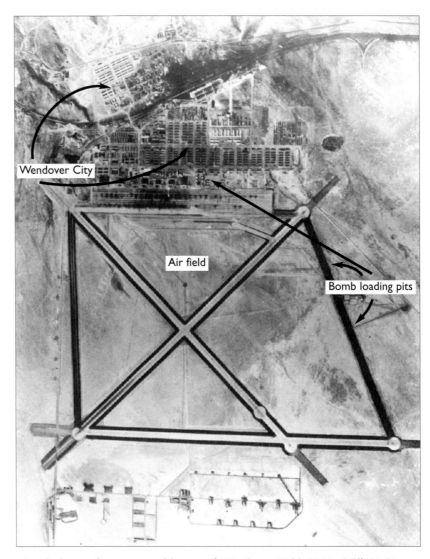

Aerial photo of runways and layout of Wendover Field, 1946. *(Hill Air Force Base)*

The beautiful city of Potsdam is located on the Havel River, sixteen miles southwest of Berlin, Germany. It is known for its public gardens, broad squares, and cultivation of winter violets. On July 17, 1945, Potsdam was the location of a famous conference of the world's most powerful leaders: U.S. president Harry S. Truman, British prime minister Winston Churchill, and Russian marshall Joseph Stalin.

The purpose of the meeting was to approve earlier agreements, dividing German territory among the allies. Also, the British and Americans prepared an ultimatum to Japan which demanded their unconditional surrender or the allies would begin an unprecedented reign of death.

While at Potsdam, President Truman received a coded message. The atomic age had dawned in the far-off desert of Alamogordo, New Mexico. At 5:29 a.m., July 16, 1945 at a place called Jornado del Muerto or

"Journey of Death" with the *"brilliance of one thousand suns,"* an atomic bomb was detonated with a blast of 20,000 tons. It was seen 450 miles away and heard 200 miles away.

President Truman now knew the U.S. was capable of bringing World War II to a rapid close without landing troops on the Japanese mainland. He and General George Marshall reckoned this *"special bomb"* would save hundreds of thousands of American troops.

The allies immediately issued the unconditional surrender message to the Japanese, warning of *"utter devastation of the Japanese homeland,"* *"a rain of ruin from the air."* The Japanese government ignored the ultimatum in silent contempt. President Truman felt that he had no choice but to proceed. Other political reasons

A nose wheel collapsed causing this landing accident for pilot Blaine Hansel and his crew, March 1944. *(Charles Freudenthal)*

pilot in leading raids on occupied Europe over the English Channel and was the pilot entrusted to fly General Mark Clark and General Dwight D. Eisenhower when the allied forces began their assault on Germany.

In February 1943, Colonel Tibbets was assigned home to the states from Europe to work with the B-29 bomber project which was in a *"shambles."* He had *"almost 3,000 hours of flying time"* and knew the basics of instrument flight at a time in aviation history when most pilots knew little about using an instrument panel while flying under foul weather conditions and the ground could not be seen.

for dropping the bomb were revenge for Japanese atrocities on our troops, justification for the enormous expenditure of time and money used on the *Manhattan Project*, scientific data to be derived about the bomb's effects, and keeping Russia out of Japan and the surrounding region while displaying to them our military capabilities.

President Truman was not fully aware of the atomic bomb building operation, called the *"Manhattan Engineering District,"* until twelve days after he took office on the death of Franklin D. Roosevelt in April 1945. In 1939, famed physicist Albert Einstein joined scientist Leo Szilard in writing a letter to Roosevelt urging him to develop a nuclear weapon as there was evidence that the Nazis were close to completing one of their own. The project started with a few thousand dollars but quickly escalated into a massive, top-secret undertaking.

The man who was chosen to assemble an *"elite bombing force,"* train them and lead them on an atomic strike to end the war was Lieutenant Colonel Paul W. Tibbets Jr. He was already a distinguished

Tibbets trained to *"fly blind"* and practiced emergency landing procedures in the advanced instrument flight training program with the 19th Transport Group in Milwaukee. He came away from the training with an endorsement of personal clearance to *"fly an airplane any time under his own authority."*

In July 1943, Tibbets reported to Wichita, Kansas, where some of the ordered 1,664 B-29s were scheduled for production. Boeing was developing the huge experimental aircraft called the B-29 bomber but had lost their chief test pilot and ten of their top technicians in a crash of a B-29 on a test flight.

Crash debris near Wendover. *(Utah State Historical Society)*

An emergency landing of a B-24. The muddy salt flats stopped you in a hurry. If you could walk away from any landing, it was said to be successful. *(Lynn Kenley)*

The B-29 had a reputation of being *"awkward and unwieldy."* The B-29 had four 2,200-horsepower R-3350-23 Wright engines which often overheated in flight and sometimes caught on fire, especially when flying high and carrying a heavy payload. In his book *Return of the* Enola Gay, Tibbets wrote: *"With its wing span of 141 feet and length of 93 feet, it was a giant compared with the B-17, which had corresponding measurements of 103 and 75 feet, respectively."*

The B-29 aircraft could not be flown in tight formations as with the B-17 Fortress in raids over Europe. Control of the aircraft was difficult in the thin air of high altitudes such as 30,000 feet.

Even with its problems, a bomber of the size and range of the B-29 was needed for use in the Pacific theater of action. Tibbets related: *"The strategy was to reconquer the islands seized by the Japanese in the early days of the war, and to be ready for a massive assault on the enemy's homeland as soon as victory had been won in Europe.*

"The B-29 involved many innovations, including a pneumatic bomb-bay door opener which opened the doors in less than a second and closed them in three seconds, thus reducing the time the open doors could act to slow the plane down while on the bomb run."

An advantage of the B-29 was that one gunner was able to control several of the five guns mounted on the outside of the airplane. Also, the cabin was pressurized so the crew could work without oxygen masks. The B-29 could fly higher, faster, and farther than the B-17. The B-29 had a tricycle landing gear which made it easier to see the airstrip below while taxiing and easier to handle on the ground. *"It was also the only plane capable of carrying a terrible new weapon, still under development,"* that few knew about including Colonel Tibbets.

Working sixteen-hour days, Colonel Tibbets spent the next year in experimental flights designed to correct flaws in the aircraft and in training pilots to fly the B-29, including two women WASPs (Women's Air Service Pilots), who performed superbly.

Fortuitously, Tibbets discovered that the B-29 handled much better without armament. He had borrowed an aircraft from Grand Island, Nebraska, which

> "All night long planes used the runways nearest our barracks. Every time one took off the whole barracks shook. One would think these liberators were disintegrating right over our heads. This interferes with our sleep."
>
> —Byron Dussler, Wendover Field

This crash of a Martin B-26 was caused by mechanical failure of the landing gear. Note minimal damage to the plane, but the co-pilot was killed by a broken, flying propeller piece. *(Lynn Kenley)*

Oppenheimer was the director of the Los Alamos, New Mexico, laboratory where the bomb was under development.

Tibbets learned that 100,000 workers and scientists worked in factories in Hanford, Washington, and Oak Ridge, Tennessee, and the laboratory in Los Alamos, New Mexico, sites where atomic bomb components were being manufactured and assembled. Astonishingly, most of the workers involved did not know what they were producing. The cost was two billion dollars for *"the most frightful weapon ever devised."*

"The problem of delivering it on target now needed urgent attention." That daunting task was given to 29-year-old Colonel Paul W. Tibbets. The first bomb would not be available until the summer of 1945, allowing nine or ten months to prepare.

The military immediately gave Tibbets broad authority to assemble and train a self-contained military unit prepared to safely deliver the 9,000+-pound

was without weapons or armor plating and weighed 7,000 pounds lighter. Tibbets said, *"The difference proved to be an important though unexpected payoff in its defense against fighter aircraft."* He said that a pilot could therefore turn in a much shorter radius than a captured Japanese Zero used in a simulated attack. This proved helpful later on when the atomic bombing run was being planned, anticipating enemy fighter resistance.

On August 31, 1944, Colonel Tibbets's focus changed. He *". . . was transported into a strange new world in which the most incredible miracles of science replaced all the realities"* of his military experience. He received a phone call to report to General Uzal G. Ent, commander of the Second Air Force, in Colorado Springs, Colorado, and was ordered to come with his bags packed.

Tibbets straightforwardly passed a short but penetrating series of questions. He also had been subjected to a thorough background check prior to going to Colorado.

Tibbets was subsequently given a sensitive, highly secret task that needed to be concealed from everyone including his family members and co-workers. The secret atomic bomb development program was briefly explained. Major General Leslie R. Groves commanded the *"Manhattan Engineering District"* or the *"Manhattan Project"* and nuclear physicist J. Robert

Boeing B-29-55-MO "Superfortress"

Crew:	9-14 persons
Engines:	Four Wright R-3350-23 radial; 2,200 hp ea.
Wingspan:	141 ft 3 in
Length:	99 ft 0 in
Height:	27 ft 9 in
Weight:	Empty, 70,140 lbs; max, 135,000 lbs
Speed:	Cruise, 220 mph; max, 365 mph
Range:	5,830 miles
Ceiling:	32, 000 feet
Armament:	Twelve .50-caliber machine guns; up to 20,000 lbs bombs
Cost:	$605, 360 (average B-29 unit cost in 1944)

Source:
http://www.hill.af.mil/museum/photos/wwwii/b-29.htm

B-29s in production at Boeing plant. *(www.childrenofthemanhattanproject.com)*

bomb. He was given fifteen B-29s and nearly 1,800 support personnel. The self-contained composite group would include maintenance, technical and engineering units, an ordnance squadron, military police, a medical unit with specialists in radiology, and troop transport aircraft.

An isolated site for training *"the atomic air fleet"* needed to be selected. The site had to be one where security could be maintained. Three sites were possibilities: Wendover, Utah, Great Bend, Kansas, and Mountain Home at Boise, Idaho.

Tibbets flew first to Kansas and then to Wendover, Utah, and he liked Wendover's remoteness. He selected it over the other two sites. Wendover, surrounded by miles of salt flats, was populated by only about 100 people. There were adequate maintenance facilities and the runways could handle the B-29s. The machine shops were excellent and the place was equipped.

There was only one east-to-west highway passing through and only one railroad. The housing was substandard, but would do for the few months the group would reside there. The P-47 fighter training squadrons had already been phased out, so there were almost no other military personnel present.

Colonel Tibbets set up headquarters in Wendover on September 8th and the 393rd Squadron personnel arrived on September 11th with their commander, Lt. Col. Tom Classen. Classen became deputy commander of the composite group. The chain of command from above was short. There were only two levels between Tibbets and President Roosevelt, and later Truman. They were Secretary of War Henry Stimson and General Leslie Groves, who headed the atomic bomb program.

The 393rd Bomb Squadron came from Harvard, Nebraska, with flight and ground crews for fifteen

Wendover Field fire station. *(Gertrude Tripp)*

B-29s. Tibbets selected them on recommendation of General Ent. There were three B-29 squadrons detached from the 504th Group and brought in. They came in under a cloak of secrecy and slipped in *"virtually unnoticed."* They were just another squadron sent to Wendover to be trained.

Colonel Tibbets brought in members of the former B-17 crew he had flown with in Europe. He brought in Tom Ferebee, bombardier, staff sergeant George Caron, tail gunner, Dutch van Kirk, navigator, and Staff Sergeant Wyatt Duzenbury, flight engineer. They served as trainers for their counterparts on other planes.

Bob Lewis, co-pilot, came from Tibbets's training in the B-29 testing program. Other key people were brought in on recommendations, including Kermit Beahan, bombardier, James van Pelt, navigator, and Jacob Beser, radar specialist, with Charles Sweeney, George Marquardt, and Don Albury as pilots. Still others were part of the 393rd and are named later in this chapter.

As members of the various units arrived at Wendover Field, their gazes fell on a large, white, painted sign which read:

"WHAT YOU SEE HERE— WHEN YOU LEAVE HERE— LET IT STAY HERE!" It was imperative to have the utmost in security on and off the base. It was necessary that every man must have that impressed on them. They were not so much as to speculate or hint at the nature of the operation or that it was any different from any other military operation.

One of the security measures was to have the men on base wear badges. The men of the 509th wore blue and red if assigned to highly restricted areas. The rest of the airmen on base wore grey badges.

William "Bud" Uanna brought approximately thirty special agents to infiltrate all aspects of the operation and to see that there was *"no information leakage."* Phone calls, mail, and off-duty conversations of the men were monitored. *"The agents swarmed over the town of Wendover and the airfield."* They were everywhere: in the mess hall, pumping gas at local service stations, driving garbage trucks, even on the flight line. Barbed wire was installed to keep people out of restricted areas. *"If a car stayed more than one night at the State Line Hotel, the license number was taken and checked out."*

A view inside the barracks at Wendover Field. *(Charles Freudenthal)*

Secrecy was of the utmost importance at Wendover Field. *(509th Pictorial Album)*

Bombs are ready to load into B-29s to be dropped over enemy targets. *(509th Pictorial Album)*

Even so, soldiers were used to such restrictions and didn't take them seriously. For that reason, Col. Tibbets authorized a large number of Christmas leaves as part of a security check. Some men only made it to the airports or train and bus stations of Salt Lake or Elko, Nevada, or bars adjacent to the departure places. Because of unguarded conversations, unknowingly with planted security agents, their furloughs were cut short by telegrams ordering them back to Wendover, where they received tongue lashings from the colonel himself and were put under house arrests.

A few were transferred out, seven to Alaska. One pilot was not allowed to disembark at Wendover Field after returning from home where he showed his plane to his parents. He was sent to Alaska.

Generally though, the men were *"good soldiers and patriotic."* They finally were told at a meeting in the base auditorium theater that they were there for a special overseas mission which could end the war. With that revelation, the men understood the reason for such tight security. Colonel Tibbets further told them to *"Stop being curious."*

According to author Jim Hubbard in the *Wendover Relay*

B-29 training at Maxwell Field in Alabama. *(Maxwell Air Force Base)*

Enola Gay crew which dropped the atomic bomb on Hiroshima, Japan. Standing: Lt. Jeppson, Capt. Lewis, Gen. Davies (not part of crew), Col. Tibbets, Maj. Ferebee, Capt. Parsons; kneeling: S/Sgt. Duzenbury, Sgt. Stiborik, Maj. van Kirk, S/Sgt. Caron, Sgt. Shumard, PFC. Nelson (not shown, Jacob Beser). *(Maxwell Air Force Base)*

of June 21, 1984: *"The forming of the composite group essentially made the 509th a small isolated and self-supporting air force, again good for security. The core of the group was the 393rd.*

"The high priority First Ordnance Squadron was housed on the south side of the airfield away from all other activities. The area was fenced off and classified as 'most restricted.' Ordnance units have always worked with weapons and explosives, but these were different. Three, oddly-shaped bomb casings were assembled: the Thin Man (the Uranium bomb, used on Hiroshima), named after Roosevelt; the 'Fat Man' (the Plutonium Bomb, used on Nagasaki) named after Churchill; and the Pumpkin [there were many pumpkins], a practice bomb filled with conventional explosives. 'Thin Man' was later referred to as 'The Little Boy.' Strangers flew in almost daily carrying design changes. They were from a secret place known only as Site Y." [James Les Rowe said he directed assembly of the bombs at Wendover. He said that two weeks prior to August 4, a *Little Boy* bomb had been delivered from Wendover to Tinian by a B-29 pilot who was his neighbor. He

clearly stated that the second bomb was assembled in thirty-six hours on August 12 and loaded on a plane at Wendover on August 13, 1945. He claimed that a third bomb was returned and disassembled at Wendover on August 16. Colonel Paul Tibbets stated that the first two bombs were delivered directly to Tinian for assembly there, with the main components coming by ship. A third atomic bomb was sent from Wendover but called back. Historian Charles Hibbard researched declassified material and said the first two actual bombs were never at Wendover. Hibbard stated, *"No one in an official position believes that Captain Rowe assembled the bombs. They would not have permitted a civil engineer to assemble the bombs and they would not have completely assembled one before it was loaded on a plane headed for Tinian. I [Charles Hibbard] have other publications, which confirm how the bomb material was shipped to Tinian in separate crates and on special planes and the cruiser Indianapolis. There is a lot of the atomic bomb history which has not been published, and because of the extreme secrecy will probably never be known."*

Jim Hubbard continued, *"Colonel Tibbets and Radar Officer Jacob Beser were the only two men in the 393rd who knew that their work was atomic related. No flight plans were filed when they made their many mysterious trips from Wendover. They were headed for Los Alamos—the highly secret Site Y.*

"Having this awareness of the atomic project created special problems for both men. Beser was working with scientists at Los Alamos in the designing of a miniature radar to be placed inside the bomb casing. As his knowlege of the bomb and radar unit increased, the lieutenant's personal security became a genuine concern. He was assigned a project agent to be with him at all times while off base."

At Wendover, the married men were allowed to

Cpl. Rao Bateman (left) and an unidentified crewman of the 603rd Air Engineering Squadron, 509th Composite Group standing beside #82, the *Enola Gay*. (Phyllis Bateman)

bring their families, but they were not to mention the nature of the mission to their families. Colonel Tibbets followed the same rules with his wife. He told her that the scientists on base were sanitary engineers. One day, she called one of them and had them unplug a bathroom drain. The man had a Ph.D in physics, but completed the job anyway and laughed about it later.

Throughout the Army Air Force, special orders were to give priority to *"Silverplate."* The code name *"Silverplate"* was used by the 509th to obtain equipment or needed services if refusal for such requests was forthcoming. The use of *"Silverplate"* brought immediate results when given. The authority to use the code came directly from the White House.

Tibbets took care of his men while they were stationed at Wendover. He wanted them to work well, and he knew they were being subjected to rigorous training, with long hours and constant security checks.

On one occasion, Tibbets told mess officer Charles Perry to use the word *"Silverplate"* if he had any problems obtaining food. He tried it one day when he became frustrated with a food supply depot. *"His goods*

arrived within hours. The 509th was the best-fed unit in the services."

Fresh fish were transported from New Orleans, Miami, and San Francisco. Tropical fruit was flown in from 1,000 miles away. An 1,800-mile round trip to Portland, Oregon, to obtain coffee cups was flown. He intervened if his men got into trouble with the police in Salt Lake City *"over traffic violations or rowdy behavior."*

In November 1944, Dora Dougherty and Helen Gosnell joined the group. Dora was a veteran pilot, who along with Didi Moorman had flown with Tibbets in the B-29 testing program. She had great skill and flew the B-29 when many men pilots were skeptical of the new bomber because of its poor reputation early on. Dora flew a transport plane while stationed at Wendover. Tibbets liked the women pilots because they never seemed to get sidetracked en route to and from destinations.

The men and women of Wendover Field celebrated Thanksgiving on November 30, 1944. Many suffered food poisoning and needed hospitalization after eating Thanksgiving Day dinner in the mess hall. The

Colonel Paul Tibbets was in charge of the 509th Composite Group and piloted the *Enola Gay*. Colonel Tibbets is shown in the middle, with navigator Dutch van Kirk on the left and bombardier Tom Ferebee on the right. *(Gertrude Tripp, Utah State Historical Society)*

The *Enola Gay* B-29 Superfortress on Tinian Island from which the atomic bomb was dropped. *(Gertrude Tripp)*

menu listed turkey noodle broth, celery hearts, pickles, olives, roast young turkey, giblet gravy, cranberry sauce, savory dressing, whipped potatoes, buttered peas, boiled onions, Waldorf salad, parker house rolls, pumpkin pie, hot mincemeat pie, ice cream, fruit punch, coffee, assorted nuts and candy, fresh fruit, cigars and cigarettes. Dinner music was provided by the 593rd Army Air Force Band.

The 509th Composite Group was officially activated on December 17, 1944, when all of its components were unified. The five squadrons consisted of 225 officers and 1,542 enlisted men. Christmas in Wendover for the 509th included turkey and ham surrounded by *"mounds of vegetables,"* mincemeat pies, and Christmas puddings. The main gate was guarded by extra MP's—snowmen with military hats and tree branch carbines. Church services were held that morning in the base chapel.

Ralph C. Berger, aircraft engineering technician, 603rd Engineering Squadron, had two memories of Wendover. *"One was the State Line Hotel, Bar and Casino. Two or three times a week, when my work was done in the evening, I would walk across the field, out the west gate into the State Line which was in Nevada. I would stay until*

Thanksgiving dinner 1942 at Wendover Field, Col. Dippey standing. *(Hill Air Force Base, Byron Dussler)*

about eleven p.m. playing blackjack. I would win a bundle and lose a bundle. In the end I just about broke even, but I had a great time. I remember, behind the bar were stacks of silver dollars on the wall.

"The other thing was the midnight Christmas service, December 25, 1944 at the base chapel. Most of my friends had gone home for the holidays. When I came out of the chapel, it was a very cold and crisp night and I took a walk. As you know, the airbase was surrounded by mountains. They were playing Christmas carols and the music was reverberating off of the hills. It was beautiful, but this was one time I was really homesick in the service."

Comedian Bob Hope and singer Bing Crosby signed on as members of the United Service Organizations or USO in the summer of 1943. The voluntary agency was organized to provide entertainment for servicemen and Hope served with it for seven years and beyond. He always brought along pretty girls to sing and dance. They were a main ingredient for success at the army camps.

Chow time with regular helpings of powdered eggs, lamb, dehydrated vegetables, and C rations. *(509th Pictorial Album)*

Time Magazine featured Bob Hope on its cover and said, *"From the ranks of show business have sprung heroes and even martyrs, but so far only one legend. That legend is Bob Hope."* He was the icon of the times, America's favorite comedian.

Hope and his friend Bing Crosby visited Wendover more than once and Hope named it *"Leftover Field."* Crosby called it, *"Tobacco Road with Slot Machines."* Local Wendover citizens were able to watch the USO entertainers perform on the open-air stage also.

Hope's jokes generated laughs wherever he went, including Wendover. When Bing was along, he poked fun at Hope with jokes such as *"Welcome home (from Europe), Ski Snoot. My, my, look at you. No more pot tummy. How'd you manage?"* Hope : *"I didn't. During an air raid, it went 'round back to hide."*

Hope got huge laughs for quipping about things that were on everyone's minds. Concerning blackouts he said, *"Well, Los Angeles had its first blackout the other night. Every electric light in the city went out. I saw one guy standing in the street and laughing like anything. I asked, 'What are you so happy about?' And he said, 'At last I'm not alone. Look! This month nobody paid their electric bills!'"*

And concerning shortages he said, *"The shortage of everything is worrying me. This morning when the bank sent back my check, it was marked, 'Insufficient rubber.'"* Hope's corny jokes made people laugh and forget about the war for a few minutes, even in Wendover. Base Sergeant Major Byron Dussler was not impressed with Hope & Crosby. He wrote home that they were a flop.

The 509th pictorial album stated *". . . Wendover really wasn't so bad. The fellow who actually looked for something to do on his off-hours usually found it. For instance, when a man contemplated a three-day pass, he didn't just stuff a few unmentionables into an over nite bag and take off. Not at Wendover.*

"First of all he checked bus and train schedules. Then he went to the PX and stocked up on cigarettes, candy bars and aspirin. His friends took him to the station and saw him off. His destination ordinarily was one of three places; Salt Lake City, Utah, Ely or Elko, Nevada, any one of which was at

Wartime Shortages

The war had a direct effect on both civilians and military personnel by war-caused shortages. The government imposed rationing of chocolate bars, sugar, coffee, rubber tires, and anti-freeze. No domestic automobiles were produced after early 1942. Newspapers of the day advertised that Castor oil was in the medicine chests of every GI and that Gillette's razor steel was in use as bayonets in the war effort. Radio commercials of a New York cemetery were timed to coincide with news bulletins of heavy casualties overseas.

The wartime effort required materials to be used for making items used by the military. Silk was made into parachutes instead of stockings. Molasses, corn syrup, or honey replaced sugar. People drove slower so that they wouldn't wear out their tires as new tires were not available. Rubber for tires came from Japanese-held territories and consequently was scarce, although essential for military vehicles and planes. People were allowed to buy only two pair of shoes annually. There were shortages of many ordinary items such as soap, paper, matchbooks, and batteries. The supply of newly-invented zippers vanished.

The government set up a program of rationing so that everyone would get some of whatever was available. War ration books containing stamps were issued to all. Each person was given sixty-four red stamps for meat, fish, and dairy foods and forty-eight blue stamps for processed foods every month. The stamps were referred to as points. People went to schools to receive their stamps where they waited in line at long tables. Then families faced the difficulties of finding the scarce, high-priced items. Victory gardens and home canned fruits & vegetables helped. Rationing of coal & heating oil cut consumption by a third. Rationing was reportedly not as severe at Wendover because the base & railroad were considered essential to the war effort.

Along the highway leading in and out of Wendover before the war were thousands of tires. Tires blew out easily in the early days of making balloon tires containing tubes. They were a throw away item, not worth fixing. When the war effort commenced, the tires became valuable scrap and quickly disappeared from along the highway. They were picked up to be re-used in making new rubber tires. Burlap, scrap metal, and baling wire were other items collected for recycling.

least 125 miles away. Several days later he returned—'beat.' But he was happy.

"Pre-war Wendover boasted a thriving population of 103—about one person per slot machine. Spike Birdzell, the mayor [townboard councilman] of the town went out of his way to make the soldiers at home in Wendover. 'After all, he reasoned, 'the boys went out of their way to get to Wendover.'

"Spike had his own little place of business—just plain 'Spikes,' he called it. He served the boys well, always having tasty food and delicious drinks on hand. For those who like to dance, he furnished the dance floor and the music. Now, if somebody had ever figured out how to get the girls to come ...

"Then there was the State Line Hotel, with its typically western bar and casino. If several of the Wendover boys had a hunch they were walking with Lady Luck, they'd go up to the State Line in the evening and throw silver dollars around until the State Line proved their hunch to be wrong.

Dancing at the base service club was one way to meet the girls who came from Ely, Elko, and Salt Lake City. *(509th Pictorial Album)*

"But if a soldier stationed at Wendover didn't leave the base, he still could find plenty to do. There were regular weekly dances at the service club. Girls came by bus from Salt Lake City, Utah, Ely, Elko, Wells, and McGill, Nevada, and from other Intermountain settlements within a radius of 150 miles. The 509th men who attended those dances were grateful to the girls who gave so freely of their time, efforts and interest.

"Nothing was more refreshing than a dip in Wendover's outdoor swimming pool. There were regular swimming schedules. One day would be for enlisted personnel only. The next day, the depth of the water would be lowered to three or four feet—Lieutenants can't swim —and officer personnel would go for a dip.

"Two post theaters were always ready to afford an evening of pleasant entertainment. Everybody, it seemed, had the 'show habit.'

"Down by the base hospital was the library. This wasn't an ordinary library, by any means. It was different, not because of the reading material it offered but because of its friendly atmosphere. It was fur-

The base library offered music and relaxation while reading a good book. *(509th Pictorial Album)*

Training for survival at sea in Wendover Field pool. *(Gertrude Tripp)*

nished with deep, comfortable lounge chairs, and its patrons felt free to speak with friends without receiving that 'hush-hush' look from the librarian. Besides stocking all of the standard works and latest novels, the library offered a music room and a collection of recordings for the enjoyment of Wendover men. Bach and Basie were equally popular.

"There was something about Wendover. People liked the boys stationed there. And when the 509th left, they left friends. They would remember those friends, and they would remember Wendover."

Rao Bateman was stationed at Wendover Field as part of the 509th. He and his wife, Phyllis's experiences, though unique, gives another glimpse of what it was like for married couples. On July 2, 1943, Rao H. Bateman of Logan, Utah, was inducted into the army air force as a private at Fort Douglas in Salt Lake City, Utah.

Almost a month later, Rao was sent to Wendover Field via special chauffeur from Hill Field in Ogden, Utah, where he was working. He served as a sheet metal engineer in the 603rd Engineering Group of the 509th Composite Group. Rao riveted airplane parts together.

He was stationed in Wendover for a year and nine

months. He had recently married Phyllis Parrish of Ibapah, Utah. She followed him to Wendover and worked as a clerk typist in the army supply at Wendover Field.

Phyllis ordered supplies for certain sections. The most frequent order was for Plexiglas. It was always in demand. It was needed for airplane repairs and parts. She trained military wives who were hired to help. It was frustrating because of the high turnover rate. Help was short-lived with soldiers continuously being transferred.

Housing was scarce, so for a week or two upon her arrival, Phyllis lived with her cousin Marjorie West and a friend, Rhea Weaver. The cousins boarded and worked at The Beanery Restaurant. The Beanery was the eating place and station for the railroad workers of the Western Pacific.

Then for a short time, Phyllis lived with friends Thelma and Will Lee and family in their small tent house. The Lees were formerly of Ibapah, her hometown. The Lee home in Wendover consisted of two rooms—a bedroom and a kitchen. The house was a tent with a board floor and was heated with a wood cook stove.

Rao and Phyllis Bateman eventually obtained a two-room apartment to rent, #155 in the housing rentals. It was furnished and had a kitchen, bath, and

A little R and R in the base pool with the girls was a refreshing relief from the heat of the desert. *(509th Pictorial Album)*

114

bedroom. They used a coal and wood stove to cook and heat the place. A pretty dish, a present from Rao's sister, fell off and broke on the cement floor simply because the fridge in operation vibrated.

The Batemans purchased food at Ray Peterson's and Hamilton's markets. Meat, gas, sugar, and tires were among the rationed items. Phyllis's parents brought them fresh bread, meat, and butter from the Ibapah ranch. Because of the Parrish's gift of fresh beef, they, together with their army friends Keith and Sue Wertz used their ration stamps for other things, and at the same time enjoyed having steak fries. They had many chuckles because of the puzzled and wanton looks of their neighbors, who couldn't figure out how they could save enough ration stamps to buy steaks so often.

They spent evenings playing cards with the Lees of Ibapah and eating pinenuts. Once in a while, they would play pool on Sundays at housing headquarters. It

Wendover grocery store during World War II. *(State Line Casino, Bill & Anna Smith family)*

was closed for army personnel on that day but their friend, Millie Lyman, was in charge of housing and gave them permission to use the facility.

They often attended the public movies at the base theater. While waiting for everyone to be seated, the usual song which blared was *"Drinking Rum and Coca Cola."* Soon the showhouse darkened and during the first few minutes cartoons and newsreels were played before the main feature. Some of their favorite movies were *Casa Blanca, Gone with the Wind, Trail of the Lonesome Pine,* and *East of Eden.*

They traveled to Logan, Utah, via Greyhound bus on furloughs and Phyllis' parents took them to Ibapah, Utah, over weekends. They walked to and from the base where they both worked until they eventually saved enough money to buy a used 1941 Chevrolet coupe. They called it, the *Green Wave.* Automobiles were a scarcity during war time.

They drove the new car to Logan on a visit to Rao's folks

KP duty brought men to their knees. "Dobe Doc" had a pig farm seven miles southwest of Wendover. He shipped 200 to 300 pigs from Iowa and fed them corn supplemented by the waste food from the mess halls on the base, according to Brent Peterson. *(509th Pictorial Album)*

and decided to get their driver's licenses. They flunked the test, but Rao was given a permit because the police officer said one of them had to be able to drive. Times were different then!

Immediately prior to leaving Wendover, Rao was confined to the base and they gave up their apartment. Phyllis made other living arrangements until Rao was shipped overseas with the atomic bomb group in May 1945. Phyllis drove the *Green Wave* home to Ibapah to live with her parents for the next six months and raised thirty orphan lambs to pass the time.

Rao was sailing across the Pacific Ocean to Tinian Island in the Marianas when there was a submarine alert on his ship. He wrote home about it and his brother Harold put it in the Logan paper. The *Logan Herald Journal* reported that Rao was traveling on board the submarine *Alert*. Rao received much ribbing

Rao & Phyllis Bateman were typical of thousands of young couples stationed at Wendover Field during WWII.

A Saturday party where bunks were removed and barracks scrubbed. Byron Dussler recorded that the bunks were dirtier after they were taken out into the foggy, sooty air. He said the men were lectured on sanitation and use of a broom, but didn't have a broom to sweep the floor. *(Hill Air Force Base & Byron Dussler)*

Wendover Field bowling alley. *(509th Pictorial Album).*

from his air corps group, especially his sergeant, as he was from Logan, too.

Other memories of Wendover living conditions of 509th crew members include that of Wesley P. Peterson, staff sergeant, 390th Air Service Squadron. He said, *"I vividly remember being temporarily quartered in some pyramidal tents and when a heavy windstorm leveled our tent one night, we hauled our cots into the nearest latrine and spent the rest of the night there. In fact, we spent the following night there as well until we could be assigned new accommodations.*

"Then, of course, I remember those often greasy eating utensils—the divided metal trays—that gave us a case of the 'G.I.s' periodically. The coal-burning, pot-bellied stoves in the barracks that blew up occasionally also come to mind."

Charles Perry, mess officer, 393rd Squadron recalled *"arriving with our two-month-old son before our belongings did. 'Cappy' slept in a bureau drawer, his diapers were attached to the clothes line with safety pins. Many, many times the washings had to be redone due to the soft coal [dust & smoke] that was in the air. One day I looked out and sheep were everywhere. They were coming down from the mountains."* Another officer, Cecil N. King, said that diapers froze on the drying line. He and his wife *"were young, healthy, in love and in a high adventure."*

Despite the less than ideal living conditions, the 509th made a great contribution to the war effort. Colonel Tibbets's experience in test flying the B-29s at Wichita, Grand Island, and Alamogordo enabled him to make necessary modifications on his fleet of B-29s.

He removed over 7,000 pounds of installed weight in weapons and armor plating resulting in increased flying altitude of the aircraft and decreasing the strain on the engines.

Flying higher put the bombers out of range of most anti-aircraft fire and they could out-maneuver the Japanese Zeros, should that become necessary. The flight mechanics considered the stripped-down bombers a crazy idea. They called the bombers, *"Sitting Target One"* and *"Sitting Target Two."*

After modification, the planes were ready for intensive training over Utah, California and Nevada. The training involved bombing accuracy, maneuvering away from the explosion, and navigation over long distance water flights. The training involved night bombing practice. On one dry run over San Francisco, pilot Charles McKnight and his crew climbed to 30,000 feet to begin the bombing run and a replacement blister blew out where the gun turrets usually were. Everything that wasn't tied down blew out of the hold. The crew had on seat belts so they were safe.

Colonel Tibbets remembered that *"flight procedures had to be changed. . . without telling the crews why the changes were necessary. Why the jolting 155 degree diving turn after the bomb was released? This gave seven to eight miles separation at the time of impact. Why the need for so much distance?"*

The practice bombs were blockbuster casings called *"flying pumpkins"* because of their unusual shape. They were built with the same outer design as the

Number 82 backs up to upload the bomb. There were three bomb pits at Wendover Field. *(Maxwell Air Force Base)*

atom bomb and ballasted to weigh the same. They were used *"to test detonators"* and *"measure fall rates."* Altogether 155 test units were dropped from October 1944 to August 1945.

Project W-47 was the designation for the assembly and testing of the inert bombs, according to James Les Rowe. An ordinance test unit of the 216th Army Air Force Bomb Unit worked on the bomb shapes, fusing, detonators, release mechanisms, etc. They also constructed the pits with hydraulic lifts used to hoist the gigantic bombs into the aircraft bomb bays. The pits in Wendover and one at Kirtland Field in New Mexico were the only ones in existence in the United States where the atomic bombs could be loaded into the B-29s. The only other pits were on the islands of Tinian and Iwo Jima.

The bomb bays of the B-29 aircraft had to be modified to accommodate the one huge bomb they would be carrying. The bomb was held in place by a single hook, which was adapted from one used by the Royal Air Force with their British blockbusters. The hook-up was manufactured and fitted to the B-29's at Wendover.

"Little Boy" was the name given to the gun-type bomb dropped on Hiroshima, Japan, on August 6,

"Little Boy" atomic bomb used over Hiroshima, Japan, August 1945. Much more took place at Wendover than is on the books with regard to the assembly of the nuclear bombs. We may never know the complete story because many of the facts are classified. There were 155 test assemblies at Wendover during the bombs' development. *(www.childrenofthemanhattanproject.org)*

1945. The bomb was the only one of its kind, an enriched uranium weapon weighing 9,700 pounds. It involved a uranium (U-235) projectile wedge fired through a gun barrel at a larger uranium (U-235) target piece. The two uranium masses striking together formed a critical mass with a resulting atomic chain reaction.

The bomb was ten feet long and measured 28 inches in diameter. It had an explosive force equivalent to 15,000 tons of TNT. It had to be lifted from a pit into the belly of a B-29, in this case the *Enola Gay* piloted by Col. Paul Tibbets. The efficiency of the weapon was described as poor, utilizing 1.38% of the uranium fuel actually fissioned. It was set to be triggered by a radar echo when it fell to an altitude of 1,850 feet.

Crew of *Bockscar*. Standing l. to r.: Capt. Kermit Beahan, Capt. James van Pelt, Lt. Charles Albury, Lt. Fred Olivi, and Maj. Charles Sweeney. Kneeling l. to r.: S/Sgt. Edward Buckly, M/Sgt. John Kuharek, Sgt. Raymond Gallagher, Sgt. Albert DeHart, and Sgt. Abe Spitzer. *(www.childrenofthemanhattanproject.org, Joseph Papalia; originally from U.S. Army Air Corp, National Archives.)*

"Fat Man" was a plutonium fueled bomb, similar to the one detonated July 16, 1945 at the Trinity site in New Mexico. *"Fat Man"* was dropped on the city of Nagasaki on August 9, 1945. This implosion-type fission bomb weighed 10,800 pounds and was ten feet, eight inches in length with a diameter of sixty inches. The 13.6-pound bomb was about the size of a softball and had the explosive force of 21,000 tons of TNT. A 5,300-pound envelope of non-nuclear high explosives imploded on a hollow sphere filled with plutonium into an inner core of beryllium and polonium, triggering a nuclear reaction. It was ten times as efficient as *"Little Boy,"* but did less damage because it was dropped on a less populated, hilly area. It was delivered by the B-29 *Bockscar*, piloted by Major Charles Sweeney.

A large atom bomb would not fit under the fuselage of the B-29 aircraft so the bombs were lowered on specially prepared cradles into pits. Then the plane could be rolled atop the loading pit and the bomb winched into the bomb bay, using a hydraulic mechanism they devised. These pits were designed and perfected at Wendover Air Field. (One bomb pit was excavated for historical purposes as a Boy Scout Eagle Project in 2001.) There were three pits built at Wendover Field.

The base machine shops were busy making constant changes to the bombs' shape and weight. These changes were dictated by the scientists flying back and forth from Los Alamos. The practice bombing runs also produced changes to the dynamics of the bomb shape. The bombardiers made suggestions which made for more accurate bomb drops.

At first, the bomb crews could not consistently hit the three hundred foot aiming circle; some fell within the circle and some landed outside. They were concerned with precision and accuracy because bomb drops were done visually, as radar was still too uncertain.

Tibbets discovered that his bombardier, Ferebee,

"lifted himself off his seat to bring his eyes to the sight. The movement was no more than an inch or two. But it was enough. Each time he lowered his eyes to the sight, his head was at a slightly different angle to the viewfinder."

At 30,000 feet, the slight difference in angle worked out to a several hundred feet error on the ground. The problem was solved by constructing a padded headrest for the bombsight. From then on the bombs were dropped with *"consistent accuracy."* Both bombs were equipped with tail parachutes to slow their descent, allowing the B-29s time to get away.

The composite group began to assume *"impressive proportions."* It was a massive undertaking requiring united effort in many areas. The 1027th Air Materiel Squadron consisted of three officers and fourteen enlisted men. *"The mission of the 1027th was to anticipate, procure and issue all air corps, quartermaster, signal, chemical warfare, and ordnance supplies and equipment for the 509th."* The rigid training program of the 1027th Air Materiel Squadron was described in the *509th Pictorial Album* as the sound of firing carbines and pistols, marching feet, pounding hammers, and whining saws.

The following several pages contain descriptions

Bockscar was used to drop the second atomic bomb, *"Fat Man."* (Maxwell Air Force Base)

taken liberally from the 509th Composite Group's *Pictorial Album* written and published in 1945-46. *"Sixty per cent of the men of the 603rd Air Engineering Squadron had been stationed at Wendover for some length of time before activation. They had already been working as a team, thus eliminating months of training along these lines."* They could *"efficiently repair or manufacture any piece of equipment or airplane part with the least amount of man-hours expended."*

The engineer's drafting department had up-to-date blueprints. The tech supply department procured aircraft parts and issued tools, maintenance equipment and mechanics' clothing. The machinists manufactured what couldn't be procured. The engineers built mobile repair units which could move from place to place in order to repair minor damage or major plane parts. They could install or repair the newly developed Curtis electric propellor which had reverse pitch and synchronization. This made it possible to use the propellor as a brake in stopping on a shorter runway, making the B-29 even more versatile.

"Fat Man" which was used to bomb Nagasaki, Japan on August 6, 1945. *(www.childrenofthemanhattanproject.org, Joseph Papalia; originally from U.S Army Air Corp, National Archives.)*

C-24 on flightline preparing to leave Wendover for Tinian. *(Maxwell Air Force Base)*

The 603rd Engineering Squadron also managed the instrument shop where all instruments and indicators were kept functioning properly. The electrical department worked in close conjunction with the instrument shop. The complex electrical systems of the B-29 were repaired and modified.

The bombsight department calibrated and repaired bombsights, stabilizer gyros, and automatic pilot equipment. The armament and central fire control department took care of all the B-29 guns and central fire control equipment.

The radar repair shop inspected and maintained the aircraft radar system. The auxiliary power plant repair shop was responsible for the gasoline generators. The generators were used on each aircraft for han-

dling the extra load of electrical devices used on bombing runs or takeoffs and landings. There were also sheet metal, paint, woodworking, fabric, parachute, radio repair, telephone, teletype and office repair shops in the 603rd Air Engineering Squadron.

Wendover Field welding shop. *(Richard Campbell)*

Takeoff of 509th Air Echelon as it departs Wendover Field, Utah. *(Maxwell Air Force Base)*

There were 233 personnel in the 603rd. The squadron *"was billeted in an area apart from the group headquarters so it could be close to the line."* Their work in stripping the armor plating and guns and turrets from the bombers went unexplained as to why they were doing it. Had old man Tibbets completely lost it, they wondered?

The First Ordnance Squadron worked *"with top scientists on the atomic bomb program for over nine months in a military unit unique to all standard army organization. Under the leadership of Major Charles F. H. Begg, the squadron's personnel represented a group of picked officers and enlisted men from all branches of the armed forces."*

So exacting were the technical and military security requirements for the squadron that only twenty percent of those having basic qualifications for the work were accepted. All of those taken into the organization were told their jobs would be hazardous due to the experimental stage of the work, and many volunteered their lives if the test program necessitated it.

Quoting from the 509th *Pictorial Album:* "During the fall, winter, and spring of 1944-45, these men toiled day and night in all phases of work to insure that test work on

the atomic bomb was carried out according to schedule. This often necessitated improvision of equipment and tools inasmuch as mass production of these items had not caught up with the accelerated test program."

The 1395th Military Police Company provided for security of personnel and equipment of the 509th group. The 128 men of the group were equipped with small arms, submachine guns, machine guns, and M-1s.

They underwent a strenuous ongoing physical training program. Bayonet practice, Judo training, and hand-to-hand combat skills were taught. They received instruction and practice in operating motorcyles on rough terrain.

The military police learned to install booby traps and defend against smoke and gas grenades. They were skilled in traffic control and use of convoys. Swimming and camouflage tactics were studied. All the while, they were performing guard duty for the 509th.

The military police guarded the main gate and all entrances to the military base. Fourteen-year-old Lloyd Hall got a job delivering newspapers on Wendover Air Base to earn money to buy a new bike. He had a special pass to get him through the front gate of the base.

Marching near Wendover Field. (*Maxwell Air Force Base, 509th Pictorial Album*)

He always took along his dog Shep.

One night as Lloyd was leaving the base, Shep ran away down the railroad tracks. He soon returned barking loudly. Lloyd followed him along the tracks on his bicycle. Shep had heard a GI yelling for help when no one else had. The GI was tied up and lying on the railroad track. Lloyd hurriedly returned to the MP guard shack and enlisted their help. One guard grabbed Lloyd and pulled him into a jeep. Loyd's dog bit the MP to protect Lloyd. The GI was rescued twenty minutes before a train went through, and Lloyd went home. As for the soldier, was he out on the tracks as a joke or was it sabotage? The answer is unknown.

The next morning Lloyd was summoned to the Provost Marshall's office. He was sure he was in trouble for his dog biting the soldier. When he went into the office the officer said, *"I don't know how to give an award to a dog, but if I could I would give your dog a citation for saving the soldier's life."*

Other 509th unit components were from the 393rd Bomb Squadron, the 390th Air Service Group, and the 320th Troop Carrier Squadron.

The 393rd Bombardment Squadron's history informatively summarized their stay in Wendover.

"The 393rd Bomb Squadron had completed two-thirds of its training in the 504th Bomb Group, and was starting to prepare for overseas, when word came that we were headed for Wendover instead of the Pacific. Rumors were plentiful, but this time no one knew the answers. Then about the middle of September 1944, by troop train, private cars, and a few by plane, the squadron personnel arrived in the middle of the salt flats. Nebraska never looked like this!

"Several days were spent in getting oriented, and finding out how often they could get to Salt Lake. And then came the news. At a meeting of all members of the unit, Col. Paul W. Tibbets was introduced. They were told about a highly secret project on which they were to be engaged; if successful, the war could be concluded a year earlier than the most optimistic expected.

"Absolute security was drummed into them from the very start. No mention of any special program was ever to be made to unauthorized personnel, not even to families. It looked as if the 393rd was in for something different.

"Primarily because there wasn't much to keep them occupied, all personnel were given leaves and furloughs. Then began the long wait for new planes, something to fill up the

Ground echelon lined up to leave Wendover for Tinian. *(Maxwell Air Force Base)*

great open spaces on the ramp. By the end of October they had two B-29's, a start towards the ultimate fifteen.

"Because Wendover had been a fighter field, the facilities, equipment, and supplies available were not suitable for the very heavy bombers. The new planes were slow in arriving, and there was usually plenty of time to order and procure all necessary items for maintenance and upkeep. There were shortages in critical personnel; but by the end of November this situation was well in hand. The southwest corner of Wendover Field was the focal point of the top secret operation.

"Flying commenced again in the last two weeks of October. Emphasis was on bombing, and navigation missions, and a 3,000 mile over water navigation hop. At this time there were absolutely no ground school facilities on the base, and therefore it was the responsibility of the squadron to train their own men for combat. By the end of December 1944, the 393rd could rightly be called a self-trained organization.

"The squadron was re-organized to suit the requirements of this special project, and the biggest change was the slashing of our crews to fifteen in number. The planes themselves had to be modified, with resulting changes in the number of combat personnel for each plane. At times this secret project could be irritating. This was especially true when restricted areas were fenced in, and a special pass was required for admittance;

it always seemed like a long walk back to the barracks when you forgot that red pass.

"December saw the 509th activated. From their arrival at Wendover they had watched the building up of the parts of this new group, and all were gradually assimilated into it.

"For some time they had heard of rumors of a trip to Cuba to perform some highly specialized training. This rumor was correct. The first part of January saw ten B-29's take off for Batista, and warmer climes. Others followed over the next month or so."

A routine physical exam was essential anytime crews were sent overseas, even to Cuba. One first lieutenant flippantly poured tincture of green soap he found in the men's room into his urine sample. The next day he flew to Cuba. He soon received a letter from the flight surgeon which grounded him.

The letter indicated that the urine sample revealed: a) linimentum saponis mollis and b) tinctura saponis viridis (tincture of green soap in urine). It further stated that this was a very rare and unusual disease which must be observed and treated daily by the medical officer of the day.

The 393rd history continued: *"Cuba was pleasant that time of the year. The weather was ideal for flying, and*

Wives waving goodbye as the 509th leaves for Tinian. Note the new water tank (which was painted orange and white) toward the west (background) built by the Army Air Corps at Wendover. *(Richard Campbell)*

sunbathing, and Havana was a great place for relaxation. It was amazing how a few trips into Havana improved the linguistic ability of the fellows. Cuba looked like heaven after Wendover. Wives and girlfriends received alligator shoes or purses or perfume from the local PX or the city. Rum and cokes were purchased at Sloppy Joe's.

"It wasn't just a vacation down there, however. Everyone was busy enough maintaining and flying the planes in bombing and navigation missions. Batista wasn't adapted especially for B-29's, particularly as many as were training there in January.

"The squadron was run as it would be in combat, with simulated combat missions to Berinquen, Bermuda, Virgin Islands, and up to Norfolk. They seemed to have plenty of spare time, but accomplished a very intensive schedule. Base personnel complimented the 393rd on their excellent training record and their behavior.

"The next few months, after returning to the states, were spent in supply and administrative processing, including an armful of shots, in preparation for overseas. There were frequent trips to Omaha for new planes and shakedown mis-

sions on these planes to put them in shape for combat.

"A series of bivouacs in rough country near Wendover were carried out. Use of field equipment, including K and C rations, field latrines, shelter halves and entrenching tools was a feature. Another was the formation and use of motor convoys, normal and blackout, and control of traffic.

"A field maneuver with half of the unit seeking to defend a position against the assault of the rest of the organization saw men using grenades of the smoke and tear gas type. Installations of booby traps were another feature.

"Another bivouac was held in March on Pilot Mountain, 30 miles from Wendover. This was a real example of conditions in the field. The organization moved into camp despite snow and cold and pup tents were erected. Defenses were prepared.

"If the men of Wendover failed to explore the hills lying to the north and west of camp, they missed a great part of the beauty of that section of our country. With a touch of imagination, one can return in fancy to the exciting days of the American Indian. For in these hills, the American Indian lived, hunted, fought and died.

509th ground echelon boarding the train bound for the west coast. *(Maxwell Air Force Base)*

"The men of the 509th, as part of their overseas training, took long hikes into the hills and valleys of Utah and Nevada. A few blisters? Tired backs? Sore feet? Yes. Even so, those hikes were fun—lots of fun.

"A range was established for firing practice and sighting of weapons. Further instruction in use of machine guns was given and all members of the unit fired the weapons. Experience was a superb teacher and everyone learned how to use his equipment to its best advantage. An L-5 from the base came over to simulate air attack[s] and to photograph the bivouac area. These photos were studied later to show defects in camouflage and concealment tactics. This bivouac marked the climax of the training program.

"The last part of April they went to Wendover depot to see the ground echelon off. In May the advance air echelon departed in C-54s, and in June and July the combat planes of the group and squadron left Wendover for Tinian.

"Getting to the war would take more than the two or three days necessary to fly the bombers to the Pacific. There were also 1,800 men and a quantity of supplies to move overseas.

"As each group prepared to leave, there were certain procedures they went through, including physicals, re-equipping

and one last furlough. When a soldier is asked to make out a will, when he is required to assume all sorts of ridiculous positions before an Army doctor, when he must get rid of all his excess and worn-out clothing, when he is obliged to wear his 'dog tags' to bed, then that soldier is being processed for overseas shipment.

"There were still a few days left before the men of the 509th moved from Wendover to the port of embarkation. Since they now were confined to the post, they decided to have a little get-together right on the base.

"Each squadron in the group named the time and place. On the appointed evening, the boys got together. The cooks prepared a variety of good substantial sandwiches—cheese, salami, and baked ham.

"There was plenty of music and song. Men who hadn't known one another previously were singing close harmony together. When the beer kegs were empty, the men went to their barracks, but they continued to make harmony.

"Things had taken shape; training was completed; processing was accomplished. But there was one bit of unfinished business—a last three-day pass. Salt Lake City braced herself, and the 509th moved in.

"What the men of the 509th failed to take in on their

last pass just wasn't worth taking in. They visited the magnificent Capitol building which stands at the head of the green Salt Lake Valley. They strolled through peaceful Memory Grove, just below the Capitol. They marveled at the architectural splendor of the Mormon Temple and of luxurious Hotel Utah.

"Then they loitered down Main Street and pretended they were on Main Street back home. They window-shopped. They eyed displays of civilian clothing, choosing their favorite suit just for fun.

"They ate in restaurants, ordering the best food they could get, or maybe just a milkshake. They teased pretty waitresses and gave them generous tips. Some took their Salt Lake

Goodbye and good luck in the South Pacific. *(Richard Campbell)*

girl friends dancing. And they'd leave the dance early—so they could take the long way home. Those Utah nights were clear and crisp. Then, before they realized it, their passes were just about up. But the men of the 509th felt certain they had packed 72 hours chock full of Salt Lake City one more time.

"The men of the 509th ground echelon heard the shrill whistle of the Charge of Quarters. The sun had not yet risen. But this was no morning to be late. After early breakfast, formation was called, roll call taken, and duffle bags piled high on trailer.

"The base band was standing in formation on Main Street. The leader raised his baton and gave the down beat. 509th troops fell in behind. Along Wendover Field's Main Street the men took one last look at the post library, where so many of them had spent pleasant hours of leisure. They passed the PX, then the base cafeteria. There would be no cafeteria overseas.

"They marched by the chapel and the service club and out through the gate. All along the way to the railroad station people stood and watched and waved goodbye. Goodbyes were said to wives and friends. Men felt that familiar pang of leaving those dear to them behind, yet here was the chance to do something that might bring them back home a little sooner. Thoughts

like that would always make the men feel a little better. No one could say just how long the group would be overseas.

"With duffle bags over their shoulders, the men boarded the train. Fifteen minutes later Wendover was out of sight. All thoughts were now turned to what lay ahead.

"Once on the train, one could sense the tenseness of the atmosphere. The 509th Composite Group was really going overseas this time. Some were fortunate enough to be on the Air Echelon, whose two and a half day trip included stops at California, Hawaii, Johnston, Kwajalein and Tinian." Two days later, the ground echelon pulled into the Seattle port of embarkation.

In April 1945, Colonel Tibbets had given the code word that processed the order to move overseas to Tinian in the Mariana Islands where the bombing operation was staged. Tinian was nicknamed "Manhattan in the Pacific" and was a welcome change from the Wendover desert. The *S. S. Cape Victory* sailed on May 6 from Seattle with 1,200 men, arriving on Tinian on May 29.

In the early part of May, Colonel Tibbets flew to the Martin Aircraft plant in Omaha to select his personal B-29 to be used on Tinian. The plane was guarded and given special attention during assembly and was flown to Utah by Captain Robert Lewis and his crew. Lewis was the last of the 509th to leave Wendover on June 14. He buzzed the airport tower, *"tipping the left wing of the massive bomber within inches of the runway"* in a farewell salute to Wendover.

On July 16 at a test site code-named Trinity in New Mexico, the atomic bomb test was successfully tested. The explosion was explained away as an ammunition magazine explosion to those who heard or saw it from a distance.

The 509th was long gone to Tinian, but highly secretive and crucial work continued in Wendover. Project W-47 was under tremendous pressure to complete assemblage procedures on the timing mechanisms of the *"more and more complex versions of the Little Boy and the Fat Man bombs [test assemblies],"* according to James Les Rowe. Navy Commander Parsons, who was in charge of the Los Alamos nuclear team, personally came to Wendover and extracted a promise from Captain James L. Rowe that he would have the bombs operable for drop by the end of July, a projected eight-month project reduced to less than a month. The team

had to work day and night to accomplish the goal.

Deak Parsons came to Wendover earlier. He was there to check the atomic bomb proximity fuses which were designed to explode at certain altitudes. 393rd Pilot George Marquardt flew Parsons and two other engineers over Wendover where they tested the fuses at different altitudes. Marquardt commented that the fuses sounded like a cap gun as they exploded. Parsons was the only person who knew how to arm the bombs.

During the last week in June, a near calamity occurred. Due to the extreme secrecy of the assembly project, a heavy tarpaulin was draped over the *"Fat Man"* prototype bomb unit while transporting it from the storage building to the loading pit. To keep from disclosing the shape, 2 x 4 lumber was placed on top of the bomb underneath the tarp. A wooden splinter on one of the boards snagged and tripped the end loop of an arming wire on the bomb.

Technician Lt. Leon Smith and the project leader, Captain James Les Rowe, immediately jumped into the pit while telling the rest of the crew to run. The two men grabbed wrenches and removed seven of eight bolts so they could swing open the plate cover-

---

The 393rd Squadron consisted of fifteen B-29s marked with a black arrowhead in a circle. They bore false markings: "497th Group insignia which was a large A painted on numbers 71, 72, 73, and 84. Airplane numbers 77, 85, 86, and 88 displayed 444th Group markings with a colored belly band while numbers 82, 89, 90, and 91 had 6th Group tail insignias and airplanes 83, 94, and 95 were marked with the 39th Group tail markings."

The pilots listed with each plane were nominal assignments. In other words, they sometimes switched plane assignments. The fifteen new, especially outfitted B-29s had arrived in May 1945 to Wendover Field for use by the 509th Composite Group, 393rd Squadron.

Aircraft number 71 was piloted by Captain John Wilson and was dubbed *Jabbitt III*. Number 72, Serial 44-27302, *Top Secret* was piloted by Lt. Charles McKnight. Number 73, Serial 44-27300, *Strange Cargo* was under command of Lt. Joseph Westover. Number 77, Serial 44-27297, *Bockscar* was piloted by Captain Frederick Bock. Captain Robert Lewis and Colonel Paul Tibbets piloted the *Enola Gay*, number 82, Serial 44-86292. Captain Ralph Taylor piloted *Full House*, number 83, Serial 44-27298 and Captain James Price piloted number 84, Serial 44-27296, named *Some Punkins* after the atomic mission. Number 85, Serial 44-27301, *Straight Flush* was captained by Claude Eatherly. Number 86, Serial 44-27299, *Next Objective* was piloted by Lt. Ralph DeVore. Number 88, Serial 44-27304, *Up an' Atom*, named after the mission was commanded by Captain George Marquardt. Lt. Charles Albury and Major Charles Sweeney captained number 89, Serial 44-27353, *The Great Artiste*. *Big Stink*, named after the atomic mission was accomplished, number 90, Serial 44-27354, was piloted by Herman Zahn. Number 91, Serial 44-27291, *Necessary Evil* was piloted by Lt. Norman Ray. Lt. Col. Tom Classen commanded number 94, Serial 44-27346, *Spook*. Captain Edward Costello piloted number 95, Serial 44-86347, *Laggin' Dragon*. The airplane commanders lived together in a quonset hut on Tinian and had been together for two years with no one injured or killed which was unusual during the war. The men of the 393rd still alive in 2003 continued to correspond in a comradery lasting sixty years.

Taken from "Field Order #13" by George Marquardt and conversations with Mrs. Bernece Marquardt.

ing the timing mechanism and quickly reset the timer. The whole thing took less than a minute.

Had such a hazard occurred a month later, the bombs might have been full of nuclear material instead of conventional explosives and would have exploded, obliterating Wendover *"and the end of World War II could have occurred later than it did and in a far different manner,"* according to Captain Rowe. Of course, the Project W-47 unit did not know at the time the exact nature of the bombs they were working on, including Captain Rowe. As mentioned before, Rowe's version is disputed by Wendover Field historian Charles Hibbard whose research indicates that Rowe was in Wendover, but that only test assemblies were there, not atomic bombs.

Sometime in the early summer of 1945, a train pulling four flat cars arrived in Wendover. Western Pacific section foreman Brent Peterson remembered that the cargo was covered with heavy canvas. There were MPs riding on each corner with loaded machine guns at the ready. Petersen wondered in hindsight if atomic bombs or pumpkins were aboard.

Nagasaki mushroom cloud. *(www.childrenofthemanhattanproject.org, Joseph Papalia)*

Meanwhile, after nine days on the sea, on July 26, the *U.S.S. Indianapolis* anchored at Tinian and off-loaded its cargo, a wooden, fifteen-foot long crate and a *"monstrously heavy bucket"* that had been chained to the steel deck of a ship cabin. The wooden crate containing the uranium atomic bomb, *"Little Boy"* was immediately put in air-conditioned storage. Three days later, the *Indianapolis* was sunk by a Japanese submarine. Three hundred men were killed instantly and 900 floated in the waters, but only 321 survived in the shark infested waters. Due to the secrecy of the mission, a rescue effort to save the survivors was not launched until five days later. A best-selling

book, *In Harm's Way* by Doug Stanton, tells the story.

On Tinian, Colonel Tibbets decided to name his plane No. 82, the *Enola Gay,* in honor of his mother, who had visited him while he was stationed in Wendover. On August 6, 1945, the *Enola Gay* left Tinian at 2:45 a.m. with twelve crew members, 7,000 pounds of fuel, and a 9,700-pound bomb named *"Little Boy."*

Two other planes accompanied the mission, including a weather plane and another with camera and scientific equipment. Number 89, *The Great Artiste,* piloted by Major Charles W. Sweeney, held sci-

In the next few days the military installations in some or all the cities named in the photograph will be destroyed by American bombs. These cities contain military installations and workshops or factories which produce military goods. The American Air Force, which does not wish to injure innocent people, now gives you a warning to evacuate the cities named and save your lives. America is not fighting the Japanese people, but is fighting the military clique which has enslaved the Japanese people. The peace which America will bring will free the people from the oppression of the military clique and mean the emergence of a new and better Japan. You can restore peace by demanding new and good leaders who will end the war. We cannot promise that only these cities will be among those attacked, but some or all will be, so heed this warning and evacuate these cities immediately.

Hundred of thousands of leaflets containing the above message were dropped over Hiroshima and Nagasaki, Japan, prior to dropping the atomic bombs. *(www.childrenofthemanhattanproject.org, Joseph Papalia)*

entific measurement equipment and Number 91, "*Necessary Evil,*" piloted by Captain George W. Marquardt contained scientific and photographic equipment. Captain Marquardt, later developed cancer in his cheek due to radiation exposure on the mission. He and his crew circled the Hiroshima site three times taking photos after the bomb was dropped. The photos for the most part did not turn out because the photographer failed to remove the camera lens cover. All the planes had previously filled several bombing missions on July 20 and 26, dropping 10,000-pound "*Pumpkins*" filled with TNT over the Japanese empire.

Two thousand miles later, "*out tumbled 'Little Boy'*" on target over Hiroshima. Navigator "Dutch" van Kirk had skillfully guided the *Enola Gay* exactly on target and within 17 seconds of schedule. It was

8:15 a.m. The *Enola Gay* went into a 155-degree diving turn to the right and 43 seconds after the bombbay door opened, at a pre-set altitude of 1,890 feet above the ground, the bomb exploded. There was an incredible fireball followed by shock waves.

Colonel Tibbets recalled: "*We were not prepared for the awesome sight that met our eyes as we turned for a heading that would take us alongside the burning devastated city. The giant purple mushroom, . . . had already risen to a height of 45,000 feet three miles above our own altitude, and was still boiling upward like something terribly alive.*

"*. . . The city we had seen so clearly in the sunlight a few minutes before was now an ugly smudge. We were all appalled . . . As we viewed the awesome spectacle below, we were sobered by the knowledge that the world would never be the same. War, the scourge of the human race since time began, now held terrors beyond belief. I reflected to myself that the kind of war in which I was engaged over Europe in 1942 was now outdated.*"

A 1995 *Newsweek* article elaborated in part: "*The Little Boy bomb generated an enormous amount of energy in terms of air pressure and heat. In addition, it generated a significant amount of radiation (Gamma ray and neutrons) that subsequently caused devastating human injuries.*

The people who saw the Little Boy bomb said 'We saw another sun in the sky when it exploded.' The heat and the light generated by the Little Boy were far stronger than bombs which they had seen before. When the heat wave reached ground level it burnt all before it, including people.

Bombing runs and observation tower at the Wendover range in 1954. *(Hill Air Force Base)*

The strong wind generated by the bomb destroyed most of the houses and buildings within a 1.5 miles radius. When the wind reached the mountains, it was reflected and again hit the people in the city center. The wind generated by Little Boy caused the most serious damage to the city and people.

The radiation generated by the bomb caused long-term problems to those affected. Many people died within the first few months and many more in subsequent years because of radiation exposure. Some people had genetic problems which sometimes resulted in having malformed babies or being unable to have children.

It is believed that more than 140,000 people died by the end of the year. They were citizens including students, soldiers and Koreans who worked in factories within the city. The total number of people who have died due to the bomb is estimated to be 200,000."

Three days later another atomic bomb, *"Fat Man"* was dropped on Nagasaki from *Bockscar* flown by the crew of Major Charles Sweeney. *"Fat Man's"* enriched plutonium components had been ferried to Tinian Island on board the 509th's B-29s. (An official version given in *Project Y: The Los Alamos Story* states: *"The active component of the Fat Man came by special C-54 transport. The HE components of two Fat Men arrived in two B-29s attached to the 509th Group, which had been held at Albuquerque for this purpose. In all cases, the active components were accompanied by special personnel to guard against accident and loss."*)

Years later, *Newsweek* summarized the bombing of Nagasaki: *"Though the amount of energy generated by the bomb dropped on Nagasaki was significantly larger than that of the Little Boy, the damage given to the city was slighter than that given to Hiroshima due to the geographic structure of the city. It is estimated that approximately 70,000 people died by the end of the year because of the bombing."* Before bombing Nagasaki, leaflets telling the populace to leave the city were dropped by the Allied forces.

Wendover Air Force Base in 1973. It was renamed in 1947, then inactivated October 1, 1949, and in 1950 became part of the Ogden Air Materiel Area. *(Hill Air Force Base)*

On August 14, Japan surrendered and the war was over, and so was the killing. A third and last available atomic bomb had been assembled and dispatched from Wendover just prior to the surrender. An operations order was sent to drop the third bomb on Kokura, Japan, on August 15. Colonel Tibbets said no definite plan had been made as to the third bomb drop other than General Curtis LeMay (former commander of Wendover Field) told him to *"get it out here,"* meaning to Tinian.

Captain John Wilson met with Captain George Marquardt's wife Bernece in the Hotel Utah coffee shop and told her that he was leaving Wendover with the third atomic bomb and swore her to secrecy. After Japan surrendered, the B-29 Wilson piloted, that was carrying the bomb, was summoned back to Wendover where the *"Fat Man"* bomb *"was disassembled and the nuclear components taken back to Los Alamos."*

On the back cover of his book *Return of the* Enola Gay, Paul W. Tibbets, Brig. General USAF Retired, is quoted as saying, *"On August 6, 1945 as the* Enola Gay *approached the Japanese city of Hiroshima, I fervently hoped for success in the first use of a nuclear type weapon. To me it*

On August 25, 1990, a 509th memorial dedication, "A Celebration for World Peace" took place at the Wendover, U.S.A. visitors' center. *(Gertrude Tripp)*

meant putting an end to the fighting and the consequent loss of lives. In fact, I viewed my mission as one to save lives rather than take them.

"The intervening years have brought me many letters and personal contact with individuals who maintain that they would not be alive if it had not been for what I did. Likewise, I have been asked in letters and to my face if I was not con- science-stricken for the loss of life I caused by dropping the first atomic bomb. To those who ask, I quickly reply, 'Not in the least.'"

A persistent rumor over the ensuing years has some members of the *Enola Gay* crew committing sui- cide or having various mental problems as a result of the guilt they felt over dropping the atomic bomb. In a 1966 interview, Paul Tibbets stated emphatically that such rumors were *"a bunch of bunk."* In retrospect,

Mrs. Bernece (George) Marquardt, who knew most of the crew members, confirmed Tibbets's statement in May 2003.

Three interesting sidebars are noted: Fifty-seven years after Japan's surrender, on August 3, 2002, Japanese blueprints for a crude atomic bomb, which was origi- nally scheduled for completion by 1945, were revealed by the widow of a Japanese scientist. Secondly, in September 2002, Bradley Rush discovered 509th atom- ic pilot Lt. Charles Albury's dogtag on the Wendover Field airport. Rush also claimed to have uncovered a buried bomb the size and shape of one of the atomic bombs. This claim has not been substantiated, although the FBI visited Wendover in the spring of 2003. Thirdly, it is interesting to note that Manhattan Project director J. Robert Oppenheimer stated in a telegram to General Leslie Groves that he could have had nineteen more atomic bombs ready by November 1945 if Groves had wanted to wait to drop the bombs.

As the war came to an end, Wendover Field *"con- sisted of 668 buildings, including a 300-bed hospital, gym- nasium, swimming pool, library, chapel, cafeteria, bowling alley, two movie theaters, guard house and 361 housing units for married officers and civilians."* The expanded base had cost the government about $13 million. The 216th Bomb Unit was transferred to Oxnard, including some of the buildings and all the nuclear bomb building tools and equipment. The bomb loading pits were filled in and covered over. By early 1946, no sign of the nuclear bomb assembly activities remained at Wendover.

Garn Anderson of Wendover commented in ret- rospect on life in Wendover in World War II. He said, *"This small town felt the impact of World War II prob- ably greater than any small community in the United States. Going from a 'sparsely settled' village to a city of almost 20,000 inhabitants was an amazing transformation.*

Sir Winston Churchill stated on August 16, 1945: *"There are those who considered that the atomic bomb should never have been used at all ... rather than throw this bomb we should have sacrificed a million Americans and a quarter of a million British in the desperate battles and massacres of an invasion of Japan. The bomb brought peace, but man alone can keep that peace."*

"Living quarters were almost non-existent necessitating converting sheds, garages, wash houses into housing. The Federal government 'was compelled' to build barracks and apartments at a rapid rate. A large supermarket was built as were a drug store, barber shop and beauty shop, bakery, nursery, a new school to replace the two-room building, a ladies ready-to-wear store in addition to the Tri-State Mercantile. There was a commissary on base and a hospital with attendant physicians, nurses and dentists. All of these were of benefit to the citizens of Wendover . . . [The hospital saved people's lives including Mary and Spike Birdzell's]. *One more benefit was the additional water the army piped into the city which helped Wendover in future years."*

Wendover bombing range July–August 1954, 461st Bomb Wing. *(Hill Air Force Base)*

A movie was made in 1952 entitled *"Above and Beyond"* which depicted life in Wendover during the war. The movie was based on a story written by Colonel Paul Tibbets and was serialized in the *Saturday Evening Post* after the war.

The stars of the movie were Robert Taylor, playing the part of Colonel Tibbets and Eleanor Parker as his wife. Some of the outdoor scenes were filmed on location at Wendover Field. Another interesting sidelight: early morning fires demolished the Wendover officers' club three times in a sixteen-month period during the war.

Author Richard Menzies in the *Nevada Magazine* summed up what happened to the airfield and Wendover after the war. He reported that *"the military presence diminished, the economic boom faded, and the little town of Wendover commenced a gradual decline, each year looking more and more like the tar paper and tin-roof railroad shanty town from which it had sprung. For many years the main industry was a potash recovery plant situated east of town on the Bonneville Salt Flats.*

"The primary tourist attraction was also the salt flats, where each August fast car enthusiasts from around the world would converge to field test their hot rods. During Speed Week, motel rooms in town would be booked solid, and occasionally a line might even form in front of the State Line, but nothing approaching the epic queue [line of persons] of 1942."

The base was used after the war for various reasons by different commands of the air force. *"Wendover Army Air Base was transferred to the Ogden Air Technical Service Command (Ogden Air Logistics Center) on December 31, 1945,"* according to the Wendover Air Base website.

Wendover was used to evaluate captured rocket types and munitions, and new weapons systems were tested. Starting in 1944, the German V-1 *"Buzz Bomb"* was tested at Wendover and the similar USAF JB-2 was developed, using minor changes to the *"Buzz Bomb."* It was so named because of the noise its pulse jet engine made. It traveled at 480 mph.

The Germans launched the V-1 rocket at England a week after D-Day in Europe. It was used as a vengeance weapon and it struck targets indiscriminately *"due to a crude guidance system."* Consequently, it killed many civilians. Fortunately, it hit only 50% of its targets. Captain Rowe of the W-47 bomb building project felt that the *"Buzz Bomb"* testing at Wendover was used to divert any curiosity away from Project W-47. The *"Buzz Bomb"* testing continued after the war, however.

The USAF was preparing to use the JB-2 at tar-

Wendover Willie V-1 rocket. *(Hill Air Force Base)*

In October 1945 Charles Freudenthal, who came to Wendover in 1943 with the 489th Bomb Group, was told to report immediately, if not sooner, back to Wendover following his return from Europe. He was given his choice of jobs at Wendover and he chose air and tech inspector on the "Buzz Bomb" project. He said that the bombs were launched with only enough fuel to fly within the boundaries of the base. A P-80 jet followed thirty seconds behind each launch in case they needed to shoot down errant radio-controlled bombs that might accidentally leave the range.

gets in Japan by launching them from B-17s. No strikes were made as dropping the atom bomb ended the war and soon after the project ended. Note: A V-1 dubbed *Wendover Willy* was on display at Hill Air Force Base Museum in 2003.

The national missile program had its origins in Wendover. A rocket systems test facility was activated at Wendover soon after the war. In 1946, ground-to-air pilotless aircraft were tested at Wendover. This

Individual KP duty after chow, 1954. *(Hill Air Force Base)*

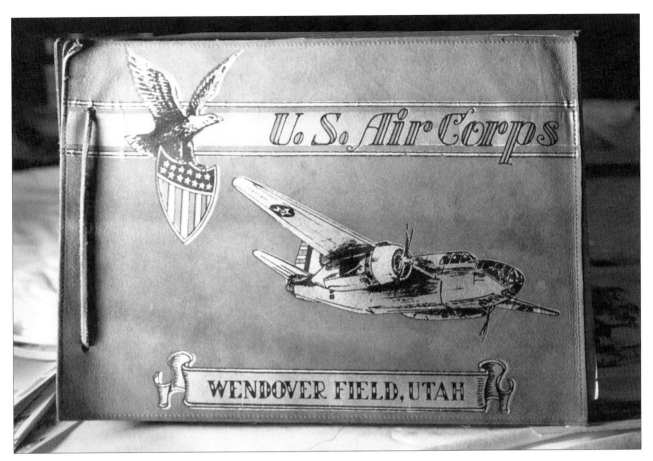

Donn Frisk's leather-bound photo album he purchased at the PX in Wendover while he was stationed there in 1941-43. The plane is a B-26. *(Donn Frisk)*

became known as the historic GAPA project headed by Boeing. It *"resulted in the first supersonic flight of an American Air Force vehicle."* The flight was executed on August 6, 1946.

Other missiles tested at Wendover were *"the Hughes TIAMAT MX-798, the 'ROC' and the 'Tarzan.'"* Subsequently, the missile program transferred to White Sands, New Mexico. The GAPA launch site and block-house were placed on the National Register of Historic Places in 1980.

In March 1947 Wendover was transferred to the Strategic Air Command for bombardment group maneuvers. Often thirty planes would leave Wendover for a ten-hour flight after which they would drop their bombs on the bombing range. Also in 1947, Wendover Army Air Base (formerly Wendover Field) was renamed Wendover Air Force Base. On October 1, 1949, the base was inactivated and eventually placed under the command of the Ogden Air Material Area in 1950.

In the early 1950s, the 25th Air Depot Wing from

Hill Air Force Base used the facilities for aerial gunnery practice. Training in low-level support operations of ground units with B-26s and B-57s soon followed in December 1953 by the 461st Bombardment Wing of the 9th Air Force, Tactical Air Command, and on July 14, 1954, *"Operation Sandstorm"* began at the Wendover base. This consisted of a six-week practice in *"rocketry, bombing, gunnery, armed reconnaissance, maximum-range and low-level navigation, transition flight training, and formation flying."* Several million dollars were spent by TAC in renovating the facilities over the next four years.

Tactical Air Command took over jurisdiction of Wendover Air Force Base on October 1, 1954, until January 1, 1958, when command was returned to Ogden Air Material Area (OOAMA). The base was renamed Wendover Air Force Auxiliary Field later the same month. The Department of the Army and the Air Force used the ranges and the air space jointly by agreement over the next few years.

The range became Hill Air Force Range in 1960.

"B-24L, 44 50030, 1944-45 Wendover, Experimental Ship bombing" is the word-for-word caption written by crew chief A. E. Inselsberger. Was this a rumored backup to the B-29s in the event their design for carrying the bomb failed? *(Gwen Inselsberger)*

The range was used from 1955 as an isolated area *"for testing air munitions, including missiles, the Minuteman ICBM, 'smart bombs,' and shelf tests of stored munitions, as well as for hazardous material storage,"* according to Charles Hibbard in the *Utah History Encyclopedia.*

In August 1961, the air force inactivated Wendover Air Force Auxiliary Field, with Hill Air Force Base assigned *"caretaker status"* for the installation. In 1971 the state of Utah tried unsuccessfully to promote the Great Salt Lake Desert as a future space port for the space shuttle flight program, including both launch and return.

In 1973, an air-to-ground gunnery range was built and in 1985 an Air Combat Maneuvering Instrumentation System was installed. This system allows simulated weapons engagements by fighter-bombers.

Air Force Systems Command took control of the range on January 1, 1979, and renamed it the Utah Test and Training Range and its management began by the 6545th Test Group at Hill Air Force Base. This group managed and evaluated *"unmanned vehicles, cruise missile recovery and systems management, support of manned air vehicles, and missile testing and evaluation."* Beginning in May 1980, the Air Launched Cruise Missile and the Ground Launched Cruise Missile were provided support at the range.

"Then in August 1977 [or June 16, 1976 in the *Utah History Encyclopedia*] *Hill Air Force Base turned over most of Wendover Air Force Auxiliary Field to the town of Wendover, Utah, retaining only a 164 acre radar site on the old base. The military career of this remote yet important airfield was at an end,"* even though the range continued to be in constant use.

An aborted attempt to rescue hostages at the U.S. Embassy in Tehran, Iran, revealed a glaring need to train military personnel for similar contingencies. Wendover offered the ideal situation of remote desert wilderness for such training. War games to prepare Rapid Deployment Forces were conducted at Nellis Air Force Base, Nevada and at Wendover, Utah. The games were dubbed *"Red Flag."* Over 9,000 men and women were deployed at Wendover's Decker Field during the 1980s. They used the same un-airconditioned mess halls, hangars and barracks as the airmen of World War II. Age and decay were taking their toll, so the field was abandoned by the military after 1988.

The conditions at Wendover airfield had changed by 2003. It was owned by Tooele County. One hundred buildings remained of the original 668, including the control tower, fire station, operations building, three squadron buildings, and six hangars.

The *Enola Gay* hangar was used as part of Historic

Wendover Airfield. The 509th held its 56th reunion in Wendover and Salt Lake City on August 2 to 5, 2001, with several hundred veterans and their families in attendance. Female WWII pilot Dora Dougherty came back for the first time along with Didi Moorman, who had also trained with Colonel Tibbets.

Plans were in the works to restore or re-create and display many of the training devices used at Wendover in World War II. Historic Wendover Airfield, Inc., a non-profit organization was organizing the effort and soliciting financial assistance, donated labor, etc. They felt that the size, scope and condition of the airfield would permit a re-creation of a historic monument *"unmatched anywhere else."*

In conclusion, there were thousands of servicemen who trained at Wendover and distinguished themselves in battle in Europe, Asia, and the Pacific. Several were awarded Distinguished Service Crosses and some earned the Medal of Honor. Many gave their lives in the cause of freedom.

A Lament to the Boys from Wendover

We are the boys from Wendover Field
Earning our meager pay
Guarding the folks with millions
For one sixty-five a day.

Out in the windswept desert
Wendover Field is the spot
Fighting the terrible dust storms
In the land that God forgot.

Out in the brush with rifles
Eating and drinking the dust
Doing the work of a chain gang
And too damn tired to cuss.

Out with the snakes and lizards
Here's where the boys get blue
Out in the windswept desert,
Two thousand miles from you.

All night the winds keep howling
It's more than one can stand
Hell folks, we're not convicts
We're defenders of this land.

For the duration we must stand it
Many years of life we'll miss
Don't let the draft board get you.
And for Heaven's sake don't enlist.

Out on this Utah desert
Wendover is the spot
Fighting terrific heat waves
In the land God forgot.

We're up at five each morning
Digging in the sand.
No, we're not convicts.
We're defenders of this land.

We spend our leisure hours
Writing to our gals,
Hoping when we return again
They're not married to our pals.

We have washed a million dishes
And have peeled as many spuds
We have our hands all blistered
From washing dirty duds.

All the inspections we have stood
Are worse than we can tell
I hope it is nice in Heaven
For I know what it's like in Hell.

When this old life is over
And we work no more
We'll do our final dress parade
On the bright and golden shore.

Then St. Peter will greet us
And suddenly he will yell,
Come in you boys from Wendover
You've served your time in Hell.

5.

Crossing the Great American Desert

"The stretch of I-80 across the salt flats between Wendover ... and
Salt Lake City is only a bore and a bother if motorists are uninformed of
all the history which has transpired here."

—Phillip I. Earl

The mountain men and trappers were the early explorers of the west. These first explorers blazed crisscrossing trails over the vast western wilderness in search of bonanzas. They, in many cases, followed trails used for centuries by Native Americans. Some were seeking precious metals and, later on, trade routes to California.

Others such as Jedediah Smith were searching for a fabled western passage to the Pacific in the form of the non-existent San Buenaventura River. The legendary lost cities full of riches and the river highway to the Pacific were not to be found, but the streams and valleys of the west were well-stocked with beaver.

At the time, beaver pelts were in great demand on the east coast and in Europe among the wealthy. Fur from the beaver's soft underbelly was trimmed, beaten, and fashioned into felt hats. A beaver pelt was worth up to $10 in the 1820s.

Mexican, American, and British fur companies quickly established outposts along major rivers and later in the mountains and watersheds of the Great Basin. There was rivalry between companies and also between the nations of America and Britain.

Consequently, according to historian Dean L. May, the *"British Hudson's Bay Company decided to keep the Americans out by eliminating their reason for being there. If the beaver were trapped out, there would be no valuable com-* *modity to attract American settlement and the land would be left to the British."* That is the reason why *"some of the earliest trappers to work in the mountains came to Utah country even though more accessible parts of the West were still rich in beaver."*

The Ashley-Henry fur trading company paid as much as $200 in yearly salary to recruit farm boys to hunt and trap in the Rocky Mountains. Some came west, paying their own expenses and working alone for a promise of greater profit. One of those who signed on the Ashley-Henry group was a young surveyor named James Clyman. He became well acquainted with the area surrounding future Wendover.

In 1831 French-born, West Point educated Captain Benjamin Louis Eulalie de Bonneville took a leave of absence from the military to explore the Oregon country and ply the fur trade. His three-year expedition experiences were published by Washington Irving in 1837 including that of his chief lieutenant Joseph R. Walker. Walker led a scouting party of forty men throughout the territory including the salt flats. He named the salt flats in honor of Bonneville even though Bonneville never saw the area.

These rugged men of the fur trade brought to the east reports of fertile lands and mild climates in Oregon and California, thus stirring the imagination of midwestern farmers. Notwithstanding the dangers

Wagons pulled by oxen similar to the Donner-Reed wagon train. *(Utah State Historical Society)*

and almost insurmountable costs involved, a flood of emigrants began wending their way westward over desert and mountain by the mid-1840s. They came on horse and mule-back, on foot sometimes pulling hand-carts, or in wagons of various shapes and sizes.

George Donner advertised for help in making the journey west in the *Sangamo Journal* on March 19, 1846. His ad read: *"Westward ho! Who wants to go to California without it costing them anything? . . . Come, Boy! You can have as much land as you want without costing you anything. The government of California gives large tracts of land to persons who move there. The first suitable persons who apply will be engaged."*

It was spring in Springfield, Illinois, and the streets were muddy as the Donners and the Reeds prepared to leave for California. James Reed owned a furniture-making business and the Donners were farmers. The Reeds and Donners were well-to-do and had a good life in Illinois but the lure of free land in a sunny climate and the prevailing political climate of Manifest Destiny created an excitement to go west. Manifest Destiny was a doctrine of territorial expansion with the goal *"to possess the whole of the continent which*

Providence has given us, for the development of our great experiment of liberty. . . ."

There was also a sense of daring in the prospect of *"encountering hostile Indians"* and the *"threat of war with Mexico."* A further sense of excitement came in the thrill of adventurous travel coupled with a race against time in order to arrive in the autumn before the snows of winter closed the passes of the Sierra Nevada Mountains. It was now or never for the Donner brothers, George and Jacob, who were approaching sixty, and for James Reed, in his mid-forties and a personal friend of Abraham Lincoln.

Several months were spent in preparing for the journey. James Reed designed their main wagon to be luxurious. It had doors at the side with portable steps leading into it. Reed built decking extensions providing additional space over each wheel. He installed a stove complete with a chimney protruding through the canvas roof.

Reed made sure the interior had a space for a small library, sewing basket, and cushioned bench seats with springs to absorb the shocks and bumps of travel on the unpaved wagon roads. There was a precious mirror, a feather bed for their ailing grandmother's comfort, and an overhead loft for the children to sleep in. The customized wagon became known as the *"Pioneer Palace Car."*

The two Donner families and the Reed family had three wagons apiece. One wagon was to haul food and other supplies. One was to live in, and one was used as a moving van, full of furniture, farm tools, fabric, and dried food.

The food necessary for the trip included an estimated 200 pounds of flour, 150 pounds of bacon, 20 pounds of sugar, 10 pounds of coffee, and 10 pounds of salt. They also packed varying amounts of trinkets for trading with the Indians, plus cornmeal, jerked meats, beans, fruit, tea, baking soda, vinegar, pickles, and mustard. They also carried coins, jewels, and textbooks. The Donners were said to have *"a quilt with ten thousand dollars in cash sewn inside."*

> "Indeed, if I do not experience something far worse than I have done, I shall say the trouble is all in getting started."
>
> —*Tamsen Donner wrote to her sister on the trail early in their trek.*

The travelers set out on April 15, 1846, from Springfield, Illinois. They covered upwards of fifteen miles per day at first. They stopped at night near streams of water or springs where they could water their animals, wash clothes, and obtain drinking water. The men tended the animals, hunted for game, and repaired the wagons. The women laundered, cooked, tended, and mended.

Breakfasts were hominy grits and bacon. Lunch was jerky and dried fruit. Meat or fish and bread were the main course for dinner. Fresh milk and butter came from the cows. Songs were sung and kids played games around the campfire. Rain storms brought muddy ruts and leaky canvas roofs on the wagons.

In June 1846 on the trail, Tamsen Donner wrote a letter to her sister in which she said, *"Indeed, if I do not experience something far worse than I have done, I shall say the trouble is all in getting started."*

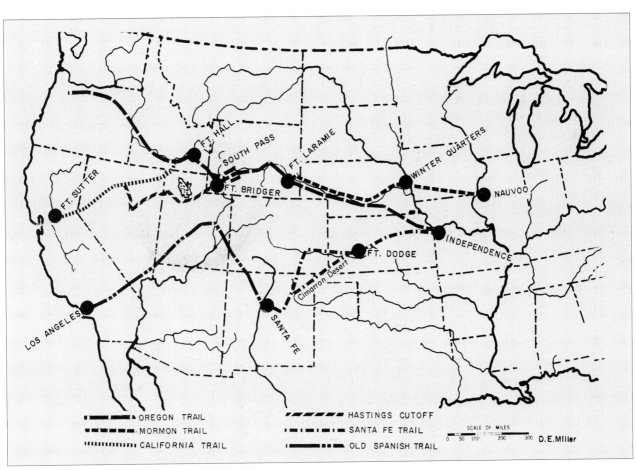

The *Hastings Cutoff* from Fort Bridger, by-passing Fort Hall as shown on David E. Miller's 1964 map. *(Utah History Atlas)*

Bonneville Salt Flats. Note the ripples in the salt.

earlier promising to come back and lead any group west following his shortcut.

Reed and the rest were aware of Captain John Charles Fremont's expedition of 1845 with Kit Carson as a guide, wherein Fremont completed the route from Skull Valley to Pilot Peak. They reported in written accounts that they had completed the route with little difficulty, although they were without heavy, slow wagons. Fremont named Pilot Peak, elevation 10,716 feet (near present-day Wendover), on this expedition.

On the hot summer day of July 20, 1846, the Donner wagon train reached *"a parting of the ways"* on their journey west to California. They had crossed the continental divide formed by the Rocky Mountains, experiencing a gentle rise and fall on each side. The travelers had to decide whether to go left to Fort Hall and follow the main road, time-tested by thousands of emigrants headed west to settle Oregon and more recently California, or turn right and save nearly 400 miles by following what came to be known as the Hastings Cutoff across the salt desert. They were at the halfway point on their 2,500-mile journey from Illinois to California.

The party was about to make a perilous decision. The majority of men and boys over the age of fourteen voted to take the shortcut. The decision was far from unanimous however. The women tended to disagree that the shortcut was the route to go but they were not allowed to vote. One young bachelor teamster earlier hired by the Donners left at that point and traveled the Fort Hall route.

The majority sided with James Reed who argued that the cutoff would save them a month in travel time. Reed reinforced his argument by reading a letter from Lansford Hastings who promoted the shortcut in his guidebook entitled *"The Emigrants' Guide, to Oregon and California."* Lansford sent the letter eastward a week

Fremont was scouting a route to California from the Salt Lake valley. It is interesting to note that historian Jesse Unruh stated that *"California rather than Oregon became the first goal of the majority of those traveling westward after 1846."* Even though the journey would cost more than it would to buy the finest Illinois farm land, *"the dusty roads to the west swelled with the flocks, herds, and wagons of Midwestern farmers."*

The Donner party would probably have known too that Jedediah S. Smith had successfully crossed the southern edge of the salt desert with two fur trappers in 1827. Smith's written report should have been forbidding enough.

Smith wrote *"After travelling twenty days from the east side of Mount Joseph, I struck the southwest corner of Great Salt Lake, travelling over a country completely barren and destitute of game. We frequently travelled without water, sometimes for two days over sandy deserts where there was no sign of vegetation, and when we found water in some of the rocky hills, we most generally found some Indians who appeared the most miserable of the human race, having nothing to subsist on (nor any clothing) except grass-seed, grasshoppers, etc. When we arrived at the Salt Lake, we had but one horse and one mule remaining, which were so feeble and poor that they could scarce carry the little camp equipage which I had along; the balance of my horses I was compelled to eat as they gave out."*

Other published encounters with the salt desert occurred in 1833 as mentioned earlier when explorer Joseph Walker and a detachment of soldiers sent by Captain Benjamin L. E. Bonneville circled the northern edge of the desert going from Wyoming to California and also in 1841 when thirty-four members of the Bartleson-Bidwell wagon train *"skirted the north end"* of the desert.

The Bartleson group lost their oxen and abandoned their wagons before reaching the fresh-water springs at the base of Pilot Peak. They journeyed past Silver Zone Pass west of Wendover and on to Johnson Springs. They continued their journey on foot until they reached Sutter's Fort in California.

Historian Dean L. May noted: *"No whites before them [meaning the Bartleson group] had driven wagons*

Mirages on the Salt Flats

Edwin Bryant gave a detailed description of three mirages his group encountered at various points along their journey across the salt plain. He began his description from the vantage point of a trail on the western side of the Cedar Mountains: "From the western terminus of this ominous-looking passage we had a view of the vast desert-plain before us, which, as far as the eye could penetrate, was of a snowy whiteness, and resembled a scene of wintry frost and icy desolation. Not a shrub or object of any kind rose above the surface for the eye to rest upon. The hiatus in the animal and vegetable kingdoms was perfect. It was a scene which excited mingled emotions of admiration and apprehension...."

Later in the morning as they drew nearer the desert, Bryant recorded: "Pausing a few moments to rest our mules, and moisten our mouths and throats from the scant supply of beverage in our powder-keg, we entered upon this appalling field of sullen and hoary desolation. It was a scene... entirely new to us,... frightfully forbidding and unearthly in its aspects ...."

Bryant described in great detail each mirage. The first illusion commenced with the grandeur of forested lands with lakes interspersed among the groves. There were palatial gardens and ornamented, "beautiful villas." Then "a vast city" with marbled columns and magnificent "domes, spires, and turreted towers" arose "upon the horizon of the plain." The phenomena appeared as an indescribable dream which he said could not be adequately portrayed in written prose. Bryant finally observed that the first mirage occurred where irregularities on the surface of the plain were apparent.

The second mirage was in the form of a "gigantic moving object" at a distance of "six or eight miles." It was moving parallel to their group and because of its enormous size caused considerable speculation among them. It was postulated that it was the "ghost of a mammoth" or a lost "cyclopean nondescript animal." It followed them for over an hour then disappeared over the horizon.

Later in the afternoon "... there appeared upon the plain one of the most extraordinary phenomena, I dare to assert, ever witnessed." In summary, Bryant saw fifteen to twenty men and horses moving diagonally toward him and his party of men. Some were on foot and some were mounted.

Soon there were "... three or four hundred and [they] appeared to be marching forward with the greatest action and speed." Bryant called others of his group to come forward and he asked if they saw the same. They had seen the army but one man said he noticed that the figures appeared and disappeared over time and were nothing but optical illusions.

Bryant decided, after an hour of experimentation wherein he learned that the phantom moved in the same direction and at the same speed as he did, that the figures were their "own shadows, produced and reproduced by the mirror-like composition impregnating the atmosphere and covering the plain." Even so he noted that the apparition "excited those superstitious emotions so natural to all mankind."

A century later, a soldier during World War II noted seeing similar illusions on the salt flats. In 1941 Private Byron Dussler wrote: "What fantastic mirages one sees... I saw an enormous lake, with islands in it of orange colored rocks rising abruptly from the water. On the shores reeds and rushes grew, but all the colors were wrong. Only in dreams could one see such an unnatural place. Of course, it was unapproachable; it always receded into the distance, or else, disappeared altogether. I saw distant trees, but as we drove toward them, they vanished."

Such encounters are common when crossing the great white plain!

across the Great Salt Lake desert or refreshed themselves at the Pilot Peak springs. But most important, they were the first sizeable immigrant party to make their way across the continent from the states to the Far West. Theirs was, by any measure, an epic journey."

It is not known whether the Donners knew of these excursions but surely Lansford Hastings must have. Three weeks before the Donners reached the crossroads and while still at Fort Laramie, famous mountain man and surveyor James Clyman warned the Donner party of the dangers associated with the cutoff.

Clyman had explored the trail with Hastings in early 1846 and wrote in his diary: *"This is the most desolate country on the whole globe, there being not one spear of vegetation, and of course no kind of animal can subsist."* James Reed's response to Clyman was: *"There is a nearer route, and it is of no use to take so much of a roundabout course,"* referring to the main route through Fort Hall.

Consequently, the group lead by George and Jacob Donner and James Reed followed Hastings's advice. They went south west to the Salt Lake valley and on to the west desert. Hastings made the route sound easy in his *Emigrant's Guide*, saying, *"The most direct path would be to leave the Oregon route, about two hundred miles*

east of Fort Hall; then bearing west-south west, to the Salt Lake; and thence continuing down to the bay of San Francisco."

Hastings mentioned that the salt desert was forty miles to cross and could be done in two days' time. He had not been over the route himself when he published his recommendations in 1845. One bit of advice included in his pamphlet which the Donners did not heed said *"emigrants should, invariably, arrive at Independence, Missouri, on or before the 15th day of April, so as to be in readiness to enter upon the journey."* The Donners were only just leaving Springfield, Illinois, on April 15th.

Hastings rode east in the spring of 1846 to divert traffic across his proposed cutoff. Using Fremont's recommendations (and Fremont's personal fame) that wagon trains could traverse the new trail and with the promise of personal guidance, Hastings sent a letter east and persuaded *"four companies of immigrants"* to pull *"away from the main stream of traffic and head southwest toward Echo Canyon. They were soon to find that Hastings promised much more than the terrain could deliver."*

The first group was the Bryant-Russell party made up of nine men on horseback. They found rough going

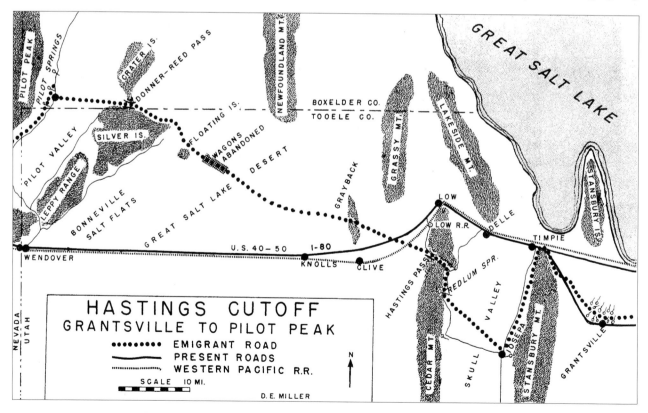

Hastings Cutoff used by the Donner-Reed Party in 1846. (*Utah History Atlas, David E. Miller*)

as they passed through Weber Canyon. On August 5 they began the forty-mile crossing of the desert to Pilot Peak and made it from there to California. Mountain man James Hudspeth told them as they looked across the desert to Pilot Peak, *"Now boys, put spurs to your mules and ride like Hell!"*

The Bryant-Russell company was followed by a larger group of forty wagons lead by Swiss immigrant Heinrich Lienhard along the same route down Weber Canyon and onto the salt flats on August 18.

Last fresh water before entering the Great American Desert. *(Utah State Historical Society)*

Lienhard's company passed twenty-four wagons that had been left on the desert by the Harlan-Young wagon train who crossed the salt August 16-18. Lienhard's group thought they saw an apparition in the form of a monstrous black snake but eventually came to know that it was a group of men with oxen, mules, and horses coming back to recover abandoned wagons.

> "Here by early morning light, the Donner party got their first close view of the great desert and came face-to-face with 'the elephant,' that mystical beast so frequently mentioned in pioneer journals as the symbol of disaster."
>
> —Charles Kelly

Mr. Lienhard said that his leading yoke of oxen was in danger of breaking their horns on the wheels of the wagon ahead of his. They were attempting to seek shade in the wagon's shadow. Lienhard wrote in his journal of the Hastings Cutoff that it *"might much better be called Hastings' Longtripp."*

The Donner wagon train was, thus, one of several groups of the summer crossing the Great American Desert. They made steady progress until they got to impassable Weber Canyon (Utah). By now they had grown in numbers to eighty-seven individuals, even

though they had lost the mother of Margaret Reed, Sarah Keyes, in Kansas where she died. They had stocked up on supplies at Fort Bridger and missed several warnings about the hazardous trail ahead.

Letters written by Edwin Bryant to his friend James Reed were not delivered to Reed by Jim Bridger. Perhaps Bridger wanted emigrants to take the shortcut giving him the business he needed to keep his trading post open. Perhaps Hastings had paid Bridger to promote his route. The fact remains that Bryant sent several letters saying the cutoff was almost impossible, even for his own men who were riding mules with no wagons. *"Reed never received those warnings."*

At the top of Weber Canyon, they found cliffs on either side of a river. They waited while James Reed went to find Hastings. Hastings refused to return and help them as he was busy helping others cross but suggested a new route through what later was named Emigration Canyon. *"He took Reed to the summit of the Oquirrh Mountains and pointed out the way they should go."*

They had lost over a week of precious time waiting, and more days lowering their wagons over the canyon walls after which they had to hack their way through dense thickets *"day after torturous day"* at the rate of two miles per day. They spent nearly a month following the shortcut and their energy was gone as

Pilot Mountain as travelers saw it when they drew closer. *(Utah State Historical Society)*

were much of their food supplies. Their oxen were not fit to cross the next obstacle, the salt desert.

They also lost one of their number when twenty-five-year-old invalid Luke Halloran died. They buried him near the black rock on the shore of the Great Salt Lake. Luke had been abandoned by another wagon train and mother Tamsen Donner had insisted that he come with the Donners. He gave the Donners a trunk containing $1,500 just before he died. The money would be no help to them in getting through what lay ahead.

The shore of the salt lake became their road as they made their way farther west through salt marshes and came to the clear waters of Twenty Wells (Grantsville) where they refreshed themselves, grazed their animals on the *"fine grass,"* and filled their vessels in preparation for what they thought were forty miles of salt desert.

John Breen later wrote *"We should have wintered there,"* referring to the beautiful Tooele Valley. Instead, they harvested grass in bundles for the upcoming desert and filled the maximum load of two or three wooden, ten-gallon barrels per wagon with water. They knew it would not be enough as an individual ox can drink twenty gallons a day. They realized they would have to ration the water.

As the eighty-six individuals traveled on they came to a board with a paper attached. The paper had been picked to pieces by birds but Tamsen Donner pieced it together. It read *"Two Days Two Nights Hard Driving Cross Desert To Next Water"* in Hastings's handwriting. They noted the *"two nights"* part of the message which meant that the desert was farther across than they had been led to believe.

After skirting the Stansbury Mountains, they reached fresh water near Iosepa in two days more of travel where they rested again for a day while gathering grass and filling containers with water. They continued on across Skull Valley through the low Hastings Pass of the Cedar Mountains and onto the salt desert.

Author Charles Kelly noted: *"Here by early morning light, the Donner party got their first close view of the great desert and came face to face with 'the elephant,' that mystical beast so frequently mentioned in pioneer journals as the symbol of disaster."* Pilot Mountain was still sixty miles ahead. It would take them six more agonizing days and nights to get there.

Sandy dunes were encountered first; then the hard, glistening salt flats came next. The clouds of alkali dust were suffocating to their lungs and caustic to their skin. The hardness of the salt crust was deceiving. Underneath, the clay was wet and mucky. The wagons were heavy and sank in the sand and mud below the salt crystal surface. The mud clung to the hooves of the oxen in *"great gobs"* making every step difficult for the already exhausted oxen.

The Donner party spent the next four days and nights in agonizing travel to cross the sixty miles of salt flat. The oxen expended enormous effort as they were forced across the mire. The people hallucinated, seeing mountains looming up in the middle of the desert and expecting shady trees, green grass, and cool springs to quench their thirst; none of which materialized. Desert mirages ahead falsely provided hope of shimmering lakes of water. Still, *"the desert stretched on."*

The Reed entourage was lagging far behind with their heavy wagons and a decreasing supply of water. James Reed saddled his horse and rode ahead to find the end of the desert and water. Before he left he instructed his family to suck on sugar lumps moistened with peppermint oil or to suck on flattened bullets. He also admonished them to drink milk from their milk cows. As he moved along the way, he was alarmed by what he saw. Those ahead had already unyoked their oxen and were pushing them forward to find water, leaving their wagons behind. Reed rode eight hours straight across thirty miles of salt before he came to water.

Mr. Reed returned the next morning with some water for his family. His teamsters by now had unhooked the oxen and begun driving them to water. The oxen soon stampeded and disappeared over the desert following the smell of water. By nightfall the Reeds were desperate and decided that they must walk, leaving behind all their belongings. The children began to fall from weariness and thirst. They came to the Jacob Donner wagon and found them asleep.

The Reeds spread a shawl on the alkali sand and cuddled close as a bitter, cold wind howled across the desert. They laid another shawl over the children and Mr. Reed summoned their five faithful dogs to lie on top of the children to provide further warmth. Virginia Reed who was a twelve-year-old child at the time later wrote in a letter to her cousin, *"if it haden bin for the dogs we would have Frosen."*

They slept for a time until they were awakened by the dogs barking. They heard a strange rushing sound which turned out to be a thirst-crazed steer bolting *"by in the dead of night."* James Reed drew his pistol to protect his family if the animal should charge them, but it ran off into the dark. The children were upset and they slept little the rest of the night.

The next morning, Mrs. Reed and the children joined the Donners in their wagon for the remainder of the ride to Pilot Springs. Historian Dean May picks up the rest of the journey. *"Out of the mud they slogged at last and onto a low, rocky pass between Silver Island and Crater Island, two fantastically stark and rugged outcroppings. Here was relief at last; a few stunted sage and greasewood bushes seemed to testify that the lifeless flats were behind. There's a small spring under a ledge here, but they did not find it. No matter. They pressed on believing that Pilot Springs was just ahead.*

"But as they topped the low pass, they gazed with horror at ten more miles of mud flats stretching between them and water. With men and animals near exhaustion and with the spring-fed willows in plain sight but so desperately far away across flats, crossing those ten miles must have been sheer agony.

"Emigrants and animals slogged twenty-eight miles to water beyond the area where many could pull wagons no farther." The remaining starving oxen were unyoked and slaughtered for a little meat. Milk cows were put under yoke with little success. The bedraggled travelers stumbled forward on foot. Eliza Donner later recalled, *"mothers carrying their babes in their arms, and fathers with weaklings across their shoulders."*

They could see snow-capped Pilot Peak as it loomed larger and larger until they spotted the green at the foot of the mountain where the spring was located. Upon reaching it, they finally were able to lie down at the edge and drink of the cool fresh water, and the children to play in it and bathe in it.

Three charred wheel hubs from the remains of James Reed's Pioneer Palace wagon. *(Utah State Historical Society, Charles Kelly)*

They found fresh water at last at Pilot Springs. *(Utah State Historical Society)*

Some wanted to immediately move on west, but the Reeds wanted to search for their oxen. They spent a week in fruitless search but couldn't find their animals. By the end of the week, the camp was known as the *"Mad Woman Camp because all the women were mad with anger."* They were tired of waiting.

The Reeds had to settle for retrieving one wagon full of their provisions. The Pioneer Palace wagon was left behind with all its furniture and other luxuries. They buried much of it in the salt to prevent theft. The unbroken looking-glass was among the cache they abandoned hoping to return one day and reclaim it. They divided their provisions with others of the company and moved on.

Dean May described the result of the crossing. *"Some wagons were recovered by teams backtracking from Pilot Springs; five were left forever in the desert. There is no record of how many animals were lost; one survivor put it at thirty-six. James Reed entered the desert with nine yoke of oxen, two to a yoke. He left it with one ox and a cow. 'Losing nine yoke of cattle here,' he later wrote, 'was the first of my sad misfortunes.'"* Reed was later banished from the train for killing another emigrant in an unfortunate argument.

The delays in crossing the Wasatch Mountains and the salt desert were costly. But, there were more heartaches to come. They became snowbound while crossing the Sierra Nevada Mountains in late October,

while only 100 miles from their destination at Sutter's Mill. *"Many perished of starvation and exposure. Others survived by cooking and eating their boots, harness, and the flesh of dead members of the party."*

Forty-four individuals lived to reach California. Most of the survivors lived long, prosperous, and productive lives. The James Reed family had a fine home and servants in California. George and Tamsen Donner and Jacob and Elizabeth Donner perished in the Sierra Nevada Mountains, but their children were adopted by the Reeds, a Swiss couple, and some of their older siblings who married young. John Breen amassed a fortune in the gold rush of 1849. And so the stories go of the survivors' lives.

Virginia Reed summed up the crossing when she wrote to her cousin, *"O Mary I have not rote you half of the truble we have had but I have rote you anuf to let you now that you don't now what truble is . . . but Don't let this letter dishaten [dishearten] anybody never take no cutofs and hury along as fast as you can."*

There were others who followed the trail across the salt, but most were discouraged after the tragedy of the Donner party. Author Dean May said, *"News of the Donner tragedy circulated among westering emigrants, but did not entirely dissuade travel over the salt desert. Gold fever lured some 500 people over that route in 1850, though few with wagons."*

Captain Howard Stansbury led a government survey party in 1849 along the Bartleson route to Pilot Peak. He returned eastward along the route of the Donner group. He found the remains of their wagons, property and oxen.

The California 1849 gold rush created a flood of travelers. Some of them brought and abandoned wagons and oxen on the salt flats. In 1854 Lieutenant E. G. Beckwith surveyed for a railroad route farther south on the edge of the salt desert, and in 1859 Captain J. H. Simpson looked for a better route south of the salt flats through Callao and Ibapah. His route became the one used by the Pony Express and Overland Stage. *"The salt flats were left to wind, sun, and memories."*

In 1884, 29-year-old Thomas Stevens arrived on a transcontinental bicycle ride. He pedaled his 50-inch, front-wheeled bike around the northern end of the Great Salt Lake as he followed wagon roads across the alkali flats. He ended up walking a third of the distance. No one, so far, had dared to cross the southern route used years before by the hapless wagons of the Donner party.

In 1896 publisher William Randolph Hearst planned a publicity stunt to send a message via bicycle from San Francisco to New York. He had William D. Rishel of Salt Lake map a route across the salt flats.

Rishel at the time *"considered himself the toughest hunk of bone and muscle west of the Mississippi River."* He was a champion cross-country wheelman or bicycler from the state of Wyoming during the 1880s. He was also president of the Cheyenne Bicycle Club. Bicycle clubs were popular in the early 1880s.

Big Bill Rishel was in charge of a leg of a relay race between Denver and Washington, D.C., in 1894. The relay race was run to demonstrate the use of bicycles for dispatch in the army. The experiment proved successful enough to warrant promoting a transcontinental relay between San Francisco and New York.

The U.S. Army, Stearns & Co. which manufactured a Yellow Fellow bike, and William Randolph Hearst, owner of the *San Francisco Examiner* and the *New York Journal,* cooperated in the undertaking. They enlisted Big Bill Rishel to map out the trail between Truckee, California, and Kearney, Nebraska.

Rishel found that the old wagon roads across the Nevada and Utah deserts were forgotten so he decided to use the railroad right-of-way. The ride began on a summer day in 1896 in San Francisco amidst the fanfare of bands. The first part of the journey was on the existing roads. In Nevada, his riders used the shoulders along the tracks or bumped along over the ties.

Author Charles Kelly reported that *"Rishel rode up and down the line on trains preparing relays and checking his riders. Sometimes they got into difficulties and Bill had to take over. On one such occasion, trying to make up lost time, he was riding at night when he ran into a trestle and wrecked his bicycle. He had to carry it on his back to the next station."*

By the time they reached Utah, the race was way behind schedule. Bill decided that the race must take a

Big Bill Rishel on his bicycle. *(Utah State Historical Society)*

shortcut across the salt desert rather than following the railroad north around the desert and the Great Salt Lake.

The desert stretched before him for sixty miles of level surface. He took a trial spin and found it to be *"smoother than pavement."* An old-timer tried to dissuade him, telling him that it would be suicide to attempt the crossing. There were forty miles of salt followed by sixty miles of rolling hills and only one small spring along the way, if he could find it.

Bill decided to risk it himself, not asking the other relay riders to join him. Charles A. Emise volunteered to go with him. They set out at 2 a.m. with two canteens of water and two sandwiches each. The moon was bright and the miles went by fast at first *"with little effort."*

At dawn, the men were still moving forward easily. They stopped and ate a sandwich and downed a canteen of water. As they continued on, the sun grew hot and they were surrounded by a mirage of shimmering liquid. Suddenly, Bill lurched forward as his bike tire was grabbed by sticky, slimy mud.

There was nothing to do but trudge forward carrying their bikes on their backs. Sometimes Bill carried both bikes. They emptied their canteens under the hot sun and continued to plug along. They found a succession of mud and sand followed by short stretches where they could ride.

They came to a series of sand dunes after they had covered fifty miles and the going got even slower. The hours went by endlessly and they became obsessed with finding the small spring they had been told about. The hills looked completely barren with no sign of green. Emise finally noticed a small animal trail and followed it in the hope it would lead to water. It did after following it for a mile or so. The spring, Cook's Spring, was only a tiny drip.

It took them half an hour to collect a cupful and four hours to quench their thirst. They ate their remaining sandwiches and continued on their way for the last forty miles of the journey. Their last hurdle was the hordes of mosquitoes and other insects which attacked them when they reached the marshy areas near the Great Salt Lake.

They reached Grantsville at midnight after twenty-two hours on the salt desert. They had achieved a first. The first southern crossing of the Great Salt Desert on bicycles! Rishel understandably felt that the desert crossing was impractical for the cyclists and so he surveyed a course around the north end of the lake. *"Six hundred cyclists, riding in relays, completed the transcontinental trip in thirteen days."*

Rishel later promoted a shortcut across the desert as an automobile route. In 1907, he looked west from the edge of the salt flats and observed that the *"whole desert was covered with a sheet of water."* He gave up the idea of the road until he did some more investigating and found that the sheet of water was *"only a magnificent mirage."* A conductor on the newly-built Western Pacific Railroad informed him that there was no water on the desert.

Eighteen years later the road became a reality. Governor George Dern cut the tape in a ceremony which opened the Wendover Cutoff/Victory Highway across the Salt Flats. It was described as a graveled road protected from undermining water by a mud-filled trench (see chapter one).

Since that time, west desert crossings have become uneventful. The 120-mile westward journey from Salt Lake City to Wendover takes motorists ninety minutes on a smooth ribbon of freeway. Air-conditioned cars make the journey one of comfort whether in the heat of summer or the bitter cold of winter.

6.

The Bonneville Speedway
"A Wild Ride on a Sea of Salt Somewhere in the Middle of Utah's Desert"

"I can't begin to compare the salt flats with the pictures.
It looks exactly like something you'd expect to find on the moon. It's really
eerie . . . It's like no other experience on earth. The salt is so white and so flat and
the cars are so fast that you have trouble believing it's all real."

—Wester Potter in *Utah Historical Quarterly*, Fall 1997

The Bonneville Salt Flats have been described as one of the most unusual places in Utah, if not the world. The first impression of British racer George Eyston was of being on Arctic ice with a hot African sun glaring dazzlingly down. He noted that the immensity of the place was overwhelming.

Others have surreallistically felt they were on a moonscape or some other planet. The salt is hard enough in places that it can be cut with a chain saw. The salt can also be treacherously thin in other areas, and the mud sticky underneath.

Modern travelers who stop at one of two eastbound or westbound rest stops seven miles east of Wendover will read a plaque which describes the Bonneville Speedway. It reads in part: *"Bonneville Speedway. Eighty feet wide, ten miles long with a black stripe down the middle* [the desert where the speedway is located is one hundred fifteen miles in length and is 40 miles wide in comparison]. *Due to the curvature of the earth, it is impossible to see from one end of the course to the other.*

"Timing of world land speed runs is under the jurisdiction of the U.S. Automobile Club. World land speed record times represent an electronically timed average of two runs over the measured mile within a one hour time period—one run in each direction.

According to the plaque, *"The first land speed record on the Bonneville Salt Flats was set September 3, 1935, by Sir Malcolm Campbell. His speed was 301.13 m.p.h."* Campbell was the first person to go over 300 miles per hour. He said of the speedway: *"These vast salt flats are the future testing grounds of those inevitable developments in racing engines on whose results we shall base the practical everyday lessons which will govern the motor car and, to a certain extent, the aeroplane."*

The world of racing on the salt flats had its beginnings many years prior to 1935. Bill Rishel, the first man to cross the salt flats on a bicycle, was involved in the origins of the race track on the salt flats. In 1911 Rishel and his Wendover friend Ferg [Ferdinand] Johnson raced a Packard touring car at unheard of speeds of up to fifty-four miles per hour. Rishel remembered: *"We were all alone in the world. The immensity and the solitude were overpowering and the velocity of the car was fantastic."*

Rishel also accompanied A. L. Westgard of the National Trails Association on a car run over the salt

Teddy Tetzlaff on the salt flats with his Blitzen Benz in 1914 next to goggled Governor William Spry. *(Utah State Historical Society)*

beds. The nationally regarded Westgard declared Bonneville *"the greatest speedway on the Earth."* His declaration fell on deaf ears at the time.

Attempts at setting unofficial land speed records on the salt flats began as early as 1914. Teddy Tetzlaff was a nationally known race car driver who traveled 141 miles an hour for the first unofficial speed record for a measured mile on the salt flats. He drove a Blitzen Benz race car. He also drove Utah governor William Spry on a high speed ride over the salt flats.

Barnstorming across the United States was popular at the time and Ernie Morrass took his fleet of eight or nine race cars all over the country. They competed on horse racing tracks at state fairs and such. Auto racing was just coming into vogue in the east and in Florida. He owned a Blitzen Benz which set a record for traveling a mile in a little over twenty-five seconds at Ormond Beach (later Daytona Beach, Florida).

A group of sportsmen in Salt Lake set up an exhibition run on the salt for the Blitzen Benz. They sold 150 tickets and billed it as a *"thrilling, soul-gripping speed contest."* Spectators were encouraged to bring their own watches and *"get the kick of a lifetime."*

A flagman was placed at each end of a measured mile. The official timer stood at the half-mile position where he could see the flag at each end. He clicked his watch when the first flag dropped and again when the second flag moved down. The speed of 141.73 mph was an unofficial world's record by one-fifth of a second. There was no official sanction of the record.

World War I set back further attempts on the salt for another eleven years until 1925 when Ab Jenkins, driving a Studebaker, beat a special excursion train by ten minutes in a race across the flats (see story in chapter one). After that time the Bonneville Salt Flats

Race driver Wilbur D'Alene with his *Marmon Wasp* racer on the salt flats in 1914. He raced a 19.2-second half mile. *(Utah State Historical Society)*

attracted racers from throughout the world and became the site of numerous land speed records. The attraction for these racers was and is due to the hard, flat, and expansive surface.

It all started in 1910 for young Utah carpenter David Abbott Jenkins when he headed west to Reno on his Yale motorcycle at sixty miles per hour, determined to witness a prizefight. He may have been the first to ride a motor vehicle across the salt flats as he bumped and jumped along the wooden railroad ties. He claimed that it was a bigger thrill than racing his automobiles on the salt.

Newsreel movies were rolling on the salt in the 1930s to record for posterity the historic world land speed records. *(Marvin Jenkins)*

In 1932 Ab Jenkins raced his automobile an average speed of 112.935 miles per hour over a 24-hour period without relief. He traveled 2,710 (2,827 according to George Eyston) miles during those 24 hours. This record was not recognized by the American Automobile Association. He slept on a cot in the upstairs of the Western Pacific Railroad Station because there were no other facilities in Wendover. The following year on August 6-7, 1933, he drove a stripped down (fenderless & windshieldless), 12-cylinder Pierce Arrow in setting the 24-hour record of 117.77 miles per hour. This time it was official. He had discontinued his bread-and-butter cross-country racing in 1931 in the interest of safety because he said that highways were becoming too crowded.

Captain George Eyston and Ab's son Marv recalled that Jenkins used a note pad and pencil attached to the horn to communicate with his pit crew. He would scribble a note and toss it to the crew as he neared the pit. Notes might say *"How do my rear tires look?"* or *"Get me a pint of ice cream,"* or *"Mouse on the backstretch; catch it."* His replies came as written notes on a chalk board. Incidentally, he tried retrieving a sack of ice cream while traveling at 100 mph and obliterated the bag and its contents. On top of that, it numbed his arm for several hours!

It is amazing to note that 54-year-old Ab set the 1933 endurance record and many subsequent records alone, without relief drivers. He

Official timers at the starting line. *(Marvin Jenkins)*

Smoothing out the raceway in 1937. Inset: Blair Lamus, who helped design and maintain the speedway. *(Marvin Jenkins)*

itable gesture for which he became well known." When he finally climbed from his car, the crowd was amazed because he was clean shaven. He had used a safety razor and tube of shaving cream slipped to him during his last pit stop by his son Marvin.

In those early years Jenkins and his crew erected a tent city on the salt for six weeks at a time. He hired a chef to feed upwards of eighty-five people per day and he always had a plane on hand in case of an accident. The track was lit for endurance runs by burning twenty smudge pots of oil

drove the 1933 run while enduring a violent wind and rainstorm during the 22nd hour of the race. Everyone else sought shelter in cars or under canvas, as the tents had been dropped so they wouldn't blow away. The people in their cars had to push on their brakes to prevent being blown across the salt. Half-way through the run, the black and silver roadster went *"into a wicked swerve."* Jenkins pressed forward until he came to the pit three miles away. Three minutes later he was on his way again with the fuel and oil topped off! During the race, ruts in the track had to be filled with crushed rock.

When he finished, he had beaten a French man by 103 miles for the record and word was sent to Paris, where international records have to be approved by the Federation International de'l Automobile (F.I.A.). In the meantime, a rumor reached Europe that Jenkins had been disqualified. The French motorists *"refused to believe in this record."* They declared that no one man could single-handedly drive for twenty-four hours straight going 110 miles an hour. It had previously taken five Europeans racing as a team of relief drivers to set world speed records. Jenkins felt that the salt came to the public's attention with that 1933 endurance run.

Before he finished he raced for ninety minutes more to reach the 3,000-mile mark after giving the timers *"a raised hand that pointed straight ahead—an inim-*

Mormon Ab Jenkins was interested in clean living and safety first. *(Marvin Jenkins)*

spaced evenly around the ten-mile perimeter.

One member of Jenkins's entourage was Blair Lamus. Lamus was born in California in 1902. He had only two years of high school education and he worked with his father, Ed, in road construction, the potash plant, and a general contracting business. He lived in Wyoming, Montana, and Utah. He was employed in Wendover and Knolls in 1930 by the state highway department.

Lamus and *"Jenkins met and by 1933 we find Lamus working on his own time to lay out the first race course for Jenkins. He had a part in every major speed trial from then until his death in 1955"* according to author Garn Anderson.

Anderson further informs readers that *"Jenkins was a native Utahn from Spanish Fork. He was born in 1883, dying in 1956 at the age of 73. Shortly before his death he drove a stock Pontiac a distance of 2,841 miles in 24 hours for an average of 118.375 mph. This run broke all then existing unlimited and class c stock car records, to climax for Jenkins a racing career which began in 1906."* He was popular enough that he was elected mayor of Salt Lake City in 1940 to a four-year term without spending money or campaigning.

As a racer Jenkins was interested in safety as well as the supremacy of speed. He will be remembered for his never-ending promotion of the salt flats as the place to race. He was also known as a mannerly gentleman who avoided vulgarity and vices such as alcohol and tobacco, which he attributed to his Mormon upbringing.

When racing, Ab quenched his thirst through tubes attached to two canteens of water hanging in a pocketed canvas on the door of the car. His nourishment was milk and orange juice while driving the

Ab wrote notes when he needed ice cream, orange juice, etc. and tossed the notes to his crew when he passed by the pit. *(Marvin Jenkins)*

endurance run. He used a powder puff to wipe salt and sweat from his face, eyes, and goggles. He covered his hands and face with *"a thick coating of grease,"* and wore cotton duck pants and shirt, a leather jacket, and a cotton skullcap.

Ab covered 3,053 miles in twenty-four hours at an

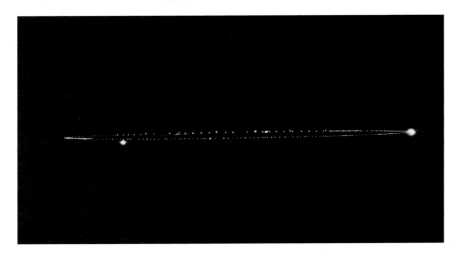

Ab Jenkins's endurance track lit at night. The night course had smudge pots every 1,000 feet and one-inch diameter "cat eyes" on four-foot laths every 100 feet. The speedway had to be re-surveyed each year and was never located in the same place exactly. There were always two round tracks, one for night and one for day, and they were designed to cross at the timer's stand. *(Marvin Jenkins)*

Pit stop for the *Ab Jenkins Special*. (Marvin Jenkins)

in a Chrysler and broke seventy-two Class B records in all. They told the press that they were impressed with the salt flats.

Sir Malcolm Campbell's single visit in 1935 helped put the salt flats on the map. However, Ab Jenkins had set the stage over several previous years and he was the one who invited Campbell to the salt flats. Jenkins visited Campbell for three weeks in Florida after sending him a professionally narrated movie film of his runs on the salt. Jenkins assured Campbell that a run of over 300 miles per hour was possible on the salt. Ab told him that he had designed a race course thirteen miles long and at least three miles wide on solid salt that had held up when driven on by a state highway truck loaded with ten tons of gravel. He convinced Campbell. The previous year, Jenkins had convinced Reed Railton, designer of Campbell's *Bluebird* and Cobb's *Railton Special*, that the salt flats was the only way to go. Speedster Captain George Eyston paid tribute to

average of 127.229 miles per hour on August 17, 1934, breaking his own record from the previous year. This time he was driving a 235 horsepower Pierce Arrow 12 called the *Ab Jenkins Special*. He had improved the previous Pierce Arrow 12 by adding a fish tail, six carburetors instead of a single dual, special manifolds, and new high compression heads. The car had an additional sixty horsepower and had gone through scores of blueprints to come up with a final design. (Note: In 2003 John Hollansworth of Arkansas owned an exact duplicate of the *Ab Jenkins Special*. Hollansworth had it built at the McPherson College of auto restoration in Kansas, and he exhibited it on the salt flats in September 2003 along with Marv Jenkins who brought the restored *Mormon Meteor III*.)

Two famous U.S. racers, Harry Hartz and Wilbur Shaw, completed a stock car endurance record on the salt a few days prior to Jenkins's 1934 run. They averaged 84.434 mph

Ab Jenkins in the cockpit of the 1935 Duesenberg, called *Mormon Meteor I*. (Marvin Jenkins)

Jenkins in September 1935 as reported in the *Salt Lake Tribune:* "*Ab Jenkins is to be congratulated not only on the records he has broken, but on his initiative in making known the speed possibilities of the salt beds . . .*"

Meanwhile Campbell was the icon of the racing world in Britain and racing in Britain was the pinnacle of the sports world in that country. He was also well-known in the United States, having set the world land speed record at Day-

The *Ab Jenkins Special,* a 235-horsepower Pierce Arrow 12 in 1934. *(Marvin Jenkins)*

tona Beach, Florida. Campbell wanted to exceed 300 miles per hour and decided it was only possible on the salt flats. When he came, he brought with him a large contingent of racing enthusiasts. His run was a social event.

"*The Cobblestone bar was filled with bearded Nevada cattlemen, French, English, and American correspondents and tourists. They took advantage of the slot machines and blackjack tables while they discussed the upcoming speed run.*

"*There were as many as 2,000 spectators on hand to witness Campbell's runs. The Cobblestone Café ran out of food. Iceboxes were set up on the speedway with 'an array of*

fresh food to rival fine restaurants,'" said George Eyston. Tents were set up for shade and sleeping. Photographers, newsreel cameras, radio broadcasters, and reporters were on hand and airplanes flew overhead, adding to the excitement. The race course was scraped ready and an 8-inch wide, black line of oil was sprayed on the 13-mile length of the course at Campbell's request. The black line was a first for the speedway.

After trying the course, he decided to attempt an official run. On his trial run he found the salt flats to be "*far superior to those of Daytona.*" The *Salt Lake Tribune's* description helped readers picture Campbell's warmup run: "*Because the flats are so expansive and the crowd was farther away from the track than it could be by using the sand dunes at Daytona for a grandstand, the run lost some of its dangerous aspects.*

"*This loss of the death-defying angle of a man riding a metal horse at a thunderous speed was supplanted by a picture of beauty. Bluebird's blue hull, glistening in the sun, rose over the horizon with a light spray of salt flying to the rear. For a moment, it appeared to be suspended in midair, looking like an airplane just taking off from the snow-white salt.*

"*On it came, the steady hum*

Ab Jenkins hung two canteens of water with tubes for drinking, along with a powder puff between the canteens to wipe salt from his face and goggles. *(Marvin Jenkins)*

The speedway track as it looked at the time Campbell made his historic run. He requested that an 8-inch wide ribbon be sprayed on the course length using diesel oil. *(Marvin Jenkins)*

like that of a bee turning into a full-throated roar as the car sped past the timing stand with the motor running smoothly and easily.

"Sir Malcolm eased his throttle a trifle as he flashed by the red banners, denoting the end of the mile and then he cut the switch, using the motor compression to help slow down the car."

Marv Jenkins, son of Ab remembered that the *Bluebird*'s engine ran rich as the mechanics hadn't compensated for the high altitude. Consequently, clouds of black smoke poured from the exhaust system. He also stated that the car made quite a racket when it started, and that it was awesome to watch.

Campbell had his forearms taped before gripping the wheel. He used a movie camera mounted in the *Bluebird* to record the indicator readings on his instrument panel. He also had a machine which produced an ink record of the acceleration of the *Bluebird*. His *Bluebird* race car was thirty-two feet long and was powered by a V-12 Rolls-Royce aircraft engine. It is

reported that on Campbell's trial runs, he found that his tires showed minimal wear as compared with being frayed and torn apart on the sands at Daytona Beach.

The 42-gallon radiator of the *Bluebird* was covered with an apron when it reached the measured mile. When Sir Malcolm saw the red flags drop, signaling the start of the measured mile, he dropped the apron to reduce air friction. He calculated that it gave him ten to thirteen miles per hour of increased speed.

A two-way amateur radio station connected the judges' stand with a courtesy car near the crowds to keep them informed. The dramatic conclusion to Campbell's four-day visit to the Bonneville Salt Flats came on Tuesday September 3, 1935.

On his first run, Campbell had difficulty when an oil film spread over his windshield, obliterating his vision, and exhaust fumes filled the cockpit causing his head to throb. The exhaust asphyxiation and the obscured vision contributed to him going into a broadside skid going 250 mph but he was able to stop short of hitting the embankment. His left front tire exploded and the *Bluebird "plunged and careened dizzily"* forward with bits of rubber flying everywhere along the way. The tire was nothing but a burning mass of rubber by the time he stopped. He could have flipped had he been on the soft sands of Daytona Beach, but on the rock hard salt the chances of flipping were greatly diminished. In fact, the salt was hard enough in some spots that tent stakes would bend when pounded by a sledge hammer, according to Ab Jenkins.

Campbell's first run in one direction was 304.31 mph. When the required second run of 298.01 mph was averaged in, he was triumphantly over 301 mph officially. The run had lasted less than thirteen seconds each way, averaging 11.95 seconds. There was a mistake in the timing and it was two hours later before he learned he had set a new land speed record.

Author Louise Ann Noeth wrote that two-way runs became a standard in 1922 *"to ensure that a driver could not gain a single direction advantage using a sloped course or following wind."* Between Campbell's first and second runs, the crew rushed as they changed six tires, including a blow-out. They hurriedly cleaned the windshield and goggles, refueled and checked fluid levels. Then off he went into the record books—with less than five minutes left to spare in the required hour!

Campbell never returned to the salt flats but he

Bringing the *Bluebird* onto the salt flats from the highway on September 3, 1935. *(Utah State Historical Society)*

The 50,000-watt, clear channel KSL radio station from Salt Lake City provided exciting live broadcasts of the salt flats record racing. *(Marvin Jenkins)*

The *Bluebird* driven by Sir Malcolm Campbell on his record-setting first run of 304.31 mph on September 3, 1935. The official two-way record set that day was 301.129 miles per hour. *(Utah State Historical Society)*

Campbell's *Bluebird* in front of the Cobblestone Cafe in Wendover, 1935. *(Utah State Historical Society)*

generously praised the course. He said: *"The course appeared to be perfect . . . It was the most wonderful sensation that I have ever felt. Here we were skimming over the surface of the earth, the black line ever disappearing over the edge of the horizon; the wind whistling past like a hurricane; and nothing in sight but the endless sea of salt with the mountains fifty miles in the distance."* Campbell retired from racing and turned to gardening and dog breeding. He was interviewed in Salt Lake the day of his triumph and he, at that time, had every intention of returning and setting an unbreakable record for the future.

The year 1935 turned out to be a momentous year on the salt flats for racing. Records were set with dizzying speed, so to speak. John Cobb set a 24-hour endurance record at 134.85 miles per hour in July after Ab Jenkins moved off the raceway to make room for Cobb. Ab left his tents, trucks, towers, and his son Marvin in place for Cobb's convenience. Cobb set twenty-one world speed records inside a week with his 450-horsepower, $100,000 Napier-Railton.

Ab Jenkins regained the record at 135.58 mph in August and also set a land speed

Ab Jenkins took a wild ride in 1935 to set a world class record on an Allis Chalmers tractor. *(Marvin Jenkins)*

record of sixty-eight miles per hour on an Allis Chalmers farm tractor. He said it was like *"riding a frightened bison."* He always felt that it was one of the most thrilling rides of his life. The tractor ride was done as an advertising stunt.

He brought Indianapolis racer, Tony Gulotta with him, to serve as a relief driver on his race car endurance runs. Augie Duesenberg supervised the maintenance of the supercharged Duesenberg racer. Duesenberg's trade-mark was walking in a circle while mulling over problems and strategies. Following Jenkins's record-setting runs, Sir Malcolm Campbell, as mentioned previously, set the land speed record on the salt flats in September for one mile at 301.129 mph with his *Bluebird Special.* Then, Captain George E. T. Eyston improved the 24-hour record by racing at 140.52 miles per hour.

Jenkins decided in late 1935 that he would have to increase the horsepower of his car to beat the British racers, some of whom had installed airplane engines in their race cars. Jenkins also turned to airplane engines to accomplish it. He purchased two Curtiss Conqueror en-

Official stands, timing shack, and observation plane on Bonneville Salt Flats Raceway in the 1930s. Tent on the left is the Salt Lake City Chamber of Commerce, the KSL and AAA stand is in the middle, and the Pierce Arrow tent is on the right. *(Utah State Historical Society)*

Racers continued to set world records at the salt flats in 1936. In April 1936, Briton Eyston set two records with a diesel-engined vehicle traveling 159 kph for one kilometer and 158.87 mph for a mile in his *"Flying Spray."* Eyston set sixty records in July including 136.34 mph in a 48-hour average in the *"Speed of the Wind."* In August and September John Cobb broke many of Eyston's records, including the 24-hour record.

Then along came Ab Jenkins in early September with *Mormon Meteor II*

Captain George E. T. Eyston's endurance car, *Speed of the Wind,* looked like a giant lizard. *(Utah State Historical Society)*

gines in New Jersey and had them *"automobilized"* as he called it. He added a flywheel, bell housing, and new clutch. The vehicle had earlier been named the *Mormon Meteor* in a Salt Lake City contest.

complete with a newly installed airplane engine. He set seventy-two new world records, including the new mark for twenty-four hours and forty-eight hours. On one of his endurance runs, Jenkins went into a 400-foot

Eyston's six-axeled, eight-wheeled *Thunderbolt* and touring car after setting a 367.110 mph land speed record in September 1938. *(Utah State Historical Society)*

skid which he called a *"wing ding"* or *"gilhooley."* He and a passenger darted in and out among spectators, tents and telephone poles. His rider was an Indianapolis racer, who hid in the cowling of the car. At the 12-hour mark, a universal joint burned out, ending the race, but not before beating Eyston's 12-hour record, upping it from 149.02 mph to 152.84 mph.

John Cobb began his race on the salt while Jenkins was out of commission. Cobb bettered Eyston's 24 hour record with a time of 150.163. Cobb was known as *"the big man with the little car."*

In 1936, Jenkins drove *Mormon Meteor II* an average of 153.823 mph for twenty-four hours and 148.641 mph for forty-eight hours. Later, in 1940, he went 161.184 miles an hour for twenty-four hours, assisted by a relief driver.

Other records set by him in ensuing years include 100 miles at 196.35 mph in 1951, 200 miles at 195.85 mph in 1950, 500 miles at 177.229 mph, 1000 miles at 172.804 mph, and 1 hour at 195.95 mph in 1950.

Jenkins summed it up by calling 1936 a year of *"intense international rivalry"* and the year of the airplane-engined cars. He set seventy-two records in 1936.

Jenkins and Eyston were first to arrive at the salt flats in 1937 but *"old Jupitor Pluvius reigned as he rained"* until September, quipped Ab. When the rain finally stopped and the race track dried out sufficiently, Ab immediately went to work establishing marathon run records in a stock car. On September 21, Ab Jenkins

George Eyston's eight-wheeled *Thunderbolt*. *(Utah State Historical Society)*

took to the salt again in the cream, blue, and orange-colored *Mormon Meteor II*. He bettered his own 24-hour record and in the process, two rear tires came off when their clincher rings loosened due to a 40-mile per hour wind. A piece of wire shrapnel from the

Restored *Mormon Meteor III* on the salt flats. The car has a Curtiss Conqueror, 12-cylinder, 1,570-cubic inch aircraft engine which averaged 3.5 miles per gallon going 200 miles an hour. The gas tank holds 112 gallons of gas and requires twelve gallons of oil. The water capacity is nine gallons. The length is 250 inches with a 142 inch wheel base. The total weight is 4,800 pounds. Firestone made the 8-ply tires with only 3/16-inch tread. The tire pressure is fifty pounds and increases four pounds at high speeds. *(Utah Salt Flats Racing Association, Cris Shearer)*

John Cobb's car, the *Railton Mobil Special,* entering the salt flats. Cobb's driving seat was in front of the four wheels. *(Utah State Historical Society)*

streamlined fender penetrated his left arm, temporarily paralyzing it. Indianapolis champion driver Louis Meyer filled in for three hours and then Ab returned, bandages and all, to finish the record-breaking run.

Then the race was on for the one-mile speed record. Captain George E. T. Eyston pushed his 14,000-pound *Thunderbolt* automobile to a record 311.42 miles per hour. *"When Thunderbolt arrived in Wendover, people were shocked by its immense size."* Ab Jenkins commented that Captain Eyston was a gentleman, a sportsman, and a pleasure to know.

Eyston's speedster was equipped with eight wheels and, though massive, it could not be detected by the photoelectric timing eye. It seems that the silver body in combination with the blinding salt rendered the photoelectric device ineffective. Eyston had to paint the car's sides black which did the trick, and on November 19 he set a new world land speed record of 311.42 miles per hour.

KSL Radio of Salt Lake City featured live coverage of Captain Eyston's run. The announcer excitedly described the run: *"The mad streak of gray is throwing out sand behind it in a*

mad race for time. This is a time for superlatives. He's coming across! [Hear] the roar of the motor. There he goes off up toward the north end through the measured mile. He's on his way. Whatever he's done, now he is done!"* On the return trip the announcer referred to the racer as the *"silver streak over against the mountain!"*

Eyston's endurance car was called *Speed of the Wind.* It looked like a giant lizard to some who saw it. He said it took six months to design his car and six more months to build it, working night and day. He beat Ab Jenkins's 24-hour endurance record by five miles an hour with the car. He remarked at how hazardous an endurance run was since any little part could fail and cause disaster.

Eyston later pointed out some of the problems he dealt with in driving the race. He recorded that each time he passed the smudge pot flares, which was every two seconds, his vision was impaired. He also noted that when he slightly increased speed, salt flakes blew turbulently around him in the cockpit. Tiny bits of salt were forced inside his tight-fitting goggles, smarting and blinding one or both eyes. In addition, the soft

Cobb's *Railton Mobil Special* on the salt. *(Marvin Jenkins)*

spots in the race track caused tremendous bumping when struck at 150 mph.

The *"unshrouded glare"* of the desert sun on salt at sunrise absolutely blinded him. Later, the intense heat of the sun was unbearable, and lastly, the salt coating on the hub caps hardened like *"nickel plating, making the thread tight."*

Captain Eyston set several records in November 1937. On November 19, Eyston set a one-mile speed record of 311.42 mph. His face was blackened by exhaust and oil on that run. He spoke of his feats to five London newspapers over the telephone and over an international radio network in the U.S. and Britain on NBC. Racing on Bonneville Salt Flats was world famous at that time.

Eyston and Cobb went at it again in 1938, exchanging the land speed record twice in two days. Cobb's ice-cooled, turtle-shaped, aluminum *Railton Mobil Special* weighed half as much as Eyston's seven and a half-ton *Thunderbolt*. Eyston raced to a record

Ice was used to cool the engine of Cobb's *Railton Mobil Special*. *(Utah State Historical Society)*

347.49 mph on September 16 and the next day Cobb *"chalked up"* 350.25 mph. The next day Eyston drove 357.5 miles an hour to again set a new record. He went faster than an army cannon projectile, according to Jenkins. Eyston tried again a few days later, but went into a death defying skid while *"6,000 spectators held their breath."*

Ab Jenkins came with *"a completely new machine"* called *Mormon Meteor III*, but standing water held him off the course in 1938. *Mormon Meteor III* held the Curtiss Conqueror airplane engine transferred from *Mormon Meteor II*, but was in a newly designed body. Jenkins had his good friend Augie Duesenberg design and build the chassis in Indianapolis. The rear fin was fitted by a gas welder, welding the two symmetrical sides together, and then it was painstakingly hand-molded by reaching through from outside holes cut in the skin. The engine was mounted backwards on the frame. It was a work of art.

In the book *The Salt of the*

Lifting the *Railton Mobil Special* body onto the chassis at the Western Garage in Wendover. *(Marvin Jenkins)*

Mormon Meteor coming into the pit at the Bonneville Salt Flats. *(Marvin Jenkins)*

Cobb's *Railton Mobil Special* and the Novi *Mobil Special* driven by Marvin Jenkins. *(Marvin Jenkins)*

1947 record-breaking run of Marv Jenkins averaged 179.434 mph, toppling eight records. Inset: Marv Jenkins, in the cockpit of the Novi *Mobile Special* is congratulated by his father Ab Jenkins. Marv claimed twenty-eight speed records in 1956. *(Marvin Jenkins)*

Earth by Ab Jenkins and Wendell Ashton, it is stated that *"After the airplane engine was moved from Mormon Meteor II to Mormon Meteor III, the original Duesenberg automotive engine was put back in Mormon Meteor II. With that change, Mormon Meteor II again became Mormon Meteor I."*

Jenkins was back on the salt in July of 1939. Three hours into the race, a universal joint began a high-pitched howl. Jenkins made a pit stop and the car burst into flames. Ab was dragged by his son Marv from the burning car with second- and third-degree burns on his right arm and leg. His leg was severely burned. He recuperated for a week in a hospital and returned to race a few weeks later, setting new records in the re-conditioned *Mormon Meteor III*. He later developed blood poisoning in the leg and required three additional weeks of recovery in the hospital.

In the meantime, he was nominated as a candidate for mayor of Salt Lake City and won by fifty-one votes without campaigning. Fifty-seven-year-old Mayor Ab Jenkins continued his marathon racing in 1940 on the salt flats *"where world records tumbled like ten pins in its wake."* Ab enlisted the services of a relief driver this time. The relief driver, Cliff Bergere, an Indy racer and stunt driver, drove ten hours of the twenty-four and his hands were blistered from keeping the car on course. Ab's son Marv served as the test driver and supervised the mechanical work also. (In the 1990s, Marv completely restored the $5,000,000 *Mormon Meteor III* to mint condition, spending 4,000 man hours and thousands of dollars of his own money to do so).

Pit stops took an average of one minute and four seconds and could be as rapid as twenty-three seconds. During a typical pit stop, the crew poured eighty-five gallons of gas into the car's gas tank, checked the tires, water, and oil, greased the car and washed the windshield. Ab was given orange juice or milk as his only nourishment.

Ab Jenkins set up stipend contracts with Pennzoil, Champion Spark Plugs, B. F. Goodrich Tire and Rubber Company, and Firestone Tire & Rubber Company. B. F. Goodrich paid him $10,000 to run on their tires. In 1933, Harvey Firestone matched Goodrich's stipend

Dunlop Tyres newspaper ad in 1936 featured the three famous British racers. *(Marvin Jenkins)*

without a contract. Jenkins ran Firestone tires after that.

John Cobb *"boosted the world's record to 367.910 miles an hour—traveling a mile in less than ten seconds."* The record was set August 23, 1939, and held until he beat it in 1947. Cobb's *Railton Mobil Special* weighed 5,000 pounds and was powered by dual Napier airplane engines capable of 1,250 horsepower. One engine provided power in front and the other to the rear wheels. The engines were cooled with ice water.

The British aristocratic racers used the Western Garage, operated by Bill Moore, as their headquarters. They had a chef named Horatio who cooked for the

Bike endurance participants race on the salt flats near Ab Jenkins's camp. Ab Jenkins in striped shirt and Brownie Carslake of Firestone Tire & Rubber Co. racing division in white shirt. Woman is Glenda Green. *(Bruce Lamus)*

forty men of the group. They relied on Ed Lamus and his son Blair to keep the track smooth and to give them advice about the salt.

Ab Jenkins's son Marv was puzzled at times by their British terminology. Cobb told him that to steer at high speeds *"It takes a bit o' correction but you don't want to yonk the wheel too hard."* The racers spoke of

dangling leads when they referred to drop cords. Bonnets were hoods and spanners were wrenches.

During the endurance races, the kids of Wendover decided to hold an endurance race of their own. There were two teams of four youths each. They even had a sponsor, Firestone Tire Company. They accomplished a 72-hour record going 1,126 miles non-stop!

Wendover youth after the 72-hour endurance run on the baseball diamond. The black sign reads *"We did 1126 miles in a 72-hour non-stop bicycle race. This dinner is given for our success."* (Bruce Lamus)

When Ab Jenkins heard of their plans, he pitched in to help. Glenda Green recalled: *"He set up a tent and we had a small table and some folding chairs. His cook shack would send over food for us during this 24 hour Speed Record Trial. The boys would ride the bicycle going around the track five times. Ab had set up the marks on the track for 1/5 mile. The girls did the timing as the boys rode the bicycle. Each boy would ride around five times. When his mile was up he would quickly throw his leg off the bike on one side while another boy got on the bike on the other side not stopping for 24 hours. After twenty-four hours were up they had ridden 121 miles. The girls kept track of the mileage. There was one flat tire that stalled the race temporarily. When it was all finished and reported in the* Salt Lake Tribune *it was a celebration. Ab Jenkins gave us a nice sweater printed on the back of it the miles and the details of the race and an Eversharp pencil.*

"That morning when we ended the race at six I had to immediately go to work to wash dishes. I had not had any sleep all night. I was exhausted but I went to work to earn my fifty cents per day." They held at least four such endurance runs.

Athol Graham's ill-fated *City of Salt Lake,* November 29, 1959. *(Utah State Historical Society)*

They used an oval-shaped course which was flare-lighted, complete with pits and timers. It was located around the perimeter of the local baseball diamond. The vehicle was a stream-lined, tubular-steeled, all-air conditioned, leg-powered bicycle.

The second world war put a hiatus on auto racing on the salt. Everyone's attention turned to the war and the war effort, and Wendover was again in the thick of things (see chapter 4). Wendover played an important part in the war, but only a handful of people knew how important while it was happening.

When the year 1947 rolled around, the salt flats were once again the focus of land speed racers. British gentleman John Cobb returned with stepped up gear ratios and newly designed tires under the watchful eye of Reed Railton, engineer. The car had the same old 1929 engines and the same basic 1935 body design. On September 16, Cobb set the speed record for the last time at 394.196 mph breaking his own 1939 record of 367.10 mph. He had a one-way run of 403 mph and said the car was easy to handle. His wheel-driven piston-engine record stood for eighteen years until 1965. He was later killed while attempting to set a world speed record on water, thus ending his illustrious career.

Meanwhile Ab Jenkins sold *Mormon Meteor III* to the state of Utah for one dollar and it was housed in the state capitol. Ab Jenkins took it out in 1950 and set twenty-six speed records including a lap of 195.86 mph. Jenkins set the 24-hour speed record for a stock

Mickey Thompson in Wendover, 1965. *(Ron Christensen)*

Mickey Thompson's four-engined racer *Challenger I* on the salt flats. *(Ron Christensen)*

car in 1956 with his son Marvin as the relief driver. Ab was seventy-three at the time. Pontiac subsequently named the car the *Bonneville* in his honor.

Ab's 24-hour endurance record held until 1989 when an eight-driver team finally broke it. His record for the 48-hour endurance run still stands. Ab Jenkins was inducted into the Utah Hall of Fame as a charter member in 1970. He was listed as #11 on the list of Utah's 50 Greatest Athletes of the Century by the *Salt Lake Tribune* at the end of December 1999.

Of his endurance runs, Frank Baker of the *Salt Lake Telegram* had this to say in 1940: *"His long grinds place prolonged tests upon mechanical parts. In reality, the human equation is probably more important in his runs than*

Donald Campbell's turbine-powered *Bluebird* made its debut on the salt in 1960. *(Ron Christensen)*

This 1950's sign was located at the east entrance to the Bonneville Salt Flats near Highway 40. *(Ron Christensen)*

Craig Breedlove's *Spirit of America*. Inset shows his car in the canal after it crashed. Breedlove said of his car in the canal: *"It was like a cartoon. The tail was sticking out of the water and there was smoke coming out of the tailpipe. It was funny."* (Utah State Historical Society)

it is in a measured mile dash, because the mile pilot makes a couple of death-defying sprints down a straightaway, whereas Ab and his relief pilot have to keep fighting for hour after hour to keep their car under control around a circular track. The mile run might conceivably be made with a robot as a pilot, but not the endurance run. It takes human blood, flesh and driving ingenuity to keep the mechanical horses functioning there . . . Drivers who have suffered agony trying to keep from dozing at the wheel should take a few lessons from the mayor. He has driven nearly a dozen 24-hour runs without relief."

The remains of the jet-engined race car *Infinity* were removed from the salt flats and stored in an empty lot on the outskirts of Wendover. *(Ron Christensen)*

Endurance runs became less popular after the 1940s, but short distance speed records were still a challenge racers wanted to accomplish. Phil Hill, Goldie Gardner, and many others set land speed records in various classes.

Ron Christensen, current Salt Flats announcer, examines the first jet car on the salt, Dr. Nathan Ostich's *Flying Caduceus,* in front of the Western Motel. A spare jet engine sits on the flat bed in the foreground. *(Ron Christensen)*

John Cobb's one-mile land speed record still held thirteen years later. But several racers had been eyeing it with the hope of breaking it. One of them was thirty-nine-year-old, safety conscious Athol Graham. The former Mormon missionary had made promising runs in 1959 of up to 344.761 mph and came back in August 1960 with thoughts of breaking Cobb's record. He had worked out several bugs in his *City of Salt Lake,* even redesigning a tie rod end the morning of his run.

He reached a speed of over 300 mph when the car started flying apart, flipped, and became airborne at the two-mile mark. Eighty yards later it bounced and went airborne for another 164 yards before sliding along on its top at high speed, and coming to a halt. Athol was flown to LDS Hospital in Salt Lake City where he died of internal injuries three hours later. Faulty body design, too fast acceleration, or perhaps improperly cast magnesium wheels caused the fatal accident. The car would race again after being rebuilt by mechanic Otto Anzjon on a shoestring budget, but it set no records after blowing a tire. The story of Athol Graham was featured in a 1963 *Reader's Digest* article.

Donald Campbell, son of Sir Malcolm Campbell, came back to the salt in 1960 and attempted setting a speed record. He sprinted to 345 miles per hour and demolished his multi-million dollar car, but came out

Walt Arfons claimed the World Land Speed record with his jet-powered *Wingfoot Express* driven by Tom Green in 1964 at 413.200 mph. Walt's brother Art took the record away three days later with a 434.22-mph average in the *Green Monster* jet car. Walt returned in 1965 with the rocket powered *Wingfoot Express II* which was powered by twenty-five JATO solid fuel rockets typically found on jet bombers to assist with takeoff. The car reached a top speed of 580 mph but the speed was not sustained through the measured mile. *(Ron Christensen)*

with only a fractured skull, cuts, and a broken eardrum. He received get-well wishes from Queen Elizabeth. With the same car, he later set the land speed record for the measured mile of 403.135 mile per hour in his rebuilt *Bluebird-Proteus CN7* in Australia in July of 1964. He eventually lost his life trying to break the 300 mile per hour jet boat speed record.

On September 9, 1960, Marion Lee "Mickey" Thompson finally broke the 400 mph barrier in his *Challenger 1*. Unfortunately he did not complete the required backup run and

Bob Summers established a new record for wheel-driven cars at 409.344 mph on November 11, 1965, at Bonneville. He was driving the *Goldenrod*, powered by four fuel-injected Chrysler engines, finally defeating John Cobb's record of 394.196 set in 1947. *(Ron Christensen)*

The *Green Monster* and its driver Art Arfons. The car resembled a spaceship from a 1930s science fiction movie. *(Utah State Historical Society)*

thus did not break Cobb's record set in 1947. His driveshaft broke on the return run.

Thompson's racer was powered by four 700-horsepower each, Pontiac V-8 engines. During his career, he set at least 295 speed records at Bonneville Speedway. He drove over one million miles in over 10,000 races, and also was an innovator and designer. *"He developed, among other things, the signal starting and foul light systems for dragstrips, the wide oval tire, nitrogen gas shocks, . . . And the Hydro-Barricade—a water safety wall for race track and highway use."* His championship skills were in such diverse categories as dragsters, sports cars, midgets, sprint cars, off-road vehicles, stock cars, and Indy cars. He was described as an innova-

Art Arfons purchased a damaged J-79 jet engine (worth $175,000 new) from the air force for $700 and repaired it. The air force tried to buy it back, but he wouldn't budge. He toyed with the engine and got it operable. He tied it outside his workshop to a chassis between two trees and fired it up. When he hit the burner, it tore loose, "torching a 50 ft swathe into the woods," and exploded a chicken coop 200 feet away.

tor, a promoter, and Mr. Speed when he was inducted into the Motor Sports Hall of Fame.

In the 1960s, jet aircraft engines became available at cheaper prices as surplus. They enabled racers to go faster with rapid acceleration. However, international racing rules stipulated that land speed records must be set with vehicles having four wheels and be powered by at least two of them.

Jet-powered racers were basically an aerodynamically designed body and engine set on wheels which were unconnected to the engine by any drive line. Jet racers were therefore ineligible for international records recognized by the Federation Internationale de l'Automobile or F.I.A. Later, a special category was

Gary Gabelich set a world speed record of 622.407 mph in his jet-powered *Blue Flame* in 1970. The day of the record, there were dark clouds, it was lightly snowing, and the salt flats flooded after the race; however, there was a break in the clouds during the race. *(Ron Christensen)*

created by the F.I.A. for the thrust-powered cars which made them legal for international speed records.

John Cobb said *"A jet-propelled vehicle would not be a motor car; it would be a sort of aeroplane dragging its wheels along the course."* *Hot Rod* magazine senior editor Gray Baskerville jeeringly labeled jet cars as *"blowtorches on wheels."* They none-the-less brought a lot of attention to the salt flats.

The anticipation was indescribable when the humongous jet-powered cars prepared to launch. The first sound was the tiny whir of a 400 amp, 36-volt electric generator used to power the electric motor which fired the jet engine. The jet rotor blades whined as they revved up in rpms to 700 and the fuel pump injected jet fuel into thirty-two injectors in the combustion chamber. A thunderous roar followed with *"accompanying tornado-like wind currents."* Just as rapidly, the roar subsided and all was quiet on the course. For those who have experienced the event either as a spectator or a racer, it is an inexpressible thrill.

An abortive attempt at the land speed record occurred on the salt on August 9, 1962 when Dr. Nathan Ostich, a *"physician to many racers"* fishtailed his $50,000 *Flying Caduceus* jet car down the raceway. After swerving and whipping in a *"crazy dance of death,"* Ostich popped his chute, lost a tire when the axle snapped, and escaped ultimately without a scratch. He had reached a speed of 331 mph during the measured mile and began his 3-spin skid in the eighth mile of the race track. Ostich fell short of his expectations to set a land speed record with a new kind of car when he declared that he had gone fast enough and parked the car for good.

Craig Breedlove tried his luck on the salt in 1962 and came away discouraged. His driving ability was questioned and discord among his team members sent him home to California. His car had not performed well either. But he would be back!

In September 1962, drag racer Glenn Leasher was killed instantly when his jet-powered car named *Infinity*

Al Teague set a new F.I.A. land speed record of 409.986 mph in August 1991. Crewman MacShaw behind car. Right inset: Teague and chief timer, the late Bob Higbee. Left inset: Al Teague in his *Speed-O-Motive*. (USFRA, Cris Shearer)

exploded in pieces across the salt flats. He had employed his parachute too soon on a trial run, causing him to go airborne briefly. It was a portent of things to come. On another trial run, apparently he decided to go for the record without inflating his tires for a high-speed run. No one knew what happened for sure, but perhaps a blow-out forced the car off the track and caused it to go airborne when it exploded.

Racing enthusiasts briefly wondered if jet cars were too dangerous for racing on the salt flats. The *Flying Caduceus, Spirit of America,* and *Infinity* were the first jet cars but wouldn't be the last. They would be followed with record-setting runs by new versions of Craig Breedlove's *Spirit of America,* Tom Green and Walt Arfons' *Wingfoot Express*, Art Arfons' *Green Monster,* and Gary Gabelich's *Blue Flame.*

Breedlove returned in August of 1963 and promptly set a record of 407.45 mph in his *"Three-ton three-wheeler that looked like a jet fighter with amputated wings,"* as aptly described by author Noeth. He utilized 85% of

Bob Higbee was a volunteer at Speed Week for more than fifty years. He never missed a year after he started coming until he died. He was one of the last to leave at the end of each Speed Week. He was the chief starter and gave a final check for safety before waving each car on to the race track.

According to author Louise Noeth, Higbee "... *spent thousands of hours all alone out on the course, more than any other racer."* He was the one who dragged the course smooth, pulling weighted land planes along the 12-mile course at 25 miles per hour. Bob passed away January 6, 2003.

the car's available thrust of 4,000 pounds. Thrust ratings in foot-pounds could be easily converted to horse-power. In setting the new record, Breedlove brought honor back to the United States since he had surpassed the record held by John Cobb for sixteen years, and ended thirty-five years of British domination in the racing scene. Ironically, the F.I.M. (Federation de l'Motorcycle, counterpart to the automobile organization, the F.I.A.) recognized the Breedlove run as a motorcycle record.

The year 1964 became a dizzying one for the land speed record. Donald Campbell set a record of 403.135 mph in Australia in July. Campbell's record was short lived however. Talmage (Tom) Green was the engineer and builder of the *Wingfoot Express* and became the driver because racer-owner Walt Arfons had previously suffered a heart attack. On October 2, 1964, always cautious Tom Green pushed the jet-powered *Wingfoot Express* to 413.199 mph over the two runs to become the fastest racer in the world. The time was amazing because a small threaded nut was ingested into the jet engine on the first run and he had run out of fuel in the measured mile also. In addition, Green was an inexperienced driver for such high speeds. On the second run he started closer to the measured mile, at a two-mile approach to conserve fuel and it worked.

Walt and Tom were scheduled to celebrate their LSR in Chicago with Goodyear executives when they heard of Walt's stepbrother's new record set three days

Don Vesco and his land speed record setting *Turbinator*. The Federation Internationale de l'Automobile (F.I.A.) granted a new designation in 2003 for "World Wheel Driven Land Speed Record" and TEAM Vesco's racecar was the first vehicle to be honored as setting the wheel-driven record. Team partner Rick Vesco commented on how technically challenging and complex the record was to set. The record of 458.481 mph was set by the Vesco brothers on October 18, 2001. According to Louise Ann Noeth, "There were very few who hold a world wheel-driven speed record in excess of 400 mph. They are the Summers brothers who in 1964 set a 409 mph record in the unsupercharged category and Al Teague who mirrored the record in 1991 with a 409 mph record but in the supercharged category. Both still reign supreme in their respective classes. Don Campbell had the turbine record which Don Vesco bettered in 2001." (*Utah Salt Flats Racing Association, Cris Shearer; www.landspeedproductions.biz*)

Nolan White set a new land speed record in August 2002. Inset: World Land Speed Record holder Nolan White in hat with Joaquin Arnett, founding member of the 1949 Bean Bandits. *(USFRA, Cris Shearer)*

after Tom's. Green and Arfons went home without celebrating. On October 5, 1964, Arthur (Art) Arfons rode onto the salt with his 15,000-pound jet-powered race car, one of many he dubbed *Green Monster.* He promptly sped across the as-hard-as-concrete salt at 434.22 mph to beat his brother.

Twenty-six-year-old Craig Breedlove was not to be outdone. He was the next racer scheduled on the salt. On October 13 he clocked in at 468.719 mph and on the 15th he exceeded the 500-mph barrier, going 526.277 mph! On his return run, his *Spirit of America* prematurely lost both of its braking parachutes. Breedlove stood on the rear brakes to no avail as they burned to a crisp. He passed by sev-

In 1976, the Utah Salt Flats Racing Association (USFRA) began sponsoring racing on the salt beds. The association was organized locally to provide more opportunities to race. They sponsor World of Speed during the month of September annually. Many of the same individuals and cars race in Speed Week and World of Speed. SCTA and USFRA follow a uniform set of rules and similar circumstances.

eral telephone poles and then snapped off the next one before shooting through a shallow lake. He went over the same 4-foot mud dike that Sir Malcolm Campbell had encountered almost thirty years before. Breedlove and his car went over the dike and buried the car's nose in the muddy water beyond. Breedlove was scared to death but lived through it all and swam to safety, having opened the canopy before plunging into the water. The car would race no more, but was eventually placed in the Chicago Museum of Science and Industry.

Art Arfons came back on October 27, 1964, and hit 536.71 mph for another new record. He said this run really frightened him. His 6,500-pound racer cost less

Inset right: Bob Duarte and his modified street roadster 188 A BGMR; inset left: Number 333 is a well-known roadster of Walsh, Walsh, and Cusack, Justin Walsh driver. Ron Joliffe and his AA street roadster number 534. *(Utah Salt Flats Racing Association, Cris Shearer)*

Local Salt Lake racer Terry Nish with his #998 streamliner. *(Utah Salt Flats Racing Association, Cris Shearer)*

Tom Thumb Special, a gas competiton coupe. Father Tom Bryant and sons, Barry and Jeff, are all in the 200 mph Club. *(Utah Salt Flats Racing Association, Cris Shearer)*

In 1957, this Kenz and Leslie streamliner was America's fastest car in its class, running 270 mph. It was powered by three flathead Ford engines. *(Ron Christensen)*

ing 17,500 pounds of thrust while Breedlove's and his brother Walt's J-47 engines had only the capability of 5,300 pounds of thrust. The *Salt Lake Tribune* commented *". . . wait until 1965. There is no telling what will happen then."*

With Breedlove and Arfons trading back and forth the top speed record, 1965 was almost a repeat of the previous year. Breedlove had built another jet-powered car with a J-79 engine named *Spirit of America Sonic I* and he set a 555 mph record on November 2, 1965. *"Goodyear still had the course reserved"* so Craig Breedlove then had his wife race the car to a maximum speed of 308.56 mph taking time on the salt away from Arfons. Earlier in September Arfons let Betty Skelton make a speed run of 277 mph to beat Paula Murphy, *"the first woman to drive a jet on the salt"* the year before at 226 mph. Both men cut the engine power for the women's runs.

On November 7, Arthur Arfons re-established the

than $10,000. He purchased a damaged J-79 jet engine (worth $175,000 new) from the air force for $700 and repaired it. The air force tried to buy it back but he wouldn't budge. He toyed with the engine and got it operable. He tied it outside his workshop to a chassis between two trees and fired it up. When he hit the burner, it tore loose, *"torching a 50 ft swathe into the woods,"* and exploded a chicken coop 200 feet away. That was his first experience with the dynamic power of a jet engine! He attached the engine to an old school bus chassis with a 1955 Packard steering column, a '37 Lincoln front axle, and a '47 Ford rear axle. Firestone developed the tires and wheels. It was 24 feet long and 74 inches wide with cockpits on each side of the engine. Arfons felt his car could go 650 mph, but he wasn't sure he wanted to go that fast.

As 1964 ended, it did so with one of the most amazing three and a half weeks in the history of land speed racing. It had become an all-consuming challenge to stay on top for Arfons. His engine was produc-

The famous Markley Brothers Lakester set a world record at over 258 mph in 1963 for open-wheeled cars. *(Ron Christensen)*

Four sanctioning entities govern national land speed racing. The four include the United States Auto Club, the National Hot Rod Association, the Southern California Timing Association, and the Federation International de l' Automobile (F.I.A.).

There is every car class imaginable among the entries. They fall into four major categories, namely *"Special Construction, Vintage, Modified, and Production. There are general rules for each category and they are related to safety of construction, drivers' attire, drivers' qualifications, basic configuration of the vehicle,"* etc.

There are two groups within the **Special Construction** category: Unlimited Streamliners and Lakesters. The Streamliners are required to have four wheels in any configuration. Two of the wheels must be covered.

The Streamliner is the most innovative class. Multiple engines are allowed. Factory produced auto bodies are not allowed. The class is known for its aerodynamically designed bodies.

Thrust power has its own unlimited class. This class has set the maximum land speed records and has only a few participants, relatively speaking. Four wheels are necessary, but winged surfaces used for lift are not allowed.

The open-wheeled Lakester classes allow only one engine and are often rear-mounted. There can be *"no streamlining, fairing or covering of the wheels and tires."* The body and axle fairing must be no wider than the *"narrowest inner vertical plane of the tires."* The width of tire tread varies.

The **Vintage** category is a fairly new classification. Auto bodies which were manufactured in large quantities of over 500 in the United States before 1948 are allowed. This class is for the antique collectors. Roadsters, Vintage Coupes and Sedans, and Vintage Oval Track make up the three groups in this category.

The modified roadsters, roadsters, and street roadsters are all grouped in the roadster class. *"The granddaddy of the classes"* is the roadster. These roadsters began racing in the 1930s and are dominated by the 1928 and '29 Ford Model "A" Roadsters. The modified roadster class generally use Model "T" bodies, and the street Roadsters must be street legal with headlights, tail lights, horns, rear fender, and must be self starting.

The **Modified** category allows foreign as well as American coupes, sedans, and pickups. Seating for four adults is a minimum generic requirement. The cars cannot be changed in height, width, and contour. All stock panels must be mounted in the original relationship to each other. Different degrees of modification determine the class each auto falls into.

There is the Competition Coupe and Sedan class, the Fuel and Altered coupe (no streamlining allowed), the street legal gas coupe and sedan class, and the production coupe and sedan which allow no modification of the body. Sports cars have several classes including Grand Touring Sports and the Modified Sports.

The **Production** category also allows foreign as well as domestic pickups, sedans, and coupes which have not been altered in height, width, or contour. These are the "typical transportation" vehicles which can be readily purchased from any auto dealer.

All stock panels must be in original configuration to each other, the same as with the modified category. *"The following must be retained in stock locations and be of the same year as the body: frame, fenders, hood, grille, rain gutters, windows, door handles, window trim, headlights, tail lights, parking lights, stop lights, radiator, both bumpers, and horn."*

There are the Production Supercharged cars which have a factory-equipped supercharger or turbocharger system installed. Grand Touring Sport Production sports cars (both blown and unblown) are vehicles originally manufactured for high speed touring in comfort and must have at least 500 of the same models produced in order to qualify.

The car categories are broken down even more according to engine size. They are divided into classes according to cubic inch displacement with Class AA 501 cubic inch displacement and over, all the way to Class K at 30.5 cid and under.

The XF engine class is for Vintage Ford/Mercury V-8 Flathead up to 3.25 cubic inches. The XX class includes XF or XO class engines with *"conversion type racing head or supercharger."* XO engines are in-line six or eight-cylinder engines older than 1959. The V4 classes are pre-1935 four-cylinder engines up to 220 cid. Many hot rodders would use the same car but change engines in order to compete in more than one class.

Fuel types must be from the approved list. Nitrous oxide, nitromethane, methanol, and gasoline furnished by the SCTA or USFRA are approved fuels. Liquid propane gas and diesel are included in the gasoline class.

In addition, frames and tires must meet certain specifications. Unconventionally designed frames must be equivalent or better than the strength of more conventional designs.

Tire specification is dependent on the speed the vehicle will be attempting. Original equipment tires with HR ratings can be used up to 150 mph. Below 200 mph VR and ZR rated tires are required, while between 200 mph and 250 mph *"shaved narrow tread super speedway tires"* are needed. Up to 300 mph requires special tires for racing with the manufacturer determining the tire construction. Above 300 is called the open record class and the tire construction is determined according to the speed that is to be attempted.

Some of the high-speed tires are forty years old or more because they are not made anymore. They have no tread as the tread picks up the salt. The salt is cool on the tires helping them to last longer. Racers nowadays sometimes use aluminum tires especially designed for individual race cars.

The drivers must meet certain requirements also. They must have a current competition license by the sponsoring organization. They must complete a medical information form. They must be helmeted with a full face shield and seat belted in along with arm and leg restraints. They are required to wear a driver's fire-resistant suit, gloves, and boots.

The cars must have roll cages. They must have sealed firewalls or heavy scattershields to protect the driver from clutch explosions. The seats can be bucket or stock, and must be anchored securely. The vehicles must have fuel shut-offs. Parachutes are required for speeds over 175 mph and two chutes for speeds over 300 mph. An on-board fire extinguishing system must be built-in.

There is a **Diesel Truck** category. Carl Heaps held the speed record in this category in 2002. He drove "The Phoenix", a 1943 International K-7 Detroit Diesel, reaching 231.356 mph in 2000.

Motorcycles racing on the Bonneville Salt Flats include an *"array of Japanese bikes,"* Triumphs, Harley Davidsons, Italian road racers, BSAs, Nortons, and Indians. Classes for motorcycles are determined by order of displacement, frame type and engine type.

Displacement classes are shown in cubic centimeters. These range from fifty cubic centimeters to over 3,000 cubic centimeters. There are nineteen engine classes under such variations as production, vintage engine, and Supercharged Engine, gasoline, etc. Frame classes include production, modified, special construction, modified partial streamlining, special construction, partial streamlining, sidecar, sidecar streamliner, and streamliner.

David Campos held the world record as the fastest motorcyclist as this book went to print. He traveled 322.149 mph on a twin Harley Davidson in the 3,000 cubic centimeter class in 1990. The Team Triumph Texas #601 bike is the world's fastest open-wheel motorcycle for the 2,000 cc and 3,000 cc at 256 mph set in 2001.

There are also novelty racers such as the bar stool racers, the monocycle (Kerry McLean's one-wheel motorcycle), skateboards, and the road trains. The road trains consist of three cars hooked together. The first car powers the train, the second car is empty, and the third car has a driver to steer it.

LSR at 576.553 mph but blew a right rear tire on the second run. His *Green Monster* disintegrated in a spectacular series of flips and rolls, but he came out with only a skinned forehead and swollen eyes as mentioned. Arfons had several cars he called the *Green Monster*. *"Art was a hot rodder in the purest sense of the word, turning junk into race cars."* according to racing enthusiast Ron Christensen. Arfons made one out of scrap iron and assembled it using an old blacksmith's anvil. Arfons worked over 5,000 hours on the car. He used Firestone tires. He raced for five decades and was inducted into the Motor Sports Hall of Fame in 1991.

In the middle of it all, the World Land Speed Record for wheel-driven cars was finally broken by driver Bob Summers and his brother Bill on November 12, 1965. They set the new 409.277 mph record shifting only into third gear with their *Goldenrod*, a 32-foot long streamliner. They had struggled in preparation to get their four fuel-injected Chrysler engines which were installed in tandem to perform optimally. Down-pouring rain, failed parts, and trips back to California added to their frustration. They worked all night before the record run to change burned out rear wheel bearings and then found a *"light, misting rain"* on the course as they started the run.

When the record was set, Bill Summers was overcome with emotions of joy and relief, and softly cried. The jet car shoot out and a plane crash overshadowed the achievement in the media, but it happened nonetheless, and the piston racing crowd was elated.

Firestone graciously had given them some of Art Arfons's time on the salt.

Craig Breedlove holds the honor of being the first man to set records faster than 400, 500, and 600 miles per hour. John Cobb in 1947 traveled over 400 mph as part of his record-setting runs but did not do so as part of an average record land speed. Breedlove's last record of 600.601 mph was set November 15, 1965, in the jet-powered *Spirit of America Sonic I*. He tried again in 1996 and 1997 at Black Rock Desert, Nevada, with a brand new *Spirit of America*, but had disappointing runs. Louise Ann Noeth comment-

A lakester begins its run from the starting line at Speed Week 1962. Most of the lakesters used a P-38 aircraft belly tank like this one for a body in those days. *(Ron Christensen)*

ed that Breedlove had crashed more times than anyone and at faster speeds without a scratch. The last time he crashed at Black Rock Desert, he was traveling at a violent 677 mph and lived to tell about it. He said speed was a *"personal, intimate experience"* as well as *"the exhil-*

aration of self-gratification." When he experienced a crash, he sensed the loss of control and *"a healthy dose of fear."*

Breedlove's record was broken October 23, 1970, by *"wild and crazy stunt driver"* Gary Gabelich at 622.407 miles per hour with his rocket-powered *Blue Flame*. Gabelich's team made nineteen runs going over 600 mph but did not have enough fuel for the return run each time. They overcame the problem by pushing the car up to 120 mph before firing the rocket. The engine was propelled by liquid nitrogen gas.

The next jet-powered land speed records were set at Black Rock Desert. Richard Noble of Britain drove the *Thrust 2* to a record of 633.468 on October 4, 1983, and Andy Green drove Noble's *Thrust SSC* 763.035 mph on October 15, 1997, breaking the sound barrier for the first time on land.

Carl Heaps is owner of the world's fastest diesel truck, the 4,000 horsepower *Phoenix*. It is an 18,000-pound, 1943 vintage International K-7. *(Utah Salt Flat Racing Association. Cris Shearer)*

All three Burkland race cars were built by Gene and Betty Burkland and son Tom of Great Falls, Montana. The 24-foot streamliner on the right was destroyed on September 22, 2001, in a rollover after going over 435 mph two days in a row. It was rebuilt in 2003. *(Utah Salt Flat Racing Association, Cris Shearer)*

The *Budweiser Rocket Car* claimed to go to Mach 1 using a sidewinder missile, but didn't meet international requirements to set a record. Its speed was recorded by a radar gun instead of the required timing lights at the beginning and ending of a measured mile.

The wheel-driven, piston-engined record stood for a quarter century until Elwin "Al" Teague of Santa Fe Springs, California, finally broke it in 1991 or did he? He clocked 378 mph in 1988, 390 in 1989, and just over 400 mph in August 1990. Nolan White of San Diego, California, actually beat Al to the 400 mph mark on a one-way run ac-complishing the feat just one day before Al did it.

On August 21, 1991, driving his supercharged *Speed-O-Motive* with a Chrysler engine, Teague squeaked by the Summers brothers' record with a two- way average of 409.986 mph. FIA rules stipulate that a new record has to be one percent faster than the old record in a recognized class, so there

were questions as to whether he really set a new record. Teague's record was ruled to be in a different class, so the record set by the *Goldenrod* in 1965 remained intact.

Al Teague was described by Louise Ann Noeth as the Jimmy Stewart or George Gershwin of salt flats racing. She called him the *"humble statesman for the sport."* He was reluctant to stand out as a hero. Other adjectives describing Teague were *"bashful"* and *"unassuming."* He hand-crafted his streamliner, spending untold hours alone in his shop in what for him was a labor of love. He was not unlike any other hot rodder except for the record where he stood alone.

Long-time salt flats racer Don Vesco of California and brother Rick of Brigham City, Utah, drove an average 458.45 mph in their turbine-powered *Turbinator*. The date the new LSR was set in its class was October 18, 2001. Sadly, racing pioneer Don Vesco died of cancer in December 2002.

The racers, under Rick Vesco's leadership joined

Vincent motorcyle pit, Lambky's *Streamliner (Utah Salt Flat Racing Association. Cris Shearer)*

forces with environmentalists, government, and business to preserve the very salt they raced on. Many years of harvesting by the potash industry had removed tons of salt, shrinking the size of the track and thinning the hard surface in some areas. Thus, the drivers inaugurated the *"Save the Salt"* campaign.

On Monday, August 12, 2002, 40-year veteran salt flats driver Nolan White of San Diego, at age 71, ran 401 mph on his first run and 422 mph on his second north to south run in the measured mile to set a record average of 413.156 mph. That made him the fastest man in the world driving a piston driven engine. On October 17, 2002, when Nolan was attempting to break his own record set in August, his car, the *Autopower* crashed, instantly turning into a tangled piece of metal. Nolan died at University Hospital

Fred and Mary Lou Larsen owned the world's fastest two- and three-liter streamliner in partnership with Don Cummins. This modified "A" Chevy roadster has set fifteen records since 1959. Fred died of pneumonia on March 24, 2003. *(Utah Salt Flat Racing Association, Cris Shearer)*

in Salt Lake three days later of injuries sustained in the crash. He had to be cut from the wreckage at the time of the accident. He had attempted to steer his car away from the freeway when it rolled after hitting a soft surface. The accident was caused by a cord holding the car's three braking parachutes, which broke as it released.

Some years the salt is smooth and hard, smooth enough to become slick. The results usually are *"rather spectacular spinouts."* When that happens there is plenty of room. Racers' wheels seldom dig in or cause their car to flip. Speedster Phil Freuduiger likened the salt flats in 1958 to a super highway.

Even so, at ultra-high speeds the small grooves and ridges where the mud comes through the crust cause the crust to be rough. As the salt has become thinner, there are some soft spots to watch out for also. Some of the racers will drive street vehi-

Looking like a helmet on wheels, Alan Richards's *Claustrophobia* was the world's smallest streamliner. *(Ron Christensen)*

Statue of Roland Free on *Black Lightening* wearing a swimming suit for aerodynamics, September 13, 1948. *(Utah Salt Flats Racing Association, Cris Shearer)*

went on to report that the first racing event was held on May 15, 1938, at dusty Muroc Dry Lake. Then World War II stopped all such activities.

After the war, the dry lake beds were increasingly the scene of car crashes resulting in injuries and death, so the car clubs looked for safer and larger venues to hold their contests. They looked to the Bonneville Salt Flats, first seeking the endorsement of AAA and then the Bonneville Speedway Association which was a committee of the Salt Lake Chamber of Commerce.

cles slowly along the entire length of the course in order to discern where the imperfections might be.

Speed Week and World of Speed

While the huge machines vied for the world's fastest and the world's endurance records, young backyard mechanics were souping up their own cars and fancying up the auto bodies with bright colors and modified designs. Many of them were from southern California and *"they tested their machines on dry lake"* beds.

The first speed events were under authority of the Muroc Timing Association. The Southern California Timing Association was soon formed with seven charter member clubs. This was on November 19, 1937, according to salt flats historian Louise Ann Noeth. She

The Southern California Timing Association (SCTA) received permission to hold their first event on the salt beds in April 1949 and scheduled *"The First Annual Bonneville Speed Trials"* on August 22-27, 1949. The first Speed Week was sponsored by *"Union Oil*

Novelty racer Kerry McLean of Detroit, Michigan, on his monocycle. Inset: There is even a category for barstools! Number L337 Barstool Racer ridden by Sonny Rossi. *(Utah Salt Flats Racing Association, Cris Shearer)*

Company, Hot Rod *magazine, Grant Piston Rings, and Service Sales of Texas."*

The first Speed Week was held in 1949 on the salt flats. The event was, and continues to be, sponsored by the Southern California Timing Association (SCTA) and Bonneville National, Inc. (BNI). Sixty cars entered the first year and by the second year ninety were pre-entered.

The second year, 1950 saw several racers go past the 200 mph mark. The first was Coloradoan Willie Young. He was driving a new streamliner owned by Bill Kenz and Roy Leslie. Young averaged 206.504 miles an hour. Both front tires were lost on his return run.

> The statement attributed to aerialist Karl Walenka, *"Whatever happens before and after is just waiting,"* applies to Bonneville Salt Flats racing. *(Ron Christensen)*

Bonneville Speed Week and also World of Speed are a racer's paradise. Anyone and everyone can have a chance at going the fastest. There is everything from eighteen-wheel transports to stock cars to motorcycles. Some have air-conditioned pit facilities, lots of spare parts, and large crews assembled to help with the race car. Others may be one or two-man teams with their car, a trailer, and a few tools.

Speed Week and World of Speed are holidays for auto enthusiasts. The participants spend a week away from the daily grind of work and city life. They come from all over the world. All year long they anticipate the one week at the salt flats. They expend vast amounts of creative energy designing their race cars and tinkering with their engines to get more power. When they arrive and wait their turn at the starting line, there is more than anticipation, there is anxiety— worry that they will do their best and fear of the ever-present danger inherent in high speed racing.

The speedway is laid out so that incoming racers can register and have their cars technically inspected at the entrance to the pit area. The unreserved pits are lined up in three rows for a quarter-mile with *"a wide access road on each side of each row of pit spaces."* There are no pre-assigned areas for the different classes.

There is no prize money in Bonneville racing even though many have spent more than $100,000 developing a roadster and many times that on a streamliner. Participants are racing to get in the record book or to better their own

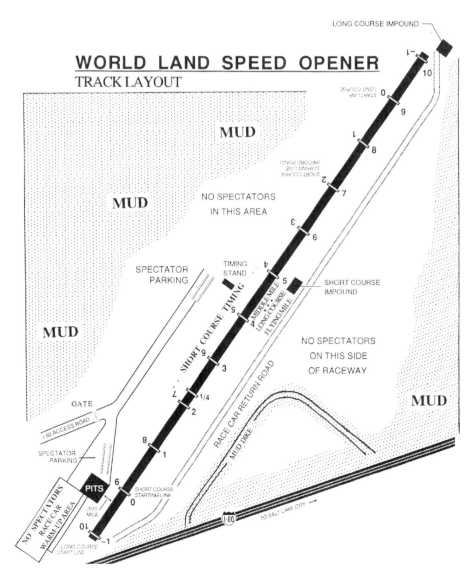

Layout of the Bonneville Speedway. *(Southern California Timing Association)*

82 year-old Lee Burkey made the 200 MPH Club on this 1000 cc motorcyle. *(Utah Salt Flat Racing Association. Cris Shearer)*

achieve their goal of speed using the leading edges of technology. It may also be the only place where cars can race competitively which have been built by hand in the family garage by shade tree mechanics.

These individualistic enthusiasts have also looked past the sheer joy of sailing across the shimmering salt at tremendous speeds. They also work hard at doing no harm to the arid desert. They change their oil with the utmost care making sure not to spill any on the salt surface. Their racing lines marked in the salt are purposely water soluable so that they will wash away with the rain.

Sadly, there are few young drivers. Almost all the salt flats racers are in their fifties, sixties, seventies, and beyond. But, they keep coming back . . .

times. They help each other as one big family, even furnishing engines to others who have blown theirs.

The experience at Bonneville has been described as *"indescribable," "remarkable," "exhilarating,"* and *"it gives you butterflies in your stomach,"* It takes a team effort of time and dedication. There is a feeling of anticipation and the excitement is shared by all. One participant claimed, *"We're just a bunch of motor enthusiasts and hot rodders having some fun. If we achieve great speed (happen to go fast), that'll be a bonus."*

The Bonneville International Speedway, just east of Wendover, is the site of the last truly amateur automotive event. Man has always had a love affair with speed. Bonneville is the place where men and women can

Beautiful sunrise reflected on the briny waters of the salt flats. *(Cris Shearer)*

188

Official One-Mile Land Speed Records, 1935 to 2003

DATE	DRIVER	CAR	CAR TYPE	LOCATION	SPEED
08/12/02	Nolan White	*Autopower*	Piston	Bonneville SF	413.156
10/18/01	Don Vesco	*Turbinator*	Jet	Bonneville SF	458.45
08/21/91	Al Teague	*Speed-O-Motive*	Piston	Bonneville SF	409.986
10/15/97	Andy Green	*Thrust SSC*	Jet	Black Rock	763.035
10/4/83	Richard Noble	*Thrust 2*	Jet	Black Rock	633.468
10/23/70	Gary Gabelich	*Blue Flame*	Jet	Bonneville SF	622.407
11/15/65	Craig Breedlove	*Spirit of America*	Jet	Bonneville SF	600.601
11/12/65	Bob Summers	*Goldenrod*	Piston	Bonneville SF	409.277
11/7/65	Art Arfons	*Green Monster*	Jet	Bonneville SF	576.553
11/2/65	Craig Breedlove	*Spirit of America*	Jet	Bonneville SF	555.127
10/27/64	Art Arfons	*Green Monster*	Jet	Bonneville SF	536.71
10/15/64	Craig Breedlove	*Spirit of America*	Jet	Bonneville SF	526.277
10/13/64	Craig Breedlove	*Spirit of America*	Jet	Bonneville SF	468.719
10/05/64	Art Arfons	*Green Monster*	Jet	Bonneville SF	434.22
10/2/64	Tom Green	*Wingfoot Express*	Jet	Bonneville SF	413.199
09/09/60	Mickey Thompson	*Challenger 1*	Piston	Bonneville SF	406.60*
09/16/47	John Cobb	*Railton Special*	Piston	Bonneville SF	394.196
8/23/39	John Cobb	*Railton Special*	Piston	Bonneville SF	367.910
09/16/38	George Eyston	*Thunderbolt*	Piston	Bonneville SF	357.50
09/15/38	John Cobb	*Railton Special*	Piston	Bonneville SF	350.25
09/03/35	Sir Malcolm Campbell	*Bluebird*	Piston	Bonneville SF	301.129

Earlier land speed records date back to December 18, 1898, when a record of 39.24 mph was set by Gaston Chasseloup-Laubat at Acheres, France, in an electric car. Many earlier records were set at Daytona Beach, Florida, until Sir Malcolm Campbell, at the encouragement of Ab Jenkins, reached the first 300 mph mark in 1935 on the Bonneville Salt Flats, establishing the flats as the world's fastest speedway.

*Mickey Thompson's was a one way only speed run.   www.landspeed.com/turbo_history.html

7.

On the Edge of a New Century

We lived ... "it out in the dusty, dirty, hot, dry, windy
old community of Wendover. Good old Wendover, the town that drew people from
all parts of the planet and forced us to become one big family."

—John Hernandez

Wendover lies on the western edge of an ancient inland sea named Lake Bonneville. The nearby Great Salt Lake is a small remnant. Thousands of years ago the climate became arid and the lake mostly evaporated and became extremely salty with no external outlet. The Great Salt Lake Desert was a part of Lake Bonneville.

The Great Salt Lake Desert, 115 miles long and forty miles wide, includes the 153 square-mile area of the Bonneville Salt Flats. The salt desert was once the floor of the inland lake and the flats are only a few feet above the high water level of the Great Salt Lake. There is no exterior drainage. It is similar to a bathtub without a drain.

The salt desert is encrusted with crystals of dry salt on the surface while underneath is a level expanse of mud and salt. It is too salty for vegetation to grow and remains barren of plant and animal life in the interior regions. The soils are described as arid, hardpan, alkaline and very thin. The vegetation is saline on the fringes. The salt areas of the flats varies in thickness from 3 or 4 feet in the middle to an edge as thin as a feather.

According to a Kaiser Chemical scientific brochure, a Shell Oil Company test hole drilled in July 1956 near the center of the salt flats revealed volcanic rocks between 1,375 and 1,400 feet in depth. Below the volcanic layer was igneous rock to the bottom of the test hole at 2,948 feet.

Between the top layer of salt and the volcanic material are layers of silt and clay of differing color. At twenty-five feet deep the clay is darker gray to black in color with *"a strong odor due to decomposing organic matter."* Blue and blue-green clay are the more common colors found under the salt. Evidence of brine shrimp are present in the lighter colored clay.

The *Utah Atlas* states that the annual normal precipitation is less than 6.0 inches (the average precipitation from 1936-75 was 4.8 in.) and snowfall is less than 10.0 inches in the salt desert near Wendover. The area falls within the desert climate zone (arid continental). The frost free season is 80 to 120 days. The January average maximum temperature is 36 degrees F. and the average minimum is 12-16 degrees F. The July maximum average temperature is 92 degrees F. and the minimum average is 60 degrees F. Winds are usually light but can gust up to 75 mph causing dust storms of salt reducing, visibility to less than 200 feet.

The altitude is 4,226 to 4,250 feet above sea level at Wendover. The latitude is 40 degrees 44 minutes north, and 114 degrees 02 minutes west longitude.

On the flats itself the elevation is about 4,215 feet above sea level. To the northwest is Pilot Mountain named by Captain John C. Fremont in 1845 while he was surveying in the area. Pilot Peak is 10,000 feet in height. Also to the north immediately adjacent to Wendover is the Leppy Mountain Range or Desert

Welcome to the Silver Island Mountains National Back Country Byway. The tour route will take you 54 miles around the rugged Silver Island Mountains. Plan to spend at least two hours to travel the entire route.

The route is suitable for most high clearance passenger vehicles. The northern part of the road may be muddy after rains, so go slow and check the route ahead. **Vehicle travel in the Silver Island Mountains is limited to existing roads and trails only.** Please stay on the tour route. Car camping is permitted within 100 feet of existing roads. All services are available in Wendover.

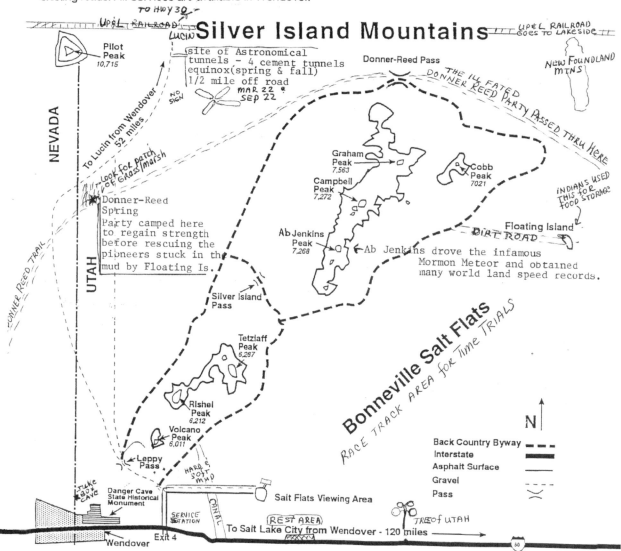

Bureau of Land Management map of the National Back Country Byway on the Bonneville Salt Flats. The Silver Island Mountain peaks are named after racers and citizens associated with the salt flats.

Hills and northeast are the Silver Island Mountains.

Five Silver Island peaks are named for famous racers of the Bonneville Salt Flats. Jenkins Peak at 7,268 feet above sea level is named for Utah racer Ab Jenkins who holds more world speed records than any other driver in the history of racing. Campbell Peak, 7,272 feet, is named in honor of Sir Malcolm Campbell of Great Britain, the first racer to go 300 mph.

Cobb Peak, elevation 7,021 feet, is named for John

Cobb who held the world's wheel-driven speed record of 394.19 mph for 18 years. Tetzlaff Peak, elevation 6,267 feet is named for Teddy Tetzlaff who in 1914 raced a record 141.73 mph on the salt flats. Graham Peak is 7,563 feet high and named after Salt Laker Athol Graham who died attempting to set a land speed record. Two other peaks are named Rishel Peak at 6,212 feet and Lamus Peak, elevation about 6,200 feet. William Rishel was the first promoter of the Bonneville Speedway, and Blair Lamus helped design and maintain the speedway, as well as helping to design and build the first highway across the salt flats.

Varying sea level lines of *"ancient Lake Bonneville are clearly visible along the eastern flanks of the Silver Island Mountain range."* A major fault line exists along the eastern side of Silver Island. South of Wendover is the Deep Creek Mountain Range with two peaks rising above 12,000 feet. Ten miles west, the Toano Range forms a western barrier in Nevada.

There are several versions for the origin of the name Wendover. It *"may have been named for a surveyor employed by the railroad named Charles Wendover."* However, Charles Wendover reportedly does not appear on the old rolls of Western Pacific employees. Another more plausible explanation originates from the livestock industry. Herds of sheep grazed in the nearby range lands and *"wended their way over"* the numerous trails available to them. Wenden is said to be an old Anglo-Saxon word meaning to go or to wend. A third notion explains that the railroad 'bends over' towards Ely, Nevada. No one knows for sure where the name came from.

Wendover is unlike other towns in Utah for many reasons. For example, Wendover is home to the 3,473 square-mile Great Salt Lake Desert where numerous world land speed records have been set. Another reason for its uniqueness results from the *"claim to fame as the place where the crew of the* Enola Gay *practiced the bombing of Japanese cities before dropping the atomic bomb in 1945."*

"Salt made Wendover" is a notable statement about Wendover. The potash industry has provided employment locally for over eighty years and the salt flat speedway has made Wendover famous for almost as long. Tourism has also been a sustaining factor throughout Wendover's history. Wendover has long served the motoring public as a stop for gas and food, or an overnight's lodging, or a place to gamble.

"Water is the key to Wendover" is another important observation about the town. Former Wendover City clerk Jean Draper explained the role of water in the desert oasis of Wendover.

She wrote in the *High Desert Advocate*: *"Although water is one of the necessities of life, unless there is an interruption of service, we pay scant attention to the fact that it is available on demand. Without an adequate supply of water this area would soon revert back to the desert it was 100 years ago.*

"Because steam engines and section crews needed water, Western Pacific Railroad Company built a twenty mile long water transmission line from Pilot Mountain to Wendover in 1903 [likely 1907]."

Draper continued *"It was no small task. The wooden stave pipe was hauled to the mountain by pack animals and the pipe trenches were hand dug and blasted out of rock and rubble. Three miles north east of town an open 254,000 gallon storage reservoir was built along with a limited distribution system to the depot and town site. Townspeople not connected to the system could fill their water barrels at the railroad standpipe. Incidentally, the standpipe is still in use today.*

"This system proved adequate until WWII when water was needed for the air base, housing and fire protection. An additional 2 cubic feet per second was leased from Johnson Springs 32 miles west of Wendover and pumped through a 12-inch pipeline to a one million gallon concrete reservoir on Three-mile Hill west of Wendover and a 480,000 gallon steel tank at the airfield. The military also constructed a 923,000 gallon open reservoir near the original railroad reservoir to store Pilot Mountain water.

"These two water sources, Pilot Mountain and Johnson Springs, proved adequate for many years, although neither source was owned by Wendover."

In January 1959, the *Tooele Transcript* reported that John Huston, movie director and real estate developer had agreed to purchase the Wendover water system from the Western Pacific Railroad. Wendover City and the Tooele County Chamber of Commerce went into action. Wendover town board president Alf Callister and the Wendover town board met a year previously with a railroad executive and had tentatively worked out an agreement to purchase the water system.

The chamber sent a telegram to the president of the Western Pacific Railroad wherein they stated *"We feel it would be unfortunate if the people of Wendover were*

> "The possibilities of Wendover's landscape are both beautiful and peculiar to the desert. From the rock outcrop at Three Mile Hill on the western edge of town, the view is almost ethereal as the distant mountain range blends with the fluid salt flats and the morning fog."
>
> —Ray Kingston as quoted by Elaine Jarvik

Wendover in 1950, looking westward. *(George Stewart)*

not extended the opportunity of purchasing and operating their own water system. We feel sure that you will show all fairness to all the people of Tooele County who have in the past displayed great confidence in your firm. Request you defer decisions of settling to outside concern. Would appreciate full particulars from your office. W. C. Tate, President Tooele County Chamber of Commerce." In the end the railroad kept its word to the city.

Jean Draper continued her narrative. *"In 1960, the Western Pacific Railroad turned the operation of the Pilot Mountain system over to Wendover. Wendover would obtain clear title after 40 years (in 2000). Fourteen years later in 1974, the Air Force turned the airfield and Johnson Springs system over to the town of Wendover.*

"However, the Air Force did not have title to a water right at Johnson Springs Ranch. After considerable litigation between the Air Force, Fred D. West, a previous owner of Johnson Springs Ranch and the present ranch owners it was judged that the ranch would receive one cubic feet per second, Fred West would have the second cfs, and if available the third cfs would be divided between the two parties.

"West eventually turned his water right over to the unincorporated community of West Wendover. By way of infor-

mation, water is not owned by anyone, only the right to use water can be owned.

"Although two excellent sources were available, neither source met clean water standards of either Nevada or Utah even though chlorination was being done. In 1974 Wendover acquired a well located at Silver Zone Pass in Nevada and connected it to the Johnson Springs transmission line. This well and a second well constructed at Silver Zone Pass in 1977 supplied good quality water until upgrading of the springs could take place.

"In 1980 the two communities completed a project which upgraded the Johnson Springs supply so it could be reintroduced into the system. That same summer Wendover replaced about two miles of old 8-inch steel Pilot Peak transmission line with new 8-inch ductile iron pipe, wrapped in plastic. And in 1981, Wendover applied to the Farmers Home Administration for funds to upgrade the spring collection system on Pilot Peak, construct a new one million gallon reservoir, replace more transmission line and install a new chlorination station. Completion of these projects brought the system into compliance with clean water standards.

"Upgrading of both systems is ongoing and costly. But efforts to obtain adequate water for this growing area in

194

Wendover in July 1993 looking west. State Line and Silver Smith in the center background. *(Steve Elton, Gertrude Tripp)*

adverse conditions is a tribute to dedicated hard working lead-ers of both communities."

In 2003 Wendover, Utah, *"accessed water from three water springs outside of the city."* Two other springs were added which brought the total water generating capac-ity to 1,100 gallons of water per minute. West Wendover uses water from four springs transmitting 2,300 gallons per minute. It was relatively cheap to deliver the water to Wendover because it was a gravity-based system.

"A TALE OF TWO CITIES"
City of Wendover, Utah

Wendover, Utah, is located about halfway between Denver, Colorado, and Los Angeles and San Francisco, California. Wendover is 125 miles west of Salt Lake City, Utah and 110 miles east of Elko, Nevada. Reno is 396 miles to the west.

By the mid-1950's Wendover consisted of a series of gas and service stations and motels. Wendover Will, a giant cowboy sign had been erected by the State Line in 1952. The sign fast became the symbol of the com-munity of Wendover. There was a barber shop, the post office and the Pastime Club remaining along the rail-road tracks.

Twain West's A-1 Service was still thriving on the Nevada side until the late 1970's. The A-1 included a hotel where Jean Draper, the A-1's bookkeeper claimed, *"for a dollar a trucker could get a towel and take a shower while his truck was being serviced."* Liquor, beer, slot machines and other gambling could be found, and the young people of Wendover were hired to work in the service station end of the business. The café served ade-quate meals for the hungry, including home-made pies.

Ripp's, Peterson's, the Tri-State Merc, and Faye & Nels' markets all disappeared at various time periods after the war. So did the Western Pacific Railroad Depot, the Beanery, the roundhouse and other railroad facilities. Howard DeVaney's garage and car dealership also closed. Many service stations came and went. Some of them were Lewis Brothers, the Western Texaco Service, the Mobil, the Flying A, the Union, and the Phillips 66. Years ago, trucks parked north of the highway occasionally lost their brakes and ended up in the Patio Motel swimming pool.

There were 400 to 500 people in Wendover in the 50's. Most of them lived in the Federal Housing proj-ect south of the highway or in the scattering of hous-es nearby.

Hot rodders filling up at the Wendover Flying A Service during Speedweek in 1962. Proprietor Paul Christensen spent most days playing pinochle with the owners of two other stations across the street. When an occasional car pulled into any of the three service stations, the owner of that particular station would hurry to help their customer. Inset: Young Ron Christensen in front of the Flying A station. *(Ron Christensen)*

Pritchett's Wendover Motel. *(Gertrude Tripp)*

Ab and Marv Jenkins at the Mobil gas station in Wendover. *(Marvin Jenkins)*

Individual citizens filled certain niches to make the town function. They all worked to make it successful, using their personal skills or position to the best of their ability. At the risk of slighting someone, a few of the many are mentioned to illustrate. Chief Ray Crawford took care to see that Wendover had fire protection as did Fred Kenley, Donald Dean, Darrell Wadsworth, John Palmer, and Robert Scobie on the base. Ray Crawford was great with the local teenagers. He allowed them to use his service station garage to work on their cars.

C. D. McCloud and Gene Craner worked hard making electricity available to townspeople. Gene Craner kept it going. Howard "Hoot" Gibson tackled the numerous water problems encountered after the city acquired the water system from the railroad. Alfred Callister had done the same job for the railroad before. Leo Waters was the railroad station and freight agent, as well as justice of the peace. Hugh K. Neilson and Lynn Poulsen were other recent justices of the peace. *"You could count on Bill Russell to keep law and order on the Utah side of the line. Dan Fernandez was the deputy of the Nevada side."*

Pete McKellar, J. Ronald Anderson and others kept the local church going. *"Anderson was the go-to-man for the boy scouts."* McKellar's specialty was home-made ice cream for everyone. He was also a first-rate prankster. At Christmas time, the tradition of lighting a gigantic tree for the town began. Gene Craner and Don Dean erected a metal A-frame tree, complete with lights on the hill north of town. It was near a translator station where electricity could be tapped. The City of Wendover continued to maintain the tree a half century later. The tradition started when Craner and Dean placed a lighted tree atop the high school, which promptly blew off. Hence, they built the sturdier metal model on the hill.

Richard Dixon collected and displayed many fine antique cars in a local speedway museum, as well as owned and operated several businesses. Locals, Bill Woffinden, Elden Williams, and Randy Croasman had cars they raced on the Bonneville Speedway. Ron Christensen grew up in Wendover where his father ran the Flying A service. Ron later set several records on the speedway. He annually produced a live, weeklong radio broadcast for the enjoyment of the racing crowd. There was definitely local representation at these national events.

Gertrude Tripp was actively involved in civic, educational and government causes over the years. Gene Jones helped people and organizations often anonomously. Anna Smith was wonderful in support of school and community projects and individual needs as well. Russ Lewis helped fund school needs and civic activities too. Among other things, Marie Johnston served on the school board and city council, made sure Wendover had a cemetery and pushed for a freeway underpass in Wendover so the north end of town could be developed.

Roy Erickson and Ab Smith were behind the Lion's Club. *"The annual turkey shoot was the Lion's Club moneymaker."* The Lady Lions held Apron and Overall dances to raise money to buy library books for the community. The books were housed in the Federal housing building. When the building finally closed, the books were given to Wells, Nevada. The Deer Hunter's Ball generated funds for the Bonneville worker's union.

The Wendover American Legion and Ladies' Auxiliary also served the citizens of Wendover, with Hazel Sorensen as auxiliary president through numerous terms. The ladies raised thousands of dollars for charitable causes, baked cookies, cooked dinners for the sick, and

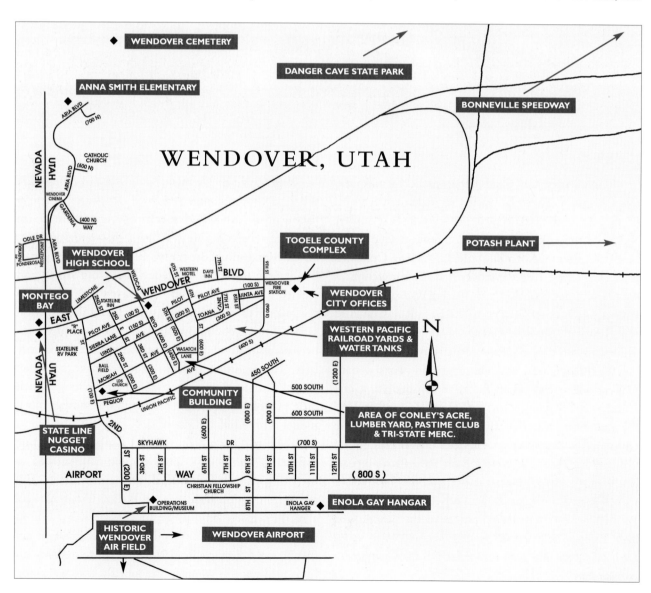

gathered donations so children could have *"mittens, hats, gloves, and scarves"* at Christmas time. They held Family Night Bingo and raised money with a New Year's Eve Sweetheart Ball. And the list goes on.

There was not a bank in Wendover, but Twain West made small loans to local people. He kept enough money on hand to cash payroll checks. His accounts receivable records read like a "Who's Who" of Wendover according to his former bookkeeper, Jean Draper. Somehow it all worked!

By 1970 Wendover, Utah had a population of 780 and grew almost 60 percent to 1,232 in 1994. 1,537 residents in 510 housing units were numbered in the 2000 census. Wendover government utilized a town-board with a town-board president for many years. It was incorporated October 25, 1950 with a population of under 500. British racer George Eyston mentioned 205 inhabitants in 1935 when he visited.

Local resident and high school junior Garn Anderson wrote a very informative history of Wendover for a sociology class in 1969. He described the town's early incorporation efforts as follows. *"During the middle 1940's the battle cry 'taxation without representation' was again heard. The residents of Wendover voiced their feelings about being neglected on the Western Utah border. Their many appeals for help with education, roads, sanitation and etc. had not been heard. Without legal community status they could do little for themselves and they felt the State of Utah would not come to their aid.*

"Mr. Lester Giffen, yard clerk for the Western Pacific R.R. and executive chairman of the Wendover Developing Association spearheaded a drive to secede from Utah and join Nevada. This never materi-

WENDOVER TOWN BOARD PRESIDENTS

Blair Lamus   Peter McKellar

Alfred Callister   John Susich   Tom Watson

WENDOVER TOWN MAYORS

Hugh K. Neilson   Glen C. Beck   Ab Smith
(also town-board president)

Brenda Morgan   Kent Peterson   Steve Perry

Wendover City Officials in 2003

Steve Perry	Mayor
Brett Shelton	Councilman
Shawn Wadsworth	Councilman
Dale Higley	Councilman
Terrence Holdeman	Councilman
Gertrude Tripp	Councilwoman
Glenn Wadsworth	City Administrator
Lamar Melville	Municipal Judge
Vaughan Tripp	Police Chief
Kirk Petersen	Fire Chief
Armando Rodriquez	Utility Foreman
Margaret L. Wheeler	Clerk/Recorder
Darlene Trammell	City Treasurer

Wendover Police Chief Vaughn Tripp.

alized but it was an interesting period in our community life, and the echoes of 'secession' and 'divorce' from Utah were heard all over the land. After it was all over Wendover remained a struggling band of people located on the Utah-Nevada border.

"The year 1950 was an important and interesting one in Wendover. The first signs of a community government began to appear. Residents were stirred with a desire to become a legal community so they could have a voice in local affairs, participate in the division of tax money and become a legal entity so they could do business for themselves. The Wendover Air Base faced further reduction and a possibility of closing entirely.

"The Western Pacific Railroad was changing from steam locomotive to diesel powered equipment. Water lines, reser-

Wendover community building was built in 1944 as a USO recreation hall at a cost of $50,000. Spike Birdzell was chairman of the Wendover war recreation committee and spearheaded the construction.

voirs, sewer lines [The military base had somewhat of a sewer system but Wendover did not install one, complete with lines and several lagoons until 1970. It was upgraded again ten years later in 1980.] and a 300 unit Federal housing program, much of which would have to be dismantled under government regulation, was at stake.

"Saving these facilities for the town was a necessity. Community control of water was a must to safeguard against private ownership and a possible 'squeeze' that might result.

"Becoming a legal entity would give status to do business with the Federal Government and qualify the community to receive some of the badly needed facilities and deal with the railroad to purchase their water line and land owned by them and leased to residents.

"A group of eleven business and community leaders formed a committee to get the 'ball rolling.' Blair S. Lamus was appointed temporary chairman. A public meeting was called on March 9, 1950 to consider the proposition of incorporating the community into a town as a solution to some of the community problems, in particular the housing problem.

"This meeting lasted nearly four hours and a lot of prepared information and reports were presented to the people. Everyone had opportunity to express themselves and present their opinions.

"A permanent committee of eleven people was elected by secret ballot and

City firemen (1974). Standing left to right: Reese Melville, Larry Lisk, Randall Melville, Bill Biondi, Ray Crawford, Fred Koska, unknown. Front: Don Hall, Lloyd Brown. *(Kirk Petersen)*

given authority to represent the people to accomplish incorporation. . . . Under date of July 15, 1950 a petition signed by a majority of the electors, 149 names, of the unincorporated town of Wendover, Tooele County, Utah was filed with the board of county commissioners. On August 7, 1950 in the regular session the commissioners approved the petition and declared Wendover an incorporated town of Tooele County, State of Utah."

The county commissioners appointed a town-board president and a board of trustees consisting of five people. They were to hold office until a municipal election could be held.

The first town board consisted of Blair Lamus president (he completed the unexpired term of his father Ed who passed away), R. Melvin (Spike) Birdzell, Peter McKellar, Jesse V. Ecton, and Clarence McLeod as trustees. John Susich was the clerk. Lind Hutchinson was thereafter appointed a trustee when Birdzell moved away and J. Rands Wiley replaced Susich as clerk.

Garn Anderson continued *"In November of 1951*

Fire Chief Ray Crawford. *(Kerrie Supanich)*

Tony Kerbovich and Earl Lacy were local law enforcement officers.

Wendover Post Office. Recent postmasters have been Larry Supanich (1994 to present), Clayton Carter (1991 to 1994), Arloene Gieber (1986 to 1991), Glenda Green (1961 to 1986), & Frances Russell (1959 to 1961).

the first election was held. The five member board ran unopposed on the Republican ticket and were the first elected leaders of Wendover."

The new community began 1952 with $1,420.66 in cash on hand. By today's standards, the new government was slow to begin passing regulations. The first ordinance was enacted the following summer, August 10, 1952 when a curfew on the sale of beer went into effect. Beer could not be sold during a six-hour period from 2 a.m. until 8 a.m. The first beer license was granted to the Western Service.

Preston Nuffer was responsible for the water system operations and billings of Wendover City for many years. He served as town clerk and his home was his office, using a ninety-nine-key adding machine and an old manual typewriter. When Jean Draper took over as clerk she moved the office into a *"little, old two-room building"* on the spot where the new city-county complex stood in modern Wendover. She was followed by Margaret Wheeler who started in 1976. Jean Draper returned as city treasurer in

1978 until 1987. She was followed by Adrian Linam and Darlene Trammell.

John Susich (1960-1974) and Thomas Watson (1974-1977) later served as town board presidents. On the 25th of March 1982, Wendover became a third class city with a population of 1,099. At that time, the town board president, who was Hugh Neilson (1978-1985), became the mayor with a city council. Mr. Neilson was succeeded by the following mayors: Glen Beck (1986-1989), Albert "Ab" Smith, (1990-1993), Brenda Morgan (1994-1997), Kent Peterson (1998), and Steve Perry (1998-present).

As mentioned, the chief of police in Wendover in 2003 was Vaughn Tripp. There were four patrol officers and two reserve officers on the force. The department had five patrol cars, a SWAT van, and an animal control van for one animal control officer. There was one Utah Highway Patrol officer stationed at Wendover City Hall also. Past police chiefs were Maurice Clark (1982-1983), Gary Blauser (1983-1984), June Carter (1984-1990), Angel Barboza (1996-1998), and Vaughn Tripp (1990-1995 and 1998-present).

The fire chief in 2003 was Kirk Petersen. The fire department of Wendover consisted of fifteen volunteers who received little or no compensation. There were

Wendover City and Tooele County Complex located at 910 E. Wendover Blvd.

one chief, one captain and three lieutenants. Facilities included the Wendover Fire Station and the Airport Fire Station leased by Tooele County.

The fire department owned two fire trucks, a patrol car for the chief and a Wildland International truck. They also own an antique fire truck which is used for displays and parades. Past fire chiefs of the Wendover Fire Department have included Fred Kenley (airbase), Ray Crawford for many years, and Don Hall.

City of West Wendover, Nevada (Formerly known as Eastline)

When Wendover, Utah, was incorporated in 1950 the residents of Wendover living in Nevada wanted to be included in the incorporation. That was not possible at the time. Thus the Nevada side of Wendover remained without city status. (Note: see Wendover Secession section elsewhere in this chapter.)

The Wendover, Nevada, residents had an elected constable and later a deputy sheriff of Elko County. Dan Fernandez was deputy sheriff for a considerable time in Wendover, Nevada, followed by Deputies North, Latta, and Earl Lacy Jr. Twain West of the A-1 and Bill Smith of the State Line offered to voluntarily assess a fee on each of their slot machines in order to pay for a deputy sheriff and justice of the peace. The Elko County commissioners liked the idea and followed through with the proposal. The unincorporated Wendover, Nevada, town was under the jurisdiction of the justice of the peace at Montello, Nevada. Eventually the *citizens "were successful in getting the district split so they could have their own justice"* in Wendover, Nevada. Leo P. Waters was justice of the peace as was Chet (Chester) Howlett, a brother-in-law of Bill Smith of the State Line. Chet served for many years.

Author Garn Anderson noted that West Wendover *"was a precinct, holding their own elections, functioning under Elko County, Nevada, entirely independent from Wendover, Utah. This was a unique situation and a good example of the problem of government where a group of people are located straddling a state line ... ."* Both cities held separate courts and operated separate jails but worked *"closely in apprehending those who"* broke the law.

During the 1980s a West Wendover Advisory Board held regular meetings to address the needs of the unincorporated Wendover, Nevada, community. Among the original advisory council members were Fred D. West,

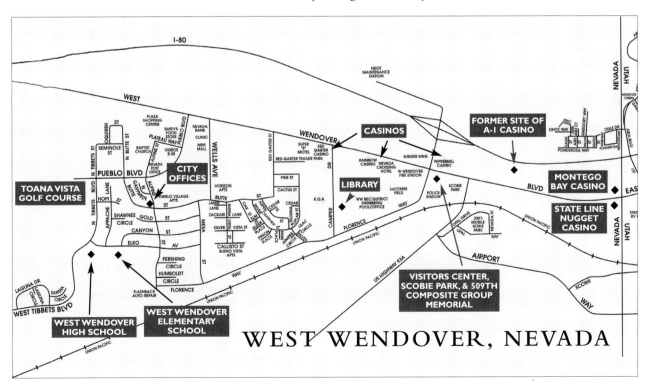

WEST WENDOVER, NEVADA

WEST WENDOVER MAYORS

Walt Saunders   Reese Melville   Josephine Thaut

Photo not available of Mayor Donna Crook. *Above photos courtesy Linda and Jerry Brown*

Jim Smith, and Bob Scobie. They met regularly with the Elko County commissioners. They addressed such matters as water and sewer, recreation, fire protection, emergency services, schools, and communications with other government entities on the county, state and federal levels.

The *Snapshot*, a February 2002 publication of West Wendover's community development department detailed the beginning of West Wendover. It stated, *"In 1991, a great historical event took place as the residents of Wendover, Nevada, now over 2,300 strong voted for self-rule and incorporated the City of West Wendover, Nevada. This formation of a city government was an important step for the residents and the community."* Funds generated locally would now be used on the local level and in addition, the citizens of West Wendover, Nevada, would have a direct voice in how the municipal government operated instead of having local services administered by Elko County, Nevada.

The City of West Wendover was incorporated in 1991 on July first and quickly boomed to a population of 5,000 and a 13% growth rate during the last five years of the twentieth century. There were *"five high class casino establishments providing year round world-wide quality entertainment, dozens of small businesses which ... found opportunity not only through eager customers but through a cooperative local government"* wrote Chris J. Melville in his ten-year history of West Wendover.

The West Wendover City government included a mayor, a five-member city council and city manager with support staff. The city operated a fire department, a police department, and public utilities departments. The administrative offices were located at 801 Alpine Street in West Wendover. Their motto, written on a round logo, reads: *"City of West Wendover, Nevada. Come Grow With Us."*

The city encouraged growth by providing a state-of-the-art, outdoor community swimming pool, the 18-hole championship Toana Vista golf course, and the tree-shaded Scobie Park. They achieved 100 percent recycling of waste-water, 75% recycling of solid waste, and sponsored several beautification and tree planting programs throughout the city.

Most homes were new and were beginner to modest in size and price. The 2000 census enumerated 1,626 housing units in West Wendover and a population of 4,721. Elko County School District operated West Wendover Elementary School with 680 stu-

West Wendover Post Office.

West Wendover City Office.

West Wendover City officials in 2003

Josephine E. Thaut	Mayor
Irene Thompson	City Clerk
Chris J. Melville	City Manager
Jeff Knudtson	Fire Chief
Richard "Fritz" Weighall	Police Chief
Tom Stratton	Utilities Director

Toana Vista Golf Course.

dents in 2002 and West Wendover High School which included junior high age students.

Police Chief Ladon Murray headed the West Wendover police department when it was formed on July 1, 1991. The department started with six police officers and two civilians. By 2002 the department had grown to sixteen officers and three technicians with four divisions. The four divisions were administration, patrol, investigation and animal control. They were involved in civic programs which provided youth sporting activities, neighborhood watch, gang resistance training, etc.

The fire department has been in operation since January 1993. Jeff Knudtson was fire chief. In 2002 the station owned an air truck, a rescue squad, and three each of pumper trucks and command vehicles. They also manned a hazmat truck and a brush truck owned by the Nevada Division of Forestry. There were two full-time professionals and twenty-four volunteer firefighters.

The public works department was under the control of the Elko County Town Board at the time of West Wendover's incorporation. On July 1, 1991 the department was transferred to West Wendover. The department is responsible for the water system, storm drains, snow removal, fleet management, streets, sewer, property maintenance and building approval for new construction. The water distribution system consists of water lines, a main spring and five wells. There were two supervisors, clerks and four technicians in 2002.

The city added the utilities department in July 1999 with six employees. The department is responsible for wastewater treatment, waste disposal and water quality. An in-house state and federally certified laboratory assured the community of environmentally safe drinking water.

Past mayors have been Donna Crick who was involved in the incorporation effort and then was elected the first mayor in 1991. Crick resigned and Walt Saunders was appointed to finish the term. He was re-elected and served until 2000 when he resigned. Reese Melville served as mayor until 2001 as an appointed official. Josephine Thaut was elected in June of 2001 and reelected in June 2003.

Gaming: Wendover's No. 1 Industry

Surrounded completely on all sides by desert, Wendover welcomes gamblers coming from the east as the first gambling opportunity and provides a last chance for gamblers going east. The major landmark on the Nevada side of the town is a sixty-four-foot metal

Peppermill Casino.

A new State Line Nugget Hotel and Gambling Hall logo was added to Wendover Will, in 2003 when ownership of the State Line changed.

Red Garter Casino

and neon cowboy that waves hello with one hand and points to the State Line Nugget Casino with the other.

It is a fact that gaming *"is and always will be Wendover's life blood. The industry employs up to 80 percent of the city's work force, it generates over 75 percent of the city's taxes directly and in one way or another the health of every other business in Wendover is linked to gaming,"* according to an August, 1995 business supplement to the local paper, *The High Desert Advocate.* Even so, the work force of

casino employees is transient with a fifty percent turnover per year.

Wendover relies on the Utah's Wasatch Front to keep the casinos in business and Wendover enables the state of Utah to remain free of any form of gambling. One study reported that 80% of the 650,000 people comprising Wendover's annual tourist trade comes from Utah. Sadly, gamblers sometimes lose their paychecks and even cars. Local minister Chris Lund spent $12,000 in a recent year on $15 bus tickets to provide people a way home. The local schools also provides free lunches to the children of employees who gamble away their paychecks.

Besides gambling, West Wendover has a golf course, shows, dancing, inexpensive meals and organized bus trips from the Salt Lake metropolitan area. There is an abundance of motel rooms and several gas stations to supply the needs of visitors.

A gaming boom began when developers, rancher Dick McDougal, Robert Berry, and Peter Laxalt built the Nevada Crossing. Within six years there were four new casinos built and operating besides the State Line Casino. They were the Rainbow Casino, the

A-1 Cafe in West Wendover *(Gertrude Tripp)*

The Rainbow Casino and Hotel. Wendover's first stop light can also be seen. It was installed in March 2003. The $250,000 plus cost of the semaphore was funded by Peppermill, Inc. which owned the Rainbow, Montego Bay and Peppermill resorts in Wendover.

Peppermill Casino, the Red Garter, and the Silver Smith. Jim's Casino was replaced by the Silver Smith. This expansion led to the creation of a new city called West Wendover.

Looking back, author Richard Menzies mused *"One day in the spring of 1975 a strange billboard appeared on the far end of town. 'Welcome to West Wendover' it read. At the time, many of us who saw it dismissed it as somebody's idea of a joke, because as far as the eye could see beyond that billboard lay a vast wasteland of shadscale and rabbit brush, populated primarily by snakes, scorpions, badgers, jackrabbits, and ring-tailed lizards."*

Former Silver Smith, now Montego Bay. It was open as the Silver Smith from 1984 until December 2002 when new ownership took it over.

Earlier, the main buildings beyond the State Line belonged to Fred West (who came originally as a squatter on BLM land), and later his ex-wife Edith and son Twain in the form of the now defunct A-1 Café and Motel and adjoining Texaco service station; plus the Hideaway Club and a couple of small dwellings. Bob Tiley's Club Bonneville with cabins and a swimming pool utilized natural hot pools west of the water tower rock. Fred West's 1,200 acres of land was sold for development as West Wendover in 1981. Also, Joe Ayala's Nevada Club operated just north of the State Line until the club burned. In 1977, the U.S. Air Force had deeded the air base and water supply to Wendover. The water supply at Johnson Springs ranch made possible the expansion in West Wendover.

Remodeled A-1 was operated as Jim's Casino from 1972 until 1984. *(Gertrude Tripp)*

Montego Bay Casino Resort marquee was installed in April 2003.

1997 State Line expansion. *(State Line Casino/William and Anna Smith family)*

After the West Wendover billboard was erected the desert literally blossomed as a rose. A truck stop, a Smith's Food King, strip mall, library, bank, post office, $9 million high school, Burger King, Arby's, Pizza Hut, liquor store, etc. emerged. Nearby was an eighteen-hole golf course dubbed Toana Vista. There were a medical clinic, city offices, rodeo grounds, Robert Scobie Park, subdivisions of beautiful homes and a Utah State University Extension building, where college degrees could be earned (this program was moved to the high school in 2003).

Gene Jones retired as general manager of the State Line in 1984, and continued as CEO for several more years. *(Gene Jones)*

A dedicated monument to the *Enola Gay* was prominently displayed in front of the Wendover USA Visitors/Convention Bureau on the west side of the street across from the Peppermill. Inside the bureau, visitors could see displays of Wendover Air Base and its crews as well as obtain information about special events such as Deer Widow's Weekend, the Border Town Bike Challenge, and time trials on the Bonneville Salt Flats. Old Highway 40 came alive and was renamed Wendover Boulevard.

West of the State Line Nugget and Montego Bay across the hill and next to an Interstate 80 exit stood the ever expanding Peppermill. It was known locally as the place to party due to the rock dance bands that perform there.

Southwest, down the street from the Peppermill was the Rainbow. Stereo music was piped throughout the well-lit parking lot. The interior decor presented *"plants and stars mingling with rainbows and drifting clouds."* Besides the ever-present gambling tables and slot machines, inside were several eateries including the Rainforest, *"complete with dense tropical foliage and babbling brooklets."* The Rainbow hosted guests in 298 suites.

Further west, the Red Garter had the façade of an old west frontier town. It had a 24-hour special ham and egg breakfast and the Garden Court Restaurant, complete with a fountain in the middle and the feel of dining outdoors. Free shuttles ran along Wendover Boulevard for casino hoppers. Some patrons preferred to walk along east-west sidewalks connecting all five casinos.

A new casino, the Keys Resort & Casino was in the planning stages adjacent to Toana Vista Golf Course. It would include over 380 rooms, a nightclub and casino, a health club and spa, vacation ownership villas, meeting and convention facilities, and a 2500-seat amphitheater and state-of-the-art recording studio. There was also planned in the new casino, childcare, miniature golf, a historical museum and water sports.

The oldest Wendover casino was the State Line. The early history of the State Line is found in chapter two. Just Hallen wrote *"The bicentennial year of 1976 was the 50th anniversary of the State Line. Its continuous ownership by the Smith family during these many years is especially noteworthy in these days of large corporate opera-*

tions." The Smiths would continue ownership for another 26 years, until 2002.

An expansion plan became reality in 1981 with a new convention center, enlarged gambling area, additional rooms and the opening of the three million dollar State Line Inn on the Utah side. Jim Smith had remodeled the A-1 into Jim's Casino in 1972 over the hill and that was expanded into a new hotel and casino across from the State Line.

The new casino was called the Silversmith and opened in 1984 the same year Gene Jones retired as general manager. Jones was named the CEO at the time. *"Big-name stars are regular attractions at both the State Liner Lounge and Silver Smith Cabaret, and between shows good food and drink is always available in a variety of settings."* Guests walked between the two establishments via an elevated skybridge, a crosswalk, or through two underground tunnels.

The year 1997 saw another major expansion to the tune of $45 million that added another 250 guest rooms and 55,000 square feet to the casino floor space. Bill Smith's tiny, one-pump gas station, with one light bulb out front had now mushroomed into an 850 room resort.

The last expansion proved to be the undoing of

Wendover & airport looking east to the salt flats in 1959. *(Utah State Historical Society, Leonard J. Arrington)*

the State Line Hotel and Casino. The State Line Corporation filed for bankruptcy in January 2002 in order to restructure their debt. Michael Devine, a grandson of Bill Smith took over as CEO after the expansion to try to save the company. In October 2002 after a brief bid by the Isle of Capri Casinos, the Peppermill Casino agreed to purchase the Silversmith, and Generation 2000 purchased the State Line for $55 million in a bidding war with two other companies. On December 20, 2002, the State Line's name was changed to the State Line Nugget Hotel & Gambling Hall and the Silver Smith became Montego Bay Casino Resort.

Current Wendover Airport, 2002. Buildings and tower were built during World War II.

Wendover & airport in the foreground with the Leppy or Desert Hills to the north in 1959. *(Utah State Historical Society, Leonard J. Arrington)*

Wendover Airport (Decker Field)

Wendover Airport dated back sixty years to World War II. It played a critical role in training pilots and crewmen of the Army Air Corps and those who delivered the atomic bomb (see chapter four).

Previous airport manager Chris J. Melville in the *High Desert Advocate* noted that *"past activities/facilities on site included vehicle and aircraft maintenance, mess halls, stores, power generation, sewage disposal, warehousing of munitions, supplies and spare parts, barracks for enlisted personnel and officers, and entertainment, recreational, medical and church facilities. All [were] activities and amenities associated with a typical community."*

Following the war, the Wendover Airport saw continued use by the military. It was the site of missile testing, Strategic Air Command training, and intermittent use by Air Force Reserve and Air National Guard units from Hill Air Force Base, and also from other states.

Development and testing of ballistic missiles, bombs, glide bombs and missile guidance systems were performed. The supersonic X-15 aircraft were dropped from other airplanes for experimental flights over the area.

Radar systems were perfected and stealth spy planes utilized the range. The effect of lightning on space shuttle booster rockets was analyzed near Wendover Airport. Reserve and active military units trained and deployed near the airfield vicinity. The military operations in Afghanistan in 2002 were simulated at Wendover before going into actual battle.

Wendover Field was deeded to Wendover in 1977 after being declared surplus by the U.S. military. An airport master plan study was completed in 1991. The study documented all existing buildings, complete with a historical description and photograph of each building.

The completed information was sent to the Library of Congress archives in Washington, D.C. Future needs and uses of the airport consistent with the historic preservation of buildings was outlined and upgrades were suggested.

Federal funding obtained by previous airport manager Chris Melville provided the means to complete a *"1.3 million dollar up-grade to runway 12-30. This project included an asphalt overlay of 100 x 6,400 feet over the original concrete pavement, the installation of edge lighting, runway end identifier light (REIL's) and precision approach path indicator system (PAPI)."*

A historic properties management plan was begun in December of 1992. On February 1, 1993, the airport at Wendover was given a limited operating certificate from the FAA. This certificate allowed the large passenger aircraft to touch down in Wendover. Casino charter flights became a reality when a DC-9 filled to capacity landed at Wendover on March 1, 1993. The charter was sponsored by the State Line Casino.

The second 9,100-foot concrete runway was upgraded soon after and enabled larger airplanes with *"greater range and the ability to reach more distant cities"* to fly into Wendover. The *"second runway was certified in April 1993."*

A second daily flight into Wendover was added and the potential of as many as 58,000 to 60,000 passengers

The abandoned *Enola Gay* hangar was designated for renovation as a museum center in conjunction with the Historic Wendover Airfield.

deplaning in Wendover yearly was then possible.

In 1994, using federal dollars, flood lighting, a beacon light, taxiway signs, a commercial service ramp and a lengthening of runway number 12-30 to 8,000 feet was achieved. In 1995 an expensive *"regenerative air vacuum sweeper"* was purchased to remove foreign objects from the runway and taxiway areas.

Air service to and from Salt Lake City was added in 1994-95. At that time Wendover ranked *"second only to Salt Lake City International in the State of Utah."*

It was placed on the National Register of Historic Places in 1974. The airport *"is the only remaining site in the United States that can be preserved with the entire front line of hangars and number of original buildings"* said a Historic Wendover Airfield, Inc. brochure. One hundred original buildings remained of the 668 that were built during World War II.

In 1995 the Historic Wendover Airfield Museum was commissioned by the City of Wendover. The *Enola Gay* hangar was designated for renovation as the museum center. Plans were for the museum to depict Wendover Field's history from 1940 to the present. It was to be a living history museum complete with a collection of memorabilia on display, tours and videos.

In August 2001 the 509th Composite Group held their reunion on site. The Confederate Airforce flew in a B-29 and a B-24 and provided rides and hands-on looks originating at the *Enola Gay* hangar. Inside the hangar were dioramas and exhibits of uniforms, photos and other items of historical importance. In September 2002 the airport was the sight of a huge air show attend-

509th Composite Group Memorial in West Wendover.

Reilly Wendover potash plant in 2002.

rooms. Efforts were being made in 2003 to revive air shuttles which were available until 1997 from as far away as Oregon, Texas, and the midwest.

Ample fuel was available to refuel jets and conventional aircraft. Wendover airport boasted *"exceptional emergency response capabilities and personnel far in excess of the requirement for an airport of its size."* Fire equipment included a T1500 Oshkosh truck, a 50-foot ladder truck, four structural engines, and two brush trucks. A wall of honor near the front entrance credited the long-time air field fire crew

ed by thousands of people. The event became an annual affair sponsored by the Historic Wendover Airfield.

The mission statement of Historic Wendover Airfield said that it was *"dedicated to preserving the efforts of ordinary soldiers and citizens during the extraordinary events of World War II. By maintaining the originality and authenticity of the facility, a historical experience will be recreated on this, the largest most original and unique airfield that played a critical role in the development of the Army Air Corps and the birth of the atomic age."*

Contributions by individuals and by major corporate sponsors were being solicited.

Wendover Airport was operated by Tooele County in 2003. The county advertised the airport as being an *"ideal hub for military uses."* There are two instrument approaches with one runway being 8,000 feet long by 150 feet wide and the other 8,000 feet by 100 feet. Both runways are capable of handling cargo and passenger service.

The main terminal contained conference rooms, a pilot's lounge, an airfield museum with photos and dioramas of Wendover Field during World War II. Airport shuttle buses linked the airport to nearby casinos including restaurants, fast food establishments, and 1,900 motel and hotel

dating back to World War II of Chief Fred Kenley, Donald Dean, Darrel Wadsworth, John Palmer, and Robert Scobie.

Wendover airport was the scene of several brief test flights of Utah State University's commemorative Wright Flyer replica, adding *"another historic moment to its storied past."* The flawless test flights were conducted March 10-13, 2003, in preparation for a national centennial flight July 3rd in the Wright brothers' hometown of Dayton, Ohio, which was attended by President George W. Bush. Former Utah Senator Jake Garn was present and taxied the plane down the Wendover Airfield runway.

Reilly Wendover to the east along old Highway 40.

Scrapers collect and load the mineral deposits to be shipped by truck to the potash plant at the Bonneville Salt Flats. *(Gertrude Tripp)*

ry dating back to the start of World War I. However it was not until the late 1930s that a successful commercial potash operation was achieved by a firm known as Bonneville Ltd. While improvements in operating techniques, pond design and equipment have been incorporated as they became available it should be understood that the basic technology developed in the late 30s and early 1940s by Bonneville Ltd. for potash production has not been changed significantly." (See chapter one for a more complete early history of the potash plant.)

Potash is a common commercial name used to denote potassium salts. Potassium minerals include potassium chloride, potassium sulfate, and magnesium sulfate. Potassium chloride is the most useful form.

The USU Wright Flyer was the only replica endorsed by the Wright Foundation, an organization of the brother's descendants which oversees the family legacy. Utah State University was loaned one of only four original blueprints owned by the Wright family in order to insure the accuracy of the replica. The modern USU replica was made of modern materials to ensure that it was light, safe and strong. These technological advancements would have been available today to the Wright brothers.

December 17, 2003, marked the 100th anniversary of powered flight. Wendover Airfield was selected to fly the maiden voyage of the commemorative biplane because of its historical significance, and connection to Jake Garn. Garn's father was a pilot at Wendover Field in World War II.

Potash Production at Wendover

A scientific paper written by M. William Lallman and Glenn Wadsworth in 1976 informatively stated: *"Potash production from natural brines of the Bonneville Salt Flats has a comparatively long histo-*

Potassium *"reacts readily with both oxygen and water."* Ninety-five percent of potash production is used as a fertilizer for agricultural purposes and the rest is used to make ceramics and glass, textiles, detergent soaps, chemicals, welding flux, drugs, and dyes. It is used as an ingredient in oil wells.

Potash was originally made by North American Indians. They boiled wood ashes in pots and utilized

Mineral deposits are being loaded for transport to the nearby potash plant. *(Gertrude Tripp)*

Potash Production Process Near Wendover

Step one in potash production is **brine collection** which depends on four inches of rainfall annually in an ideal situation to move the brine. Natural gravity causes the brine to move through the collection ditches with supplemental pumps. Ditches are dug with a dragline equipped with a bucket. The ditches are constructed to a depth of about 20 feet and are made 5 or 6 feet wide. The brine is 23 percent salt and one percent magnesium chloride as it is pumped at 5,000 to 10,000 gallons per minute into an 8,000-acre pond where evaporation takes place. About six inches of sodium chloride builds up per year until it reaches a layer four feet thick. From the primary pond, it is moved to a 500-acre harvest pond using elevator machines with paddles (later replaced by pumps). Motorized graders move the precipitate into windrows and scrapers collect and load the mineral deposit to be shipped by truck to the purification plant and later to the nearby railroad.

Salt and high temperatures are hard on the equipment which includes *"drag-lines, scrapers, crawler dozers and motor graders."* Salt *"causes equipment to rust away."* It also crusts on equipment making it impossible to loosen nuts, bolts, and pins. Salt is especially hard on wheels, bearings, tracks, idler arms, and other moving parts.

Clear water must be used in frequent cleanings in tandem with short interval oil changes, and lubricating with grease. Preventive maintenance also includes visual inspections. Engine overhauls, transmission rebuilds, and machining of new parts are all handled at the shop facilities on site.

Author Garn Anderson introduces step two in potash production, that of **brine concentration** after it is collected. He explains: *"Through a solar system of evaporation, the original brine is concentrated from a worthless product to a solid material containing 30% potassium muriate. Utilizing the sun's rays to perform this magic condensation of worthless brine into valuable potassium muriate has been a major factor in cutting refining costs. It is estimated that 5,000 tons of coal per day for 300 days would be required to accomplish the same job which the sun does in three months. A system of brine elevators moves the brine through several stages of evaporation ponds."*

Step three involves *"**Selective precipitation and collection of the potash ore**. After the original concen-* tration process, the product is further refined by flotation, giving a finished material of approximately 95% pure potassium muriate content.

"The process of extraction and refining requires several steps, namely heavy media process, flotation process, crystallization, compacting, and treatment. Wet grinding with ball mills followed by screening liberates the sylvite mineral (native potassium chloride) which is intergrown with halite crystals" (sodium chloride or rock salt). This is part of the concentration operation.

The last step is **concentration and processing of the concentrates.** In dry, evaporated form, the potash and salt ore are crushed and mixed with a salty solution called brine. The solution is pumped through number 10 mesh screens which are the size of window screens. *"Larger particles diverted by the screen go to heavy media. Smaller particles drop through and go to flotation."*

During the heavy media process, the potash floats to the surface while the salts and impurities sink to the bottom. The floating coarse-sized potash particles are then washed and dried and removed for storage. Some of the particles do not separate and have to be re-crushed, re-screened, and sent to flotation. These particles are called middlings.

The scavenger flotation process removes insoluble materials and brine from the ore through de-sliming. The potash ore is coated with chemical regents and mixed with brine. The brine slurry is pumped inside flotation tanks and *"air is injected into the mixture."* The salts sink to the bottom while the coated potash particles adhere to the air bubbles and rise to the surface. These particles are *"skimmed off, de-brined, and dried."*

Two grades of potash were once produced during the process: standard and special standard sizes. Now only granular size is produced. High pressure compaction leads to potash flakes which are crushed and screened to the desired size of granular potash. Additional potash in the form of dust known as soluble fines is recovered in dust collectors and during the flotation process. Next, leaching washes away any sodium chloride which may have inadvertently been floated in the process. Then the resultant concentrate is *"case hardened."*

One final step for some customers involves spraying the product with *"a mixture of oil and amine before loading"* for shipment. This is done to prevent caking from being too damp or dusting from being too dry. Some customers want the mixture applied and others do not.

the potash in food gardening to make the plants grow and produce better.

In the late 19th century, Justus Von Liebig, a German chemist, discovered that there were three essential elements in plant nutrition. They were phosphate, potash (potassium) and ammonia (nitrogen). The first two, he found were contained in the ashes of burned plants. Potash is critical in producing *"healthy yields"* of major crops such as corn, coffee, rice, soybeans and potatoes.

Potash results from the evaporation of seawater leaving a bed of salt from which the potash is extracted. Most potash is mined from underground seabeds in various parts of

The brine collection ponds are lined with 14-foot-deep, clay-filled trenches to keep them from leaking. Plant manager Jesse Ecton on the left. *(Gertrude Tripp)*

the world such as Canada, Belarus, Europe, and China. New Mexico is the leading producer of potash in the United States. There are only thirteen countries worldwide which produce potash.

Another source of potash is solar evaporation mining. Israel, Jordan, Wendover and Ogden, Utah, have solar evaporation mining operations. Sulfate of potash and magnesium chloride are extracted in concentrated solution and then purified in liquid or dry form.

According to Lallman and Wadsworth, potash pro-

duction involves four steps: *"collection of naturally occurring brines, brine concentration using solar energy for evaporation, selective precipitation and collection of the potash ore, and concentration of the potash ore and processing of the concentrates."*

Annual production rates depend on quality and quantity of the brine and the evaporation rate. Weather in the Wendover area is a major factor in the amount of potash production. Rainfall determines both the quality and quantity of the brine, and the evaporation rate depends also on the number of sunny days each year.

Author Garn Anderson commented on the potash mining technique. He stated, *"To reclaim potash from the Salt Flats, a unique method has been devised. Approximately 50,000 acres of the wasteland has been criscrossed with more than 50 miles of canals which collect the low grade salt brine for storage in evaporation ponds."* (This process is explained on page 214.)

Standard Magnesium Corp. of Tulsa, Oklahoma purchased Bonneville Ltd. in 1963 to use as a magnesium production site. Their plans did not materialize as Standard Mag-

Motorized graders move the precipitate into windrows. *(Gertrude Tripp)*

Old Bonneville Limited, Inc. potash plant.

nesium was sold to Kaiser Aluminum & Chemical Corp. of Oakland, California.

Kaiser produced 100,000 tons each year of muriate of potash, manure salts, and magnesium chloride brine. They moved brine water through about 115 miles of ditches next to I-80 and the Bonneville Speedway.

Reilly Industries owned the plant in Wendover in 2004, having purchased it in 1988. Reilly Wendover was one of the largest employers for residents of the city of Wendover.

At the Wendover plant they continued to produce potash. Boxcars and railroad hoppers transported virtually all potash products in bulk to markets outside of Utah.

Reilly Industries poured millions of dollars into a salt flats renewal project called *"Save the Salt"* for five years during the late 1990s and into the twenty-first century. The company spent the money pumping salt back onto the salt flats. Eighty years of extracting mineral salts from the old lake bed were taking its toll on salt levels and therefore the quality of the beds for speed racing.

Wendover Power Company

Author Jean Draper cited Eugene Craner in a report later published in the *High Desert Advocate* regarding the history of Wendover electric power.

Craner was a stockholder in the power company when it was organized in 1947 and was also the chief electrician on the air base.

Prior to 1947 Wendover businesses generated their own power and the power to nearby neighbors as well. During World War II the air base also produced its own power.

Most everyone else did without. They used kerosene lamps for lights and heated their homes with wood and coal stoves. The kitchen stoves also cooked food and heated water through a water jacket or an adjacent water tank fed through a pipe inside the stove walls.

In 1947 C. D. McLeod, general manager of Western Service Station, formed the Wendover Power Company with ten initial investors. The company had a franchise to furnish power north to Grouse Creek and south to Baker, Nevada; west to the Nevada line and east to Knolls.

Shortly after the company was formed, McLeod bought the shares of eight other stockholders. He became company president, Craner was vice president and the only other stockholder, and McLeod's wife was the secretary and bookkeeper.

Mr. Craner did most of the work. He dug the holes for the power poles by hand. McLeod would help set the poles but refused to climb them. The company purchased their electrical materials from *"a defunct mining company."* They generated power using three Caterpillar engines set up at the Western Service Station.

They started out with thirteen customers. The meters were old and could be reversed so the meter ran backwards. The power company actually owed the customer money in some cases so a surcharge of 13 cents per kilowatt hour was soon added. The surcharge apparently worked in stopping the reversals and so was reduced to three and three-quarter cents per KWH.

At the close of World War II, the power company

purchased the air base power plant as the lowest bidder at a surplus auction. As the power plant became obsolete, Wendover Power was forced to hand-manufacture replacement parts in order to stay reliable.

McLeod first offered to sell Wendover Power to Wells Rural Co-op in 1958. It took several years to obtain financing and permission from the Utah Public Service Commission before the sale could take place. Wells Rural completed the purchase on January 11, 1962 at the price of $170,000.

Compactor at Bonneville Limited, Inc. *(Gertrude Tripp)*

The new company provided an *"ample supply of reliable power"* for everyone to hook up to. Consequently all individual power plants were abandoned in favor of the modern power supply which continued to the present time. Power was not produced on site but a 138-kilovolt transmission power line supplied twenty-five megawatts to Wendover and West Wendover.

Jean Draper concluded: *"Power like water is a silent servant that is only missed when not available. With power shortages plaguing other areas of the west, we can be grateful to farsighted people who brought electricity to Wendover."*

Microwave Stations Near Wendover Bombed

During the late 1950s and the 1960s, society in the United States went through extreme changes. The civil rights movement was in the forefront of the news. Great strides were being made in the space industry. Inflation lead to spiraling prices.

The Cold War was at its height and caused great anxiety for Americans. The U.S. was sometimes on the brink of war with Russia. The Bay of Pigs invasion was a fiasco in April 1961 when President Kennedy tacitly approved Cuban exiles' bid to overthrow Castro's regime. *"Americans were nervous about the future and that anxiety bred suspicion."*

To add to the anxiety and suspicion, an act of *"sabotage took place in our own back yard."* On the night of May 28, 1961, several bombs were set at three critical microwave repeater facilities in the vicinity of

Wendover and the salt flats and by morning all three locations were in ruins.

The first set of four bombs was placed around the walls of the repeater building at Cedar Mountain just south and west of the Great Salt Lake. Twenty minutes later, another set of explosives was set at Knolls, Utah, inside a brick building. The Barro microwave station was next, but it was by-passed. Three more bombs were placed at strategic locations at Wendover Notch, twenty-eight miles further and three miles past Wendover. The timers were set to go off simultaneously at 4:40 a.m.

At 4:42 a.m., a total failure code was received at the repeater office owned by Bell of Nevada in Elko. Shortly after, other alarm codes indicated a major problem to the east. All communications from coast to coast were cut off. Television circuits, long distance telephone operations, and military information were stopped. Because microwaves travel in straight lines, it was necessary to build a series of repeating stations within line of sight of each other with no intervening obstacles. Repeater stations across the salt flats boosted incoming signals and re-transmitted them coast to coast them in a fraction of a second.

The bombing was a major disaster! By destroying these repeater stations, America's transcontinental communications were rendered inoperable. Definitely, it was a serious case of sabotage!

Several people in Wendover were awakened by the

Wendover High School, home of the Wildcats. At right is World War II Elementary.

"tremendous blast." A truck driver sleeping below the site was awakened by a *"thunderous boom."* He saw bits of Styrofoam from the demolished antennas *"floating down like snowflakes."*

It looked like a war zone. George A. Phelps, a local supervisor for the phone company described the aftermath in an article entitled *"Wendover Blast."*

The Elko County sheriff dispatched deputies to protect underground cable stations throughout the county. Those that arrived at the bombed-out site at Wendover Notch found small fires still burning. Hundreds of personnel became involved almost immediately. Portable equipment and technicians were flown in from three west coast cities. The FBI, the local sheriff's department, the National Guard, and the Pentagon joined the Bell System in emergency repair procedures and in investigating the bombings.

They needed to find out who had committed the attacks and why. It could have been part of a subversive plot to overthrow the U.S. government. It may have been an act of vandalism or it could have been an enemy test to determine the resiliency of the communications network. No one knew.

Troops were called out in eleven states to guard telephone company facilities. An investigation immediately began of the bombed out facilities.

Four days after the blasts, technicians had substitute equipment up and *"operating at partial capacity."* One week after the disaster, full service was restored. The microwave route was complete with *"receivers, transmit-*

ters, transmission lines, antennas, power supplies, and a surveillance-alarm system" in place. Eventually the stations were rebuilt with steel trusses and concrete block and all new equipment.

On June 19, 1961, two men and a woman were arrested on a yacht in Ensenada, Mexico. They were linked to the bombings after a check was made with the FBI. The two men were each eventually sentenced to eight years in prison.

This two-man army *"exposed the vulnerability"* of one of America's most vital communication networks at that time. AT&T *"spent many millions of dollars over the next few years providing new alternate routes, sophisticated equipment, elaborate emergency plans and restoration exercises."*

Education

On the Nevada side, a one-room school sat on State Line property with Lloyda DeVaney as the teacher for grades one through eight. The school was closed after World War II. The last teacher had been Irene Fernandez.

Molly Smith taught the first school classes in Wendover, Utah, in a small house on Second Street. About 1920 a little red school was built by Tooele County School District. Grades one through six were taught in this school. The building was also used for church by the Church of Jesus Christ of Latter-day Saints. There was not a play area at first until towns-

Old Wendover Junior High School. *(Gertrude Tripp)*

Sheryl Lynn Kellogg

David Kikumoto

Glenna Morgan

Mike Spillman

Starr Tilbury

Ra Nae Mauer

Kathleen Tripp

Douglas Earl Tucker

Verna Tucker

The class of 1967 was the first to graduate from Wendover High School. The event represented a major milestone in the history of Wendover. *(Sheila Stewart, Crystal Yearbook)*

people filled in a gulley, and poured a concrete slab with cement hauled by Pete McKellar's wagon from Tooele.

The building was remodeled so that it contained two classrooms. Grades one to four were taught in the east room. The teacher was Mary Birdzell. Carrol Madsen (also the custodian) taught grades five to eight in the west room. Restrooms were in the rear and the supply room was located on the southwest corner. Later, a small library was begun in the back of the school with both donated and purchased books.

Gladys Casperson wrote a brief history of Wendover schools in which she stated: *"Teachers were able to get any supplies they wanted. All they had to do was ask. They had no playground duties. School started at 9 a.m. The children played by themselves at recess, they went home for lunch, and as soon as school was out they went home."* She did not explain where they got the supplies.

Casperson further explained: *"Teachers were paid $110 per month and an extra check for $10 because*

> Wendover is very much a part of our soul and we cannot forget where we came from. Wendover truly had much to do with who we are today.
>
> —John Hernandez

Wendover was considered a rural school. Early teachers were Mary Birdzell, Mrs. Kirkham, Mr. & Mrs. Carrol Madsen, Mrs. Bean, Mr. & Mrs. Bevans, and Lola Jeffries. Mr. Elwin Cammack was principal."

Development and expansion of Wendover Field during World War II created a need for a new six classroom elementary school. The federal government built the building and then turned it over to the Tooele County School District for staffing and administration in 1943–44. It was deeded to the district in 1945.

Each of the six classrooms housed two grades. First and second were combined and so on through the eighth grade with a ninth grade class added later on. The northern two classrooms were actually one big room with a folding door divider. This room could be used for PTA meetings and parties. Refreshments could be served at meetings from an adjoining kitchen. The government built a nursery school next door for the mothers who worked on base. The nursery school became a junior high after the war. In 1955 a brick gymnasium was built next to the junior high.

In 1968-69 a thirteen-member Kindergarten class was added to Wendover Elementary. The elementary school served Wendover for fifty-five years. Mobile classrooms had to be utilized when Wendover's population increased.

"Anna Smith Elementary School was built in 1998 on a hillside in one of Wendover's newest neighborhoods, and children can see the vast expanse of the ... region below from its rooms and outside play areas." There were 213 students enrolled in 2002-03 in the brick building which is located on 11.9 acres. The 42,420 square foot school was dedicated October 6, 1998 at a cost of $6,000,000. The staff of the elementary included a principal, thirteen teachers, and three special programs instructors.

Earl Arnoldson was the first principal followed by Dr. Kent Parsons. The mascot was the Salt Bear and the school colors are royal blue and white.

In 1964 an independent report to Tooele County School District done by the University of Utah made the following statement: "There is no senior high school beyond the tenth grade in Wendover and none is recommended. Patrons there could probably demand a senior high school and get it. That is not recommended. Students will receive a much better education in a better educational environment if they can go to school somewhere else, preferably at another high school in the Tooele District."

The report suggested that the $30 a month allowance for transportation be increased. Most students from Wendover attended Grantsville High School after 9th grade. Students boarded with

---

Ron Christensen remembered: "I attended Wendover Elementary School during the period when the Wendover Air Force Base had been reactivated. Nearly 2,000 airmen were stationed there during that period and the base was a beehive of activity with aircraft constantly flying in and out of the base which delighted all the school children ... mostly the boys. School days were punctuated with an occasional sonic boom from the many jet fighters that buzzed the town and rattled the windows. With the runways less than a mile away, we could hear the roar of the jets as they took off and catch a glimpse of them out our windows as they flew over the school. It was all extremely exciting and inspired nearly all of us to build an armada of plastic model aircraft ... jet fighters, of course.

"Below the windows, along the wall of each classroom were rows of 6" by 12" cubby holes, one for each student which was meant for storage of school books and supplies. For us they were hangars for our jet plane models! You could always tell which of the cubbies belonged to the girls because those were the ones that didn't have jet planes sitting in them, poised nose out, eagerly awaiting recess so they could fly the school grounds, engaging in fierce dog fighting with other aircraft. Of course there were casualties of this dog fighting and if you were unfortunate enough to be hit, you had to make a forced landing. It was always best to attempt to maneuver your injured craft to the area near the tricky bars where the soft sand made for a more successful emergency landing. And that was where I came in. I had elected to build a Sikorsky helicopter which was the designated rescue craft and I would swoop in and retrieve the pilot of the downed jet which was, of course,

deep inside enemy territory. Sometimes the rescue involved lowering a tether while hovering overhead. Our recess activity was all great fun.

"Our teachers however became annoyed at times as we had to run down the hallways in order to maintain air speed with our high performance aircraft. They just didn't understand the aerodynamic requirements of the jets we were flying. Sound barrier passes in the halls were often met with aircraft confiscation by the enemy (teachers) and held until the war ended (school let out).

"When the air base reopened in 1954 the runways were heavily populated with F-86 jet fighters as that was the most popular Air Force jet of the day. Shortly afterwards the up-dated and faster F-100s began to replace the aging F-86s and about the time the base closed down a few years after that the F-104s and the delta-winged F-102s made a brief appearance."

Ron Christensen also remembered constructing rocket launchers of 10" water pipe. The rockets were made of aluminum TV antenna tubing with an arrow attached and gunpowder from live .50 caliber shells furnished the rocket propellent. A detonator made of old airplane instruments ignited the fuse and the rockets would go up to 1,000 feet in the air.

Other Wendover diversions Wendover youngsters participated in included threatening to throw boulders off the overpass at passing trains, rolling a tire full of cement into the Patio Motel pool, and setting fire to a tank of flammable liquid at the government administration building. The children then pretended not to notice the fire as they sat nonchalantly at a nearby gas station.

Grantsville or Tooele families. Some went to schools where their own extended family lived or where their families purchased a second home for the purpose of educating their children.

The Tooele School District apparently agreed with the report. The parents were rudely told things like *"You women should go home and have more babies"* and *"The district will build no more monuments to tax payers"*.

Residents in Wendover did not agree with the report or the comments. They went into action, including electing local resident Marie Johnston to the district school board. They petitioned the school board and after several heated meetings their persistence paid off in 1965, at least for a new junior high. During the year while the brick school was being built, high school students were bused sixty miles to Wells, Nevada, leaving at 7:30 a.m. and arriving home at 4:30 p.m. The busing arrangement was planned to be a permanent solution for the high school students. The community building was used to teach grades seven to nine. The old junior high had to be torn down in order to build the new junior high.

The new junior high was completed in the summer of 1966. Before school started, *"it was decided that the new building should be used as a senior high as well as a junior high school."* There were initial concerns that the building had enough room for both.

The classroom areas were originally large, open, and built in the round. This proved unsatisfactory and partitions were built to create individual classrooms within months. A shop was added in 1971 in a location away from the classrooms. The same year a science room and art room were added. The art room has since been used as a math room and then a history classroom. A new metal-framed gym to augment the old one was

Anna Smith Elementary

West Wendover Elementary School

West Wendover High School; Fred Gordon was principal in 2003. *(Jerry and Linda Brown)*

built in 1974. English and music modular classes were built in 1979.

The first class to graduate from Wendover High School was in May 1967. There were nine students in the graduating class. They were Ranae Mauer, Starr Lavonne Moore Tilbury, Kathleen Carol Tripp, Verna Marie Tucker, Douglas Earl Tucker, Martin Earl Spillman, and Charles David Kikumoto.

Some of the principals of the Wendover schools since 1940 have been Herman C. Coray, Mr. Wright, Darrell Willey, Elwin Cammack, Eldon Puckett, Roy West, Thomas Irvine, Wayne Shields, Max Welker, Zenas Burroughs, Don Halliday, Wally Gurney, R. Cargile, and John Butterfield. More recently Randy Houk, Robert McArthur, Gary Brogan, Mr. Alejandro, Bruce Knowlton, Dolene Pitt, Leonard Marshall, and Steve Lawrence have been principals. Earl Arnoldson and Kent Parsons have served at Anna Smith Elementary.

Marie "Pokey" Green editorialized on her educational experience due to the lack of a local high school. "It was a very sad day when I left at age fourteen and went away to school. I felt sad and happy all mixed into one. It would be a great adventure, and it was, but I got homesick. I missed Mom and Dad and the love of a home. Dormitories cannot compare to a home and family. We packed up the clothes and the instruments and left the precious animals behind. I missed my dog and parrot but even more missed the family atmosphere. It seemed like a harsh reality and no one there to overlook my foolish antics of learning

"Part of me raged at the going-away-to-high school. There were enough kids in Wendover to have a high school but the people in Tooele controlled all the money. And of course they had a swimming pool at the school in Tooele and all the kids in Wendover had to go away. It seemed so unbalanced, so ruthlessly unfair. The politicians would call meetings of the school board and the meetings were held in Tooele. They would notify Marie Johnston half an hour before the meeting was to begin. That made it impossible for her to get there to deal with engineered inequities. She tried often though. Ultimately, she succeeded in getting a high school for Wendover but not until 1967, the year I graduated. I still wonder at the integrity of so called good upstanding people who will support such inequities at the expense of children. The inequities continue to this day even though there is a school in Wendover. The apportionment of monies for years seemed so inequitable. Looking back it has all turned out well and by going away I was able to have some music lessons that were unavailable in Wendover.

Marie earned a Ph.D at the University of Utah in 1988. She said: "One time a supervisor from Tooele came to Wendover when I was working as a substitute teacher and tutor and he said, 'Students from rural areas are not as bright as those from urban areas and they do not test as well either.' I was flabbergasted. He did not know that I was a product of Wendover and that there were many bright kids who were reared in Wendover and benefitted greatly from the rural environment. He seemed to despise the Wendover and Ibapah school kids. He was above them and theirs. He had made that remark to the wrong person and I knew that he would indeed rot in hell from disparaging my precious town and all that it had brought to so many of us.

"In the end we are the defenders of the place. Perhaps not as good at it as Marie Johnston and others but defenders nevertheless. Many Wendover folks cherish the memories and the opportunities that do not exist elsewhere. And until our dying days we will keep those fond memories. And wonder if our burying will be at the foot of Needle Point Mountain where we climbed to the heights and rode our horses round about. Or will it be in some city cemetery where cars are loud, grass is too prevalent and no smell of sage in bloom fills the air. Days of my youth in the desert went very slow and now days in the city speed by like a runaway horse. I long for the slowness of time like in my youth and for the fitness of body that made it possible to climb all those mountains around Wendover and swim out to the middle of Blue Lake and run the full length of the hardpan at Nine Mile Hill.

"I will carry it all in my heart and wish the same sweet memories for others who read the stories in this book. Looking back I think there are things that kids growing up in rural settings gain. Mostly it is the connection with the earth and nature. It is also the connection with self-learning. We went to work as youngsters and learned how to work. And we learned how to play and to be together and make good things happen.

"Very few people from outside Wendover ever have any sense of appreciation for the place. But there are many advantages held secret in the wide open spaces of the small town and surrounding area. Always the secrets will remain in my heart as an adult and the advantages will be forever appreciated as gifts from beyond like the sweetness of the gentle winds that cool the heat from the desert."

West Wendover Visitor's Center adjacent to Scobie Park.

Bob Scobie

Wendover High School had twenty-five staff members in 2002, including a principal, thirteen teachers and five special program teachers. It was built to accommodate up to 500 students. There were 200 students in grades seven to twelve enrolled in 2001-02 school year. Athletic teams and other Wendover High School entities were known as the *"Wendover Wildcats."* In 2003, Tooele School District purchased adjoining land to the west of the high school for use as athletic fields. The price was $500,000.

West Wendover Elementary School was a modern facility with a new gym and soccer field. There were thirty-two teachers, a principal and twenty-three support personnel for a population of 713 kindergarten through sixth-grade students. The school was originally built to house 500 students, so 200 students were housed in pre-fabricated modular units.

Sixteen certified teachers provided the instruction at the modern West Wendover Jr./Sr. High School as part of an overall staff of forty individuals. There were 415 students attending seventh through twelveth grades in 2001-02. West Wendover High School was known as the *"Home of the Wolverines."* A $17 million junior high was planned for completion in 2011.

The Wendover Education Center offered extension classes from the University of Nevada in Reno and from Utah State University until January 2003. After that, the two high schools offered classes from their respective state universities to students qualifying for university credit while still in high school.

Even though Wendover has been small and the educators have been transient and varied in qualifications and abilities, the opportunities have been there for those who wanted an education. The tiny Wendover high school has produced *"lawyers, plumbing engineers, physicians, an oral surgeon, several CPAs, a college coach, an architect and designer, teachers, a dentist, managerial positions, a colonel in the Air Force, and many others."*

Scobie Park, Wendover Cemetery & Elko County Branch Library

Scobie Park provided residents and passersby with shade, lawn, picnic tables and a playground for kids at the junction of Wendover Boulevard and Highway 93 to Ely. It was named for Robert Scobie a longtime resident of Wendover. He worked for the Wendover fire department on the base from 1950 until retirement in 1972.

A transient room tax in Nevada was assessed over the years but West Wendover had received very little of those funds even though a considerable amount of money had been collected. The money was supposed to be used for recreational purposes. Bob Scobie was instrumental in getting those funds released for the West Wendover park and equestrian park. That was the basis for naming the park after Bob Scobie.

Garn Anderson once stated, *"Through all these years, till the air base, Wendover had no doctor or cemetery … . The townspeople claimed Wendover to be the healthiest place in the county because few people ever died here."*

Well, that situation finally changed! At least now people can be buried there officially. Through the per-

Growing Up as a Youth in Wendover

The recreation of the local youth growing up in Wendover was aptly described by John Hernandez on the Wendover Reunion website in 2002. He reminisced about *"our time in school and the long, hot summers so full of life and endless possibilities."* He remembered *"the generation of the 60's and 70's and early 80s."*

He wrote about *" ... draggin' Main in search of whatever the night held."* He reflected on *" ... relationships that formed and dissolved."* He talked *" ... about being employed as dishwashers, busboys, waitresses, service station attendants, motel maids, drive-in workers."* He mused *" ... about the gas stations which were oases for the weary travelers moving east or west on Interstate 80 (Highway 40).*

"When the tourists would stop we would be there at Ray's Chevron, the Shell station, the Conoco and the Kwiky Mart, the Texaco truck stop, Mobile, Amoco, the 76 and others (there were eleven viable stations in Wendover at one point in the 50s and 60s). We would interact, assist and accommodate those pilgrims with relief and service. Occasionally, we gently persuaded some travelers into purchasing shocks, tires, water pumps and if you were a great sales person like myself, a quart of Kwik Kool."

Hernandez nostalgically reminded potential reunion attendees about *" ... Dixon's Dairy Queen, Darrell and Dan's drive-ins and the Stateline Casino/coffee shop, the Western Café, A-1 (later Jim's) and the foods that sustained our lives. ... Yes, there was always plenty to eat."*

He wrote of *" ... the uniqueness of Wendover. Going to school in a community/x-movie theatre building or riding buses to Wells, Nevada each day while a new school was being built. Going home for lunch. Playing basketball in one of the smallest gyms in the state. A playground made of asphalt. Going to school where the kindergarten and the 12th grade were located on the same ground. We walked or drove to school, no buses. Having Principals and teachers that never lasted very long. The teachers that we did have were old, young, thin, tall, drunk, heavy, psycho, loud quiet, incompetent and incompetent, and then there was Bruce Campbell.*

"Our telephone numbers were only four digits long (my family's # was 2001). Wendover had a large motorcycle park right in its back yard going in every direction. Sun tanning on nature's finest tanning beds, the salt flats. We had a dead man's curve. We could view the curvature of the earth or make out with our date on three-mile hill.

"Playing little league baseball on alkaline salt beds that would reach temperatures in excess of 100,000 degrees. The hard flat salty surface of our playing field would tear through cotton baseball uniforms, embedding salt into the abrasions that were sure to occur with each slide into base. Ouch!!! We have the salt flats, a geographical phenomenon, 40 square miles of salt, void of any life form except the occasional lizards, snakes, and black stink bugs that would venture across along with a jackrabbit or two or three or four.

"Wendover was not a typical community as there were many things we did not have like a local newspaper, movie theatre or a bowling alley, a clinic, dentist, a doctor or hospital, a golf course, or a graveyard. But we had a Bums' Jungle, the stockyards, the railroad, the Beanery, the Air Force base bringing with it historical glory, and the home to Enola Gay."

Hernandez continued, *"We had a red water tank and a black water tank and one orange and white checkered one on a mountain. We had mountains, Needle Point, Big Bear Claw, 116, Flat Top, 158, Elephant Mountain, Poulsen's Mountain and Pilot Peak. We had caves, Danger Cave, Indian Cave, and Limestone Cave. We had the BNG, the canals, with awesome minnow fishing, The Reservoir, and Lone Tree. We had Buela Burgers (if you wanted to travel to Montello). We had a Duner.*

"We had a big store and a little store. We had Little Kennecott. We had a nine-mile. We had a potash plant and a salt plant. We had a Hideaway. We had a dump with a deputy. We had Pete Petersen and his pigs and a Mosquito Pete. We had a floating Island and a Silver Island. Excuse me, we did have a movie theatre, one in our infancy, thank you Mr. & Mrs. Waters, or the one that was just a sixty mile drive away.

"We had chipmunks, pigeons, horned toads, ring-neck lizards, scorpions, tarantulas, wild horses, antelope, coyotes, salt bears and a Blue Goose; long gone before our time but full of mystery and curiosity.

"We had tradition and culture. We had the Golden Green and Sweetheart's Ball. We built and played on stilts, and go-karts. We captured chipmunks for pets in our own patented cages we built out of wooden fruit and vegetable crates. We slept out and raided gardens. We had weekend summer dances with hometown bands, like the Meteors, and the Rideways.

"We went rabbit, arrowhead and deer hunting. We made sling shots (flippers as we called them) and cut strips out of car inner tubes to fling our rocks that were placed in a leather pouch, usually from the remain of somebody's shoe. We swam in Blue Lake, ... and the various motels pools: the Patio, Lewis Brothers, the Western and Poulsen's pools during those hot, arid summer months. We had the 4th of July fireworks, shooting off one skyrocket at a time.

"Each summer the world's fastest automobiles and motorcycles converged on Wendover to supply us with t-shirts and STP stickers to last a lifetime. Well, they hardly supplied them to us. It was more like we begged for them and they gave them away just to get rid of us. These eccentric racing types came from California and various other locations and created their own Salt City on the Bonneville race way.

"We had Russ Lewis' summer steak fries, and Dixon's end of the season free Dairy Freeze give-aways. We had train wrecks, which mobilized the entire community to travel to the wrecked train site to provide assistance in a search and rescue. 'Search and rescue' might be giving the wrong impression. How about, 'search and haul away' as much of the wrecked train cargo to our homes before the railroad inspectors arrived.

"We would collect pine cones for the pine nuts when they were in season. We played community bingo during Thanksgiving for turkeys, groceries and other give-aways. We had a turkey shoot.

"We would cut down our own Christmas trees from Silver Zone and the Toana mountain range. We had Santa on a fire engine. The day after Christmas we would start our Christmas tree collection campaign. We attempted to collect every tree in the community.

"We would store these trees until the New Year. Then dragging the trees to the empty lot south of the black water tank we would ignite the trees at sunset for our annual bonfire that would send flames high into Wendover's dark, cold, winter sky announcing to the world that a celebration was taking place.

"A celebration of another year, survived by our isolated existence in the middle of a desert. The fire then heated our tired, cold, overworked bodies, while we gorged ourselves on hot dogs, marshmallows, chips and soda pop. After the last tree was thrown on the fire and it burned down to glowing embers, we would all reluctantly go home and prepare to face another year in Wendover."

Marie & Larry Johnston. Civic-minded Marie Johnston was chairperson of town reunions, spearheaded the securing of the Wendover cemetery, fought for a freeway underpass linking the north side of Wendover to allow for expansion, was a member of the Tooele County Board of Education in a successful effort to get a high school, and served as a city council woman. (Dale Stewart)

Wendover Cemetery

sistence of Marie Johnston, Hazel Sorensen, Mark Tripp, Glen Wadsworth, Glenda Lacy, Ron Green, Mayor Ab Smith and others, Wendover was able to obtain land for a cemetery north of town. The land was near Needle Point and was received from the Federal Bureau of Land Management.

There were ten acres designated for use as a cemetery. It was dedicated by Dale Stewart. It was fenced with a tree or two planted but no lawn. It officially came into being in June of 1990. Mae Pettit was the first burial in the cemetery.

Another civic improvement was the library. The state of Nevada gave final approval for a library to be constructed on 2.25 acres of land in March of 1986. The library was completed at a cost of about $276,000 in 1986. It was called the *West Wendover Branch Library*.

Metaphor, Tree of Utah

Twenty-six miles east of Wendover stands the *Metaphor, Tree of Utah*. The sometimes controversial sculpture was the brain-child of Swedish artist Karl Momen. He wanted a *"thing of beauty growing from the salt."* He knew of people's fascination with the vast, empty salt plain and the fact that a person can see the curvature of the earth from Three-Mile Hill west of Wendover.

Momen spent $2 million of his own money in constructing the tall rock tree. He made the tree of *"255 tons of cement, 1,800 ceramic tiles, [and] 5 tons of welding rod."* The tree reaches skyward to a total of 87 feet. There are six spheres topping the tree all coated with minerals and rocks found within the state of Utah.

There are no parking facilities on the state-owned land. The tree can be seen clearly on the north side of I-80 at mile marker 25 by passing cars. It was dedicated on January 18, 1981, with Utah's governor accepting Momen's donation to the state of Utah. It is on land deeded to the state by the Federal Bureau of Land Management.

Metaphor, Tree of Utah

Population

The area population of the whole of Wendover was approximately 7,700 persons in 2002 according to the West Wendover website. On the weekends tourism causes a quadruple jump in population and travelers during the week double the population on a daily basis.

Wendover, Utah homeowners lived in older homes dating back to World War II and earlier. The north side of the freeway had an area of newer development, mostly single family homes but also of modular homes.

Most of the housing on the West Wendover side was modern and up-to-date due to the more recent development of the city. Much of the housing was comprised of single family dwellings. There were also custom-built homes on larger lots. There was also multi-family housing in the form of apartments, condominiums, and town houses.

Most of the employment in Wendover stemmed from the tourism economy generated by the casinos. The potash fertilizer industry was the second leading provider of income for the communities. Other jobs related to lime mining and the public service sector in the local schools and other governmental entities.

In 2003 West Wendover annexed *"some 96,000 acres"* of which 15,000 acres would be set aside as the port of West Wendover.

Health Care Services

Throughout most of Wendover's history there were only sporadic medical services available. Lack of medical care was a major concern to locals. Dr. Joseph Peck worked for the Western Pacific Railroad in 1917 and stayed on in nearby Gold Hill, Utah, for a short time during World War I. There was likely nothing available for the Wendover folk until World War II when the air base was in operation. Only recently has medical and dental care been available on a regular basis.

Hilda Hewitt Wiley used the base hospital to deliver her first baby at minimal cost and furnishing her own supplies. Jean Draper moved to Wendover in 1954 and remembered that there was a registered nurse named Jane Ervine, a licensed practical nurse, Leah "Chris" Christensen, and an unlicensed woman by the

> "Wendover was not just a town; it was a school on life. Wendover taught us more about living than most people will ever learn in a lifetime in other communities."
>
> —John Hernandez

name of Billie Campbell taking care of the health care needs of Wendover citizens. A pharmacist named MacGrew filled prescriptions ordered from Salt Lake area physicians.

By the early 1960's, Wendover had acquired a station wagon for use as an ambulance. It was housed at the Western Service and driven by Western's garage mechanic Bill Richie, fireman Donald Dean, or Utah Highway Patrolman Tony Kerbovich. Sick or injured persons could be taken to Salt Lake City *"post haste."*

The large family of Phil Garrett needed medical for their many young ones and persuaded Dr. David Wray and Dr. Hubert Burton to visit Wendover on a weekly basis via a small plane. Their offices were located in a motel room at the Wendover Best Western.

Luana Dean made the appointments each week. For more extensive care, patients had to travel to Bountiful where the doctors practiced.

Jean Draper recalled: *"The system worked well for my family. Thursday morning I would ask, 'How are you feeling?' If the answer was 'okay' they went to school. Thursday being doctor day."* She said she was a scoop-and-run mother. If her kids coughed, she scooped them up and ran them to the doctor.

The mid-1970s brought changes in medical care. A clinic housed in a World War II building was opened under the auspices of the University of Utah and was staffed by a physician's assistant or a nurse practitioner. In addition, Wendover purchased an ambulance and trained emergency medical technicians to staff it. It was closed when West Wendover opened a clinic on the Nevada side of the line. Laura and Larry Lisk purchased the ambulance from Wendover and continued to operate the ambulance service.

West Wendover Clinic offered the full services of a family practice. West Wendover Ambulance Company extended the reach of the clinic to onsite emergency situations. The clinic was open seven days per week with two doctors available assisted by nurse practitioners and other support staff. It was open eight hours per day.

On the Utah side the Women's Health Clinic offered full social and medical services to meet the needs of women. It was licensed by Tooele County, until it closed in January 2003 due to funding cuts.

Excavating Danger Cave by layers. *(University of Utah Archaelogy Department)*

Hands and Knees or Danger Cave, and Indian or Juke Box Cave

Early inhabitants of the Wendover area prehistorically were nomadic within a territory due to *"the arid climate and harsh conditions"* of the west desert. They moved from place to place and survived by hunting small animals and harvesting seeds and roots.

Their other main activity was seeking shelter. The Fremont, Paiute, Ute, Goshute, and Shoshone groups all lived in the area dating back approximately 11,000 years. *"There are dozens of caves"* used as shelter by prehistoric humans in the mountain range near Wendover, according to Kevin Jones, Utah State Archaeologist in 1997. The caves would have been a cool refuge from the stifling heat of summer and a warm, seamless enclosure during the bitter cold of the area's winters.

One of the major sites for identifying and quantifying archeological and anthropological data of the early inhabitants of the area is Danger Cave. The cave is located one mile northeast of Wendover on the Leppy Hills (Desert Hills). *"It was variously known as 'Hands and Knees Cave' and 'Lamus Cave' before a rock fall almost crushed*

an excavation worker. Thereafter it was known as 'Danger Cave.'"

The cave was carved out of limestone with a high ceiling. It measures 60 feet wide and 120 long and holds a steady temperature of 68 to 70 degrees. The cave's elevation is 4,325 feet above sea level. The cave entrance lies 200 feet below the Stansbury level of old Lake Bonneville. The cave entrance was originally mostly blocked by debris from cave inhabitants so that explorers had to enter by crawling on hands and knees.

Robert Heizer of the University of California performed brief test excavations in 1937. Further excavations were undertaken by E. R. Smith from the University of Utah in the late 1930s and early 1940s. Smith's work halted when the cave roof fell in 1941.

Jesse Jennings of the University of Utah lead extensive examinations of the cave in 1949-51 and 1953-55 despite the suffocating, dusty working conditions which were less than ideal. Breathing could not

Looking south toward Wendover air base with excavation soil from Danger Cave piled by a truck. *(University of Utah Archaeology Department)*

228

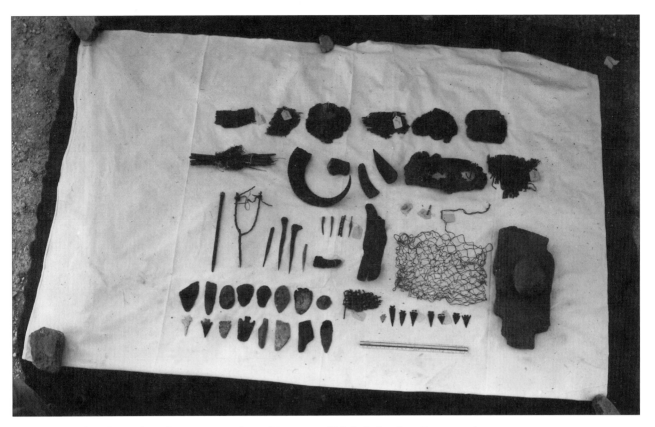

A sampling of artifacts taken from Danger Cave. *(University of Utah Archaeology Department)*

be done without respirators, masks had to be worn at all times, and touch instead of sight was often the rule. Even with portable generator powered fans and electric flood lights most of the screening work had to be done outside the cave.

Sixty-five plant species still in existence in the area were recovered from the cave, along with wood scraps, charcoal fire pits, and remains of various animals. Jennings found items probably used for food including dog, bobcat, desert fox, jackrabbit, antelope, bison, and mountain sheep. The animals were obtained using arrows, Atlatls, snares and traps, all of which were found in the cave.

Jennings also unearthed varied artifacts including beetle wings, textiles, *"leather scraps, pieces of string, nets of twine, coarse fabric, basket fragments, and bone and wood tools such as knives, weapons, and millstones."* Sandals made of woven grass and animal skin clothing remnants were among the finds.

Danger Cave is one of the oldest archeological sites in North America. Archeologist Francine Weiss noted: *"It is clear that many questions concerning Great Basin prehistory remain unanswered. Danger cave was the*

first site to provide a chronological framework for the arid West ..." The excavation by Jennings revealed that the human population of the desert area was sparse. There were maybe thirty people in a unit of extended family.

Jennings felt that the *"pattern of life was a cyclic wandering, but it was not a truly nomadic one."* The groups did not wander aimlessly but rather within a defined territory, dictated by food resources of plants and animals, and was seasonal in nature.

Jennings observed: *"The quest for food required most of the energy of the group."* They were hunter-gatherers. The cave was used as a shelter where they could roast meat and eat seeds and pinenuts.

Jennings wrote that the *"twin hallmarks"* of this group of people *"were the basket and the flat milling stone."* Seeds were harvested, milled into flour and parched among hot coals in baskets on flat stones lining the baskets. Small animals were cooked intact on the fires. In addition to spending time hunting and gathering, they manufactured and used plant fibers for *"nets, bags, and ropes"* plus winnowing baskets, water jugs, robes and blankets.

Jennings concluded: *"It is difficult for modern man to*

First Little League team in Wendover. Back left to right: Al Linares, unknown, James Williams, Mike Spillman, Gene L. Jones, Barry Jones, unknown, Tom Freeman, unknown, Lyons, Dale Stewart. Front: Kenny Linares, Garn Anderson, Mickey Holder, Craig Lyons, unknown, unknown, unknown, John Parks, Earl Tucker. *(Al Linares)*

conceive of a life so directly and continuously focused on sheer survival as the Desert culture was. In such situations there is little leisure, and almost no certainty about the morrow. No long-term building projects, no complicated rituals, no extensive amassing of personal property nor any long range plans can be undertaken in such circumstances."

Danger Cave was vandalized both before and after Jennings' excavations. Pot hunting disturbed the area and graffiti was written on the cave outcrop. The City of Wendover applied to the National Park Service for National Historic Landmark status for Danger Cave and received it in March of 1984. Further excavations were done in 1986 by professionals led by David Madsen of the Utah Geological Survey. It was later designated a United Nations World Heritage Site.

In 1997 the cave was closed at the entrance for protection against further vandalism. In June of 2002 the cave was again examined during a six-day excavation by scientists from the University of Nevada-Reno, the Desert Research Institute, the Utah Division of History, and the Utah Geological Survey. They were digging along the back wall of Jennings' quarry to determine how rapid climate changes effected humans and plants.

Professor Jennings also excavated Raven Cave twenty-five miles north of Wendover and nearby Juke Box Cave (Indian Cave) with less spectacular results. Jennings' work is well-known and is taught as part of archaeology courses in modern colleges.

Juke Box Cave or Indian Cave is located about 2½ miles to the northeast of Wendover. It originally was called Indian Cave and Picture Cave by locals. The cave was planned for use by army personnel during World War II as a bar and dance hall. Spike Birdzell local café owner, helped pour a concrete floor but the military thought it was too dangerous to use.

The teenagers of Wendover reportedly used the cave after the war as a place to party. Marriage proposals and graduation parties took place in the coolness of Juke Box Cave. It was out of town and a place to get away from parents. Sharon Scott was one of the teenagers. She said, *"When we went there we always showed great respect for it, leaving nothing behind."* Dale Stewart said it was too dusty inside to do much when he was a teenager.

The cave was excavated by Jesse Jennings of the University of Utah in the late 1940s and he wrote anthropological papers reporting his findings, similar but not as extensive as those of Danger Cave. Dave Madsen of the Utah Geological Survey did further investigations in 1998 as he studied climate trends in the Great Basin. Juke Box Cave is part of Danger Cave State Park, a part of the Utah State Parks system, but it has not been developed due to lack of funding.

Evidence of looters in 1997 caused state officials to erect an iron gate over the entrance to Juke Box Cave. The gate was funded from a private donor. The cave was once again vandalized with spray paint in May 2003.

A Fourth of July parade in Wendover

The Wizard of Wendover

Robert Golka, an individual with 1½ years of education at a Massachusetts college, became interested in producing and harnessing ball lightning. He saw a potential energy source from ball lightning as did Tesla. He came to Wendover Air Base to set up his lab in an abandoned airplane hanger, renting it for $1 per year from the Air Force.

During his experiments in 1981 at Wendover, Golka felt that there was internal heat reaching 5,000 to 10,000 degrees but that the balls did not radiate any heat. He also felt that the balls were *"similar to miniature nuclear bombs."* There was one difference, he felt that the ball's explosive energy could be *"released in specific quantities."* Mr. Golka wanted to harness the lightening. The problem was in keeping the energy from bouncing around.

While in Wendover, he upset some of the locals. One man put it this way: *"This joker that has moved in down there—they should have castrated him. I think he stole all of the copper out of it* [the hangar] *... Whoever give* [sic] *him permission to come in here should have been sent down the road right away!"* Golka's experiments proved inconclusive. At the same time, the Air Force encouraged him to abandon his activities and he left.

Recreation

The West Wendover Recreation District was organized in the mid 1980s for the purpose of managing the 18-hole championship golf course. The recreation district expanded later on to manage the Robert F. Scobie Park, the LaCombe Triune baseball/soccer fields, and an equestrian park. The district sponsored events in biking, swimming, culture, rodeoing, and running throughout each year. An outdoor Olympic-sized swimming pool with video games, ping pong or basketball also was available. Drag racing was held at a strip on the old air base facility.

Wendover offered annual events such as the Bordertown Mountain Bike Challenge. There were 15-, 50-, and 75-mile races and a high speed 1.5 mile downhill race from Wendover Peak. The Cinco de Mayo festival featured fiestas, dances and a parade.

Speed Week on the salt flats occurred the third week in August, World of Speed in September, and World Finals in October for car and motorcycle race enthusiasts. Amateur and professional racers competed to set new land speed records. The Bureau of Land Management managed the Bonneville Salt Flats to insure that the scenic, recreational, and geologic resources were protected. Racing events were open to the public but the BLM charged an admission fee.

Wendover Airfield held a Second Annual Fly-in &

Air show on September 28, 2002. World War II vintage aircraft were flown in. Rides were available. There was judging of aircraft complete with awards. Contestants competed in a *"flour bombing contest."* Humvees and Apache helicopters from the 19th Special Forces were brought in. Thousands were in attendance which showed great potential in holding future annual events.

The Hawk Watch International Goshute Research Site *"is one of the West's premier spots for observing hawks and other migratory birds."* The Goshute Raptor Project ran yearly from August 15 to November 15. Close to 42,000 raptors had been banded at the site since 1980 in an effort to get an annual count. The home range was located twenty-four miles southwest of Wendover off Highway 93 near Ferguson Springs.

> "Most travelers going through the Wendover area would already assume that the towns in the middle of the desert are one isolated city."
> —Jacqueline Cheney

Mountain biking, hiking, and cross-country cycling trails were abundant in the nearby foothills, deserts, and mountains. Desert scuba diving and fishing for bluegill and large-mouth bass were year-round sports at nearby Blue Lake, named for its light blue, slightly salty water. Blue Lake is a 9.7-acre, brakish, geo-thermal, spring-fed hot springs. It is fifty-eight feet deep and has water temperatures ranging from sixty-nine degrees at the top to eighty-three degrees at the bottom. Hot pots bubble up and are visible on the lake bottom. Visibility varies from ten to twenty-five feet. Diving schools and law enforcement agencies train at Blue Lake. Metal sculptures of a praying mantis, hammerhead shark, turtle, scorpion, and rhinoceras adorn the lake, above and beneath the surface. A boardwalk and metal ladder aide divers. Hermit Gilbert McCollough, alias *"Mosquito Bill"* resided in a cave at what used to be called Salt Springs in years past.

Drivers followed a 54-mile loop called the Silver Island Mountain National Back Country Byway. The isolated route passed the Donner Reed trail with markers and geologic formation are evident from Lake Bonneville.

Wendover Secession

Wendover is *"peculiarly located"* with part being in Utah and part being in Nevada. In 1913, it was noted that when somebody needed arresting in Wendover, it was necessary to have sheriffs from both Nevada and Utah present so that the suspect couldn't quickly flee over the border to the other state.

The local Wendover saloon in 1913 was built straddling the states with a white line running through the center designating the state line. The news article stated that *"wanted men keep mighty close to the line when either sheriff is in town."* What made it even worse was the lawlessness evident there. Tooele County Sheriff Harris considered Wendover to be the *"toughest town in the state."* Having one jurisdiction instead of two might have helped.

As early as 1946 there was talk of Wendover, Utah, seceding to Nevada. The following two entertaining newspaper articles from the *Deseret News* on September 9, 1946, illustrate the mood of the times.

"Neglected little Wendover, Utah, tired of receiving the horse laugh from Utah in its attempts to 'secede' from the state, today appealed to the governor of Nevada to set up a 'refugee camp,' so its residents could move over into a 'liberal American, constitutionally-run state.'

"The forgotten town expressed the desire last June to get out of Utah because it couldn't compete with Nevada's liberalism only a stone's throw away. Then, during the last session of the legislature, they sent a telegram asking that the state 'cede' the town to Nevada.

"Governor Herbert B. Maw commented at that time that Wendover had about as much chance as Salt Lake City of getting out of Utah, inasmuch as it would take an act of Congress and the consent of both states to change the boundary line.

"So today Lester Giffen, president of the Wendover Development Association sent a letter to Governor Vail Pittman of Nevada asking for that state's help. 'If you establish a refugee camp, we can move into a liberal, American, constitutionally-run state, hold our present jobs, support ourselves and enjoy our right of life, liberty and the pursuit of happiness,' Mr. Giffen wrote.

"He pointed out that the appeal to the Utah legislature and Governor Maw had been 'flatly turned down,' and that no mention was made of what Wendover could do to get a high school or sewers. Mr. Giffen, a Wendover railroader, also said that a suggestion had been made that if Wendover, Utah

Fred, Hilda, and Percy Hewitt on the Utah-Nevada state line at Wendover in 1926.
(Molly Hewitt Taylor)

residents did not like Utah and preferred Nevada, they move to Nevada …

"Governor Maw said today that although the Senate had referred the Wendover telegram to him, he hadn't received it, but that his original comment still stood. 'Congress set the boundary lines and they would have to change it,' he declared. 'If we start changing boundary lines Utah would want that north-western corner that went to Wyoming when that state joined the union and also the northern rim of the Grand Canyon from Arizona. If Wendover wants to fix all those things up at the same time, it would be all right with us.'"

On October 30, 1947 the *Deseret News* reported- *"Wendover, Utah's most rebellious city, which tried in vain to secede from the state last spring, now has petitioned Congress to make the area 'an autonomous district of Shangri-La' and relieve it of Utah's 'oppressive conditions.'*

"The little town which sits on the Nevada state line declares that under Utah's strict laws it can't compete with Wendover, Nevada, and its more liberal way of life. Utah wouldn't consent to the town's seceding from the state last spring, so now it apparently is trying other measures."

The unification issue came closer to reality in 2001 when the U.S. Congress became involved. In the spring of 2001, Utah Congressman Jim Hansen and Nevada Congressman Jim Gibbons introduced House Resolution 2054 which allowed Congress to approve a shift in state boundary lines as long as the state legislatures affected by the boundary lines approved also.

The law specified a five-year time period until 2006 to work out the details.

The Wendover boundary shift proposal made the front page of *The New York Times*. Such a shift would be the first since West Virginia became a state separate from Virginia in 1863 after Virginia seceded from the Union during the Civil War.

Government officials of the two Wendovers met in October 2001. The two city councils subsequently applied for a federal grant and hired consultants to study the pros and cons of unification. They *"also appointed 19 residents to serve on study committees."*

A Congressional delegation went to Wendover in late November 2002. At the November meeting more than fifty residents and business executives met together. *"West Wendover Mayor Josephine Thaut proposed local ballot referendums."* The two city councils organized citizen committees to look at issues such as how to handle bonded indebtedness owed by the Tooele County School District and costs incurred by the Tooele County Commission to modernize Wendover airport. Other problems to be looked at were related to police, fire, utilities, school services, *"state loyalties,"* and community redevelopment.

Not all citizens of Wendover and West Wendover were in favor of annexation. Taxpayers of Elko County, Nevada, were concerned about taking on Wendover, Utah's, indebtedness with the Wendover Airport to the tune of $3.4 million. Although neither city had any general obligation debt, Wendover, Utah, had three water revenue bonds to be paid by the revenues of the city water system.

It was felt by some citizens that inter-local agreements could be worked out to avoid duplicative services without having to annex Wendover, Utah, into Nevada. There was initial talk of a *"ban against casinos on the now-Utah side"* to avoid competition for the established resorts, but that proposal was dropped.

The report concluded that there were many benefits to annexation despite the concerns. In actuality Wendover, Utah, residents reportedly stood to save over $1,400 per year in property taxes in addition to paying no state income tax in Nevada. West Wendover would increase its general fund revenues and property tax increases generated from developed vacant sites.

High school graduation requirements would change for former Utah students to meet Nevada standards. Students would lose Utah residency status needed to get in-state tuition at nearby Utah universities but would be able to attend Nevada universities qualifying for in-state tuition.

One city government could operate more efficiently and less costly than two. Three water service agencies combined into one should have the effect of reducing water rates for all residents. Health and social services programs, police, fire, utility, public school systems, and courts would be combined for the benefit of all. The recreation district of West Wendover which had served both communities anyway would receive more revenues and thus be able to make additional improvements. Also, the transfer of the airport to Nevada would remedy numerous disagreements between the two communities with regard to zoning and airspace.

The unity issue remained unresolved in 2004. Both communities had previously agreed that Wendover, Utah, and Wendover, Nevada, should have the last word in the reunification plan. On election day November 6, 2002, annexation came one step closer to reality when citizens of both communities voted to unite. The Utah side voted 110 to 61 in favor of the shift and West Wendover residents voted 248 to 191 in favor of the merger.

The next steps would involve both states and their legislatures. An interstate compact would have to be drafted and agreed upon. Nevada legislative procedures were somewhat complicated and would take several years to accomplish.

The proposed new boundary would extend about 3.75 miles east of Wendover, avoiding the Utah Port of Entry location. Land totaling 9,935 acres would be added to Nevada with no major land use changes. Reilly Industries and the Wendover airport would fall within the new city limits. However, Tooele County was not in favor of giving up the vast acreage involved in the airport and the potash plant.

The merger would not likely happen until 2007, at the earliest, if at all. There were still many unresolved issues. In late 2002, a new dispute seemed to sour the whole prospect of unification when West Wendover played hardball politics, at least from Wendover, Utah's perspective. The new owners of the State Line Nugget were allegedly told their liquor license would be revoked as well as their business license unless they switched their water system to West Wendover and purchased their water from the Nevada side. The same thing could conceivably happen with the casino's sewer account in the future.

The account represented about $135,000 in revenues to Wendover, Utah, and could possibly bankrupt the city if it were lost to West Wendover. Somewhere between 15% and 25% of Wendover's city budget came from the State Line water usage. Some predicted that Wendover, Utah, would need to disincorporate should they lose the water account. The next few months would tell the tale.

The squabble over connecting the State Line to the West Wendover water system had historical as well as economic significance. When the City of Wendover took over the Pilot Mountain water system from the Western Pacific Railroad in 1960, there were no distribution water lines to carry the water to individual residents. People were allowed to tie into the water line if they wanted to furnish their own pipes and fittings. *"It was a real mess with lines running every way imaginable."*

The State Line Casino and the A-1 Service decided to help. They were hauling their own water from the railroad standpipe which was located north of the depot. The State Line water truck hauled water steadily eight hours a day, seven days a week. The same railroad standpipe continued to be used by stockmen and others in modern Wendover also.

The two casinos loaned the City of Wendover $25,000 from the State Line and $5,000 from the A-1 in order to install a main water line between the east end of town and the State Line on the west. The A-1's water came from a pipeline buried under U.S. 40 and connected to the State Line water tank. All businesses along the main thoroughfare were also connected and became the first metered customers. Subsequently, the loans were repaid by deducting one-half of each month's water bill charged to the two benefactors. The arrangement was a perfect example of pulling together in a small community.

However, old Wendover with its closely knit group of citizens who relied on each other so readily was quickly disappearing. At the same time, the population was multiplying and spreading westward across the Utah-Nevada boundary line. The two communities continued to meet in an attempt to iron out their differences and become one city within Nevada. Tourism and gambling were the watchwords of the times and of the future in modern Wendover. The A-1 and family-owned State Line were gone, replaced by newer, larger corporations. The railroad simply passed through. The bustling, noisy rail yard of yesteryear was a distant memory. The goliath military city with its soaring, graceful war birds and secretive code names was a mirage, touching reality only in the remaining rows of decaying edifices and aging airmen's reminiscences. The potash industry reliably continued on. At the same time, the unique racing brotherhood met each year on the world famous Bonneville Speedway with their sleek powerhouse racing machines, anticipating their ever-memorable triumphs over speed. And a small group of long-time residents linked the past to the present.

"*Off-setting the negatives* [of living in Wendover] *were the distant vistas, incredible sunsets and the quiet solitude of the desert at eventide. I took a lesson from my children, to grow where I had been planted. My most cherished blessings in the past forty-seven years have been the friendships I have made in Wendover. Those dear people who like myself came to Wendover for economic reasons but stayed on to build a community,*" said Jean Draper in the *High Desert Advocate,* a local newspaper.

With the previous insightful perspective by Wendover author Jean Draper, virtually the first century of Wendover's written history ends. There's been a whole lot of living in that little town!

One final bit of philosophy about history: someone has said, "*The past is prologue.*" History repeats itself. Indeed, "*History is bunk right up until it repeats itself.*" Looking back doesn't mean we are re-treating into the past. Rather, we are preparing for the future. We find the clues to where we are going by examining where we have been.

History comes in booms and busts, in cycles, whether it is the history of the world or of communities or of individuals. We have read in these pages how the Wendover citizenry of the past reacted to change. How will they respond to the potentially extraordinary times of the future? The answer will come with the passage of time.

Appendix A

PARTIAL LISTING OF WENDOVER, UTAH & WEST WENDOVER, NEVADA RESIDENTS, FORMER AND PRESENT

Ackerman, Janet
Adams, Ralph
Adams, Don & Francis
Adams, Stirling
Allen, Lenard & Maud
Andrews, Rachel
Andrus, Brenda
Allen, Bryan
Alllen, Clyde & Josephine
Allison, Bob & Esther
Andersen, Barry & Judy
Andersen, Howard and Sandra
Anderson, Charles D.

Anderson, Ada & Chunky

Anderson, Coreen
Anderson, Donald & Chris
Anderson, Garn
Anderson, Harold
Anderson, Kathleen
Anderson, Lowell
Anderson, Otto

Anderson, J. Ronald & Melba

Anderson, Robert and Judy
Anderson, Roland
Anderson, Todd Eugene
Anderson, Tom
Anderson, Varian and Ada
Andrus, Dale & Vicky
Antry, Kenny & Sue
Arias, Della
Arnoldsen, Earl
Arthur, Robert and Tamra

Arthur, Robert

Asper, Richard and Janet
Augura, Orland & Ruth
Aviles, Bobbi

Ayala, Joe & Lupe

Baker, Harvey & Nannette
Ball James E. and Terre
Bangs, Hewitt & Beulah
Barnes, Ellis
Barrus, John
Bartlome, Anna
Bartlome, Jerry & Anna
Bartlome, Jerry & Judy

Baker, David M.

Bayles, Butch
Bean, Gary & Cathy
Beardsley, Gracie
Beck, Glenn & Ann
Becker Larry & Eilene

Beer, Cathem

Behl, Katherine Ann
Bennett, Don & Bunnie
Bennett, Josie & Alpi
Bermejo, Fred & Florence
Birdwell, Marvin
Birdzell, Pat
Birdzell, Spike & Mary
Black, Allen
Black, LaRene
Blake, Richard and Mary
Blanchard, George & June
Blaner, Fred & Eliza
Bolinder, Les & Doll
Bostock Don & Barbara
Bostock, Gordon
Bostock, Ron & Ruth

Birdzell, Mary Lou

Bostock, Shane & Anda
Bostock Tom & Bobby
Bostock, Thomas & Lori Ann
Boyd, James E.
Brant, Errol
Brothers, Arthur & Fran
Brown, Gary
Brown, Jerry & Linda
Brown, Linda
Brown, Lloyd & Lillian

Brown, Mert & Violet

Brown, Rocky & Tammie
Brown, William and Dorothy
Bru, Kierstien
Bru, Ingrid Diane
Brun, Gig & Linda
Bryant, Mary Ellen
Bumgarner, Bob & Mabel
Burg, Jeanne
Burgess, Charles & Reenie
Burrows, Zenos and Terry
Burt, Nathan & Jane
Bushman, Carolyn
Butterfield, John & Judy
Calaghan, Dennis
Callister, Melvin Dale & Leila
Callister, Troy
Cameron, Mary
Campbell, Bob & Louise
Camron, Mell
Cappa, Mike
Carder, Betty J.

Callister, Alf & Chloe and Jane Irvine

Campbell, Billy & Clarence

Carello, Matilda Esse
Carroll, Dave & Blanche
Carter, Augustus "June"
Carter, Clayton & Brenda
Carter, Jared & Emily
Casperson, Gladys

Castagno, Ken & Heather

Cathy, Charles H. & Betty Ruth
Cerna, Abel
Charles, Irene
Chavez, Cirro
Chichis, George & Tessie
Christensen, Ron
Christensen, Sharon

Christensen, Paul & Lucille

Christensen, Tom & Chris
Christensen, Weldon & Carol
Christiansen, Francis & Grace
Chuensiri, Pirote
Clancy, Peter & Aurea
Clard, Corma Hazel
Clark, Guy & Helen
Clark, Lonnie & Delsie
Claw, Ned & Velma
Cloward, George & Macine
Coalon, Charles
Condie, Paul and Gay
Conley, Joseph & Caroline
Conrad, Jim & Jackie
Cook, David & Evelyn
Cook, Gerald
Cooley, John W.
Copelan, Howard & Corrine
Corham, Roy & Leah
Cornett, Virgil and Wilma
Coulson, Sam & Doris
Cowan, Ron & Sandra
Craner, Roy & Dorthy

Craner, Eugene & Betty

Crawford, Mike & Ann
Crawford, Ray and Karen
Cress, Justin & Rebecca
Crowley, William & Bonnie
Dahlstrom, Derek

Dahlstrom, Gary & Elaine

Dahlstrom, Lance
Dana, Michael
Daniels, Gary & Vanessa

Danvers, Tracey
Daudna, Judy
Daum, Carole Ann
Daum, George
Daugherty, Jim & Rose
Davis, Jack & June
Dean, Bruce & Cindy
Dean, Georgia

Dean, Luana & Donald

Devaney, Ruth & Fred

Dennis, L. J.
DeVaney, Howard & Lloyda
Devine, Dave & Billy Ann
Devine, Frank Blaine
Devine, Michael & Rita
Dilleshaw, Stacey
Dixon, Richie & Kim
Dixon, Stephanie
Dorado, Miguel
Doran, Hector

Dixon, Caren & Arthur Richard

Dotson, Louis & Mary
Douglas, John & Mary
Dowdy, Steve & Jackie
Dowling, Mrs.
Draper, Birdel Jr.

Draper, Jean & Birdel (Bird)

Draper, Russ & Brenda

Druhl, Ralph & Virginia
Dugan, Louis & Nellie
Dulong, Edward & Barbara
Duncan, James
Duncan, Rose
Dunlavy, Mike & Karen
Durham, Keyth & Donna
Eastwood, John
Eby, Dave & Dede
Eby, David & Patricia

Ecton, Jesse & Geneva

Ekker, Matt & Debbie
Eller, Henry
Elliot, Edson & Sarah
Elliot, Franklin "High" & Elizabeth
Elliot, Lynn & Jenn
Elton, Steve & Julia

Ekker, Matt

Ericksen, Dovie & Roy

Ennis, Roger & Heather
Esparza, Faustino
Espinosa, Betty & Frank
Espinosa, Frank & Margaret
Excell, Max T. & Glenda
Fait, Elwin
Faust, Frank
Fedin, Donald and Rose
Fernandez, Dan & Irene
Field, Lee & Henrietta
Fineout, Elmer and Alice
Fione, Gloria
Fione, Norman
Fisher, Ryon
Flinders, Leon
Flores, Elias
Flournoy, John W & Patricia
Ford, Boomer
Francis, Shawn & Nancy
Frandsen, Burke & Sherrie
Forsberg, Penny
Freeman, Billy
Freeman, Thomas and Evelyn
Freeman, Tom and Rae
Garcia, Cindy
Garfield, Tom & Essie Mae
Gentry, Vickie

Garrett, Phillip F.

Gibson, Hoot & Pam

Gerhardt, Robin
Gibson, Howard and Bonnie
Gibson, Howard and Pansy Rae
Gieber, George and Arloene
Giffen, Grace
Gill, Harold
Gillett, Guy
Gonzalez, Luis & Gloria
Gonzalez, Ralph
Gonzalez, Tammy
Gonzalez, Tracy
Graham, Wayne
Green, Clayton & Glenda
Green, Goldie & Nancy
Green, Malin

Green, Marie "Pokey"

Green, Marion Clayton

Green, Marion Jr.
Green, Shannon
Greenhalgh, Wendall
Gregory, Phillip & Lyn
Gregory, Shaun & Mellisa
Gonzalez, Tracy & Pam
Goudy, Margaret
Griego, Jose
Griego, Maniluez & Siria
Griesdale, Grant & Jan

Griffith, Jennnifer
Grossman, Rodney
Grossman, Virginia
Guinn, Ginger
Guitierrez, Aaron & Leah
Guitierrez, Robert & Carla
Gutierrez, Jesse & Kathy
Gutierrez, Joe & Jo
Gutierrez, Jose & Eufenia
Gunter, Michael & Sandi
Gurney, Walden
Hale, Archie & Helen
Hales, Frank and Ruby
Hall, Dale
Hall, Don & Shirley

Hall, Don & Ruby Monjar

Hall, Earl and Afton

Halladay, Don
Hamilton, Bill & Delores
Hamilton, Candy & Gram
Hammond, Mont & Iona

Hammond, Monte G.

Haney, Harold & Sandy
Haney, Mindy
Haney, Ricky & Paula
Hansen, Brad & Terry
Hansen, David
Hanson, John B & Rose

Heath, Earl & Violet

Hardy, Kathy
Hargrove, Harold & Myrtle
Herron, Larry & Jan
Harrigan, Thomas & Suzanne
Hart, Cliff & Debbie
Haslam, Clyde & Beatrice
Hawk, Randy
Hayes, Harry & Betty
Hayes, Tom & Helen
Heed, Harry & Venita
Hensley, Roger & Lynne
Hernandez, Chono
Hernandez, Joe & Annie
Hernandez, Joe & Bobbie
Hernandez, John
Hernandez, Sandra
Herrera, Herman & Lillian
Herron, Larry
Hess, Greg
Heugly, Leisha
Hewitt, Percy and Letty
Hicktor, Mrs.
Higley, Dale & Betty
Hildago, Roger & Victoria
Hitt, Sandra
Hobbs, Byron & Darlene
Hobbs, Hilton
Holdeman, Terrance
Holden, Jimmy
Holt, Richard
Honey, Butch & Sandy
Hougard, Jon & Stacie
Houghly, Brian & Leisha
Houser, Jay & Diane
Hubbard, Jane
Hudson, James & Grace

Howe, Dean & Gene

Howlett, Chet & Elaine

Hughs, Mable & Sy

Hughs, Max & Dovie
Hungate, Gene & Nell
Hunter, Carol
Hussey, Tom & Kathleen
Hutchinson, Lind and Myrtis
Irvine, Tom & Jan
Ivie, Charles
Jacobsen, Matthew
James, Robert & Gladys

Jensen, Auer & Doris

Jensen, Douglas
Jensen, Elizabeth
Jensen, Jack
Jensen, John & Lizzie
Jensen, William
John, Molly
Johnson, Ferdinand & Lillian
Johnson, Leah Mae
Johnson, Mary
Johnson, Robert G.
Johnston, Bill
Johnston, Marie and Lawrence
Jokan, Alex & Jiggs
Jolley, Linda
Jones, Barry & Kim
Jones, Brent
Jones, Carol & Marlene

Jones, Gene & Sue
Jones, Wayne & Taunya
Joynt, Jeffrey & Nancy
Julian, Gary & Pat
Kanakos, Knick & Delores
Karas, Jack & Ellen

Jones, Barry

Jones, Leah

Jones, Gene
Kearney, Ralph and Wilma
Keiser, Les & Mary
Keith, Tho & Shawnee
Kellogg, Joseph and Verna
Kelly, Harold & Norma

Kemp, Norvin & Voris

Kenley, Fred and Annie
Kennedy, David
Kennedy, Elizabeth
Kerbovich, Tony & Katherine
Kerbovich, April
Khavari, Manoochehrl
Kibler, Lewis and Verna
Kido, Kiyoji & Minora
Kimber, Russ
King, Cherie
Kinzie, John

Kinzie, Sam & Heather
Kirkham Deila
Kirkham, Hugh P.
Knudson, Richard
Knudtson, Jeff

Koska, Betty & Manfred (Fred)

Lacombe, Dwayne & Mandie
Lacombe, Robert & Gina
Lacombe, Roger
Lacy, Earl & Mary
Lacy, Earl III & Glenda
Lacy, Rick & Virginia Gutierrez
Lamb, William
Lambert, George & Janice
Lamus, Blair & Nel
Lamus, Bruce
Lamus, Nelson "Ed" & Martha "Gram"
Lamus, Nelson and Rosa
Lander, Mike

Lange, Betty Ruth & Harold

Lara, Carolyn
LaRock, John & Lillie
Laub, Kunt
Lavelle, Eugene and Verna
Lawrence, Steve
Lee, Eloise
Lee, Ordie & Mae
Lee, Cheryl
Lee, Robert and Betty
Leland, Tobina
Leo, Ivan & Mary Lou
Lewis, Cody
Lewis, Gary & Heidi
Lewis, Don & Mary Lou
Lewis, Ronnie & Ann
Limke, Terry & Carol

Lewis, Mitzi

Lewis, Russell R.

Linares, Al & Ruth

Linam, Dean & Adrienne
Linam, Terry & Barbara
Linares, Danny Keith & DeAnna
Liotiris, Nick & Susan
Lisk, Larry & Cheryl
Lisk, Ryan & Dennis
Lisk, Laura
Lobato, Lucille
Longson, Charles & Kelly
Loosemore, Lester
Lopez, Diana
Lopez, Don L.
Louis, Henry
Lords, Elsie
Lovel, Steven & Adell
Luby, Thomas and Delores
Lund, Chris & Pat
Lutes, LeRoy & Sherry
Lyman, James "Ace" & Millie
Lyon, Ivan and Vera
Lyons, Frank and Gayla
Macintires
Madsen, Buss & Faun
Madsen, Vern & Shirley
Magson, James & Ethel

Lyman, Millie & Glenda Green

Mair, William E.
Mair, William L.
Malone, Daniel
Malone, Doug & Elaine
Malone, Jerry

Malone, Doug

Manahan, Hildred
Mangum, Peggy
Mansor, Kevin
Marquez, Carlos & Rosa
Martin, Gay
Martinez, Dorothy
Martinez, LaMar and Eusebio
Mascaro, Greg & Kathy
Mascaro, Paul & Nonie
Massey, Bill
Massey, Belindai

Matthews, Patricia & Daniel

Mauer, Leonard and Joy
Maxfield, Garff & Bonnie
May, Michael
Maycock, Lea Ann
McCloud, Mac & Chris
McCown, James & Jenny
McEntire, Donald

Mauer, Leonard

McGarry, Herbert & Frances
McGillizray, Gene
McGrew, Mac
McKee, Roy & Mildred
McKellar, Charles
McKellar, Glenn & Gert
McKellar, John
McKellar, Peter & Hildred
McKellar, Warren
McLachlin, John
McLead, Leatha
McQueen, Bill & Pat
McQueen, Jack & Guineivere
Meiklejohn, William
Melville, Cheryl
Melville, Chris

Melville, Dixie

Melville, Helen
Melville, LaMar and Carol
Melville, Randall & Natalie
Melville, Reese & Beth
Melville, Roberta
Memlendez, Florencio
Merideth, Paula
Merl, Bradley & Lorraine
Merritt, Joyce
Middlebrook, Earl & Francis
Miera, Mike and Stacey
Mikesell, Chris
Miller, Berl
Minner, Melvin and Viola
Mitchell, Mark
Monahan, Jim & Hildred
Monjar, Ed & Ruby
Montoya, Errol & Galla
Moon, Velma
Moore, Cecil

Moore, Lenard
Moore, Mason & Carrie
Moore, Richard & Susan
Moore, William Bud
Moore, William & Lorene

Morgan, Barbara & Glen

Morgan, Billie & Brenda
Morgan, Connie
Morgan, Grant
Morgan, Marsha
Morgan, William S.
Mori, Jahyiro & Turee
Morley, Shane & Kim
Morris, Vicki
Morton, Art & Louise

Moss, Bud & Pena

Mueller, Steven
Munsee, Edward & Mary
Munsee, Eugene
Murphy, Bernice and Deverle
Murphy, Carol
Murphy, David & Annette
Murphy, Jared & Cecelia

Murphy, Everett & O'Nae

Murphy, Kirk & Radine
Murphy, Kyle & Heather
Murphy, Lane & Wendy
Murphy, Vaughn & Mary
Murray, Ernest & Nellie
Nance, Val & Cheryl
Navarro, Stephen & Rebecca
Neilsen, Hugh K.
Nelms, Dick & Connie
Neilsen, Kay & Ruby
Nelson, Von & Sylvia

Nielsen, Verl & Earnie

Nieman, Larry & Jodean
Nongyuan, Musel
Norris, Clara
Nuffer, Preston & Mae

Nuffer, Preston A.

Nyrehn, Neldon
O'Hanlon, Lois
O'Neal, Claudia
O'Neal, Jim & Mildred
Oakes, Jesse & Patricia
Oglesby, Bob & Marilyn
Oliverson, Garth & Sonja
Olson, Larry and Nina
Olson, Mark & Julie
Openshaw, Rose
Orgill, Raymond & Erma
Page, Karen
Palafox, Hector & Lori
Palafox, Mario
Palafox, Jose
Palmer, Raeldon and JoEllen
Pankratz, Charlie & Ted
Pantelakis, George M.
Parker, Samuel & Barbara

Parker, William & Verna
Parkin, Jerry & Diane
Parks, Walt & Barbara
Parra, Augustino & Elena
Paulis, John & Mary
Paxton, Mechelle
Peasnall, Frank and Jeanette
Pechart, Louis & Margaret
Peck, Dr. Joseph
Pedersen, Lars
Pendleton, Claudia
Pendleton, Dirk
Perez, Gregory & Maria
Perez, Michael & Cathy
Perkins, Linda
Perly, Gregory and Marie
Perry, Steve & Barbara
Pete, Harlan & Debbie
Pete, Lorraine
Peterson, Brenton
Peterson, Darryl & Penelope
Peterson, Kent & Barbara
Peterson, Kirk & Christina

Peterson, Neil & LaFaye

Peterson, Ray & Shirley
Peterson, Richard
Pettit, Coleman
Pettit, Linda
Pettit, Mae
Phizacklea, Fred & Tamie
Phizacklea, James & Jean
Pierren, Frederic & Vickie
Pitts, Kenneth & Jill

Pinaire, Olive & Joe

Porter, Bruce
Porter, Chris
Portella, charlotte & Ricky
Portwood, Roland & Bonnie
Poulson, Beckie

Poulson, Gwen & Lynn

Pritchett, Frank & Olive

Pruitt, Ray & Frieda

Price, Jake & Tammy
Priest, David & Brenda
Prowden, Joe
Pruitt, James
Quintero, Roberto
Rainey, Sam & Joan
Ramirez, Ishmael & Lucero
Ratliff, Bill & Marge
Ratliff, Bill Jr. & Jackie
Ratliff, Glenn & Patti
Ratledge, Jarid
Redd, James
Reilly, Jamey
Reyes, Henry & Janice

Reynolds, Clarence & Agnes
Reynolds, Mont & Barbara
Rhoades, Christopher & Mai
Richert, Steven
Richey, Charlene
Richey Bill
Richey, Benny Jack
Richey, H. L. & Mary

Richey, Mary

Richey, Phillip & Glenna
Richey, Ruth
Richey, Sam & Fayma
Ring, Donald
Ringholz, Michael
Rippetoe, Eldon & Dorothy
Rippetoe, Gary
Rippetoe, Royal
Rivers, David & Sue
Roach, Mark & Carol
Roberts, Harvey & Cathrine
Robertshaw, George & Vicky

Robertshaw, George

Robertshaw, Walt
Robertson, Danny
Robertson, Poncho & B.J.
Robinson, Calvin & Tanya
Roblyer, Vernon and Velda
Rodd, Sam
Rodgers, Sharon
Rodriguez, George
Rodriquez, Armondo
Rodriguez, Arosmo & Angelica
Rogers, Mildred
Rogers, Will & Boots
Rohmer, Brett & Kay
Rojas, Jaime

Rothburn, Ralph & Lillie
Rowley, Allen & Barbara
Rumsey, Kenneth
Rusk, John & Elfiedo

Russell, Frances & Bill

Salazar, Bertha
Salazar, Pedro
Sanborn, Richard
Sandberg, Larry
Sandoval
Santillanez, Bea
Santillanez, Ralph
Savedra, Sandra
Sawyer, Cornelius & Lucy
Sax, Virginia

Scobie, Robert

Schooley, Traci
Sessions, Thomas & Julia
Settle, Douglas
Sharp, Allan & Kelly
Sharp, Oliver & Edna
Sharp, Roland & Linda
Sharp, Todd
Shea, Tom & Peggy
Sheilds, Wayne & Carol

Sheilds, Wayne

Shelton, Brett

Shelton, Brett & Shirlee
Shelton, David & Lettie
Shelton, Vaun and Velda
Shepherd, Gerald
Shepherd, John & Louise
Shepherd, Lynn
Shepherd, Ranae

Shepherd, Randy & Karen

Shepherd, Rhea
Shepherd, Wayne
Shepherd, Willie & Joyce
Shindlin, Jesse & Ila
Skinner, Dale and Linda

Skinner, Dale

Simone, Henry
Sitek, Allen
Smith, Albert & Bessie
Smith, Carol
Smith, Coral & Janette
Smith, James & Charlee
Smith, Gordon & Deana
Smith, Hal & Pamela
Smith, Marion
Smith, Samuel

Smith, Bessie

Smith, Shirley
Smith, Teckla
Smith, Walt & Turdy
Smith, William & Anna
Snively, Kenneth & Mildred
Snodgrass, Pam
Sorenson, Clair & Letha

Sorenson, Hazel & Frank

Spatheth, Clint & Dean
Spatheth, Elsie
Spencer, Howard & LaRae
Spillman, Bob & Nina
Spillman, John
Spillman, Lennie
Spillman, Martin
Spillman, Merle & Ruth
Spillman, Michael & Tammy Jo

Spillman, Mike & Sharon

Spillman, Monica
Stachan, D.L
Steele, Francis & Bernice
Steele, Jacob
Stewart, Garth & Donna
Stewart, Gordon & Deanna
Stewart, Melvin

Steele, Ruth

Stewart, Sheila & Dale

Stone, Arby & Erma
Streetman, Homer & Reva
Stratton, Tom & Kelly
Sullivan, Virgil & LaRay
Supanich, Larry & Kerrie
Susich, John and Ruby
Sutton, Bill & Leta
Sutton, Donald
Swaney, Francis & Violet
Sweat. Dennis & Debra
Sweat, Karl & Hope
Sweat, Raymond and Rhea
Symes, Don & Diane
Tangaro, Gene & Ida
Tangaro, Nick & Cameron
Thaut, Josephine
Thoburn, Andrus Merritt
Thompson, Charles and Sharon
Thompson, Irene
Thompson, Mearna
Tiberglieu, Leo & Ellen
Tilbury, George & Bonnie
Tilley, Robert
Todecheene, John
Tolly, Jack & Lois
Trammel, Jim & Darlene
Trammel, Matthew
Trezona, Richard & Nellie
Tripp, Don & Cheryl
Tripp, Gilbert & Barbara
Tripp, M.B. and Emma
Tripp, Marion & Evelyn
Tripp, Tina

Tripp, Bailey

Tripp, Don

Tripp, Mark & Gertrude
Tripp, Vaughn & Sylvia
Trivet, Bob & Angie
Troyan, Viola
Trujillo, Ben & Rosalba
Trujillo, Leo
Tucker, Art & Mary
Tucker, Doug & Emily
Tucker, Vigil
Tyroff, Fred & Laura
Vigil, Mary
Vinson, Dale & Alice
Vinson, Jay
Vollmann, Ron & Carolyn
Wade, Janese
Wadsworth, Christy

Wadsworth, Darrel & Loneta

Wadsworth, Glenn & Tammy

Wadsworth, Shaun & Kristy
Walker, Max
Walters, Willard & Lylia
Warren Leishman
Waters, Billy and Rita

Waters, Naomi & Leo

Watkins, LeIsle
Watkins, Tom
Watkins, Wayne & Deon
Wayman, Paul & Linda
Weaver, Garth

Weems, Blanche

Weighall, John and Carma
Weighall, RichardFritz
Welker, Max
Wertz, Merle & Jean
West, Fred & Lynn
West, Twain & Irene
Wheeler, Leo & Sebrina

Wheeler, Margaret & Richard

Whiting, Charlton & Janet
Wiley, Rands and Hilda
Wilken, Pam
Wilkinson, Francis & Alyce

Willey, Darrell
Williams, Eldon & Marge
Williams, Joe & Jeannine
Wilson, Anna

Wind, Harold & Thora

Wind, Harry & LaDawn
Witt, Esther A.
Woffinden, Todd
Woffinden, William & Thelma

Woffinden, Thelma

Wollack, Henry & Philis
Wong, Sammy
Wood, Larry & Elaine
Woodruff, Cris & Eva
Works, Robert
Worthy, Herbert & Lorraine
Wroths
Zemel, Hope
Zacharias, James & Linda

Appendix B

WENDOVER AREA NEWSPAPERS AND MOVIES

Wendover Times
Deeanna Croasmun, editor;
established March 10, 1995,
to present

Wendover Herald
S. A. Juenke and
Larry Henderson, publishers;
S. A. Juenke, managing editor;
Alex Wilder, editor,
1986

High Desert Advocate
founded by Harry Copelan;
Howard Copelan, publisher & editor,
1984 to present

Wendover Relay
Brenda Robertson Draper,
publisher & editor ,
ca. 1983 to 1985

The *BLISTER Wendover News and World Report*;
Marie "Pokey" Green, publisher,
ca. 1978
photo not available

Salt Flat News
Richard Nahum Goldberger, editor,
Salt Flats Publishing Corporation,
publisher; ca. 1970 to 1975

Salt Tablet
published Semi-Monthly by
and for the Enlisted Men at
Wendover Field, Utah;
ca. 1942 to 1945

WENDOVER AREA MOVIES

Wendover has served as a backdrop for several Hollywood productions. Here is a list of recent movies that were filmed fully or in part at Wendover Field, with their release years.

Above and Beyond (1952)

Birds of Prey (1973)

Damnation Alley (1977)

The Philadelphia Experiment (1984)

Promised Land (1988)

Warlock (1989)

Wind (1992)

Independence Day (1996)

Mulholland Falls (1996)

Con Air (1997)

Money Plays (1997)

Midsummer Murders (1997)

Letters from a Killer (1998)

Flat Earth (1999)

The Runner (1999)

Slow Burn (2000-01)

The Ballad of Big Al (2001)

Joy Ride (2001)

The Core (2003)

The Hulk (2003)

Touched by an Angel (1996, 1998, 1999, 2001)

Sources:
http://www.wendoverairbase.com/hollywood.html
West Wendover Visitor's Center, Kerrie Supanich.

BIBLIOGRAPHY

Chapter 1. WENDOVER'S BEGINNINGS

Anderson, Garn. "The History of Wendover, 1908-1969." Typescript, March 17, 1969.

"Bloodless Duel Fought over Line of Two States." *Carson City News*, February 20, 1913.

Blow, Ben. "The Victory Highway." *Good Roads: The Journal of Highway Engineering and Transportation,* LXVI, No. 6, June 1924.

Casperson, Gladys. "A Brief History of Wendover Schools." Typescript, n.d.

Christensen, P. C. "An Irish Lass vs. Wild Desert Town." *Frontier Times,* January 1966.

Clark, George. "The Victory Highway." San Francisco, Brochure, 2002.

Draper, Jean. "The Wendover Story: History of the Town." Typescript, n.d.

Earl, Phillip I. "This Was Nevada: Phone Line's 75th Anniversary." *Free Press Extra,* Elko, July 25, 1989.

"History of the U.S. Highway System from Dirt Paths to Superhighways." http://gbcnet.com/ushighways/ history.html (9/12/2001).

Jardine, William M. "Linking the Atlantic with the Pacific." *Motor Land,* July 1925.

Johnson, Ferdinand. "Early History of Wendover." Undated manuscript.

Justice's Docket. "Wendover Justice of the Peace Court Proceedings, 1911-1921." Utah State Historical Society.

Knowlton, Ezra C. "History of Highway Development in Utah." Salt Lake City: Utah State Department of Highways, 1961.

Lamus, Blair. Letter to Illeana Z'Vara, 1951.

Lodor, A. E. "Across the Great White Way." *Motorland,* March 1924.

Means, Howard C. "Some Interesting Features in the Construction of the 'Wendover Cutoff' in Utah." Address at annual meeting of American Association of State Highway Officials held at San Francisco, California, November 17-20, 1924. Published in *American Highways,* January 1925.

Noeth, Louise Ann. *Bonneville Salt Flats.* Osceola, WI & Hong Kong: MBI Publishing Company, 1999.

Petersen, Jesse G. "The Lincoln Highway and Its Changing Routes in Utah." *Utah Historical Quarterly,* vol. 69, number 3, Summer 2001.

"Salduro Work was Program." *The Salt Lake Tribune,* June 14, 1925.

"Transcontinental Telephone Service Began in 1914, But Who Remembers?" *The History Blazer.* Utah State Historical Society: Salt Lake City, May 10, 1995.

Webb, Henry J. "Still the Fearful Drive of 100 Years Ago." Unidentified newspaper, Salt Lake City, Sunday, June 22, 1958.

Wendelboe, Lee. *A Will to Live.* Providence, Utah: Watkins & Sons, 1981.

Z'Vara, Illeana. Letters written to early Wendover residents asking for historical information. Typescripts, 1951.

Chapter 2. A COMMUNITY WITHOUT PARALLEL

Anderson, Garn. "The History of Wendover 1908-1969." Typescript, March 17, 1969.

Copelan, David. "Main Street: Bright Lights on the Border." *Nevada Magazine*, vol. 52, no. 1, February 1992.

Eyston, George, and W. F. Bradley. *Speed on Salt: A History of the Bonneville Salt Flats, Utah, USA.* London: Charles Scribner's Sons, 1936.

Lallman, M. William, and Glenn D. Wadsworth. "Kaiser Chemicals' Bonneville Potash Operation." Salt Lake City: Society of Mining Engineers of AIME, 1976.

McKellar, George A. "History of McKellar Ranches in Wendover, Utah." Typescript, n.d.

Tripp, Gertrude, ed. "Thro' the Years." Wendover Ward Relief Society, 1974.

Chapter 3. THE WESTERN PACIFIC

Bateman, Ronald R. *Deep Creek Reflections: 124 Years of History at Ibapah, Utah.* Author, 1984.

Bridges, R. W. "Dick." "Eighty Candles on the Final Cake." *Mileposts*, March 1983.

Hall, Shawn. *Old Heart of Nevada: Ghost Towns and Mining Camps of Elko County.* Reno/Las Vegas, University of Nevada Press, 1998.

Kneiss, G. H. "Fifty Candles for Western Pacific." *Mileposts*, 1953, http://www.wprrhs.org/wphistory.html (1998-99).

Myrick, David. *Railroads of Nevada and Eastern California* rptd. Reno: University of Nevada Press, 1993.

Peck, Joseph H., M.D. *What Next Doctor Peck? The Hilarious and Heartwarming Tale of a Struggling Doctor's Early Practice on the Desolate Utah Salt Flats.* Englewood Cliffs, NJ: Prentice-Hall, 1959.

Van Cott, John W. *Utah Place Names.* Salt Lake City, University of Utah Press, 1990.

Wendelboe, Lee. *A Will to Live.* Providence, Utah: Watkins & Sons, 1981.

"The Western Pacific Sacramento Northern and Tidewater Southern Railroad Companies Timetable No. 6," April 27, 1980.

Wilson, John, and Alan Radecki. "A History of the California Zephyr," http://calzephyr.railfan.net/history.html.

Chapter 4. WENDOVER FIELD

"Army Air Forces at Fort Douglas and Wendover, Utah." Typescript, Fort Douglas Military Museum.

Arrington, Leonard J., and Thomas G. Alexander. "World's Largest Military Reserve: Wendover Air Force Base, 1941-63." *Utah Historical Quarterly,* vol. 31, no. 4, Fall 1963.

Bateman, Phyllis. "Wendover Memories." Manuscript, 2000-01.

Correll, John T. "The Decision that Launched the *Enola Gay.*" *Air Force Magazine,* April 1994, http://www.afa.org/enolagay/07-02.html (April 1994).

Dussler, Byron. "Letters Written from Wendover Air Field, 6 August 1941 to March 1946." Typescript.

Freudenthal, Charles H. *A History of the 489th Bomb Group.* Minneapolis, Minn., Author, 1989.

Frischnecht, Scott. "Interview with Mr. Fred G. Kenley." July 16, 1981.

Gierhart, Diane. "Reflections: A Collection of Memories–Wendover, 1942-1945." Pamphlet, 1990.

Gwyn, Thomas Elmer, "Wendover Army Air Base, Utah." Manuscript, April 10, 1965.

Hibbard, Charles. "History of Wendover Army Air Field, Utah." *Utah History Encyclopedia,* http://www.online-utah.com/wendoverairfieldhistory.shtml (1994).

"Historical Documentation of Brig. General Paul W. Tibbets, Jr., September 1966." Oral history interviews conducted by the Air Force Historical Division, Arthur Marmor.

"History of the Wendover Army Air Base and 315th Base Headquarters and Air Base Squadron." Typescript, 7 December 1941 to 31 December 1942.

Holzapfel, Richard Neitzel. *Utah: A Journey of Discovery,* Layton: Gibbs Smith, 1999.

Hope, Bob, with Melville Shavelson. *Don't Shoot, It's Only Me.* New York, G.P. Putman's Sons, 1990.

Hubbard, Jim, "Fifteen Came to Wendover." *Wendover Relay,* June 21, 1984.

Huntington, Tom. "Dawn over Trinity." *American History.* April 2000, http://www.Historic Traveler.com (April 2000).

"Joseph Papalia Collection, 509th Composite Group." http://www/childrenofthemanhattanproject.org/collectionscg-jpap/pages/jpap_gallery_ol.htm

Knebel, Fletcher, and Charles W. Bailey II. "No High Ground." *Reader's Digest,* Nov. 1960.

Krauss, Robert, ed. "Wendover Memories. 509th Composite Group 56th Reunion 1945-2001." Wendover Historic Restoration, August 2001.

Laub, Bill. "Third Pilot at Hiroshima." Pamphlet, n.d.

Launius, Roger D. "Home on the Range: The U.S. Air Force Range in Utah, a Unique Military Resource." *Utah Historical Quarterly*, 59, no. 4, Fall 1991.

Launius, Roger D. "One Man's Air Force. The Experience of Bryon Dussler at Wendover Field, Utah, 1941-46." *Utah Historical Quarterly* 54, no.2, Spring 1986.

Launius, Roger D. "The United States Air Force in Utah: The Case of Wendover Field." Monograph, Fort Douglas Museum, 1985.

Marquardt, George. "Field Order #13." Pamphlet, n.d.

"Nevada League of Cities Seeks *Enola Gay* Plane at Wendover." Associated Press, 29 August 1997.

Newton, Eric. "What's the Top Story of the Century?" http://www.newseum.org/century/century_essay.html 2003.

Ossip, Jerome, ed. *509th Composite Group Pictorial Album. First Atomic Bombardment.* Tinian & Roswell, N.M. :The 509th Composite Group, 1945.

Ransom, Jay Ellis. "Wendover: Home of the Atom Bomb." *The Ruralite,* November 1973.

Rowe, James Les. *Project W-47: A Never Disclosed Chapter in the A-Bomb Story.* Livermore, CA: JA. A. Ro Publishing, 1978.

Thomas, Gordon, and Max Morgan-Witts. *Enola Gay Mission to Hiroshima.* England: White Owl Press Limited, 1995.

Tibbets, Paul W. Kenneth Leish Interview. Typescript, Tampa, Fla., December 1960.

Tibbets, Paul W. *Return of the Enola Gay.* Columbus: Mid Coast Marketing, 1998.

Truslow, Edith C., and Ralph Carlisle Smith. *Project Y: The Los Alamos Story.* Tomash Publishers, Los Angeles/San Francisco, 1983.

"Wendover Field." http://www.hill.af.mil/museum/history/Wendover.htm (2002)

The Wendover Times, 1999-2004.

Wensyel, James W. "Home Front." *American History,* June 1995.

"World War II Activities," http://www.wendoverairbase.com/ww2act.html (2002)

Chapter 5. THE GREAT AMERICAN DESERT

"A Bicyclist Challenges the Great Salt Lake Desert." *The History Blazer.* Utah State Historical Society: Salt Lake City, April 1, 1996.

Calabro, Marian. *The Perilous Journey of the Donner Party.* New York, Clarion Books, 1999.

Cressman, L. S. *Prehistory of the Far West Home of Vanished People.* Salt Lake City: University of Utah Press, 1977.

Hawkins, Bruce R., and David B. Madsen. *Excavation of the Donner-Reed Wagons. Historic Archaelogy along the Hastings Cutoff.* Salt Lake City: University of Utah Press, 1990. Originally published: Salt Lake City, Utah: Western Printing Co., 1930.

Huchel, Frederick M. *A History of Box Elder County.* Salt Lake City: Utah State Historical Society Box Elder County Commission, 1999.

Jackson, Donald, and Mary Lee Spence, eds. *The Expeditions of John Charles Fremont.* 3 vols. Supplement, Map Portfolio, Urbana, Ill., 1970-84.

Kelly, Charles. "First Emigrant Train." *The Desert Magazine,* March 1946.

Kelly, Charles. *Salt Desert Trails: A History of the Hastings Cutoff and Other Early Trails which Crossed the Great Salt Lake Desert Seeking a Shorter Road to California.* Salt Lake City: Western Epics, Inc., 1996.

Kelly, Charles. "They Saw the Elephant." *Salt Lake Tribune,* May 28, 1950. (Reprinted in *Wendover Review,* July 1, 1983.)

May, Dean L. Utah. *A People's History.* Salt Lake City: University of Utah Press, 1987.

Miller, David E. *Utah History Atlas.* n.p. 1964.

Morgan, Dale, ed. *Overland in 1846: Diaries and Letters of the California-Oregon Trail, vol. 1.* Lincoln/London: University of Nebraska Press, 1963.

Morgan, Dale, & J. Roderic Korns, eds. *West from Fort Bridger: The Pioneering of the Immigrant Trails across Utah 1846-1850.* Revised and updated by Will Bagley and Harold Schindler. Logan: Utah State University Press, 1994.

Murphy, Virginia Reed. *Across the Plains in the Donner Party.* Ed. Karen Zeinert, New Haven: Linnet Books, 1996.

Smith, Jedediah S. *The Southwest Expedition of Jedediah S. Smith. His Personal Account of the Journey to California, 1826-1827.* Ed. George R. Brooks, Lincoln and London: University of Nebraska Press, 1977.

Chapter 6. THE BONNEVILLE SPEEDWAY

Embry, Jessie, and Ron Shook. "These Bloomin' Salt Beds: Racing on the Bonneville Salt Flats." *Utah Historical Quarterly,* 65, Fall 1997. The subtitle for this chapter, "On a sea of salt somewhere in the middle of Utah's desert," is quoted in this article.

Eyston, George and W. F. Bradley. *Speed on Salt: A History of the Bonneville Salt Flats, Utah, USA.* London: Charles Scribner's Sons, 1936.

"FIA History of Land Speed Record Holders—Unlimited Division." *History of Land Speed Records.* 4 June 2000, http://www.landspeed.com/turbo_history.html.

Jenkins, Ab, and Wendell J. Ashton. *The Salt of the Earth: Ab Jenkins' Own Story of Speed.* St George, Dixie College Foundation, 1993.

Jennings, Jesse D. "Salt and Speed." Wendover Lion's Club, 1973.

"The Mormon Meteor III." Mormon Meteor home page, http://www.ti.dixie.edu/meteor/meteor.htm.

Noeth, Louise Ann. *Bonneville Salt Flats.* Osceola, WI & Hong Kong: MBI Publishing Company, 1999.

"The Rocket Car: Spirit of America Book," chapter 15. http://www.spiritofamerica.com/book/chapters/c15.html.

"Southern California Timing Association 2001 Rules and Records." Lancaster, SCTA, 2001.

Author's note: The local people were not always positive about the racers, especially when the "Save the Salt" campaign was launched which blamed the potash plant as the cause of salt loss, thus threatening the livelihood of townspeople. Brenda Draper let her strong feelings be known in a letter to the editor of the *High Desert Advocate* in May of 1990: "… No one anywhere could be more proud of the beauty and heritage of the Salt Flats than the people who live here. Those things are an intrinsic part of our culture. I find the present conflict between the racers and Reilly [Industries] somewhat ironic. For years, the town of Wendover has welcomed the racers with open arms. We have looked forward to race week and seeing 'old Friends' again. The racers have consistently for years asked favors from the potash plant in using tools and equipment. When the racers needed specialized work done, they weren't hesitant to ask for help from the machine shop at Reilly. Now all of a sudden the potash plant is the villain and the residents of town are ignorant hicks. If [they are] looking for a campaign perhaps [they] could take on the people who designed and built the ridiculous Tree of Life monument on the Flats. One of those people somewhere along the line presumed that man could improve upon the majesty and grandeur of the Flats with his vanity."

Steve Sweat echoed similar sentiments in another May 1990 letter to the editor when he said in part: "I have lived in Wendover for 22 years and I love it here. You have to really love Wendover to live here. I really hate to see the racers come to Wendover. The last 22 years I've seen how they treat Wendover and its people. They definitely don't love it here. For those who claim to be so interested in conserving something, they sure don't show it. Many racers leave their trash and don't clean all the salt off their race cars …"

Chapter 7. ON THE EDGE OF A NEW CENTURY

Draft, "Wendover, Utah/West Wendover, Nevada, Annexation Study." Applied Development Economics, Inc. , July 2002.

Draper, Jean. "Journey into History: Wendover Schools." Typescript, n.d.

Draper, Jean. "The Wendover Story: History of the Town. Historical Economic Developments." Typescript, n.d.

Earl, Phillip I. "Nevada: Then and Now." *Pahrump Valley Gazette*, June 11, 1998.

Harmon, Gordon L. "Desert Dive." *The Salt Lake Tribune*, December 18, 2003, pp. 1-2.

Hernandez, John. "Wendover Reunion 2002." http://www.wendoverreunion.com/report.html (2003).

Jennings, Jesse D. "Danger Cave." *Anthropological Papers.* Salt Lake City: University of Utah Press, 1957.

Jensen, Elsie Lord. Letter to Illeana Z'Vara, 1952.

Langberg, Michael. "Lick Salt and Heat Corrosion with Daily PM." Unidentified newspaper article, August 28, 1979.

Lavine, Greg. "Building on the Wright Idea." *Salt Lake Tribune,* March 20, 2003.

Liddel, Joseph T. "9 Make Wendover History." *Deseret News,* May 26, 1967.

Mascaro, Kathryn. "Wendover High School, 1979-1980: Home of the Wildcats." Typescript, 1980.

Melville, Chris J. "City of West Wendover Ten Years Your City." Typescript, 2001.

Melville, Chris J. "The Wendover Airport: Like Its Past, Its Future Contains Endless Possibilities." *High Desert Advocate,* August, 1995.

Menzies, Richard. "Wild about Wendover." *Nevada Magazine*, vol. 57, no. 5 (Sept.-Oct. 1997).

Miller, David E. *Utah History Atlas,* 2nd ed. Salt Lake City, 1968.

Moreno, Richard. "Wendover Not Just another Border Town." *Nevada Appeal*, April 26, 1998.

"Nevada, Utah Towns Fighting over Uniting." Associated Press, Nevada Appeal/Tahoe.com, May 29, 2001.

Phelps, George A. "Wendover Blast: May 28, 1961." *Northeastern Nevada Historical Society Quarterly,* 1, 1991.

Reeve, W. Paul. "Danger Cave Near Wendover Provided Clues to Ancient Utah Dwellers." *History Blazer,* June 1995.

"Reilly Industries, Inc., Company Information: Reilly's History." http://www.reillyind.com/content/htm/company-information/history.html.

Rigert, Michael. "Flyer Tested at Historic Airfield for 100th Anniversary of Flight." *Tooele Transcript Bulletin* 109:83, March 13, 2003.

Smith, Christopher. "Telling New Secrets, Danger Cave Opens Fresh Chapter on Past." *The Salt Lake Tribune,* June 12, 2002.

Snow, Nick. "Potash Firm Seeks Treasure in Briny Water." *Deseret News*, July 31, 1976.

Snapshot. City of West Wendover, February, 2000.

"The Story of Potash." http:www.imcglobal.com/general/education_corner/potash/history.htm.

"Tooele School War Declared." *High Desert Advocate,* February 14, 1996.

Tree, Harvey. "Winds of Change." *High Desert Advocate,* October 21, 1998.

Utah: A Guide to the State. Hastings House: New York, 1941.

Wahlquist, Wayne L., ed. *Atlas of Utah.* Provo: Brigham Young University Press, 1981.

"Wendover Airport Master Plan." Typescript, 1991.

INDEX

A

Ronald Rao Bateman was raised in the small western community of Ibapah, Utah, sixty miles south of Wendover. He is the son of Rao H. and Phyllis P. Bateman, who were stationed in Wendover during World War II with the 509th Composite Group. Ron holds an EdS. degree from Utah State University and has been employed as an educational audiologist for thirty-two years. He is a businessman, educator, and writer and is involved in ranching. He also serves in his church and scouting.

He is the author of *Deep Creek Reflections: A History of Ibapah, Utah, 1859-1984*; *Of Dugouts and Spires: The History of South Jordan, Utah*; two articles in the *Utah History Encyclopedia*; and edited a large family history volume. In addition, he wrote the narrative for a Utah sesquicentennial monument. He and his wife Beverly C. Bateman reside in South Jordan, Utah. They are the parents of Jodi Bateman Kimball, Jonathan (Leah), Jana (Mike) Christiansen, Jeffrey (Sonia), and have nine grandchildren.